WITHDRAWN

The Soderini and the Medici

The Soderini and the Medici

Power and Patronage in
Fifteenth-century Florence

PAULA C. CLARKE

CLARENDON PRESS · OXFORD
1991

Oxford University Press, Walton Street, Oxford OX2 6DP

Oxford New York Toronto
Delhi Bombay Calcutta Madras Karachi
Petaling Jaya Singapore Hong Kong Tokyo
Nairobi Dar es Salaam Cape Town
Melbourne Auckland

and associated companies in
Berlin Ibadan

Oxford is a trade mark of Oxford University Press

Published in the United States
by Oxford University Press, New York

© Paula C. Clarke 1991

British Library Cataloguing in Publication Data
Clarke, Paula C.
The Soderini and the Medici : power and patronage in
fifteenth-century Florence.
1. Italy. Florence. Politics. Role of Medici (family), history
I. Title 320.94551
ISBN 0–19–822992–5

Library of Congress Cataloging in Publication Data
Clarke, Paula C.
The Soderini and the Medici : power and patronage in fifteenth-
century Florence / Paula C. Clarke.
Includes bibliographical references and index.
1. Florence (Italy)–Politics and government–1421–1737.
2. Soderini, Niccolò, 1401–1474. 3. Soderini, Tommaso, 1403–1485.
4. Medici, House of. I. Title.
DG737.8.C57 1991   320.945′51′09024–dc20   90-49433
ISBN 0–19–822992–5

Typeset by Cambridge Composing (UK) Ltd
Printed and bound in
Great Britain by Bookcraft Ltd
Midsomer Norton, Bath

Alla buona memoria di
Maureen A. Lally

Acknowledgements

I would like to take the opportunity here to thank the Rothermere Fellowship Foundation for the generous financial assistance that it gave me while I was preparing the thesis which forms the basis of this book. I must also express my gratitude to the University of London for the travel grants which contributed to research trips to Italy. It is impossible to give such specific thanks for the numerous intellectual obligations which I have contracted over the years. While some have been acknowledged in the notes, these by no means recognize all the debts incurred. Special mention is owed to Nicolai Rubinstein, who for so many years patiently followed the progress of this manuscript, always ready with suggestions and advice. Dale Kent kindly read an earlier draft, offering suggestions regarding its reorganization along with much appreciated encouragement to continue with it. The staffs of the archives and libraries have almost invariably been of valuable aid, especially those at the Archivio di Stato in Florence, where so much of the research for this book was done. Finally, my parents deserve particular thanks for the constant support and interest which they have given to this work, which they have therefore helped in so many ways towards completion.

Abbreviations

All references are to the Archivio di Stato, Florence, unless otherwise indicated, and all dates are in the modern style.

Florence
Archivio di Stato:

Carte Strozz.	Carte Strozziane
Cat.	Catasto
Corp. relig. soppr.	Corporazioni religiose soppresse
CP	Consulte e Pratiche
Dieci, Miss.	Dieci di Balìa, Missive interne
Dieci, Delib.	Dieci di Balìa, Deliberazioni, Condotte, Stanziamenti
Libri Fab.	Libri Fabarum
MAP	Archivio Mediceo avanti il Principato
MSS	Manoscritti
Notarile Antecos.	Notarile Antecosimiano
Provv.	Provvisioni, Registri
Pupilli	Ufficiali dei Pupilli avanti il Principato
Sig., Dieci, Otto	Signori, Dieci di Balìa, Otto di Pratica, Legazioni e Commissarie, Missive e Responsive
Sig. Leg. e Comm.	Signori, Legazioni e Commissarie
Sig., Miss., Min.	Signori, Missive, Minutari
BNF:	Biblioteca Nazionale Centrale
Coll. Passerini	Collezione genealogica Passerini
Conv. Soppr.	Conventi Soppressi
Magl.	Manoscritti Magliabecchiani

Mantua

ASMa	Archivio di Stato, Archivio Gonzaga

Milan

ASMi, SPE	Archivio di Stato, Carteggio generale Visconteo-Sforzesco, Potenze Estere

Modena

ASMo   Archivio di Stato, Archivio Segreto Estense

Venice

ASV, Sen. Secr.   Archivio di Stato, Senato, Deliberazioni Segrete (Senatus Secreta)

Contents

Introduction

The following work is intended first and foremost to demonstrate how politics worked in fifteenth-century Florence, and the factors bringing about the constitutional change for which the period is well known. These political changes consisted principally of the rise of the Medici family to a position of predominance never before enjoyed by any Florentine clan, and a concomitant shift towards a more oligarchic government. In these developments much the same issues were at stake, and the same factors operating, as had been the case in earlier Florentine history. As before, constitutional change was the result of the endemic conflict which characterized the Florentine ruling group, and which centred round perennial sources of contention, such as finance and taxation. Foreign policy also created dissension when it involved citizens' economic and political interests. Whatever the issue in question, however, office-holding ultimately became the crux of the struggle, for it was only through influence in government that citizens could achieve their political goals. Moreover, public posts were themselves frequently the subject of conflict, as they brought not only political influence but social prestige, occasional salaries, and a better chance to pursue private interests in public fields, whether justice or government finance.

The Florentine constitution of the fifteenth century represented a compromise between groups within the city's society, and one which had repeatedly been remodelled throughout the city's history. The principal features of this constitution (if a loose body of statutes can be so termed) were established in the late thirteenth and early fourteenth centuries, when the commoners or *popolo* emerged victorious over the city's

old aristocratic families. Their victory widened the circle of
political power to include the leading popular families, but it
also made possible an extension of political influence to a yet
larger section of the citizen body. The principal unit of
organization of the growing commercial élite which dominated within the *popolo* was the guild, and consequently their
victory brought with it the adoption of the guild as one of
the basic units of political life. This in turn raised the
possibility of extending political privileges to the whole guild
community. However, the inherent conflicts of interest
between prominent merchants and bankers on the one hand
and lowly tavern-keepers or belt-makers on the other,
ensured that a conflict over political participation would
continue.

   Although the political system gradually worked out in the
last decades of the thirteenth and the beginning of the
fourteenth centuries granted a share of political power to
members of the lesser guilds, it maintained the major political
weight in the hands of the city's wealthier manufacturers,
merchants, and bankers. Thus, it failed to satisfy the political
aspirations of the lower sections of the citizen body while
forcing the upper levels of the community to share their
power with lower-ranking citizens. Consequently, unsatisfied
ambitions remained, and the bounds of political power were
by no means clearly defined. On the one hand, the leading
families continued to assert their right to a predominant role
in politics, but less prominent citizens repeatedly sought to
win a greater say in government. Thus, the fourteenth and
fifteenth centuries saw continued political conflict, which
often achieved little more than a temporary shift of power in
one direction or the other, but which meanwhile won for the
city that reputation for constant change which Dante made
so famous.

   In part, this constant tinkering with the city's constitution
was a result of continued immigration into Florence, which
brought into the municipal arena new citizens who might
either become involved in the quarrels of great rival families,
or seek a political voice for themselves against the exclusive-
ness of the older clans. In part, it stemmed from the shifts in
the city's economy, which at times strengthened the position

of the great commercial houses and at times gave additional weight to the demands of the less wealthy. However, neither of these factors would have so contributed to political fluctuations if the Florentines themselves had not recognized the mobility inherent in their society, and from the start made it an essential feature of their political regime. Unlike other cities such as Venice, the Florentines did not try to fix permanently the group of citizens who possessed the right to participate in political life. Rather, in a more egalitarian fashion, they recognized that citizens' fortunes rose and fell, and that new citizens could emerge with sufficient wealth and influence to merit a share in political life. Therefore, they developed the practice of redefining their political class every five years or so, allowing such changes to express themselves. In these revisions, no citizen, no matter how eminent, was guaranteed a renewal of his political rights, while any citizen could in theory be proposed for the right to hold almost any public office.[1] In practice leading citizens rarely lost their qualifications to office (except at moments of political crisis) and the most prominent families maintained a sizeable representation within the city's ruling group. Yet, at the same time, new citizens and new families did enter public life, and consequently the composition and goals of the government could and did change. This in itself proved the source of conflict, as leading families saw their influence diluted by the entry of new men into political life, and sought repeatedly to reassert their ascendancy, particularly when policies inimical to their interests were proposed. On the other hand, the egalitarian elements in the Florentine constitution and the openness of her political group, at times encouraged even citizens of the city's labouring classes to seek to share in municipal politics, or to vindicate their sometimes neglected interests by striving for dominance within the governing group.

Despite the fact that their political system thus gave rise to

---

[1] Leading families ensured that access to certain important offices was to a degree restricted. For example, the principal executive post of Standardbearer of Justice could not be held by a member of the lesser guilds. The Lords of the Mint were drawn exclusively from the Banking and Calimala guilds, etc.

repeated conflict among opposing interest groups, the Florentines became extremely attached to their 'constitution'. They were generally proud of its popular features, and that it included in decision-making a wider swath of public opinion than did other regimes. From the point of view of political theory, they could cite the old adage that 'what affects all should be approved by all', and argue that the real object of political life—the common good—could best be achieved by including in government a wide section of the citizen body. On a less theoretical level, the Florentines undoubtedly felt that their system was more fair, in that it allowed any citizen who demonstrated personal merit to be included within the ruling group. Moreover, their ethical sense was satisfied by the consideration that repeated revisions of citizens' political qualifications served as a stimulus to honest and effective government on the part of the members of the political class. Even the less prominent citizens outside the ruling group could content themselves with the guarantee that success on their part could lead eventually to their families' gaining a place within the higher ranks of government.[2]

Thus, Florentines tended to remain faithful to the basic institutions of the political system worked out in the early centuries of the republic. Since they were reluctant to change them, and were aware of the resistance serious alteration would provoke, during most of the fourteenth and fifteenth centuries conflicts tended to revolve around minor modifications in the system, such as the number of new men admitted to political life, or the number of guilds supplying candidates for the scrutinies. This was the case whether political conflict involved disagreements among opposing interest groups in Florentine society or rivalries among the city's leading families, or both, as was generally the case.

Both sources of conflict were evident in the political crisis of the 1420s and 1430s which brought the Medici to power and set the stage for the events recounted in the following pages. During the late fourteenth century Florence's political system had shifted in favour of a narrower oligarchy—the

---

[2] This point is made particularly well in Najemy, *Corporatism and Consensus*.

product in part of a reaction against a popular revolution of 1378. The leading figures within this oligarchy were members of old, prominent families in Florence, whose wealth, local influence, and foreign contacts made them the most powerful figures at home and abroad. As in the past, this inner circle maintained its power through modifications in political practice which shifted the membership of the ruling class in favour of the established citizens among whom they could hope to have predominant support. However, the basic features of the system guaranteed that new men would continue to enter the ruling group, and that fluctuations among citizens' fortunes would bring new and powerful families on to the political scene. By the 1420s the oligarchic group, named after its leading family, the degli Albizzi, was becoming concerned at the number of new men entering office, and at the manner in which political influence was being acquired by a family only now reappearing in the inner circles of Florentine politics—the Medici.

Although active in politics since the second half of the thirteenth century, the Medici family had gradually declined in wealth, while its connection with the revolutionary workers' uprising of 1378 had brought it under suspicion from the more oligarchic regime which had followed.[3] The participation by several Medici in plots against this regime meant that proscription further reduced their presence within the ruling group. Consequently, it was not until Giovanni di Bicci de' Medici had made a fortune in banking at the end of the fourteenth and beginning of the fifteenth century that he was able to regain a place for his family in the inner circle, where his wealth, his vast influence, and his popularity soon made him one of the leading figures.

Given the Medici's history of hostility towards the Albizzi group, it is not surprising that Giovanni should hesitate to support the plan by which this leading circle sought to reinforce its political position during the 1420s. Whereas the Albizzi and their friends wished to reduce the presence of lower guildsmen in public offices and to exercise a greater

---

[3] On the Medici before 1434 see Brucker, 'The Medici in the Fourteenth Century', 1–26.

control over entry into the ruling group, the Medici undoubtedly regarded such measures as merely concentrating power
in the hands of potential opponents. Moreover, Giovanni's
own political style had been characterized by a modesty and
restraint which had won him sympathy in all quarters. To
opt for the aggressive, oligarchic policies advocated by
Rinaldo degli Albizzi and his associates might jeopardize that
following, while the results might exclude some of the
Medici's own supporters from the ruling group.

Giovanni's decision to oppose the oligarchs' programme
was thus undoubtedly based on family interests, but it led to
a widespread conflict within the ruling group, for, apart from
the political issue originally at stake, other factors intervened
to expand and complicate the quarrel. On the one hand, the
strong personal ties within Florentine society caused friends
and relatives of the principals to rally to their side, partly in
recognition that their own interests lay in supporting their
friends' political success. Beyond this, ambition or personal
enmities caused citizens to commit themselves to powerful
figures involved in the conflict, as they hoped to use their
influence for their own advancement or protection. Moreover, other questions of public policy aroused tensions within
the governing group which, becoming intertwined with existing disputes, served to exacerbate the factional quarrel.

In 1433, after a long war against Lucca had heightened
economic and political tensions within the city, the Albizzi
group attempted to resolve the conflict by exiling most of the
Medici family. However, their victory was short-lived, as the
Medici's wide following in the city, their influence with
powers abroad, and their immense wealth created strong
pressure for their recall. Only a year after their expulsion
their supporters within the city gained a majority within the
principal magistracy, the Signoria, and the Medici were
rapidly recalled. In turn, large numbers of the Albizzi group
and their supporters were exiled, and many others deprived
of their qualifications for political posts. Moreover, in order
to secure their political position, the new regime resorted to
more radical methods of political manipulation than those
employed by their enemies. Almost all previous qualifications
to office were destroyed, and these political rights were made

to depend on the review undertaken by a special council, or *Balìa*, deliberately selected to represent supporters of the new regime. The same council was also used to pass measures against the defeated faction, including controls over government posts, by which enemies of the Medici and their friends were kept out of key appointments.

These controls were instituted as an emergency measure, but they did not disappear after the threat posed by the Albizzi group had passed. They were further elaborated until they became permanent features of the city's political system. In particular, the special councils, already common during the Albizzi period, were transformed from *ad hoc* bodies to longer-term, eventually permanent, assemblies, whose members, first chosen on a partisan basis, were from 1458 selected by regular procedures from the upper echelons of the post-1434 regime. The authority to screen candidates for the Signoria was also permanently entrusted to special magistrates called *accoppiatori*, who, although they changed in membership, nevertheless consistently represented the inner circle of the regime. Moreover, election was substituted for sortition in the appointment of some major magistracies, while their terms of office were extended.

Thus, procedures of government which had guaranteed a fairly wide citizen participation and a relatively egalitarian distribution of political offices were gradually bypassed, first for partisan motives and later with the aim of securing in authority the upper echelons of the governing group. By 1480 this process had gone so far that government policy was being formulated and to a degree executed, and some major magistrates were being selected, by only some 100 citizens out of approximately 3,000 actually eligible for public office. Thus, the Medici faction, which had gained political ascendancy as champions of the traditional constitution, had become instead the leaders in the same trend towards an oligarchic government which they had originally opposed.

Together with this volte-face went the second major political development of the fifteenth century—the rise of the Medici family to a position of pre-eminent authority. Already the principal family of the regime on their recall in 1434, in subsequent years the Medici further strengthened their position, until by the 1480s their political ascendancy was practically unchallenged. In part, this was the result of the Medici's conscious effort to win friends and supporters within the ruling group. Fully aware of the resentment which their unusual pre-eminence aroused, they sought to attach talented and willing collaborators to themselves and used all the means at their disposal to keep their friends—indeed, as many people as possible—grateful and well disposed towards them. The political changes mentioned above aided the Medici in this regard, for they possessed considerable influence within the narrowing circles who exercised political power in Florence, and were thereby better able to satisfy the political ambitions of their friends.

In addition to such patronage, the Medici won support by pursuing policies favoured by the other leading citizens of the regime. These might involve furthering trade, a shift in Florentine foreign policy, or, from the constitutional perspective, contributing to the oligarchic changes mentioned above. While these last were generally also in the Medici's interests, it was often other citizens who were most anxious to press ahead with the innovations, in a desire to guarantee their own influence over government policy or win for themselves the most powerful public posts. As in the late 1420s, so after 1434, Medici consent and assistance remained essential for the success of such measures, for they possessed such influence at home and abroad that they could create or destroy an internal consensus or provide the foreign backing which might be required for the success of the leading citizens' plans.

As will emerge in the course of the following pages, the ability to call on foreign support was one of the more important factors contributing to the Medici political success. Despite the normal harmony reigning between the Medici and the rest of the inner circle, their interests were at certain points irredeemably opposed, and, when conflict occurred, foreign support might mean the difference between political survival or defeat. Conscious of this, the Medici developed a special relationship with the Sforza family, who, although initially mere mercenary captains, became the rulers of Milan in 1450. Despite the Sforza's close relations with other prominent figures in Florence, they always recognized the superior financial and political assistance which the Medici could render them, and their consequent commitment to the Medici connected internal conflicts in Florence more directly with the Italian, and even European, political scene. From 1451, Medici influence over foreign policy ensured that Florence remained allied with Sforza Milan, forcing citizens who wished to undermine Medici authority to seek contacts with rivals of the Florence–Sforza axis.

From the early 1450s, such rivals could most easily be found in Venice or in minor Italian powers, such as the Este rulers of Ferrara and Modena. In fact, the Florence–Sforza alliance of 1451 had seemed to some a betrayal of Venice, as previously the Florentines had been regular allies with the Venetians against the expansionist ambitions of the Visconti Dukes of Milan. Instead, from the early 1450s the Florentines found themselves fighting against Venice on behalf of the Duke of Milan, for the Venetians had succeeded in making themselves masters of much of Lombardy and were determined to see that their acquisitions were not threatened by the emergence of another powerful opponent in that zone. Although peace was made among the warring parties in 1454, the alignment established in mid-century remained intact for the following twenty years. Indeed, the Florence–Sforza alliance proved one of the more permanent realities of fifteenth-century Italian politics, as did the continuing distrust between Venice and Milan. Meanwhile, the tendency of the King of Naples to side with the Milan–Florence coalition meant that the Venetians became increasingly isolated in Italy. By the 1460s they were anxious to break up the alliance ranged against them, and in particular to renew friendship with Florence. Their failure to do so they blamed on the Medici, and consequently the Venetians and their satellites became prepared to lend themselves to the plans of those who wished to overthrow Medici supremacy in Florence.

It was not until 1474 that Florentine–Venetian friendship was re-established, as deteriorating relations within the Milan–Naples–Florence alliance caused the Medici to abandon the existing triple league for a new one with Milan and

Venice. Meanwhile, these same worsening relations meant that for a period in the 1470s the King of Naples became a potential source of support for anti-Medici currents in Florence, as the King sought to separate Florence from Milan with menacing implications for the Medici. Nevertheless, the Medici managed to overcome these threats, and, by maintaining control over Florence's foreign policy, were able to secure their position at home. Not only the alliance with Venice in 1474 but the subsequent league formed among Naples, Florence, and Milan in 1480 was desired and negotiated by the Medici.

Ultimately, of course, the Medici's control of foreign policy depended on the internal support which they could muster at home. To understand the sources of the Medici's long-term ascendancy, as well as the motives behind the oligarchic changes which supported it, it is therefore necessary to look at the factors which caused Florentines to further, or at least acquiesce in, both these political trends. Similarly, the nature and weaknesses of the opposition which emerged against the Medici can be clarified only by examining the position and objectives of citizens who played a prominent role within it.

The following pages constitute a contribution towards such goals by investigating the careers of two Florentines who were extremely important in both supporting and opposing Medici supremacy and the constitutional developments of the period. Both these citizens—two brothers, Niccolò and Tommaso Soderini—were at different periods partisans and enemies of the Medici, and thus their careers illustrate diverse, even contradictory, reactions to the political developments of their time. In the case of the elder, Niccolò, self-defence served as the original motive for promoting Medici ascendancy, while he advocated oligarchic trends through dedication to a patrician ideal which also served his political interests. However, for a variety of reasons, Niccolò fell out with the Medici and became an opponent of the constitutional innovations which they sponsored. On the one hand, the fact that he remained outside the group which most benefited from the narrowing of power meant that he found his political and economic interests thwarted by the success of the Medici and their friends. At the same time, political principle, reinforced by personal attachments, served to strengthen his hostility. Consequently, by the later 1450s he had become an adversary of the inner, Medici, circle in the economic as well as the political sphere, and in 1466 he emerged as one of the leading figures of a movement which sought unsuccessfully to destroy both Medici primacy and the constitutional innovations which concentrated authority in their hands and those of their friends.

Meanwhile, unlike Niccolò, Tommaso became attached to the Medici only after 1434, apparently not only through political ambition but in large part as a result of the Medici's search for competent allies. Tommaso was already proving a reliable supporter of the regime when a marriage alliance established a bond with the Medici which had permanent effects on his political career. The mutual obligations implied in such ties contributed to creating an alliance in which Tommaso served for many years as a Medici supporter, while he benefited from Medici favour in the advancement of his political and business career. This connection also meant that Tommaso, unlike his brother, remained a fervent advocate of the narrower government which developed under the Medici aegis and which proved a useful instrument for advancing his own political authority. In the anti-Medici movement of 1465–6, Tommaso was therefore on the side opposed to his own brother, and made a significant contribution to the defeat of the reforming movement in which his brother played a leading part.

As a result of the Medici victory, Tommaso enjoyed a period of exceptional political prominence in the years following 1466. Nevertheless, his success in collaborating with the Medici did not prevent him from eventually seeking, like his brother, to undermine their authority when it conflicted with his own ambitions. Paradoxically, the very prominence which he won through Medici assistance ultimately brought him into conflict with them, as it placed him in a position whence he could aspire to the Medici's role of first citizens of Florence. When the opportunity offered of altering Florence's alliance system in a manner beneficial to himself, Tommaso seized the occasion, attempting to detach

Florence from Milan and form an alliance instead with Venice and Naples. However, his goal was thwarted by the Medici and their Sforza allies, and a power struggle resulted which pitted Tommaso, as the leader of the dissatisfied elements within the city, against the Medici. Ultimately, the Medici's foreign support, the strength of the pro-Milanese current, and the Medici's vast influence gave them the upper hand, and, realizing that the opposition movement could not succeed, Tommaso decided that his best interests lay in a reconciliation with the Medici. That the Medici were prepared to forget his temporary disloyalty and seek a permanent reconciliation with him is an indication both of Tommaso's competence as a politician and of the Medici's reliance on their leading collaborators' support.

Nevertheless, Tommaso's resentment of Medici primacy could never completely be overcome, for his thwarted political ambition was fed by the constant need to subordinate his interests to those of the city's leading family. It was also reinforced by the belated realization that the alterations which he had helped impose on Florence's traditional constitution had produced a form of government which contradicted his own interests and, to a degree, even his principles. Thus, while Tommaso illustrates the symbiotic relationship existing between the Medici and the other prominent citizens of the regime, he also exemplifies the inherently conflicting interests between the Medici and their principal supporters, and consequently the potential instability in the new political balance effected in 1434.

So the significance of the careers of Niccolò and Tommaso lies both in their contribution to the political developments of their time and in the fact that they demonstrate so many of the motives and responses of Florentine citizens to the consolidation of Medici supremacy and the institutional changes which accompanied it. Together, the brothers' histories illustrate the permanent tensions within the Florentine ruling group and the problems faced by any section of the regime which sought to alter the prevailing political forms and the balance of power which they embodied. While such problems were perennial within the Italian city-state, it is only during the lifetimes of Niccolò and Tommaso Soderini that sufficient evidence becomes available for such a detailed description of city-state politics, and therefore of the origins of that constant flux of political institutions which was typical not only of Florence but of so many cities of medieval and Renaissance Italy.

1. The Origins of the Soderini–Medici Bond

Niccolò and Tommaso Soderini's initial connection with the
Medici came about through circumstances unrelated to the
political crisis of the late 1420s and early 1430s. These
circumstances, moreover, carried them in a direction contrary to the position taken by the rest of their distinguished
clan, for the Soderini were one of those old, prominent,
patrician families who backed the Albizzi in their aim of
fortifying the political power of an aristocratic section of the
regime. The Soderini were, as Piero Guicciardini pointed out
in 1484, one of the 'old, noble, popular' clans of the city,
just below the descendants of the ancient feudal houses on
the social scale.[1] Already prominent by the twelfth century,
they had fought for the victorious Guelf cause against the
Ghibellines, and during the thirteenth and fourteenth centuries had built a fortune through the international textile trade
and banking. From the institution of the Priorate in 1282,
the Soderini had frequently been appointed to this principal
magistracy, and although their involvement in the crash of
the Peruzzi bank in the 1340s had caused a temporary
decline in their fortunes, by the later fourteenth century they
had recovered both their wealth and their political prestige.
Niccolò di Geri, for example, was a prominent figure within

---

[1] This description is contained in Piero's account of the scrutiny of 1484,
published in Rubinstein, *Government*, 323.

the reactionary Guelf Party, which during the middle and later decades of the fourteenth century attempted to strengthen the position of the older families by removing 'new men' and their own political opponents from the governing group. Consequently one of the victims of the revolutionary Ciompi rising of 1378, Niccolò ended his life in exile, but the Soderini tradition of political eminence was carried on by his cousin, Messer Tommaso di Guccio, the grandfather of the protagonists of this work. After amassing a fortune in business at Avignon during the 1360s, Messer Tommaso had returned to Florence by the 1370s and was also, if to a lesser degree than his cousin, associated with the oligarchic policies of the Guelf Party. He, however, managed to survive the Ciompi Revolution to become a powerful figure in the Albizzi regime of the late fourteenth century. According to the contemporary diarist Marchionne Stefani, he was one of a small group of individuals who 'preceded the others in directing public affairs' and who could reinforce their political position by seeing 'that arms were raised against whomever they wished'.[2]

This tradition of participation in the highest social and political circles of the city was carried on by Messer Tommaso's son Francesco. In about 1415 Francesco had married a daughter of the wealthiest citizen of Florence, Messer Palla degli Strozzi. Although Palla later distinguished himself by his refusal to take up arms in the Albizzi cause, he was nevertheless a prominent figure in the regime's inner circle, and considered sufficiently on the Albizzi side to be exiled by the victorious Medici group in 1434. Another Soderini, Niccolò's son Giovanni, also maintained close relations with some of the most eminent statesmen of his day, including the powerful Niccolò da Uzzano. As Niccolò da Uzzano was one of the leaders of the Albizzi faction until his death in about

[2] Stefani, *Istoria fiorentina*, 412–13. On the Soderini family in general, see Litta, *Famiglie*, disp. 141 (not always accurate, however), and Ammirato, *Delle famiglie*, 118–36. On the Soderini's involvement in the Peruzzi company and their subsequent possession of their own company involved, among other things, in papal finance, see in particular Sapori, 'La compagnia dei Peruzzi', 196, and Renouard, *Relations*, e.g. 47, 112, 116, 225, 258, 260, 300–1, 619.

1432, his influence must have confirmed the attachment of Giovanni and his family to the more patrician Albizzi camp.[3]

However, the Niccolò and Tommaso Soderini with whom we are to deal did not fall within quite the same tradition. Although descendants of the eminent Messer Tommaso, their prospects were profoundly affected by the fact that their father was illegitimate, the son of a French woman whom Messer Tommaso knew while in business at Avignon. Although Messer Tommaso had acknowledged Lorenzo as his son, brought him back to Florence and arranged for his support, Lorenzo was never to gain the status of his legitimate half-brother Francesco. He was apparently never promoted to public office, while legal handicaps prevented him from inheriting much of his father's huge estate.[4] Moreover, his opportunities for a marriage alliance, with all its implications for social and political connections, were markedly inferior to those of Messer Tommaso's legitimate children.[5] Lorenzo's efforts to rectify this situation were never completely successful, for although he was eventually legitimized and gained the right to inherit an amount determined by his father, his deteriorating relations with Messer Tommaso meant that his hopes of obtaining a substantial proportion of the Soderini wealth were never realized. Indeed, by 1400 Messer Tommaso was so badly disposed towards Lorenzo that he cut him completely out of his will.[6]

---

[3] On Francesco Soderini, see Cavalcanti, *Istorie*, i. 530–1, 542, and Litta, *Famiglie*, disp. 141. The connection between Giovanni Soderini and Niccolò da Uzzano was symbolized by Giovanni's marriage to Niccolò's daughter Gismonda: Dainelli, 'Niccolò da Uzzano', 37.

[4] On illegitimate sons' handicaps regarding inheritance, see Calisse, *Storia*, iii. 145–6.

[5] Lorenzo married Ghilla, daughter of Tommaso di Ser Manetto Cambi, who, although prominent in his guild of the Medici e Speziali and successful in gaining appointment to the Signoria, was nevertheless of a standing far inferior to the Strozzis'. Ghilla's dowry was, for example, only 325 florins. For dowries of 3 or more times as large given or received by the Niccolini family, see Klapisch, 'Parenti, Amici e Vicini', 958, 963–5.

[6] Information regarding Lorenzo is taken, except when otherwise stated, from the investigation and condemnation in Atti del Podestà, 4018, fos. 5ᵛ–10ᵛ. Another copy, destroyed in the flood of 1966, was published with some deletions by Brucker, *Renaissance Florence*, 162–6, and the author very kindly supplied me with a copy of his transcript of the original. Messer Tommaso's will is in Notarile Antecos., V79, unpaginated, 25 Aug., 6 Sept. 1402. For Lorenzo's efforts to gain legitimation

However, Lorenzo was not prepared to accept this exclusion from what he regarded as his rightful patrimony. Rather, realizing that Messer Tommaso might succumb to the plague of 1400, he decided to devise a plan whereby, in the event of his father's death, he could hope to secure the whole of the Soderini estate. He would claim, he decided, that his father had actually married his mother in Avignon. Therefore Messer Tommaso's later marriage to a Florentine lady would have been bigamous, their children bastards, and Lorenzo remain the sole legitimate heir. Naturally, he was aware of the need of documents to buttress such a startling claim, and went all the way to Avignon to obtain his mother's aid in obtaining the necessary forgeries. Once these had been secured, and Messer Tommaso eventually did die in 1402, Lorenzo implemented his plan, initially with some success. However, he could not have anticipated the determined resistance put up by Messer Tommaso's legitimate heirs, who apparently possessed the backing of the influential Niccolò da Uzzano. Presumably through their efforts, the full story of Lorenzo's fraud was discovered, and his insistence on carrying his case to the highest Florentine courts merely resulted in his condemnation to execution in late August 1405 for the crime of aggravated forgery and fraud.

Lorenzo's execution left behind a young family which included his widow, Ghilla Cambi, and two infant sons, Niccolò and Tommaso, aged three and two respectively.[7] For them his death had important implications, including their removal from their home in the traditional Soderini enclave in S. Spirito. In the settlement of Lorenzo's small estate, the family's residence was sold to Messer Tommaso's legitimate son Francesco in order to repay Ghilla's dowry, and therefore she and her children returned to her father's home across the River Arno in the Santa Maria Novella quarter. There Niccolò and Tommaso spent their childhood and adolescent

---

and property, see Diplomatico, Acquisto Soderini, App., particularly 8 Dec. 1394, 25, 26 Jan., 4 Feb., 10 Dec. 1399.

[7] There was at least one other child but no information on her has come to light. There is also no proof that the additional daughters whom Litta mentions, *Famiglie*, disp. 141, were really Lorenzo's.

years, cut off from the family influences which might have drawn them too into the conservative camp.

Niccolò and Tommaso's separation from their family was to be the more important as they enjoyed, even from their childhood, remarkably successful political careers. Surprisingly, Lorenzo's history had little effect on their political prospects. Nor did the fact that they were absent from their official area of residence in S. Spirito and therefore less able to gain the local contacts who could be so important for success in the scrutinies. For, despite these handicaps, both brothers were qualified by the scrutiny councils for even the highest government offices—i.e. the Signoria and its Colleges—when they were still children.[8] Consequently, they could accumulate qualifications for all the city's offices from an early age, and begin to fill them frequently as soon as they reached the minimum ages required in each instance.[9] That they became eligible for public office so early must in large part be attributed not only to their friends within the ruling group[10] but, more particularly, to the lustre of the Soderini name and to the political inheritance bequeathed to them by their grandfather. Apart from the influence which Messer Tommaso had wielded in S. Spirito, he had been qualified for the highest executive offices, and by Florentine custom his achievement could be passed on to his descendants. His grandchildren as well as his children received a special status, or *beneficio*, by which they were included in a group often voted on before the other candidates in the scrutiny and which had a greater chance of success.[11] Messer Tommaso's

---

[8] Tratte, 46, fo. 22ʳ; ibid., 9, fo. 184ᵛ.

[9] Niccolò and Tommaso even began their careers before they reached the minimum age, and may have been exaggerating their ages for just this purpose. In 1427, for example, they gave their ages as 32 and 28 respectively (Cat., 25, fo. 457ᵛ), even though they were only 25 and 24. From May/June, 1426, both were sitting regularly in the Councils of the People and Commune, for which the minimum age was 25: Tratte, 154, fos 1ᵛ ff. On the tendency to round up ages, possibly for political purposes, see Klapisch-Zuber and Herlihy, *Les Toscans*, especially p. 359.

[10] Niccolò's and Tommaso's maternal grandfather, Tommaso di Ser Manetto Cambi, was three times the effective head of the republic, as Standardbearer of Justice, while his friend, Francesco Palmieri, was a person of importance within the ruling group.

[11] Messer Tommaso had acted twice as Standardbearer of Justice, the highest

political stand undoubtedly also accounts for the favour shown to Tommaso of inclusion in a special election bag, or *borsellino*, by which his chances of appointment to the Signoria were substantially increased.[12]

Although family inheritance thus acted to Niccolò's and Tommaso's benefit, their political success was still by no means equal to that of Messer Tommaso Soderini's legitimate heir, Francesco. Although only five years older than Niccolò, by 1426 Francesco had not only become a regular candidate for the Signoria but many times had been judged worthy to hold the highest position within it, as Standardbearer of Justice. In the late 1420s and early 1430s he was also frequently summoned to the *Pratiche*—the Signoria's informal consultative sessions attended by only the most reputed and distinguished citizens. In contrast, Niccolò was invited to these meetings only rarely, and Tommaso not at all. Finally, by the early 1430s Francesco had begun to be appointed to the prestigious role of ambassador—a considerable mark of esteem on the part of his fellow citizens.[13]

Despite Francesco's superior political success, there is no evidence of hostility between the two branches of the family during the 1420s. Thus, the contention of Machiavelli, followed by later historians, that Niccolò and Tommaso joined the Medici group through hatred of their uncle can only be an over-simplification. Instead, the brothers' separation from the rest of their family increased the likelihood that they would form connections with citizens friendly to the Medici. Their friend Nastagio Guiducci, for instance, who was a resident of the S. Maria Novella quarter and from

post within the Signoria: Tratte, 61, fo. 101ᵛ; 194*bis*, fo. 36. On the *beneficiati*, see Kent, 'The Florentine Reggimento', 589–90.

[12] In 1430, Tommaso's name was drawn from the *borsellino* prepared for the Signoria: Tratte, 198, fo. 50ᵛ. On the *borsellino* and its purposes, see Rubinstein, *Government*, 17, 45; Najemy, *Corporatism and Consensus*, 276–7, 282–90; Guidi, *Il governo*, i. 222–3.

[13] Cf. Litta, *Famiglie*, disp. 141. On Francesco's eligibility for the position of Standardbearer see Tratte, 61, fo. 82ᵛ. For his presence in the *Pratiche*, see CP, 48, fos. 20ʳ, 46ʳ, 55ʳ, 64ʳ, 85ʳ, 90ʳ. Niccolò was summoned only to the *Pratiche* of 20 March 1431 (CP, 49, fo. 132ʳ) and, as a representative of the Twelve, on 9 July 1433 (CP, 50, fo. 82ᵛ). Francesco was born 26 Feb. 1397: Tratte, Libri d'approvazione d'età, computer print-out, courtesy of Prof. D. Herlihy.

whom the brothers rented a house during the late 1420s, was active with Medici partisans in various political manœuvres, while his father played a major part in the Medici recall of 1434.[14] By the end of the 1420s Tommaso Soderini may himself have been moving into the Medici sphere, for in about 1429 he married the daughter of a citizen who had some association with that family. Before his death in 1428, Tommaso's father-in-law, Giuliano Torrigiani, was renting from Giovanni de' Medici a house immediately adjacent to the ancestral houses of the Medici clan. Although very little information regarding Giuliano survives, his physical propinquity to the Medici suggests that at least he was a friend of Giovanni's and may have come under the family's influence.[15]

Nevertheless, Niccolò and Tommaso formed no direct connection with the Medici prior to the personal incident which embroiled Niccolò in factional activity on their side. In 1429 Niccolò Soderini decided to assassinate Niccolò da Uzzano, whom Lorenzo Soderini's family blamed for the severe sentence delivered against Lorenzo in 1405. Niccolò's plan miscarried, however, as his hired assassins succeeded only in injuring their victim, and Niccolò da Uzzano brought charges against his presumed assailant, Soderini. In self-defence, Niccolò then decided to seek aid from Niccolò da Uzzano's political opponents—the Medici and their supporters. According to the subsequent confession of a Medici partisan, Ser Niccolò Tinucci, a meeting was arranged between Soderini and three prominent Medici friends (Averardo de' Medici, Ser Martino Martini, and Lorenzo Cresci), who promised Niccolò the group's full support in the quarrel now developing between him and the elder statesman.[16]

---

[14] On Nastagio's involvement with Medici partisans, see the confession of Ser Niccolò Tinucci, published in Cavalcanti, *Istorie*, ii. 403–4. His father Simone was a member of the Signoria of Sept.–Oct. 1434 and an *accoppiatore* from 1434 until 1439: Rubinstein, *Government*, 237, 244.

[15] This information regarding Giuliano is contained in his *catasto* return of 1427: Cat., 78, fo. 113ʳ⁻ᵛ. On Medici influence in the zone surrounding their residences, cf. Kent, *Rise*, 61–71.

[16] The fullest report of this incident is the court inquisition: Atti del Podestà, 4423, fos. 1ʳ–4ᵛ. I am grateful to Professor Gene Brucker for providing me with a copy of his transcription of this document, which was destroyed in the flood of

Events soon indicated why the Medici partisans were so ready to support Soderini's cause: they hoped to use it to make political capital against their oligarchic opponents. A comment by a Medici supporter suggests, for example, that they tried to destroy Niccolò da Uzzano's reputation by accusing him of having fabricated the accusation against Soderini. Tinucci also charged in his confession that Cosimo and Averardo de' Medici, as well as Niccolò Soderini, had bribed the Executor of Justice to have Niccolò da Uzzano arrested in connection with the case.[17] Further comments that Soderini was receiving considerable assistance from powerful quarters explain the Signoria's decision to intervene in order to end the political tensions being generated by the incident. In December 1429, asserting that if the case continued more serious conflicts might develop among the leading citizens, they quashed the charges which had been laid against Niccolò Soderini.[18]

Although the motive which the Signoria gave for intervening was undoubtedly sincere, other factors had also helped to bring about what was essentially a verdict in Soderini's favour. Among the Priors who composed the principal magistracy was Nastagio Guiducci, whose connections with Niccolò Soderini and with the Medici have already been mentioned. In addition, the most powerful figure within the Signoria, the Standardbearer of Justice, was Tommaso Barbadori, a Medici partisan who was, by the early 1430s, also a friend of the Soderini brothers. In fact, in 1433 he owed money to Niccolò—a debt which might have been the result of this particular incident.[19]

1966. The motive of the attack was confirmed by a letter of Francesco Filelfo of 22 Sept. 1432 (*Epistolae Francisci Philelfi*, ii. 70, no. 10), and in a highly coloured account by Giovanni di Carlo ('De temporibus suis', Vatican City, Bibl. Apostolica Vaticana, Cod. Lat. 5878, fos. 22ᵛ–23ᵛ),who, since he wrote late in the century, is not fully reliable. The incident is also mentioned in Tinucci's confession in Cavalcanti, *Istorie*, ii. 402; Kent, *Rise*, 236–9, and Zippel, *Filelfo*, 30–2.

[17] CP, 48, fo. 99ʳ, 3 Nov. 1429; Tinucci's confesssion, Cavalcanti, *Istorie*, ii. 403. Filelfo's letter, cited above, complained that not only did those who had hired the assassins go unpunished, an attempt was made to punish Niccolò da Uzzano instead. Cf. also Zippel, 'Filelfo', 30–2.

[18] Cf. the inquisition cited above.

[19] On Tommaso Barbadori's partisanship for the Medici, see Kent, *Rise*, 237,

Thus, as Niccolò had intended, his appeal to the Medici group succeeded in protecting him from the consequences of his personal vendetta. Beyond this, his involvement with the Medici network brought him powerful friends through whom he could hope to influence political decisions and achieve his personal political goals. Individuals such as Tommaso Barbadori remained permanent political connections, while, according to Niccolò's later declaration, his political influence at this stage grew to the point that 'everyone came to see him'.[20] Moreover, one letter survives from this period to suggest that Niccolò may have been using his Medici connections to increase his chances of obtaining government positions.[21] Certainly, the benefits accruing from his involvement with the Medici group and the dangers which would arise from his abandoning it kept him a firmly committed partisan even after the family's fall from favour in 1433. During the year in which the Medici were exiled from Florence and the Albizzi faction held sway, Niccolò apparently did his best to rally support for the Medici's recall. He was regarded as enough of a threat by some Albizzi supporters for them to plot to banish him along with other Medici partisans by using fabricated evidence—a plan which was, however, never effected.[22] Niccolò also suffered political proscription during this period, for, in order to strengthen their political ascendancy, the successful Albizzi group appointed a special council to carry out a scrutiny which favoured their own faction. Niccolò was one of those who lost out in consequence, for, even though he was a member of this *Balìa* (ex officio), he did not receive a majority in the scrutiny.[23]

---

352. During the 1430s, Barbadori acted as arbiter between Niccolò and Tommaso (Diplomatico, Acquisto Soderini, 7 Nov. 1432). For his debt to Niccolò: Cat., 347, fo. 299ʳ.

[20] See an undated *Pratica* of sometime between 9 and 31 July 1466: published by Pampaloni, 'Nuovi tentativi', 572.

[21] Niccolò Soderini to Averardo de' Medici, 1 March 1431, MAP, ii. 311. Cf. Kent, *Rise*, 236.

[22] Gelli, 'L'esilio', 163–6. Cf. also Guicciardini, *Memorie di famiglia*, 11, and Kent, *Rise*, 299–302, on Medici partisans' agitation for the Medici's recall.

[23] Tratte, 47, fo. 28ʳ. Niccolò's presence in the *Balìa* is recorded in Tratte, 156, fo. 182ᵛ and Balìe, 24, fo. 3ʳ.

In contrast to Niccolò, his brother Tommaso seems—intentionally or not—to have kept a much greater distance from the Medici group and from the factional conflict as a whole. Although the desire to avenge his father was attributed to him as well as to Niccolò,[24] there is no evidence that Tommaso became involved in the assassination attempt. Moreover, he was never mentioned as collaborating with Medici partisans in their political schemes. This divergence in political commitment may have been the result of a nascent conflict between the Soderini brothers, for they had separated their households by 1430, and were at odds over finances as early as 1432.[25] On the other hand, it is possible that they may have wanted to be sure that they could salvage something from a potential political defeat by maintaining at least one family member extraneous to the conflict in which the other was so deeply involved.

Whatever the motive, Tommaso's effort to distance himself from his brother's action was relatively successful. Although omitted from the *Balìa* created to confirm the Albizzi group's ascendancy, he, unlike his brother, obtained a majority in the scrutiny carried out by that council.[26] Similarly, when the Medici faction came to power in the autumn of 1434, Tommaso was again declared eligible for all public offices, even though he was not appointed to the special council established to reinforce the Medici victory.[27] On the other hand, Niccolò, as the active supporter, gained considerably from the Medici victory. A member of the pro-Medicean *Balìa* of 1434, he consequently not only voted in the new scrutiny but helped pass legislation which exiled the Medici group's major political opponents and instituted electoral controls designed to guarantee that Albizzi supporters would not gain access to key government posts. In the scrutiny of

[24] e.g. by Filelfo, in the letter cited in n. 16.
[25] Tommaso then complained that Niccolò owed him money but that he would have to take him to court in order to obtain restitution: Cat., 347, fo. 620ʳ. On the brothers' financial conflicts, see also Chap. 4.
[26] Balìa, 24, and Tratte, 47, fo. 28ᵛ.
[27] The members of the *Balìa* of 1434 are listed in Tratte, 156, and Rubinstein, *Government*, 244–53. Although the scrutiny lists of 1434 are not extant, citizens' success can be inferred from the offices which they subsequently held.

1434 Niccolò, like his brother, was successful at every level. Moreover, he was apparently elected as both *Podestà* (Governor) and commissary with custody of the fortress at Castiglione della Pescaia (one of the southernmost outposts of the Florentine dominion).[28] This double appointment testifies to Niccolò's high standing within the new regime. Moreover, as the position of *Podestà* was salaried, it may, in those economically difficult times, have served as a financial reward for his contribution to the Medici group's victory.

As the balance of power within the regime shifted in favour of a new political faction, so power relations within the family also changed. In contrast to Niccolò and Tommaso, some of the principal Soderini families suffered through their connection with the Albizzi group. In particular, before 1434 the eminent Francesco had been conspicuous within the Albizzi faction, even fulfilling the dubious honour of conducting the exiled Cosimo de' Medici to the boundaries of Florentine territory.[29] Although not exiled by the 1434 *Balìa*, Francesco thereafter lost his political prominence, for afterwards he was appointed to only one relatively minor office. Similarly, the sons of Giovanni di Niccolò and the other Soderini involved with the Albizzi suffered a political eclipse, as they became suspect to the post-1434 regime.[30] As the political mantle of the Soderini clan passed to the illegitimate, cadet branch of the family, the inferior status which had so galled Lorenzo was reversed, and Niccolò and Tommaso were placed in a position both to identify themselves with their clan's distinguished tradition and to raise their own families to a position of power never surpassed by the Soderini clan.

[28] Tratte, 67, fo. 129ʳ and the statement of Niccolò's deposit as surety for the custody of the fortress: Diplomatico, Acquisto Soderini, 29 Nov. 1434.

[29] Cavalcanti, *Istorie*, i. 542.

[30] e.g. in 1455 the *accoppiatori* removed Luigi di Giovanni's name from the election bags of the *Tre Maggiori*: Rubinstein, *Government*, 45. Francesco was elected as one of the syndics of the Captain of the People in 1435: Tratte, 80, fo. 137ʳ.

2 INVOLVEMENT IN THE ELECTORAL CONTROLS OF THE REGIME

The presence of Niccolò and Tommaso on the winning side in 1434 meant that thereafter both enjoyed active political careers which necessarily involved them in the institutional controls gradually introduced by the new regime. Although the measures of 1434 were intended to be temporary, certain elements were perpetuated. Not only did the results of the scrutiny remain in force in subsequent years; the special powers given to officials called *accoppiatori* to screen the candidates in each two-monthly drawing of the Signoria were repeatedly extended. Drawn from the inner circle of the new regime, these *accoppiatori* were able to intervene in the normal electoral process to prevent the enemies of the regime from gaining control of the Signoria, whence they might again make a bid for political power. With the exiled Albizzi leaders attempting to return to Florence by force or stealth, the leading citizens were determined to maintain this electoral control and succeeded in doing so despite growing resentment against the arbitrary authority thus exercised over major political appointments. By 1438, however, it was becoming increasingly difficult to persuade the legislative councils to prolong the *accoppiatori*'s powers, and the powerful circle around the Medici became increasingly convinced that extraordinary methods, such as another *Balìa*, would be necessary if their influence over the selection of the Signoria were to be maintained. Moreover, they were aware that other advantages might be derived from another special council. On the one hand, a new scrutiny would soon be due, and, from the principal citizens' point of view, it would be best conducted by a body favourable towards them. In addition, special councils had long been used as a means of dealing more expeditiously with controversial matters, especially finance: the possibility of passing legislation on such matters as taxation was increased by creating smaller legislative bodies more responsive to the leadership of the regime.[31] Even in 1434 this potential on the part of the

---

[31] On the use of *Balie* for this purpose during the late 14th c., cf. the

special council had not been neglected, as full powers over all areas of legislation had been entrusted to it. Now, thorny financial and military problems remaining from a recent war with Milan might, the leading Florentines thought, be most easily resolved with the help of another special council, and preferably one prepared to follow their lead.

For all these reasons, then, in the spring of 1438 the principal citizens decided to institute another extraordinary council, called the *Consiglio Maggiore*. It was to last, with permanent membership, for the unusually long period of three years, during which time it was not only to have full authority over the scrutiny and the method of appointing the Signoria, but also to vote before the other councils on the crucial questions of new taxes, war and peace, and the hiring of soldiers. The nucleus of the council was to be composed of various officials, some of whom, such as the Signoria and *accoppiatori*, represented the regime's leadership or had been screened by them. These ex-officio members were in turn to elect the remaining 200 councillors from, it was specifically stated, 'friends of the existing regime'.[32] Although this council did not prove totally amenable to the government's financial proposals, it did extend the *accoppiatori*'s powers to select the Signoria, and assumed the authority to carry out the required review of political qualifications.

While there is no indication of Niccolò's and Tommaso's response to the extension of the control over entry into the Signoria between 1434 and 1438, something of their attitude towards the political changes of 1438 can be inferred. Not only were both the brothers members of the new *Consiglio Maggiore*; Tommaso possessed a particular responsibility for the creation of the council in that he was a member of the Signoria which introduced the relevant legislation.[33] As a

interpretation of Molho, 'The Florentine Oligarchy', 23–51. On the circumstances surrounding the creation of this *Consiglio Maggiore* of 1438–41, see Rubinstein, *Government*, 15, 71. On the way in which the *Balìe* of the Medici period assumed the role of earlier special councils in this respect, cf. ibid., *passim*.

[32] The regulations regarding this *Balìa* and the measures which it enacted have been described by Rubinstein, ibid., 15–16, 71–4.

[33] The members of the *Balìa* of 1438–41 are listed in ibid., 254–63.

result, he was included ex officio in the *Balìa* and subsequently helped to select the elected section of the assembly. There is every reason to believe that he fulfilled these duties as the leading citizens would have wished. Indeed, both he and Niccolò had good reason to want to strengthen the regime of which they formed part, while both stood to gain from inclusion in the *Balìa*, in that for three years they could express their opinion on important legislation, as well as participate in the all-important scrutiny.

Apart from their formal participation in the measures of 1438, Niccolò's views regarding them are suggested in letters which he wrote at the time to a close friend, Agnolo di Messer Palla Novello Strozzi. In one of these, Niccolò asserted that the new council was 'a magnificent thing', through which, he promised, 'we will put this city in fine order'.[34] Presumably, he was thinking not merely of the council's role in finance and foreign policy, but also of the political provisions it would make. Indeed, Niccolò later commented that 'at Florence there is an extremely strong regime which will prove permanent' and 'we will eventually end up in the Venetian style, but it's happening very slowly'.[35] While Niccolò did not pass any further judgement on these political changes, it would appear that he approved not only of a permanent stabilization of the Medici regime, but also of the fact that its institutional innovations tended to bring the Florentine political system more into line with that of Venice. Presumably, by 'Venetian style' he meant that the *Consiglio Maggiore*, by confirming some 350 leading figures of the regime in power for a relatively long period, represented a step towards a more permanent, fixed ruling group of a sort which had been created at Venice in the late thirteenth century, when political participation had been restricted to the patrician families who were then members of the major legislative council. Moreover, the new *Consiglio Maggiore*, despite its temporary nature, was similar to the Venetian upper house or Senate not only regarding its

[34] Niccolò Soderini to Agnolo Strozzi, 19 May 1438, Carte Strozz., ser. 3, 130, fo. 239ʳ.
[35] Niccolò to Agnolo, 27 May 1438, ibid., fo. 246ᵛ.

numbers but in that it represented the upper stratum of the patrician families and provided them with a means of filtering legislation before it passed to the general citizen assembly.

That Niccolò should approve of a shift towards a more oligarchic system is hardly surprising, considering the tendencies repeatedly shown by Florentine patricians to strengthen their own political position by limiting participation in government by 'new men' or the lower classes. However, it serves as evidence that leading figures within the Medici regime recognized the connection between the changes they were introducing and the Venetian system, and suggests that these changes may in part have been inspired by the Venetian model. Thereby, Niccolò's remarks support Felix Gilbert's assertion that during the early part of the fifteenth century the growing admiration for the Venetian constitution evident in Florence existed principally within the Medici group, and that it was based not simply on a belief that the Venetians had solved the problem of factional struggles and political instability which had plagued Florence and produced a more stable, competent, and effective system of government than had the Florentines. Rather, as Niccolò's attitude indicates, the Venetian model was attractive to these Florentines because it was oligarchic, and seemed to prove the effectiveness—indeed, the superiority—of a narrower constitution of the sort which these citizens desired.[36]

However, Niccolò's approval of the constitutional tendencies of the inner Medici group was to disappear in the decades following 1438. Whereas he was apparently hoping for a limited shift towards a more patrician, stable government, the oligarchic leanings of the Medici group eventually went much further. Not one but two permanent councils were eventually instituted, through which the wider citizen body was almost totally deprived of a voice in government, while policy-making and much influence over the appointment of government personnel was turned over to a relatively narrow political élite. This degree of oligarchic concentration was much more extreme than Niccolò, and presumably

---

[36] For Felix Gilbert's remarks on the subject, see his 'Venetian Constitution', especially pp. 472–7.

others like him, wished, and was eventually to provoke a serious reaction within the ruling group. Thus, it is possible to discern in Niccolò's views in the 1430s not only an ideological basis for the oligarchic tendencies of the Medici regime, but also the seeds of future opposition which eventually emerged even within those groups originally most favourable to constitutional change.

The events of the 1430s represented only the beginning of the involvement of Niccolò and Tommaso in the new institutions of the Medici regime, particularly as their support for the regime contributed to their continuing appointment to posts of considerable importance. In 1440, the year when general scrutinies again became due, it was necessary to elect secretaries who would place the names of the successful candidates in the appropriate election bags. Niccolò and Tommaso were both selected for this task—Niccolò as one of the secretaries for the Guelf Party's scrutiny, and Tommaso as a secretary for the scrutiny of all offices except the Signoria and Colleges, called the *Tre Maggiori*.[37] Although both posts were merely administrative, it was important to the Medici group to ensure that any process involving political qualifications was not controlled by their enemies. They must have been anxious therefore that the posts were occupied by 'friends of the regime' and, in Tommaso's case at least, this was achieved by entrusting the election of the secretaries to the *Consiglio Maggiore*.

Once Niccolò and Tommaso had occupied a position which affected the regime's security, they, along with others who had filled the posts of secretary and *accoppiatore*, tended subsequently to be entrusted with further duties of major responsibility. Thus, they were included ex officio in a special council created in 1444 for purposes similar to the *Consiglio Maggiore*. Moreover, before that Tommaso, as an ex-secretary of the scrutiny of the general offices, was one of the citizens designated to select the membership of another short-lived council created in 1443.[38] In effect he, and to a

[37] For Niccolò's appointment: BNF, ii, iv, 346, fo. 144ʳ. For Tommaso's: Tratte, 60, fo. 238ʳ.
[38] Niccolò and Tommaso are listed as members of the 1444–9 *Balìa* in *Balìe*,

lesser degree Niccolò, were being called on to help preserve the political predominance of the Medici group, with which their own political authority and prominence were being identified.

As the foregoing suggests, by the early 1440s Tommaso rather than Niccolò was emerging as the more committed collaborator of the regime's leadership. The reasons for this are not altogether clear. Presumably Tommaso possessed a political viewpoint similar to his brother's—if anything more determinedly oligarchic—and in office he demonstrated a readiness to support the objectives of the inner circle of the regime. This attitude was probably reinforced by ambition, while the intelligence and ability which he displayed in office must have contributed to his gradual acceptance into the inner circle of the regime. The process whereby this occurred cannot be precisely traced, although his role in 1438 must have been a major step. Certainly, by the late 1430s and early 1440s, Tommaso was on terms of familiarity and confidence with several prominent citizens, and this must have been true within the political as in the personal sphere.[39] The most crucial of Tommaso's distinguished connections was with the Medici family, and in this case it was apparently the Medici who sought out Tommaso in order to establish with him the closest tie possible between Florentine families—that of marriage.[40]

The precise date of Tommaso's second marriage, with Dianora Tornabuoni, is nowhere recorded. Quite probably it followed not long after the death of his first wife, Maria Torrigiani, in the autumn of 1440, for Tommaso must have

---

26, fos. 31ᵛ–32ʳ, and in Rubinstein, *Government*, 266–7. On the creation of the special council in 1443, see ibid., 74.

[39] i.e. Tommaso was close enough to Giovannozzo Pitti to act as a witness to his wedding in May 1443: Notarile Antecos., G693, fo. 53ᵛ. Giovannozzo was not only an influential figure in his own right but a relative of the Luca Pitti who during the late 1450s was second in power only to the Medici.

[40] Tommaso's connections with the Medici were by no means new in the 1440s; e.g. in Feb. 1439 the widow of Averardo de' Medici renounced certain income from the *Monte* which she had been receiving although it was in the name of one of Tommaso's daughters: Notarile Antecos., G695, 27 Feb. 1439. Presumably Tommaso had been repaying her a loan, possibly on his brother's behalf, or assisting her financially.

wanted a mother for the small children Maria left behind.[41] In deciding on Dianora as his bride, however, Tommaso was undoubtedly taking other than domestic factors into account, for one of the most notable features of the Tornabuoni family was its close relationship with the Medici. The Tornabuoni had been partisans of the Medici from the pre-1434 period, and had become deeply involved in Medici banking affairs. Giovanni, the brother of Tommaso's wife, had become one of the Medici's branch managers and a director of the central firm. As was typical of Florentine enterprises, this business connection was further cemented by a marriage between the two families, as, about 1444, Dianora's sister Lucrezia married Cosimo de' Medici's eldest son Piero.[42] Therefore, through his marriage, Tommaso became a relative of Piero himself, and emphasized this aspect of the marriage alliance at least as much as his connection with the Tornabuoni. In fact, according to a near contemporary, Cosimo himself arranged Tommaso's as well as Piero's marriage, and he did so with the express purpose of winning the younger man's political support for his own son.[43] In return, Cosimo was willing to give Tommaso the benefits of Medici patronage, as after the marriage, this author went on, Cosimo furthered Tommaso's career by every means in his power.

Whether or not this account is totally accurate, the Soderini–Tornabuoni marriage connection was of profound political importance for both sides. On the one hand, it imbued

[41] Maria Torrigiani's date of death is stated in Tommaso's will of 10 Mar. 1462 (Notarile Antecos., M570, fo. 85ʳ) and in his statement that she died intestate (ibid., P128, unpaginated, 23 Mar. 1457). Various sources give different dates for the Soderini–Tornabuoni marriage, but it must have been arranged by 1446, as by early 1447 Dianora had already had a son: Cat., 655, fo. 842ʳ. It may well have been arranged long before, as is suggested by the union of their names under the date 1440 in a Zibaldone genealogico of F. del Migliore, BNF, Magl., 26, 145, p. 84.

[42] On the Tornabuoni's involvement in the Medici bank, cf. de Roover, *Rise and Decline*, 127, 219 ff. For the date of Piero's marriage with Lucrezia Tornabuoni, Molho and Kirschner, 'The Dowry Fund', 417.

[43] Cosimo Favilla, 'De origine', BNF, Conv. Soppr., c. 1. 145, fo. 119ʳ⁻ᵛ, published in Razzi, *Vita di Piero Soderini*, 167. As Favilla was writing late in the 15th c., his view may have been influenced by the post-1440s Soderini–Medici connection and by the habit of Cosimo's grandson Lorenzo of using marriages quite openly for political purposes (cf. Cohn, *The Labouring Classes*, 53). However, the practice was undoubtedly of much earlier origin: cf. Kent, *Rise*, 49–61.

Tommaso with all the sense of loyalty and obligation to the Medici which the strong family relationships of the time implied—a sentiment reinforced by the expectation of what Medici patronage could bestow. In turn, the marriage increased the Medici's readiness to further Tommaso's career, in the expectation that he would prove a devoted supporter. Acquiring such partisans was, as the above author suggests, of extreme importance to Cosimo, for he was fully aware of the difficulties which his family would face in maintaining their position of primacy, particularly after his own death. For both sides, then, the bond was beneficial. For the next twenty-five years Tommaso acted as a loyal collaborator of the Medici, continuing to support them in crises when many of their other friends deserted them. In turn, the Medici helped promote him to a position of immense personal influence, as the right-hand man of the city's leading family.

As Favilla suggested, the effect of the Medici connection may have been immediately visible in Tommaso's success in acquiring a series of powerful positions during the early 1440s, some of which brought him financial benefit as well as prestige, while they also implied a greater political responsibility, especially for the Medici regime's secure possession of power. In 1442 Tommaso was appointed for the first time to one of the city's principal financial offices, that of director of the *Monte*.[44] This magistracy not only administered the city's public funded debt, or *Monte*, but also supervised much of Florence's income and expenditure, which by this time was being channelled towards servicing the huge debt which had accumulated. Moreover, as part of their duties, the *Monte* Officials were sometimes called on to lend the state urgently needed funds which were afterwards repaid at high rates of interest. Although it is not clear that Tommaso was ever required to perform this task during his year in office, it is possible that he did so, and therefore that his post as *Monte* Official allowed him to make a personal profit as well as

---

[44] Tratte, 80, fo. 261ᵛ. On the lending functions of these officials, see Marks, 'The Financial Oligarchy', 132, 139–41.

bringing him political authority and prestige. Both the lending functions of the officials and their immense importance
within the city's financial system had caused the Medici
group to try and gain greater control over their appointment.
Thus, when Tommaso was appointed he was selected by a
combined process of election and sortition, which allowed
the executive, screened in part by the leading citizens, to
superimpose its control over the random appointment of
qualified candidates, without destroying the traditional selection procedure.

After winning his spurs as a financial official in supervising
the *Monte*, Tommaso was elected two years later to another
financial post as one of twelve '*Officiales Pratice et Banchi*'.
As such, he was required to produce his share of 20,000
florins required for immediate government expenditure, on
the understanding that it would be restored with interest
from taxes due to be paid seven to eight months later.[45] In
this case, Tommaso clearly made a profit from his position,
and even more clearly owed his appointment not to traditional selection procedures, but to the decision of a small
number of prominent citizens. The '*Officiales Pratice et
Banchi*' were elected by the Signoria and Colleges, of whom
the Signoria had in turn been vetted by the *accoppiatori*.

While Tommaso's appointment to such posts as *Monte*
and Bank Official signified his rising status within the ruling
group, his real arrival within the inner circle can best be
dated from his appointment in 1444 to the key position for
the Medici regime—that of *accoppiatore*. Tommaso's selection for this office was made by a group dominated by friends
of the regime—i.e. by a special council created in 1444 for
purposes similar to those of the earlier *Consiglio Maggiore*.
As in 1438, the institution of this *ad hoc* assembly was
prompted by the necessity of dealing with several thorny
issues. The spectre of a scrutiny was again beginning to haunt
the leading citizens, as it raised the possibility that their old
enemies might become eligible for key political offices. The
problem of extending the *accoppiatori*'s authority to screen
candidates to the Signoria had also arisen, as their powers

[45] Provv., 134, fos. 244^r–246^v; Tratte, 80, fo. 339^r.

had lapsed with the *Consiglio Maggiore* in 1441 and had subsequently been only partially reinstated.[46] In addition, many of the punishments meted out to the defeated faction in 1434 were now about to expire, and some leading citizens felt that appropriate action was necessary. Finally, although previous special councils had by no means always voted as the inner circle had wished, they had provided the leading citizens with a more effective vehicle for implementing their policies in foreign and internal affairs and for bypassing the resistance often posed by the more broadly based statutory councils.

Thus, in the spring of 1444 the principal citizens opted for the institution of another *Balìa*.[47] This group of some 240 citizens was granted the same powers as those possessed by the earlier *Consiglio Maggiore*—i.e. over the scrutiny, the method of selection of the Signoria, political punishments, and matters affecting the city's government. Moreover, it too was authorized to vote before the statutory councils on taxes, war and peace, and the hiring of soldiers. However, whereas the *Consiglio Maggiore* had been appointed for only three years, this *Balìa* was to last for five, from 1444 to 1449, without any change in its personnel. Its creation represented, then, a further stage in the establishment of a more fixed political élite in Florence, and in the strengthening of the authority of the inner circle within government. This was especially to be seen in the results of the scrutiny performed by this assembly, which in one case reversed the more liberal results of a partial review conducted the previous year. Moreover, it extended the political punishments imposed on the Albizzi faction, and appointed new *accoppiatori* not just to place the names of candidates successful in the scrutiny of the *Tre Maggiori* in the appropriate bags, but with the additional duty of electing the Signoria *a mano*.

It was not only Tommaso's election by this special assembly as *accoppiatore* which signalled his arrival within the

[46] i.e. the *accoppiatori* had been given authority to elect *a mano* only the principal figure within the Signoria, the Standardbearer of Justice, and the three Priors drawn from the *borsellino*: cf. Rubinstein, *Government*, 17.

[47] On the circumstances surrounding the creation of this *Balìa* of 1444–9, and its composition and powers, see ibid., 18–19, 74–5.

inner circle of the regime. The same was indicated by his appointment by the same *Balìa* for another delicate role, that of tax official.[48] Since 1434 the regime had tended to abandon the most objective forms of taxation ever devised at Florence—the *catasto*—in favour of more flexible methods of assessment. While these could be justified on the grounds that they allowed changes in wealth to be taken into account without time-consuming revisions of tax declarations, the real purpose was probably to avoid the heavy incidence of taxation on commercial wealth brought about by the *catasto*. However, the use of more discretionary taxation meant that the tax officials possessed powers which might be used punitively or with favouritism by citizens anxious to assist friends or harm political enemies. Since the strength and survival of the regime depended on its economic resources, it was important for the leading citizens of the regime to ensure that the tax officials were their friends as well as being competent and trustworthy officials. It was undoubtedly for this reason that the post-1434 regime tended to entrust their election to the *Balìe*, which were likely to appoint prominent members of the regime, such as Tommaso.

As both tax official and *accoppiatore*, Tommaso was fulfilling functions which were unpopular with many of his fellow citizens. On the one hand, by 1444 some Florentines were convinced that the perpetuation of the post-1434 innovations was endangering not only their chance to participate in politics, but republican government itself. An extreme statement of this point of view was made by Giovanni Cavalcanti, who, by the 1440s, had qualified his support for Cosimo de' Medici with bitter criticism of the type of government which was evolving under Medici leadership. According to Cavalcanti, the measures of 1444 meant the establishment in Florence of a 'tyrannical mode of government', in that the ten *accoppiatori* acted as 'ten tyrants' who 'drew [for the Signoria] whomever they wanted, and not whom the people had designated'.[49] Like other Florentines, Cavalcanti was isolating the powers of the

---

[48] Tratte, 80, fo. 343^r.
[49] Cavalcanti, *Istorie*, ii. 193.

accoppiatori as the principal means whereby a small group of citizens was subverting the popular elements of the Florentine government, and Tommaso, as an *accoppiatore*, was becoming identified as one of the worst offenders in a system which some citizens were by now openly describing as tyrannical and repressive.

Similarly, Tommaso's job of assessing taxes was bound to arouse resentment among a population always prepared to complain of discrimination.[50] In fact, when Tommaso was a tax official fear was expressed that retaliation might be taken against these magistrates by citizens who believed—justly or not—that they had been unfairly assessed. In June 1444 the Signoria informed the *Balìa* that since the scrutiny was to follow immediately after the issue of the new tax, aggrieved citizens might revenge themselves by voting against the tax officials and their relatives in the scrutiny. To guard against this, the Signoria presented special legislation by which the officials, their brothers and their sons received automatic majorities for those posts for which they had previously been qualified.[51] Thus, with the Signoria favourable to the Medici group, citizens like Tommaso could be defended from the possible consequences of carrying out unpopular governmental tasks, and this in turn must have reinforced their commitment to institutional controls.

Unlike Tommaso, Niccolò was not elected to any positions by the *Balìa* of 1444–9. Although he had been appointed to undertake responsible duties as secretary, he had apparently not become sufficiently close or committed to the circle surrounding the Medici to be selected for such a crucial office as, for example, *accoppiatore*. In part, Niccolò's personal connections had contributed to this, for, while Tommaso was being drawn into an enduring intimacy with the Medici, Niccolò seems to have lost his early contacts with the family. Niccolò's marriage in 1437 in fact allied him with a clan connected with the exiles of 1434. His bride, Ginevra

---

[50] Cf. Francesco Guicciardini's comment that his uncle Jacopo refused appointment as tax official because he could not help 'displeasing many citizens' while fulfilling these duties: *Memorie di famiglia*, 43. Cf. also Molho, *Public Finances*, 108, on action taken against tax assessors.

[51] Balìe, 26, fos. 27^v–28^v, 40^r, 42^r, 30 May to 22 June 1444.

Macinghi, was the sister of the famous Alessandra Macinghi negli Strozzi who, as widow of the exiled Matteo Strozzi, left an eloquent account of the tribulations of a family on the wrong political side in Medicean Florence. The marriage had little immediate effect on Niccolò's political career, not least because he chose to remain aloof from his Strozzi in-laws, while during the 1430s, at least, some of the Macinghi remained sufficiently acceptable to the Medici group to be included in the early *Balìe*.[52] Nevertheless, the marriage must have contributed to Niccolò's exclusion from that amorphous but powerful group around the Medici who repeatedly sought to strengthen their political position through institutional controls. Moreover, principle may have played a part in Niccolò's gradual estrangement from the Medici group, for, although enthusiastic for the innovations of 1438 and their oligarchic, stabilizing tendencies, he may have come to feel, by the mid-1440s, that the degree of concentration of power being brought about by the Medici group was excessive. In particular, he may have disapproved of the repeated extension of the *accoppiatori*'s powers, for in 1446 he formed part of a Signoria which raised the question of abolishing elections *a mano* long before they were due to expire.[53] Thus, while still a prominent member of the regime, Niccolò was probably questioning the key feature of the political changes introduced by the Medici group and one with which his brother had become closely involved. By the mid-1440s, then, the political sympathies and principles of Niccolò and Tommaso were beginning to diverge, and, although no outright conflict between them occurred for over a decade, they were beginning to carry the brothers into opposed and ultimately hostile political camps.

[52] Carlo di Niccolò Macinghi was a member of the *Balìa* of 1434, and his brother Giovachino was included in that of 1438: Rubinstein, *Government*, 252, 263. Thereafter, like Niccolò, the family appears to have become distanced from the Medici group.

[53] Ibid., 23.

2. Opposing Political Paths

The settlement of 1444 constituted a turning point not just for the Soderini, but for the regime as a whole. Now that it was clear that the controls were to be used to shift the locus of political power and not solely as a defence against the defeated faction, opposition against them became more widespread and persistent. During the subsequent two decades resistance to the new political forms surfaced repeatedly, and the battle over the constitution intensified until a temporary resolution was achieved in 1458. That this involved a further elaboration of the partisan institutions used since 1434 and a confirmation of the leading citizens' power was due in large measure to active championship of the new institutions by committed and capable citizens, such as Tommaso Soderini. During the later 1440s and 1450s, Tommaso emerged as a major figure in these political struggles, as his attachment to the Medici and his own political ambition made him a leading exponent of the restrictive institutions against which a rising chorus of criticism was by now being heard.

Tommaso's first major battle for the interests of the regime's inner circle occurred in 1449, the year in which the *Balìa* of 1444 was to terminate and with it, presumably, elections *a mano* of the Signoria. Since 1444 the *Balìa* had apparently been prolonging the *accoppiatori*'s powers, and once it was dissolved it was very unlikely that the statutory councils would prove as amenable to the perpetuation of the *accoppiatori*'s control.[1] Recognizing this, the leading citizens made attempts to prolong the term of the *Balìa*, but all of these met with indomitable resistance from the councils.[2]

---

[1] Cf. Rubinstein, *Government*, 18–19.   [2] Ibid., 19–20, 76–7.

Indeed, by the late 1440s several factors were combining to strengthen hostility to the 1444 settlement. Apart from the restrictions placed on the powers of the statutory councils and on citizens' appointments to the Signoria, the institutional controls possessed implications for the perennially controversial issue of taxation. After 1434 the Medici group had succeeded in gradually abandoning the *catasto*, but the more arbitrary forms which had replaced it were held by many citizens to be less objective and less just. In an effort to respond to this criticism, a revised assessment had been introduced in 1446–7, but complaints about the injustice of the system continued.[3] After an invasion of southern Tuscany by King Alfonso of Aragon in 1447 Florence's military expenditure, and hence the incidence of taxation, increased, and with them discontent over the method of assessment. Criticism rapidly spread to the government responsible for tax policy, and thence to the unpopular controls which so fortified the power of the inner, policy-making circle of the regime. Even some of the prominent citizens of the *Pratica* began to condemn these controls, and to suggest doing away with the hated *Balìa*, or with what some called the excessive authority of the *accoppiatori*.[4] As one commentator in a *Pratica* in the summer of 1448 asserted, in terms reminiscent of Giovanni Cavalcanti, the real source of the widespread discontent lay in the fact that the city was being governed 'tyrannically', by the *accoppiatori*, instead of 'popularly' as, he was implying, was the Florentine tradition.[5]

It was in this atmosphere of rebellion that the termination of the *Balìa* approached, and the leading citizens were faced with the prospect of a return to the pre-1444 situation and a

---

[3] The *decima scalata* was intended to be a fairer tax: Balìe, 26, fos. 150ʳ–154ʳ; Canestrini, *La scienza*, 221–5. However, it was criticized both because it retained an arbitrary element and because some wealthy citizens, including Cosimo de' Medici, thought it made them pay too much: Giannozzo Pandolfini to Bartolomeo Cederni, 17 Oct 1447, Corp. relig. soppr., 78, 314, fo. 303; CP, 52, fos. 28ᵛ–29ᵛ, 3 Nov 1447. On the criticism of arbitrariness in taxation, cf. n. 52 below and, for the pre-1427 period, Molho, *Public Finances*, 76 ff and Klapisch-Zuber and Herlihy, *Les Toscans*, 31–3.

[4] Cf. CP, 52, fos. 38ʳ, 55ᵛ, 4 Apr., 16 June 1448. Cf. also Rubinstein, *Government*, 76–7.

[5] Messer Giovanni Bertaldi, 3 June 1448, CP, 52, fo. 49ᵛ.

loss of the additional authority which they had since enjoyed. It was precisely at this point—in March–April 1449—that Tommaso Soderini was appointed for the first time as Standardbearer of Justice. Indeed, this was the first occasion on which he was eligible for the position, for he had reached the minimum age of 45 only the previous year. His colleagues, the *accoppiatori*, must immediately have qualified him for the post, and seen that his name was included the first time the Standardbearer was to be drawn from Tommaso's quarter of S. Spirito.[6] Their eagerness to promote him to the chairmanship of the Signoria was undoubtedly connected with the existing political circumstances, for the inner circle had every reason to want a friend in this powerful office at this point. As head of the Signoria, the Standardbearer wielded considerable influence over his colleagues' decisions, and therefore over legislative proposals and government initiatives. Moreover, he helped select the citizens invited to the *Pratiche*, where the fact that he chaired the sessions gave him an opportunity to affect the outcome of these crucial debates.

Tommaso had probably consulted the leading citizens before he called a *Pratica* on 16 March 1449, to discuss the principal questions then at issue, i.e. the institutional controls and taxation. Although the complete list of citizens summoned to this meeting is not extant, the fact that the consensus which they reached was reported by four of the leading figures of the Medici circle, including Cosimo de' Medici himself, suggests that the final decision was determined by a small, select group. Even these citizens, however, were not prepared in the prevailing atmosphere to try again to extend the life of the *Balìa*. Instead, they made two proposals designed to counteract the effects of its forthcoming dissolution. On the subject of taxation, they recommended that legislation should be entrusted for a year to a

    [6] Tommaso was born 12 Aug. 1403: Tratte, 61, fo. 123ʳ. He must have been declared eligible for the post of Standardbearer in the scrutiny of Aug. 1448: Rubinstein, *Government*, 53–4. The *accoppiatori* were obliged to include a minimum number of candidates' names in the election bags, but they could increase certain citizens' chances by selecting others who were temporarily ineligible to fill the post. Tommaso's appointment as Standardbearer is recorded in Tratte, 200, fo. 89ᵛ.

special assembly previously used for this purpose rather than being restored to the purview of the statutory councils.[7] As regards the electoral controls, an analogous solution was offered, as it was suggested that before resigning the *accoppiatori* should prepare special election bags from which the next six Signorie would be appointed.[8] Thus, some control over the Signoria could be exercised for an additional year, during which time the leading citizens could think of alternative approaches, or a change in the climate of opinion might allow a return to elections *a mano*.

Although the proposal regarding taxation was never presented to the *Balìa*, that of the special election bags was translated into a draft bill. The fact that it took ten days to do so suggests, however, that considerable opposition had to be overcome within the executive before agreement could be reached. That was, moreover, only the first hurdle, as much stronger objections were voiced by the *Balìa*, which rejected the proposal on two successive occasions.[9] Despite this indication that even prominent and trusted citizens of the regime opposed the inner circle's plan, Tommaso was unwilling to accept the *Balìa*'s decision as final. Instead, he again sought the opinion of the citizens of the previous *Pratica*, and followed their advice to summon another forty 'leading citizens of the regime' for discussion. If the intention was to persuade these citizens to support the recently defeated bill, the effort was a failure, for many of them roundly condemned the leading citizens' proposal. Several admonished Tommaso not to force on citizens what they so clearly did not want, while others asserted that the measure was unnecessary, and that the arguments of war and plague being used to justify it were really obscuring a different motive. As one put it, the inner circle was simply trying to prolong its

---

[7] i.e. the 131 or the 145: CP, 52, fo. 74ʳ. Both these councils were composed of a large number of official members and a smaller number of specially selected ones, and, like many special councils of the Medici period, had to approve legislation in certain key areas before it was presented to the Councils of the People and Commune: Rubinstein, *Government*, 68–9.

[8] CP, 52, fo. 74ʳ.

[9] For the *Balìa*'s resistance to tax bills, see Libri fab., 60, fos. 92ᵛ–93ʳ. The legislation on the special bags was presented to the *Balìa* on 26, 27 Mar. 1449: ibid., fo. 92ᵛ.

tenure of power at the community's expense, for 'the people want to recover their old ways and pristine liberty'.[10]

After such outspoken criticism, Tommaso decided once more to seek the opinion, and the support, of his original advisers. Since they chose to ignore the negative opinions expressed in the preceding *Pratica*, and encouraged him again to present the proposals regarding the special bags to the *Balìa*, he did so, and, although it was again rejected, he still refused to let the idea drop. Instead, he took the unusual step of summoning representatives of the special council in order to sound out opinion within it, and, possibly, to exert pressure on its members to pass the bill. However, the response from these citizens was so discouraging that even Tommaso finally decided to let the idea die.[11]

Despite the best will in the world Tommaso had not been able to achieve the political goals of the inner circle of the regime. Hostility to institutional controls had proved stronger than the leading citizens' influence, with the result that, in May 1449 the constitutional forms of the pre-1444 period were restored. Although Tommaso must have been disappointed by his legislative failure, there was one further way in which he and other leading citizens could hope to influence future government policy. Before leaving office, the *accoppiatori* were to prepare, or 'close', the election bags of the Signoria for the return to sortition. In fulfilling this duty they possessed their normal authority of determining which citizens should be eligible for the post of Standardbearer of Justice, and which name-tags should be included in the special bag or *borsellino* from which three members of the Signoria were chosen. On this occasion the *Balìa* also agreed to grant them additional authority to add some names to, and remove some from, the election bags of the Signoria.[12] All these powers they presumably used in the interests of the regime, as they saw it, while they also decided to employ their authority for their own benefit and that of their closest

[10] These *Pratiche* of 27, 28 Mar. 1449 are recorded in CP, 52, fos. 75ʳ–76ʳ. Cf. Rubinstein, *Government*, 26–7.

[11] Libri fab., 60, fo. 93ʳ, 31 Mar. 1449.

[12] Rubinstein, *Government*, 42–3. The citizens whose names were added had to have passed certain previous scrutinies.

relatives. In Tommaso's case, the *accoppiatori* placed all the tags which he had accumulated for posts in the Signoria in the bag from which the Standardbearer of Justice was to be drawn.[13] Thereby he gained the maximum chance of future appointment to this prestigious post, whence he could continue to battle on behalf of the inner circle of the regime. Tommaso was undoubtedly also instrumental in ensuring that half of his brother Niccolò's name-tags were placed in the same bag as Tommaso's and half in the select bag for the Priorate.[14] Thus, although the *accoppiatori* failed to show Niccolò the same favour as they did Tommaso, they were still prepared practically to guarantee him access to the highest positions in the republic.

However, the *accoppiatori*'s action was at best only a slight modification of the electoral system in favour of the leadership of the post-1434 regime. Some figures within the Medici group decided that much more decisive action was necessary, presumably to preserve the advantages which they had enjoyed during the era of institutional controls. On 1 May 1449 over sixty of these citizens banded together in a pact committing them to pursue the interests of the Medici group privately and informally. According to Florentine constitutional practice this also meant illegally, as they were in effect placing the interests of a faction before those of the community as a whole. However, they succeeded in concealing their partisan goals, perhaps even from themselves, by framing their rationale in terms of the same permanent republican ideal as had traditionally animated Florentines of all persuasions. They, no less than Giovanni Cavalcanti and the representatives of civic humanism, proclaimed their goal to be 'most holy and sweetest liberty'. However, their programme differed in that they asserted that liberty should be preserved and the republic maintained in its 'good and tranquil state' not only by the existing constitutional means but also by 'secret and special counsels, actions, and assistants'.[15] While they professed to aim at the elimination of

---

[13] Tratte, 61, fo. 79ʳ.
[14] Ibid., fo. 79ᵛ. On the regulations governing this closure of the bags, cf. Rubinstein, *Government*, 20, 42–4.
[15] This pact was published several times by Armando Sapori, e.g. in *Eventail*, ii.

discords among citizens and the observance of justice, it was clear that they intended these goals to serve the interests of one section of the citizen body. Thus, the signatories obligated themselves to attend to the 'preservation and advancement of this present . . . regime', and in particular to see that offices and taxes were distributed and legal cases decided as best promoted the 'greatness and happiness of the present . . . regime'. Moreover, the signatories committed themselves to keeping all the regime's friends 'on the good path'; anyone who secretly or openly 'tried anything against this present peaceful state' they swore to 'persecute . . . and see that they are punished'.

The signatories of this pact represented no easily definable political group. Many came from the regime's leadership—*accoppiatori* who had just laid down their duties or citizens repeatedly summoned to the *Pratiche*. However, several of the most prominent figures of government, such as Neri Capponi, Domenico Martelli, and even Agnolo Acciaiuoli, did not sign the pact, while some of its signatories were relatively obscure. The oath-takers did not, then, represent the regime's inner circle. Rather, the pact apparently drew together citizens who, through ambition, obligation, or fear, had become the most determined advocates of a concentration of power in the inner circle of the regime. In part, at least, they must have been citizens who benefited most from the concentration of patronage which it implied. Typical of them was the recent Standardbearer of Justice, Tommaso Soderini, who was one of the first to sign the document.

In contrast, Niccolò Soderini did not sign the pact of 1 May 1449—further confirmation that Niccolò was not within, nor anxious to fortify the authority of, the circle surrounding the Medici. Nevertheless, he remained a prominent and influential citizen within the regime, and his views

115–32, and in *Studi*, i. 412–26. Although he sees Tommaso Soderini as the major influence behind the pact, acting, he assumes, as Cosimo's agent, there is no evidence to support this view. The fact that the only remaining copy is preserved in the Niccolini family archive suggests that Otto Niccolini would be a more logical candidate for the role. However, even if Otto, as a lawyer, may have drawn up the pact, it was undoubtedly the product of a small partisan group acting collectively, as they undoubtedly had done and continued to do for years.

on most issues were in harmony with those of the Medici group. Moreover, Niccolò's abilities were clearly appreciated even within the highest circles, as his brilliant career in the early 1450s demonstrates. To this the *accoppiatori*, and particularly his brother, contributed, for once they had placed several of Niccolò's name-tags in the election bags for the position of Standardbearer of Justice, the return to sortition meant that he would eventually be selected for the post. This finally occurred at the end of October 1451, and for the following two months Niccolò acted for the first time as official head of the republic.

He took office during a time of particular tension for Florence, for in 1447 the last Visconti Duke of Milan had died, leaving no legitimate male heir. A war of succession had consequently developed between, on the one hand, Venice and King Alfonso of Naples, and, on the other, the principal claimant to the Duchy, the mercenary captain and husband of the Duke's daughter, Francesco Sforza. During the preceding decades, Sforza had established close ties with some of the leading Florentines, in particular with Cosimo de' Medici, as Francesco served as a source of military support for Florence while the Florentines, in particular Cosimo, supplied him with advice and sorely needed funds. During the war of the Milanese succession, the support of Cosimo and other prominent Florentines had enabled Francesco to gain Florentine financial backing and, with it, to take Milan in March 1450. However, his rivals for the Duchy had no intention of accepting his victory as final, and, after a Sforza–Florence alliance was signed in the summer of 1451, events were building towards war again in the autumn of 1451.[16]

As far as the Florentines were concerned, the principal question during Niccolò's term as Standardbearer was to what extent they should assist their ally. Since the city had

---

[16] On the political situation in Italy at this time, see Sacchi, 'Cosimo de' Medici', 274–85, 340–6; Rossi, 'Niccolò V', 241–61, 392–421; Jordan, 'Florence', 93–119; *Storia di Milano*, vii. 24–7. Niccolò Soderini had known Francesco Sforza from at least the late 1430s, when he was trying to use his influence to gain positions outside Florence: e.g. Niccolò to Agnolo Strozzi, 19 May 1438, Carte Strozz., ser. 3, 130, fo. 239ʳ.

already paid out vast sums in the recent war against the King of Naples, many citizens were reluctant to make further sacrifices for so distant and anti-republican a cause. In this situation, the attitude of the new Standardbearer was crucial, and, to the relief of Cosimo de' Medici, Niccolò proved to be firmly on Sforza's side. Niccolò had known Sforza since the 1430s, and, as an enthusiastic advocate of a Sforza Milan, he was now prepared to lend his efforts to convincing the Florentine councils to grant the subsidies requested by the new Duke. Although by no means always successful, Niccolò was instrumental in the passage of financial legislation favourable to the Duke, and, according to the Milanese ambassador, even succeeded in dissipating Cosimo de' Medici's temporary discouragement regarding Sforza's chances of victory.[17] Niccolò seems greatly to have impressed the Milanese ambassador, who wrote to his master that he was a 'very prudent and bold man, very affectionate to Your Lordship and much more to the preservation of the dignity and honour of this republic'.[18]

The energy and relative success with which Niccolò fulfilled his duties as Standardbearer, and the fame brought him by his leadership of the republic in this dangerous moment, undoubtedly contributed to the rapidity with which he was promoted thereafter to a series of prestigious appointments. At the very beginning of 1452 he was selected as one of the ambassadors designated to welcome Emperor Frederick III as he passed through Florentine territory on his way to Rome.[19] Immediately thereafter, in February 1452, he was given the further honour of appointment by the special war magistracy, the *Dieci di Balìa*, as ambassador to Genoa.[20]

---

[17] The financial proposals passed, frequently with great difficulty, during Niccolò's term of office are recorded in Libri fab., 62, fos. 109ʳ–129ᵛ. For the comments on Cosimo: Niccolò Arcimboldi to the Duke of Milan, 3, 5 Nov. 1451, ASMi, SPE, Firenze, 265. Cf. Rossi, 'Niccolò V', 385–8.

[18] Arcimboldi to the Duke, 3 Nov. 1451, ASMi, SPE, Firenze, 265. By 'the dignity and honour of the republic', Arcimboldi was probably referring to Niccolò's determination that Florence abide by her promised commitment to Sforza.

[19] On the Emperor's visit, see Cambi, *Istorie*, in *Delizie*, xx. 278–86; Boninsegni, *Storie*, 95–8; Petribuoni, 'Priorista', BNF, Conv. Soppr., c. 4. 895, fos. 154ᵛ–156ʳ; Palmieri, *Annales*, 162–3.

[20] Dieci, Miss., Leg. e Comm., 4, fos. 16ᵛ–17ᵛ.

This diplomatic mission marked a high point in Niccolò's career, as only the most eminent and experienced citizens were chosen for these sometimes crucial duties abroad. In this case, Niccolò was a particularly suitable choice, as he had presided over the conclusion of Florence's alliance with Genoa while Standardbearer of Justice, and was now being sent to ensure that Genoa abided by the commitment she had then made to Florence and Milan. According to Agnolo della Stufa, Florence's new ambassador to Genoa was a 'vigorous man able to start things boiling',[21] and Niccolò certainly exerted all his energies in trying to convince the Genoese that their best interests lay on the Sforza–Florentine side.

To the Genoese, his vigorous prosecution of their allies' interests was a little annoying, especially as Niccolò was so forthright in his criticism of the Doge's tendency to give his own and Genoa's security the highest priority. To the Milanese ambassador, on the other hand, Niccolò's presentations were a model of intelligence, eloquence, and force, while the *Dieci* were sufficiently impressed by Niccolò's performance to maintain him in his post at Genoa for almost the whole of 1452.[22] When Niccolò was finally recalled in December 1452 he was understandably reluctant to leave a post which made him a conspicuous figure on the international diplomatic scene. As ambassador, Niccolò had been in constant communication with princes and with the leading citizens of Florence, including Cosimo de' Medici. That Niccolò was at this time on reasonably good, if not close, terms with Cosimo is indicated by the willingness he expressed to follow Cosimo's guidance in questions of foreign policy.[23] Indeed, according to Niccolò, when he was recalled Cosimo as well as the *Dieci* wrote urging him to return and promising that he could resume his post at Genoa at a later date.[24]

[21] Agnolo della Stufa to the Duke, 13 Feb. 1452, ASMi, SPE, Firenze, 265.

[22] For the Milanese ambassador's reports on Niccolò's actions as ambassador and the Genoese attitude to him, see Sceva de Curte to the Duke, 24 Sept., 12, 28 Oct. 1452, ASMi, SPE, Genova, 407. Cf. also Niccolò to the Duke, 1 Sept., 10, 29 Oct., 12 Nov. 1452, ibid. On the Genoese attitude, Fossati, 'Francesco Sforza', 336–9.

[23] Cf. Niccolò to the Duke, 20 Aug., 12 Nov., 5 Dec. 1452, ASMi, SPE, Genova, 407.

[24] Niccolò to the Duke, 2 Jan. 1453, Milan, Bibl. Ambros., MS Z.247. Sup., fo. 3.

Niccolò was well enough regarded by his fellow citizens to be loaded with further honours after his return to Florence. During his absence he had already been appointed a member of another special council, or *Balìa*, created in July 1452 to deal expeditiously with problems arising from the war. Moreover, according to Niccolò's own account, he discovered on his return that his fellow Florentines were profoundly discouraged by the loss of some of their southern territories to King Alfonso of Naples. As he wrote to the Duke of Milan, he successfully roused them to energetic resistance, with the result that he was appointed as one of the commissaries directing military operations in the area.[25] He was not long in this post before he was appointed to the *Otto di Guardia*, the magistracy responsible for state security. As these officials were then being elected by the Signoria and Colleges, the *Dieci di Balìa* and the *accoppiatori*,[26] Niccolò must clearly have been highly esteemed by the upper circles of the Florentine regime. In March 1453, moreover, he was chosen along with four other citizens to arrange the state funeral of the city's famous and highly respected Chancellor Carlo Marsuppini.[27]

Niccolò's series of distinguished appointments was crowned in May 1453 by his reappointment as ambassador to Genoa. However, this posting was not to be a repetition of the successful performance of the previous year. If Niccolò had offended the Doge before by his severe criticism of Genoa's failure to support her allies to the hilt, this time he threatened to alienate him totally by backing one of his rivals for the leadership of the Genoese government. Niccolò hoped that replacing the existing Doge would result in greater Genoese assistance for Sforza and for Florence. However, his confidence was not shared by Francesco Sforza, who was undoubtedly aware that the claimant backed by Niccolò had

[25] Niccolò to the Duke, 2 Jan. 1453, ibid. Niccolò was mentioned as a commissary in the area in Sig., Miss., 1a Canc., 38, fos. 15ᵛ, 25ʳ, 33ᵛ, dated 3, 13, 22 Jan. 1453.

[26] Tratte, 80, fo. 27ᵛ. On the method of appointment of the *Otto* at this time, see Rubinstein, *Government*, 52.

[27] On Carlo Marsuppini's funeral: Cambi, *Istorie*, in *Delizie*, xx. 310–11; Boninsegni, *Storie*, 102; Giovanni, 'Ricordanze', Carte Strozz., ser. 2, 16ᵇⁱˢ, fo. 16ᵛ.

connections with his own enemies, and who consequently became very concerned at Niccolò's dangerous meddling in Genoese affairs. Arguing that Niccolò was going far beyond his original commission, Sforza tried to have him recalled in late August 1453 through the good offices of his friend Cosimo de' Medici. Cosimo, on the other hand, while in agreement with Sforza, pointed out to the Duke the danger of alienating such a powerful individual as Niccolò, who had, Cosimo wrote, many supporters. Nevertheless, he promised by 'some honourable excuse' to see that Niccolò was recalled, and this was successfully accomplished in September 1453.[28] Despite protesting his innocence and his constant devotion to Milanese interests, Niccolò was therefore forced to return home, knowing that he had incurred the displeasure of Francesco Sforza.

Although Niccolò's embassy had ended in disgrace, his diplomatic career was not yet over. The *Dieci* who took office in December 1453, and included Cosimo de' Medici himself, sent him on two further missions, to the lords of Rimini and Pesaro in late 1453 and early 1454.[29] However, these embassies were of minor importance, and thereafter Niccolò was never again appointed to a diplomatic post. Moreover, the later 1450s saw a relative decline in his political career: although he received the positions normally available by lot to a Florentine successful in the scrutinies, he was not appointed during the following fifteen years to any position within the Signoria. After 1454, in fact, he received only one elective position, which was granted by the statutory councils rather than by magistracies representing the inner circle of the regime.[30] While Niccolò seems, then, to

---

[28] Cf. the Duke to Cosimo de' Medici, 25 Aug. 1453, and Boccaccino Alamanni and Nicodemo Tranchedini to the Duke, 1 Sept. 1453, ASMi, SPE, Firenze, 266, and the Duke's reply of 18 Sept., ibid. The Signoria's letter recalling Niccolò referred only to his family's wish to have him at home: the Signoria to Niccolò Soderini, 25 Sept. 1453, Sig., Miss., 1a Canc., 39, fo. 143ᵛ. On the situation at Genoa in the spring and summer of 1453, cf. Colombo, 'Re Renato', 84–94; Catalano, *Francesco Sforza*, 80 ff.

[29] Cf. Notarile Antecos., P128, fo. 93ʳ, 28 Dec. 1453 and fo. 107ʳ, 11 Mar. 1454. These are notarial statements that Niccolò left on these missions. There is apparently no further extant documentation.

[30] Niccolò was elected by the statutory councils to a financial commission of

50   *Opposing Political Paths*

he gradually lost the esteem which he had enjoyed within the
inner circle. In part this was undoubtedly because of the poor
judgement and wilfulness he had shown as ambassador in
Genoa, as a result of which the other leading citizens must
have been less eager to entrust him with delicate political
tasks. Moreover, the incident may have created some suspicion between Niccolò and the Medici. In turn, the fact that
from the mid-1450s Niccolò saw himself excluded from
prestigious magistracies may have caused him to resent the
figures who most influenced political appointments, particularly when *Balìe* and elections *a mano* were in place. This
resentment must have been reinforced by personal conflicts
which developed between him and several prominent members of the Medici group. With Antonio Pucci and Otto
Niccolini, both well-known Medici friends, Niccolò seems to
have quarrelled over property.[31] More seriously, he incurred
the enmity of Piero de' Medici's brother Giovanni, who
apparently persecuted Niccolò in his private affairs.[32] Presumably, the opposition of such influential citizens contributed to the decline evident in Niccolò's political career, and
made him increasingly hostile to the group who wielded
power in Florence. Apparently opposed to the continued
power of the *accoppiatori* by the 1440s, Niccolò may thus
for personal reasons have felt an increasing revulsion against
the concentration of power in the Medici group, and a
greater impulse to maintain the more 'popular' elements of
the Florentine constitution. The continued esteem in which
he was held by the wider regime must have strengthened this
commitment, not least because a popular line was more
likely to bring Niccolò further political success. It is hardly

1456–7, apparently created to increase the income of the *Monte* and indirect taxes:
Tratte, 80, fo. 279ʳ, Provv., 146, fos. 352ᵛ–355ʳ.

[31] Niccolò quarrelled with Otto Niccolini over a farm belonging to the Macinghi
family: Francesco Caccini to Bartolomeo Cederni, 17 July 1454, Corp. relig. soppr.,
78, 314, fo. 597. By Jan. 1453 he felt it necessary to agree to arbitration with
Antonio Pucci (Notarile Antecos., M564, fo. 125ᵛ), who was described in 1465 as
a determined enemy of his: Alessandra Strozzi to her son Filippo, 2 Nov. 1465, in
Lettere, 506.

[32] On Niccolò's quarrel with Giovanni and its consequences, see Chapter 3.

surprising, then, that during the later 1450s Niccolò moved increasingly into the anti-Medici camp—a trend further reinforced by his response to internal developments in the constitutional and financial spheres.

These internal developments of the mid- and later 1450s again involved the familiar issues of political institutions and taxation, and saw the brothers play conspicuous, though opposing, roles in their city's politics. As mentioned above, after an abeyance of both *Balìe* and elections *a mano* between 1449 and 1452, a new special council was created for the ostensible purpose of providing the efficient government required during war. However, the leading citizens' objectives really went further, for the new council was also given authority over such matters as scrutinies and the appointment of the Signoria. It was subsequently used to restore elections *a mano* of the Signoria, and it placed in charge of them not new *accoppiatori* but those who had already closed the bags in 1449. While such measures could be justified on the grounds that during a war crisis it was essential to have trusted people in the principal offices, the leading citizens were also using the situation to recover their influence over the membership of a key political office, and to ensure that this power was delegated to citizens who had proved loyal to them in the past. Among the latter was Tommaso Soderini, who, as ex-*accoppiatore*, was both automatically a member of the new special council and one of the *accoppiatori* in charge of the renewed elections *a mano*.

That some of the leading citizens, at least, had long-term political objectives was yet clearer when the terms of both *Balìa* and elections *a mano* were extended in late 1453. Although peace was imminent, the Signoria, now screened by the *accoppiatori*, used the spectre of war to persuade the special council to pass this measure. However, the unpopularity of both controls was such that once peace had been signed between Venice and the Duke of Milan in April 1454 the legislative councils eagerly accepted a proposal to dissolve the *Balìa*, whose original rationale had now disappeared.[33] This action could not have been taken without the initiative

---

[33] Cf. Rubinstein, *Government*, 21–2.

of the Signoria then in office, and in particular of the then Standardbearer of Justice, Dietisalvi Neroni.

Dietisalvi had for years been a prominent Medici supporter, and a powerful figure within the regime. He had acted as *accoppiatore*, had sat in the various *Balìe* of his time, and had helped introduce and reintroduce the electoral controls which had so strengthened the authority of the regime's inner circle. However, his family had not always supported institutional controls, and, as a Milanese ambassador was later to report, he was secretly jealous of the Medici family's supremacy. By chance, a letter from Tommaso Soderini gives a fairly clear account of the circumstances of Dietisalvi's action and of how Tommaso responded to this attack from within on the Medici group's policies and power. Tommaso's correspondent was Piero de' Medici, then one of the Florentine ambassadors attempting to persuade the Venetians to strengthen the recently concluded peace of Lodi by forming an alliance with Florence and Milan. Being out of the city, Piero was unable to exercise a direct influence on events, while his father Cosimo was incapacitated by illness. It was undoubtedly because of this weakening of Medici vigilance that Dietisalvi succumbed to the arguments of citizens opposed to the existing political controls and opted for a decision of which Piero de' Medici disapproved.

With no major Medici figure able to intervene, Tommaso himself, on learning of Dietisalvi's plan to dissolve the *Balìa*, had attempted to dissuade the Standardbearer from any such action. He had, he wrote to Piero, reminded Dietisalvi that the regime's security depended on three interrelated factors: 'the *Balìa*, the election bags, and the *catasto*'.[34] Thereby, Tommaso was clearly expressing the practical connection between the special councils of the Medici period and the controls over political appointments. Moreover, he was arguing that the regime's security had a financial basis. Possibly, he meant that the *catasto*, or rather its absence, was a means of strengthening the regime's political control by

---

[34] Tommaso Soderini to Piero de' Medici, 5 June 1454, MAP, xx, 93.

helping to preserve the fortunes of citizens friendly to the Medici group.

Despite Tommaso's arguments, Dietisalvi had gone ahead with the abolition of the special council. Moreover, it was rumoured that he and other citizens—some of them, according to Tommaso, among the most prominent of the regime— were considering further steps, such as terminating elections *a mano* of the Signoria and annulling the results of the most recent scrutiny, performed by the *Balìa* in 1453.[35] However, Dietisalvi did not go on to implement these measures, whether because he feared to go too far, or because arguments of the sort which Tommaso was using finally began to strike home. By 5 June, Tommaso was able to write to Piero that the Standardbearer now seemed animated by better intentions, while opponents of the political controls were disappointed that the possibility of a return to sortition of the Signoria was rapidly disappearing.[36]

Although the danger to the Medici group thus seemed for the moment to be over, Tommaso was concerned that a serious error had been committed. Dietisalvi, he wrote to Piero, should have been suitably 'clarified' before he entered office. Now, Tommaso warned, the Standardbearer should be confirmed in the better path, 'especially', he added significantly, 'in everything he will obtain from your family'.[37] Tommaso's warnings apparently alerted Piero to the seriousness of the situation at Florence. Unable to assess events himself, Piero wrote to his brother Giovanni on 29 June that he was aware that 'our internal affairs need help' and, demonstrating considerable confidence in Tommaso's ability, expressed a hope that Tommaso would be appointed as the next Standardbearer of Justice: 'there is', he wrote, 'no one

[35] Ibid.; Salvestro del Cicha to Bartolomeo Cederni, 22 May 1454, Corp. relig. soppr., 78, 314, fo. 582: The termination of the *Balìa* caused widespread pleasure in Florence, and citizens were hoping for further changes, including the closure of the election bags of the Signoria. I am grateful to Bill Kent for drawing my attention to these letters. For his work on Bartolomeo Cederni, see his *Letters to an Obscure Florentine*.

[36] Tommaso to Piero, 5 June 1454, MAP, xx, 93; Francesco Caccini to Bartolomeo Cederni, 4, 7 June 1454, Corp. relig. soppr., 78, 314, fos. 563, 566.

[37] Tommaso to Piero, 5 June 1454, MAP, xx, 93.

who will satisfy the need as well as Tommaso'.[38] Clearly others shared Piero's view, for even before the letter arrived, Tommaso had been appointed as the next Standardbearer of Justice.

Whatever was expected of Tommaso, not even his efforts could turn the tide in favour of the restrictive institutions favoured by the circle around the Medici. The difficulties of his task became obvious when he turned to the first serious political issue with which he had to deal—the scrutiny of the general offices due to begin in August 1454. A cautious politician, Tommaso first considered postponing the scrutiny, but enthusiasm for it was so strong within the Signoria and Colleges that he decided to proceed. In doing so, however, he was expecting that Piero would shortly return from Venice, and then, he wrote, 'we will do as you say in the matter'.[39] As it happened, Piero was delayed at Venice and, although he delegated his authority to his brother Giovanni,[40] the absence of Cosimo's elder heir must have made Tommaso's task more difficult.

Presumably, not only the Medici but other leading citizens had been consulted on the plan of action which Tommaso put into effect on 19 July, when he first presented the subject of the scrutiny to the consideration of a *Pratica*. When introducing the question, Tommaso referred to the importance of avoiding the 'dissensions' which normally arose during a scrutiny, thereby providing a justification for the *Pratica* to delegate discussion of the subject to a smaller group of 'wise' citizens.[41] Although the deliberations of this smaller body went unrecorded, they must have resulted in the proposal presented to the legislative councils on 27 July, by which the recently dissolved *Balìa* would have been resuscitated to perform the scrutiny, as had been provided in

---

[38] Piero to his brother Giovanni, 29 June 1454, MAP, ix, 48. Tommaso's appointment as Standardbearer is recorded in Tratte, 201, fo. 6ʳ.

[39] Tommaso to Piero, 10 July 1454, MAP, vi, 306. Cf. Francesco Caccini to Bartolomeo Cederni, 27 July 1454, Corp. relig. soppr., 78, 314, fo. 598: the Colleges requested a scrutiny after this Signoria entered office.

[40] Piero wrote to his brother Giovanni on 29 June 1454, MAP, ix, 48, that Tommaso would have the same confidence in Giovanni as he would in Piero himself.

[41] CP, 53, fos. 105ᵛ–107ʳ.

the legislation of July 1452. However, even a temporary revival of the unpopular special council was too much for the legislative bodies to stomach, and the bill was rejected on four successive days.[42] Despite modifications, the Council of the People continued to reject the bill and, when Tommaso again turned for advice to the citizens of the *Pratica*, a majority recommended that he abandon it, on the grounds that not only had the city become too agitated for a scrutiny to be held but also that the bill was unlikely to be passed in any form.[43]

Tommaso consequently must have abandoned the idea, to the annoyance of the Colleges, who were sufficiently angry with the Signoria to block its proposals in protest.[44] Consequently, by the beginning of August Tommaso was understandably disappointed with the results of his term of office. As well as failing to achieve the leading citizens' objectives, he had incurred personal unpopularity for his stand over the scrutiny, and was finding it difficult to make headway in other areas. Increasingly, he looked to the negotiation which Piero de' Medici was conducting at Venice to salvage some glory for his term as Standardbearer. As he wrote to Piero, he was looking forward to both 'reputation and honour' from the conclusion of the alliance, but even here problems arose. At the end of August, with his term of office coming to a close and the negotiation apparently no nearer conclusion, Tommaso dejectedly wrote to Piero that he felt that he had lost more than he had gained through his appointment.[45]

None the less, Tommaso's magistracy had by no means seen the nadir of the Medici group's political fortunes. The conclusion of the Milan–Venice–Florence alliance just as

---

[42] Libri fab., 62, fos. 218ᵛ, 220ʳ. On this legislation, see also Caccini to Cederni, 27, 28 July 1454, Corp. relig. soppr., 78, 314, fos. 598, 606.

[43] Libri fab., 62, fo. 220ʳ, 31 July 1454, contains a modification allowing the Councillors to nominate some of the scrutineers. The *Pratica* of 1 Aug 1454 is recorded in CP, 53, fos. 111ʳ–113ʳ. Cf. also the *Pratica* of 31 July: ibid., fos. 109ʳ–111ʳ and Caccini to Cederni, 3 Aug. 1454, Corp. relig. soppr., 78, 314, fo. 600: because the *Pratica* advised against the scrutiny, the idea had been allowed to die. Cf. also Rubinstein, *Government*, 123.

[44] Caccini to Cederni, 3 Aug. 1454, Corp. relig. soppr., 78, 314, fo. 600: 'The Colleges don't want to pass anything as they have not yet obtained their wish'.

[45] Tommaso to Piero, 26 Aug. 1454, MAP, cxxvii, 852.

Tommaso left office, combined with the consequent hopes for a general Italian peace, strengthened Florentines' desire for an end of controls which had originally been justified by the pressures of war. The members of the legislative councils continued to express a desire for further change by rejecting proposed legislation, including essential financial bills.[46] Eventually, the inner circle recognized that they would have to make further sacrifices if government were to go forward, and therefore, late in February, it was decided that the *accoppiatori* should hand in their resignations.[47] Although Tommaso was not present at the *Pratica* where this decision was made, he was forced to consent to a measure which, although it undermined the leading citizens' position, was extremely popular throughout the city. According to Marco Parenti, himself no friend of the Medici group, the event was hailed with joy not only by ordinary citizens, who saw in it the end of the 'robberies' to which the leading citizens had become accustomed; even some of the most prominent Florentines were pleased by what they regarded as a blow to Medici authority and therefore an advantage to themselves.[48]

Once the *accoppiatori* had taken the popular step of resigning their duties, they retained their final task of preparing the election bags of the Signoria for the return to sortition. Despite the existing climate of opinion, the leading figures of the regime succeeded once more in gaining advantage by entrusting these officials with additional powers. Again, the *accoppiatori* were authorized both to add names to, and remove them from, the election bags.[49] Moreover, they again respected the claims of family solidarity by transferring their authority over the fate of the name-tags of certain prominent families to the individuals actually involved. They also claimed this privilege for themselves, as

[46] Cf. the *Pratiche* of 17, 24 Jan. 1455, CP, 53, fos. 149ʳ–153ᵛ, and Rubinstein, *Government*, 28–9.

[47] CP, 53, fos. 155ᵛ–157ʳ, 22 Feb. 1455. Cf. also the preceding discussion on 20 Feb. 1455, ibid., fos. 154ʳ–155ᵛ.

[48] Parenti, 'Ricordi politici', BNF, Magl., xxv, 272, fo. 57ʳ⁻ᵛ. On this MS, see Phillips, 'A Newly Discovered Chronicle'.

[49] Cf. Rubinstein, *Government*, 43. The *accoppiatori* were allowed to nominate the citizens from their quarter for elimination from the bags.

each *accoppiatore* proceeded to name the three members of his own family who would be eligible for the highest post, that of Standardbearer of Justice. Thereby Tommaso could ensure that all his and his brother Niccolò's name-tags for the Signoria were placed in the bag from which the Standardbearer was drawn. Meanwhile, half the tags of his eldest son Lorenzo received the same treatment, while the rest were placed in the select bag, or *borsellino*, for the Priors.[50]

The years following the termination of *Balìa* and elections *a mano* witnessed considerable conflict within the Florentine ruling group. On the one hand, the circle surrounding the Medici resented the abolition of the bases of their political ascendancy. Soon after the *accoppiatori* had resigned, some were already devising plans to recover their political authority, but action was discouraged by other prominent citizens, including the ever-cautious Cosimo de' Medici. On the other hand, the many opponents of institutional controls, encouraged by their successes of 1454 and 1455, sought further measures to counteract the advantages gained by the Medici group, such as cancelling the results of the scrutiny of 1453.[51] Although these proposals were in turn rejected, the lines of the continuing political struggle had been clearly drawn, and the conflict between the leadership of the Medici regime and their opponents eventually came to a climax in 1458 over the perennially controversial issue of taxation.

As Tommaso had implied to Dietisalvi Neroni, the *Balìe* had contributed to the substitution of more arbitrary forms of taxation for the popular and rigorous *catasto*. Once the statutory councils alone were in charge of financial legislation from 1455 and the *accoppiatori*'s influence over the Signoria removed, it became more difficult for that policy to be maintained. While wealthier citizens continued to denounce the *catasto* as an attack on the city's sources of economic prosperity, popular feeling was strongly in favour of a return

[50] The *accoppiatori*'s decisions regarding the closing of the bags are recorded in Tratte, 16, fos. 7ᵛ–32ʳ.
[51] On the internal struggles of these years, see Giovanni di Carlo, 'De temporibus suis', fos. 77ʳ⁻ᵛ; Guicciardini, *Memorie di famiglia*, 19; Parenti, 'Ricordi politici', fo. 57ʳ; Morçay, *Saint Antonin*, 257–9; Rubinstein, *Government*, 89–92.

to a form of taxation, which, it was felt, would make the wealthy pay their fair share.[52] During the later 1450s, severe tension over taxation resulted yet again in the Councils' rejection of financial bills. By late 1457, the situation was so serious that leading citizens were again entertaining the idea of seizing control of the government, and this became a determination after the advocates of the *catasto* won victory for their policy in January 1458.[53]

During this struggle over taxation and political control, Niccolò Soderini emerged for the first time as a declared enemy of the inner circle of the regime. Even though an opponent of the rigorous *catasto*, he nevertheless assumed a 'popular' stand in the heated debates over tax policy. In contrast to friends of the Medici like his brother, Niccolò advocated a form of taxation which would prove fairer towards the ordinary citizen, expressing harsh criticism of the methods proposed by others in the debate. In taking this approach, his language became at times almost demagogic. In March 1456, for example, he insisted that, whatever the tax selected, 'those who pay less should not be preyed on', while he rejected one tax on the grounds that 'the people abhor [it]'.[54] While such remarks were not abnormal even within the *Pratiche*, they clearly set him apart from the leading citizens who were battling to defend their own patrimonies, and undoubtedly made him more unpopular with the Medici group. This must have been particularly the case after the statutory councils elected Niccolò to a special financial commission, where he could try to translate his views into public policy, and may therefore have proved a thorn in the side of the Medici group.[55]

---

[52] For the argument against the *catasto*, cf. Molho, *Public Finances*, 86. In contrast, the *catasto*'s proponents denounced the arbitrary methods which had been employed and insisted that the *catasto* was more just: e.g. Carlo Pandolfini in the *Pratica* of 2 Mar. 1456, CP, 53, fos. 224ʳ–227ʳ; the prologue of the *catasto* law of Jan. 1458, in Canestrini, *La scienza*, 171. Cf. also ibid., 184–5, on the *arbitrio*'s falling more heavily on the less wealthy.

[53] On the Councils' opposition to tax bills cf. Parenti, 'Ricordi politici', fo. 58ᵛ, and Rubinstein, *Government*, 89. On the plans of the leading citizens: Guicciardini, *Memorie di famiglia*, 19.

[54] CP, 53, fos. 189ᵛ. 227ʳ, 230ʳ, 4 Nov. 1455 and 2, 3 Mar. 1456.

[55] Cf. n. 30 above.

Niccolò's outspoken comments on taxation were probably accompanied by criticism of the Medici circle's style of government. Already, in 1454, at the height of the controversy over the dissolution of the *Balìa*, he had had angry interchanges with some prominent citizens, presumably over the political issues then in dispute.[56] Now he must have made similar comments, which represented a serious threat to the leading citizens because of Niccolò's personal influence. Apart from his contributions to the *Pratiche*, Niccolò could lobby privately for his own policies among a wide circle of citizens active in the government, while his long history of success in the scrutinies meant that he was frequently a member of the bodies which had the final say in many questions of supreme political importance.

Certainly, Niccolò was regarded as a dangerous enemy by the leading citizens, who, reeling under the blow of the restoration of the *catasto*, determined to take power again into their own hands. Their opportunity came in July 1458, when Luca Pitti was selected as Standardbearer of Justice. A Medici partisan of long standing, Luca had acted as *accoppiatore*, had been a prominent figure in all the *Balìe* since 1434, had signed the pact of 1449, and was now again prepared to use his influence in favour of the Medici group. Under his leadership, the citizens of the *Pratica* immediately began to discuss the idea of political changes, and very quickly brought forward a written programme of reform. This represented a major development in the constitutional policy of the Medici group in that it would have transformed the special councils to which they had repeatedly resorted into a permanent body guaranteeing them a constant influence over crucial legislation.

Although the citizens of the *Pratica* approved this plan, it encountered strong resistance from Luca Pitti's colleagues

---

[56] Cf. Caccini to Cederni, 7 June 1454, Corp. relig. soppr., 78, 314, fo. 566, re Niccolò's encounter with Messer Manno [Temperani] at the Ponte alla Carraia, in which '*no lasciarono nulla . . . che non si dicesino*', about which many comments were made. A similar encounter occurred between Neri [Capponi] and Messer Agnolo [Acciaiuoli]. Cf. also Niccolò's call for general reforms, and for living '*iuste et honeste*': *Pratiche* of 19 Mar. and 1 Apr. 1457, CP, 54, fos. 113ʳ–114ʳ, 116ᵛ–117ʳ.

within the Signoria. In their efforts to overcome this opposition, the most enthusiastic supporters of the new departure within the *Pratica* were forced to express their justification for a measure which would have increased their own political power. One of the citizens who attempted this was Tommaso Soderini, emerging in these debates as one of the most committed advocates of constitutional reform. According to Tommaso, the proposed changes would have transferred authority from citizens who sponsored 'wicked laws' to the more prudent members of the community—i.e. the inner circle of the Medici regime. According to Tommaso, recent legislation—including the *catasto* law—was a direct attack by 'wicked' citizens on the wiser and better informed as well as a threat to the city's merchants. Moreover, he claimed, those responsible for the recent 'terrible laws' had intended to harm the 'good and outstanding citizens' and even to create civil disturbances. The projected new council was therefore necessary to foil those citizens who were 'rash and eager to do harm', and to restore control over legislation to those who were 'good and wise'.[57]

Thus, in his determination to provide a moral justification for a programme motivated by political and financial self-interest, Tommaso had fallen back on the traditional, patrician, or aristocratic thread in Florentine political thought. It was, he was arguing, the 'better' citizens who should rule the republic, and he was identifying these, with some justification, as the more experienced and distinguished members of the ruling group. That this rationale was repeated not just by Tommaso but by other citizens of the *Pratica*, suggests that the inner circle as a whole relied on this patrician ethic—one which went back to classical antiquity—as the rationale for the gradual shift of their city's constitution towards a more confirmed oligarchy.[58]

Despite Tommaso's and others' impassioned pleas, the Signoria's reluctance regarding the projected political changes could not be overcome. Moreover, with the Signoria

---

[57] Tommaso's speech of 6 July 1458 is recorded in CP, 55, fos. 44ᵛ–45ʳ.
[58] On the importance of aristocracy in 15th-century political thinking, cf. Gilbert, 'The Venetian Constitution', 470–2.

so resistant, there was very little chance that the councils would agree to the leading citizens' plan. In desperation, the inner circle began seriously to consider re-establishing their authority by extraordinary means—i.e. having recourse to a *parlamento* or full assembly of the citizen body which, since it represented the community as a whole, possessed complete legislative authority. Once again, despite the reservations of many leading citizens, Tommaso emerged as a committed advocate of this alternative. To the objections of those who feared that such a general assembly might prove recalcitrant or uncontrollable Tommaso responded that, since the plan for a permanent council had been rejected 'without any justification', a *parlamento* was the only means of assuring that the Signoria was filled with 'outstanding and prudent' men. It would not, he insisted, be a dangerous expedient, nor would it discredit the government; rather, it would prove the means of restoring the reputation which the government had already lost.[59]

By such arguments, the citizens of the *Pratica* were eventually convinced, and then only Cosimo de' Medici's consent was necessary before the plan was carried into effect. As this was immediately forthcoming, the *parlamento* went ahead on 11 August 1458, and, with soldiers surrounding the principal square, the unarmed citizens who assembled unanimously accepted the proposals read to them. These provided for the creation of a short-term *Balìa*, which would perform new scrutinies and legislate regarding the new permanent council to which the inner circle had become committed. In addition, apparently unwilling to leave the issue to the *Balìa*, the leading citizens ensured that the *parlamento* re-established elections *a mano* of the Signoria for a full five years.[60]

---

[59] *Pratica* of 1 Aug. 1458, CP, 55, fos. 61ᵛ–68ʳ. Cf. also Nicodemo Tranchedini to the Duke of Milan, 1 Aug. 1458, Paris., Bibl. Nat., MSS italiens, 1588, fo. 109ʳ; Giovanni di Carlo, 'De temporibus, suis', fo. 78ᵛ; Rubinstein, *Government*, 100–2.

[60] On this *parlamento*, cf. Giovanni, 'Ricordanze', fo. 29ʳ; Parenti, 'Ricordi politici', fos. 58ʳ–59ʳ; Nicodemo to the Duke, 8, 11 Aug. 1458, Paris, Bibl. Nat., MSS italiens, 1588, fos. 116ʳ, 117ʳ; Rubinstein, *Government*, 101–4. The legislation passed by this *parlamento* is recorded in Tratte, 17, fos. 1ʳ–7ᵛ.

Once again Tommaso was one of the principal beneficiaries of these measures. As one of the *accoppiatori* who had closed the election bags in 1455, he became an ex-officio member of the new *Balìa*, and was included in the small number of officials who selected the approximately 200 elected members of this special council. He and the other *accoppiatori* of 1455 also joined with the ten new *accoppiatori* appointed for the projected scrutiny, to carry out the elections *a mano* of the Signoria. Moreover, the old *accoppiatori* received additional duties, such as helping to choose their new colleagues and to determine the regulations governing the planned scrutinies.[61] Apart from these powers, they received other, lesser duties which were nevertheless important for the security of the regime. Along with the Signoria, for example, they were entrusted for two years with the election of the *Otto di Guardia* and with granting special powers, or *balìa*, to this body, while they were also authorized to renew the term of office of one of the city's judicial officials for the same period.[62] The delegation of such details of political management to the *accoppiatori* well illustrates the manner in which these experienced and loyal magistrates were becoming the linchpins of the Medicean political machine.

The most important task assumed by the *accoppiatori* was undoubtedly that of determining the form of the new permanent council. Authority on the subject was delegated to a committee of eight *accoppiatori*, and it was a mark of Tommaso's prominence that he was one of these eight.[63] In drawing up their scheme, which was finally approved on 29 November 1458, this commission relied heavily on the plan presented to the *Pratica* of 5 July. The new council which they designed was authorized to vote before the other legislative bodies on such key matters as electoral qualifications, public appointments, taxation, and the hiring of

---

[61] Cf. Rubinstein, *Government*, 105–8; Tratte, 17, fos. 2ᵛ–3ᵛ, 9ᵛ–10ᵛ.

[62] Ibid., fos. 4ʳ⁻ᵛ, 37ʳ–38ᵛ. They also performed such duties as helping to elect the *Conservatori delle Leggi* and the Five of Pisa and to confirm in office the associates and servants of the *Podestà* and Captain: ibid., fos. 17ʳ–21ʳ.

[63] CP, 55, fo. 89ʳ⁻ᵛ (26 Nov. 1458). Cf. Rubinstein, *Government*, 113. For the regulations governing the new council, see ibid., 113–16; Tratte, 17, fos. 23ʳ–34ᵛ.

troops, while its approval was necessary for all other legisla-tion. The membership of such a powerful assembly was of course of central importance, such that the members of the first two six-month sittings were directly nominated by the same group of *accoppiatori*, secretaries, and Signoria. There-after, its members were to be chosen by lot from citizens who were demonstrated to have been qualified for the executive (the *Tre Maggiori*) since 1434. While this group was more likely than a wider section of the citizen body to be favourable to the existing leadership of the regime, it contained many citizens who had become critical of recent policies. As a result, an additional scrutiny process was prescribed, by which those whose names had been drawn for the more exclusive position of Standardbearer of Justice would annually determine which of the larger group of *veduti ai Tre Maggiori* should be eligible to sit in the *Cento*, as the new council was called. With this additional screening process and the incentive it provided for citizens to prove their acceptability to the upper echelons of the regime, the chances were increased that the *Cento* would prove a more reliable vehicle for the policies of the leading citizens than had the ordinary councils. This probability was increased by the fact that the ex-Standardbearers were allowed to attend the *Cento*'s meetings and to vote in the elections it per-formed. Moreover, its smaller size made it a more manage-able body, while, on the other hand, the fact that its composition changed every six months made it more accept-able to citizens than previous *Balìe* had been.

Not only Tommaso but also Niccolò Soderini was among the ex-Standardbearers detailed to scrutinize the future mem-bers of this new government institution. However, whereas Tommaso could be expected to act in support of the leading circle of the regime, Niccolò was by no means so reliable. Although the leading citizens were forced to accept his presence even at the highest levels of government, he was so suspect to them that some were even considering exiling him once they had recovered power.[64] Indeed, several citizens were exiled by the *Balìa* of 1458, and among them were

[64] Parenti, 'Ricordi politici', fo. 59ʳ.

some individuals close to Niccolò, who may well have shared his point of view.[65] That Niccolò himself escaped punishment was attributed by a contemporary to the intervention of his brother Tommaso, who, it was implied, wielded sufficient influence to convince the leading citizens to continue to tolerate a person who by then constituted for them a serious risk.[66] Presumably, then, it was also Tommaso's influence which won Niccolò a place in the first sitting of the *Cento*.[67] If this is correct, family solidarity had again overridden 'reason of state', not only in Tommaso's mind but in that of the other leading citizens of the regime.

Apart from the citizens exiled by the *Balìa* of 1458, many others who were suspect to the group which had seized power saw their political rights rescinded in the scrutiny which followed. These citizens, according to Benedetto Dei, remained with 'resentful minds', seeing themselves 'deprived of every honour and emolument of office' while their enemies enjoyed 'a clear field, with honours and offices every day, and their heads always in the trough'.[68] Thus, while the regime's inner circle had succeeded in reaffirming its ascendancy more securely than ever before, it had done so at the cost of creating a large potential opposition within the city. When, as we shall see, an opportunity was eventually offered to destroy the settlement of 1458, many citizens were prepared to seize it. Then, the Medici and their friends were forced to battle yet more fiercely against Niccolò and his 'popular' current, not merely in order to reinforce their authority but for their very political survival.

[65] e.g., Niccolò Bartolini: Rubinstein, *Government*, 109. Bartolini had been involved in Niccolò Soderini's rentals in the Pisano, and had, e.g., acted as an arbiter for him and been one of the guarantors of Ginevra Macinghi's dowry.

[66] Parenti, 'Ricordi politici, fo. 59ʳ.

[67] Tratte, 17, fo. 24ᵛ. His inclusion in the *Balìa* of 1458 was presumably almost automatic, as he had sat in every such council since 1434: Balìe, 29, fos. 8–9. Cf. Rubinstein, *Government*, 287.

[68] Cronica, MSS, 119 fo. 22ʳ. Cf. Rubinstein, *Government*, 109.

3. The Crisis of 1465–1466

During the discussions which had led up to the *parlamento* of 11 August 1458, it had frequently been pointed out that there was a need for the government to encourage trade, on which the city depended for its livelihood. In particular, the state galley system had been singled out as an area requiring particular attention and an infusion of funds. Concern had also been expressed regarding the economic situation in Pisa and the surrounding district, where recurrent malaria as well as heavy taxation had seriously reduced both the population and the tax revenue flowing to Florence.[1]

Very soon after the institutional changes of 1458 had been effected, the inner circle addressed itself to these issues, and the manner in which it did so demonstrated one advantage, as they saw it, of the reconfirmation of their authority. Through the short-lived *Balìa* of 1458 a special *ad hoc* body was created, consisting of five 'Governors of Pisa', who for a year were granted extremely wide powers for regulation and reform.[2] These covered all matters requiring attention in the vicinity of Pisa—whether the state galley system which operated from its port, or the defences, agriculture, and taxation of the subject town and its hinterland. This powerful magistracy was filled not by sortition but by election, as the

---

[1] Cf. the debates of 3 July (Francesco Ventura, Carlo Pandolfini), 4 July (Tommaso Soderini) and 6 July (Luca Pitti, Francesco Neroni), 1458, and the 'Rapporto . . . sopra 'facti del navigare' following the *Pratica* of 6 July: CP, 55, fos. 29^{r-v}, 32^r, 41^v, 42^v–43^v, 49^v–50^r. On the depopulation of the countryside and the controversial issue of Florence's taxation of her dominion, cf. Molho, *Public Finances*, 26–45.

[2] The legislation regarding this commission is in Balìe, 29, fos. 22^r–23^r. The decisions of the Five were to have the same force as those of the *Balìa* itself. On the Five's replacement of the Sea Consuls at Pisa, cf. also Mallett, 'Sea Consuls', 159.

Balìa granted the authority to select these officials to the Signoria, *accoppiatori*, and secretaries of the scrutinies since 1434. Consequently, the five citizens chosen were not only familiar with questions of commerce and administration but also prominent figures within the Medici group, and included Tommaso Soderini as well as other merchant-statesmen such as Bartolomeo Lenzi and Francesco Neroni.[3]

The political position of these officials meant that the major changes made in Pisa and its hinterland would not be undertaken without consultation with the Medici. In fact, what little of their correspondence survives suggests that Piero de' Medici remained the Five's constant contact and advocate in Florence. He was useful in that he provided a means through which the Five could gain the government's attention for their problems and demands. Whether the issue was a public one, such as funds to prepare the galleys for launching, or a semi-private one of trying to avoid a posting in the malaria-infected port of Livorno, it was the Medici to whom they turned for assistance and advice.[4] In turn, since the Five remained in such close correspondence with them, the Medici were not only aware of the major decisions being taken at Pisa, but had the opportunity to exert an influence in whatever direction they chose.

After Tommaso's return from Pisa, his continuing concern for the issues in which he had been involved was evident in the high priority which he gave commercial questions even while he was acting in other government capacities. In the *Pratiche* following his return to Florence in January 1460, he took an unusually vocal role in discussions regarding maritime affairs, and, when he became Standardbearer of Justice for the second time in July 1460, he devoted considerable

---

[3] Tratte, 17, fos. 20ᵛ–21ʳ and 81, fo. 166ʳ. Elected on 31 August 1458, they were to take up their duties for one year beginning on 21 Nov. However, two, one of whom was Tommaso, were to remain in office until 20 Jan. 1460, in order to provide continuity with the next set of commissioners.

[4] Cf. the Five to Piero de' Medici and an unnamed Florentine, 14, 25 Sept. 1459, and Tommaso Soderini to Piero, 29 July 1459, MAP, ix, 506 and xvii, 219, 249. On the special interest which the Medici took in the Pisan area, cf. Mallett, 'Pisa and Florence', 409, 433–5. This was an interest which Tommaso, along with other members of the Medici regime, soon came to share: cf. ibid., 432, 435–41.

attention to the same themes.[5] His term of office witnessed the passage of much valuable legislation governing the galley voyages, incentives to settlement in the Pisan area, and the revision of the tax system in Pisa and its hinterland. Finally, Tommaso sponsored a bill which prolonged the special Pisan commission, already extended for a second year, to a third, and thereby himself became an ex-officio member of it.[6] Thus, Tommaso served consistently during these years as a spokesman for the anxiety felt by leading Florentines regarding the economy of the city and her territory, and demonstrates how concentration of political power tended to reinforce the policies of the mercantile interests which predominated within the Medici group.

While Tommaso was using his political expertise and influence to further the leading citizens' policies regarding trade, he was not failing in his vigilance for the security and predominance of the Medici group. In fact, during his term as Standardbearer, he spearheaded a manœuvre designed to prolong the leading citizens' political ascendancy. During his term, a prominent Florentine who had been exiled in 1458 because of his opposition to the Medici group's seizure of power, was apprehended and accused of conspiring against the government. Under torture, he confessed to the charges, and this revelation provided the inner circle with an opportunity to introduce measures justified by the need to ensure the regime's security.[7]

Tommaso's attitude was made clear in the speech with which he opened the *Pratica* of 9 July 1460.[8] In exaggerated terms, he presented the recently discovered plot as a dangerous threat to the government. Asserting that if the conspiracy

[5] Cf. Tommaso's comments in the *Pratiche* of 30 Mar. and 2, 14 July 1460: CP, 56, fos. 70ᵛ–71ʳ, 82ʳ–ᵛ, 91ʳ. The relevant legislation of his term as Standardbearer of Justice is in Provv., 151, fos. 127ᵛ–129ᵛ (8 July 1460), 150ᵛ–152ᵛ (24 July), 159ʳ–161ᵛ (25 July), 171ᵛ–172ʳ (7 Aug.), 192ᵛ–193ʳ (23 Aug.).

[6] This legislation stated that since the three Sea Consuls and the two Provisors of the Pisan gabelles already appointed were '*sufficientissimi*', the two offices should be combined for a year and the resulting Five possess the same powers as the last: Provv., 151, fos. 197ᵛ–198ᵛ, 26 Aug. 1460.

[7] On this incident, see Giovanni di Carlo, 'De temporibus suis', fos. 78ᵛ–79ʳ; Boninsegni, *Storie*, 127; Rubinstein, *Government*, 103, 109, 121.

[8] CP, 56, fo. 84ʳ–ᵛ.

had succeeded the city would have been ruined, he reminded his audience that the honour and even the lives of themselves and their families depended on the continuation of the 'form of government which now exists'. It was therefore their duty to support any action which would render it more secure. In this, he assured them, they would have the Signoria's full support, as he and his colleagues were totally committed to preserving the welfare of the republic.

With such encouragement, some of the assembled citizens proposed concrete measures. Elections a mano, it was suggested, should be extended for five years beyond the original five-year term decreed by the parlamento of 1458. Moreover, on Giovannozzo Pitti's suggestion, it was also recommended that the legislation provide for a new scrutiny—an addition which would not only be popular in itself, but which would also offer the possibility of an eventual change in accoppiatori. Both suggestions were incorporated into a bill which, now that the fear of conspiracy and subversion were in the air, received almost unobstructed passage.[9] Thus, the well-executed manœuvre gained the leading citizens an easy advantage, while Tommaso himself registered a notable personal triumph which must in part have compensated for the failure of his previous legislative efforts on behalf of the regime. Moreover, as the elections a mano of the Signoria were in future to be conducted not just by the new accoppiatori but also by those already in office, Tommaso's own powers of patronage remained intact.

Tommaso's promotion for a second time to the post of Standardbearer of Justice marked him as a citizen of considerable authority within the regime. His growing stature was likewise demonstrated not only by his appointment to the authoritative Pisan commission but by his inclusion, while he was Standardbearer of Justice, in a three-man delegation created to settle a major dispute in the subject town of Pistoia.[10] By the early 1460s Tommaso was a regular member of the Pratiche, while, more importantly, he also

[9] For the discussion in the Pratica: CP, 56, fos. 85ᵛ–90ᵛ. The relevant legislation is in Provv., 151, fos. 137ᵛ–142ʳ. Cf. Rubinstein, Government, 121–2.
[10] CP, 56, fo. 100ʳ (12 Aug. 1460).

attended the more informal and exclusive meetings at the Medici palace. Since at least the 1450s age and recurring illness had prevented Cosimo de' Medici from frequenting the Palace of the Signoria, where most public business was transacted. Instead, leading citizens tended to congregate at his house, where news of the day was discussed and policy formulated by that small circle of citizens who wielded the greatest political power in Florence. In 1462 a foreign observer mentioned Tommaso as one of the citizens summoned to such a meeting, while in December 1463 Cosimo ensured that Tommaso and a few other prominent citizens unable to attend were informed of the news brought back by the ambassador upon his return from Milan.[11]

Given Tommaso's relative prominence by the early 1460s, it is not surprising that in the autumn of 1463 he was appointed to that pinnacle of a Florentine's political career—a diplomatic posting abroad. On 6 October 1463, he was selected by the Signoria, Colleges, and *Cento* as ambassador to Venice, with the mission of defusing a commercial quarrel which was threatening to bring the two republics close to war. Tommaso was particularly suitable for the mission, for it involved the Florentine galley voyages with which he had been involved since 1458. Earlier in 1463, the Venetians had asked the Florentines and other Italian cities to refrain from sending their trading vessels to Constantinople. The reason formally given was the Venetians' fear that the Turks, with whom they were effectively at war, would seize the ships and use them in their fleet against Venice. Christian solidarity should, the Venetians argued, cause all Italians to terminate any activity which might favour the Turks, including direct trade with Constantinople. To the Florentines, on the other hand, the Venetian demand represented merely an attempt to undermine the lucrative commerce which they had established with Turkish-held territories in the East. As the Milanese ambassador in Florence reported, 'the Venetians are anxious for the galleys not to go because of their envy of

[11] Nicodemo Tranchedini to the Duke of Milan, 4, 5 April 1462 and 10 Dec. 1463, Paris, Bibl. Nat., MSS italiens, 1589, fos. 55–6, 316. On the 1462 incident, cf. Rubinstein, *Government*, 134.

Florence's maritime commerce, and not because of fear that the Turks will use [the ships]'.[12]

Initially, the Florentines had therefore ignored the Venetian request, but they were forced to take notice when it was repeated in September 1463 with the threat that the commander of the Venetian fleet had been instructed to prevent any ships from reaching Constantinople—if necessary by force. Although some citizens, including Cosimo de' Medici, were convinced that the Venetian threat was hollow, the Signoria decided to seek an assurance from the Venetians that their ships would not be attacked. Since Cosimo's son Piero supported this policy, it is tempting to suggest that he might have been behind Tommaso's election.[13] However, there were also other reasons why Tommaso should have been chosen. Apart from his interest in the galley system, he was, as the Signoria pointed out, a 'very prudent' citizen, while the Florentine ambassador at Rome described him as 'wise and discreet', and possessing 'great ability'.[14]

Tommaso's mission was inevitably difficult. Apparently, in September 1463 the Signoria had pacified the Venetian emissary by promising that the galleys would not go as far as Constantinople. However, they soon countermanded this decision when they began to hope that with Milanese and papal support they might persuade the Venetians to let the ships come and go in safety.[15] Tommaso therefore had to ask

[12] Tranchedini to the Duke, 27 Sept. 1463, Paris, Bibl. Nat., MSS italiens, 1589, fo. 220ʳ. On this conflict over the galleys' voyage, and the situation of Florence and Venice *vis-à-vis* the Turks, see Rinuccini, *Ricordi storici*, pp. xci–xcii; Malipiero, *Annali veneti*, 17–21; Piccolomini, *Commentaries*, 777–8, 804–5; Pastor, *History of the Popes*, iii. 312–15, 317–19; Setton, *The Papacy and the Levant*, ii. 240–70.

[13] On the Medici position, see Tranchedini to the Duke, 25 Sept. 1463, Paris, Bibl. Nat., MSS italiens, 1589, fo. 218ʳ⁻ᵛ.

[14] The Florentine Signoria to Otto Niccolini, 6 Oct. 1463, in Pastor, *Ungedruckte Akten*, 199–202; Otto to the Signoria, 25 Oct. 1463, Florence, Archivio Niccolini, 13.

[15] That the Florentines did promise in Sept. not to send the ships to Constantinople is proved by the Venetian government's letter to the captain of their fleet, 6 Oct. 1463, ASV, Sen. Secr., 21, fo. 193ᵛ, and by the Florentine Signoria's to Otto, 15 Oct.: Pastor, *Ungedruckte Akten*, 214. On 17 Oct., however, the Signoria changed its instructions to Otto and began instead to connect their contribution to the proposed crusade to their ships' safe voyage: the Signoria to Otto, 15, 17, 24 Oct. and 5 Nov. 1463, ibid., 213–16, 227–8, 233–5. Meanwhile, the Duke of Milan had agreed to support the Florentine position: e.g. the Signoria to Otto, 17 Oct. 1463, ibid.

the Venetian government to allow the voyage to go ahead as planned, and he was given a long series of arguments to buttress his request.[16] Some of these were blatantly insincere, as the Florentines had no intention of terminating their lucrative trade with the Turks. Moreover, as the Venetians insisted on hiding the economic motives behind their position, realistic discussion was made very difficult.

Tommaso's first conclusion on his arrival in Venice, based on the Venetians' warm greetings, was that they must have been expecting a message very different from the one he brought.[17] However, the Venetians must have rapidly realized their mistake and, although subsequently Tommaso did his best to argue the Florentine position, they refused even to discuss the matter seriously. 'In the part we wanted them most to clarify', he wrote to Piero, 'they are the most reticent.'[18] Eventually, informal conversations with private citizens convinced Tommaso that they were sincerely concerned that the Turks might confiscate the Florentine vessels—an indication of the effectiveness of the private pressure regularly exerted on foreign envoys. In short, everything which Tommaso saw reinforced his impression that he could get nowhere with the Venetians, and the Florentines soon agreed, for they recalled him before any conclusion was reached.[19]

Although ostensibly a failure, Tommaso's mission provided him with a means of demonstrating his dedication and competence to the Florentine government and to Piero de' Medici. Apparently, it was Piero whom Tommaso particularly wanted to impress, for he made full reports to him which emphasized the diligence with which he was fulfilling

---

[16] Cf. Tommaso's instructions of 19 Oct. 1463, Sig., Leg. e Comm., 15, fos. 103ʳ–108ᵛ.

[17] Tommaso to Piero de' Medici, 30 Oct. 1463, MAP, xvii, 384.

[18] Ibid.

[19] While the Florentine vessels probably did not go to Constantinople, they did return safely from the East with a rich cargo in Mar. 1464: Nicodemo Tranchedini to the Duke of Milan, 14, 17 Mar. 1464, Paris, Bibl. Nat., MSS italiens, 1590, fos. 73ʳ, 76ʳ. Cf. however, Mallett, *Galleys*, 69–70. Tommaso may have been partly correct concerning the Venetians' sincerity, for the Venetian government was prohibiting even its own citizens' ships from entering Turkish ports: ASV, Senato, Mar, 7, fo. 90ᵛ, 4 Dec. 1462.

his commission. In one letter he assured Piero that in his presentation to the Venetian Signoria he had omitted none of the arguments included in his instruction, and that those who heard him thought that he had acquitted himself well.[20] Tommaso may also have been behind a separate report made to Piero by the manager of the Medici bank in Venice, which similarly stated that the ambassador had performed his duties well, and that the failure of the mission could in no way be imputed to him.[21] Apparently, these reports regarding Tommaso's execution of his commission had their effect, for the Signoria praised the 'diligence and ability' which he displayed, and everyone seemed satisfied that he had done the best he could with a difficult mandate.[22]

Tommaso's mission to Venice also illustrated the potential value to the Medici of seeing that such duties were exercised by their friends. Even before setting out for Venice, Tommaso had discussed the issues involved at Piero's bedside, and had presumably learned of his views. On one occasion, he reminded Piero that he expected instructions from him and Cosimo as well as from the Signoria.[23] If they wished, then, the Medici could exercise a considerable influence over the negotiations taking place in Venice. Tommaso also gave them a degree of control over the length of the embassy, for, as he wrote to Piero, before leaving Florence he had promised to remain at Venice for 'a day, an hour or a year'; he would ask for permission to return only when Piero gave him leave. Although a relatively minor aspect of an embassy, possessing the power to cut short or prolong a negotiation could profoundly affect its outcome.

The embassy of 1463 was only the beginning of what was to be for Tommaso a long and distinguished diplomatic career. The leading citizens' satisfaction with his performance at Venice was reflected the following year in his appointment to a second embassy, this time to the papal court. In August 1464 Pope Pius II had died while attempting to realize his

[20] Tommaso to Piero, 30 Oct. 1463, MAP, xvii, 384.
[21] Alessandro Martelli to Piero, 26 Nov. 1463, MAP, xvi, 133.
[22] For the Signoria's praise, see the Signoria to Tommaso, 12, 16, 24 Nov. 1463, Sig., Leg. e Comm., 15, fos. 116ᵛ–118ʳ, 120ʳ.
[23] Tommaso to Piero, 30 Oct. 1463, MAP, xvii, 384.

dream of accompanying a sea-borne crusade against the Turks. In Pius's place, the cardinals had elected a Venetian, Paolo Barbo, who could, given his countrymen's continuing conflict with the Turks, be expected to carry on his predecessor's plan. The accession of a new Pope was traditionally followed by formal embassies from the Christian powers offering obedience and congratulations, and in this case Tommaso and five other prominent Florentines formed Florence's delegation to Rome.[24]

Although the mission was primarily ceremonial, the ambassadors performed an important task in searching out the new Pope's political position, and making him as well-disposed as possible towards their own city. As the new pontiff was Venetian, he was expected to be hostile towards the Florence–Milan coalition, but Paul II, as Barbo chose to be called, showed himself anxious to win the goodwill of these powers. In particular, he demonstrated favour towards Florence, and, for the ambassadors, this meant that various personal favours were granted along with many of the public requests they had been ordered to make.[25] As a special mark of favour, Tommaso and two other of the Florentines were even created knights by the Pope.[26]

Although by this time the rank of knighthood conferred few advantages in Florence, it was valuable because of the prestige which the title bestowed, and because of certain signs of pre-eminence which it still conferred. For example, knights were allowed to carry arms, and they and their wives could dress with greater sumptuousness than ordinary citizens. In a society which placed considerable emphasis on

[24] The Florentine ambassadors are named and their instructions recorded in Sig., Leg. e Comm., 15, fos. 125ʳ–128ʳ. On the election of Paul II, see Ammanati, *Commentariorum liber tertius*, fos. 347ᵛ–348ᵛ; Pastor, *History of the Popes*, iv. 3–12.

[25] In Tommaso's case, this meant acquiring the patronage of his parish church and a dispensation for an illegitimate son to enter holy orders: Notarile Antecos., M570, fos. 419ʳ–422ʳ, 446ᵛ–449ʳ (Feb.–June, 1465), fos. 484ʳ–485ᵛ (5 Oct. 1465).

[26] For a description of the ceremony, see Francesco Accolti to the Duke of Milan, 9 Nov. 1464, ASMi, SPE, Roma, 56. Paul II's letter to the Signoria of 20 Dec. 1464 indicates that he bestowed these knighthoods in the hope of winning support in Florence: Sig., Resp., Copiari, 1, fo. 126ʳ⁻ᵛ. His ultimate objective was thought to be a Florence–Venice *rapprochement*.

visual symbol, these aspects of the title could significantly raise a Florentine's reputation and status. Most importantly, knights also possessed the right to speak first in the *Pratiche*, where their views consequently exercised a greater influence on the outcome of the debate. It was this advantage in particular which benefited Tommaso, although in general the rank must have confirmed and reinforced his growing political power.[27]

The embassy to Rome took on greater political significance when the new pontiff, under pressure from the Cardinals and the Venetians, agreed to continue his predecessor's initiative in organizing a crusade. He therefore asked that one member of every embassy remain to participate in the discussions, and of the Florentines, Tommaso was the one selected.[28] Why Tommaso should have been chosen is not immediately obvious, as he had no experience at Rome, and was one of the more junior members of the ambassadorial party. However, he had had some contact with the Turkish question during his embassy of the previous year, while, as far as the Medici were concerned, he could provide them with a means of influencing what might prove for Florence a vital negotiation.

Tommaso maintained the same kind of contact with the Medici while at Rome as he had the previous year at Venice. The only letter surviving from the mission indicates that he kept Piero as well as the Signoria informed of what he was doing, and that he regarded Piero, as much as the Signoria, as the source of his political directives. This letter, of 6 December 1464, also illustrates the freedom with which he discussed matters with Piero. Tommaso had been left alone in Rome in late November 1464 without any mandate to

---

[27] On the rank of knighthood in 15th-c. Florence, see Salvemini, *La dignità*, especially pp. 29–70; Brown, 'The Guelf Party' 46–8. Cf. Sacramoro dei Mengozzi da Rimini to the Duke of Milan, 15 Feb. 1469, ASMi, SPE, Firenze, 276: '. . . *a simile dispute* [i.e. the *Pratiche*] . . . *fa assay li primi motori e dicituri, che sonno li cavalleri.*' Also, Sacramoro to the Duke, 24 Feb. 1469, ibid.: '*Toggono volontera qui questa insegna de militia perche li cavalleri sonno li più rechesti, li più honorati e li primi dicitori quando fanno . . . pratiche.*'

[28] The Signoria to the ambassadors at Rome, 7 Nov. 1464, Sig., Leg e Comm., 15, fo. 129^r. Cf. Pastor, *History of the Popes*, iv. 79–81; Setton, *The Papacy and the Levant*, ii. 727.

negotiate the terms of a crusade. With the cardinal-delegates insisting on discussing the issue and the Venetian ambassadors pressing for a conclusion, Tommaso had done his best, he reported to Piero, to satisfy the Pope with words. Nevertheless, he felt strongly that Florence's failure to send a mandate showed a disregard for papal wishes which would ultimately undermine Florence's relations with the Holy See. The Pope, he argued, would believe that the Florentines did not 'esteem' him, and this, in combination with Cosimo de' Medici's death and a recent spate of bankruptcies, would seriously reduce Florence's reputation abroad.[29]

While Tommaso's arguments were perceptive and his advice sound, he was clearly arguing the papal position in a manner which suggests that he had once again been influenced by the viewpoint of his host. Indeed, as some prominent Florentines saw it, the Florentine ambassadors to Rome had been so showered with favours that they had become outright papal partisans.[30] Nevertheless, Tommaso's description of the situation was sufficiently disturbing to the Florentines to ensure that instructions were immediately sent to him, and these must rapidly have restored the ambassador to a sense of his city's real interests. By the beginning of January 1465 he could report that Paul II would probably be content with little more than the 'good words', with which Tommaso had clearly been generous.[31] In turn, the Signoria appreciated Tommaso's competence and diligence; at one point they wrote to him that no one could have responded better to papal arguments than he.[32]

Tommaso's awkward task in Rome was finally terminated

---

[29] Tommaso to Piero, 6 Dec. 1464, MAP, xvi, 172.

[30] Nicodemo Tranchedini to the Duke of Milan, 25 Jan. 1465, ASMi, SPE, Firenze, 272, reporting a comment by Dietisalvi Neroni. Cf. also Tranchedini to the Duke, 29 Dec. 1464, Paris, Bibl. Nat., MSS italiens, 1591, fo. 228: Nicodemo refers to the Florentine ambassadors just returned from Rome as the Pope's *'cavalieri e partesani'*.

[31] Tranchedini to the Duke, 6 Jan. 1465, ASMi, SPE, Firenze, 272. The Florentines did eventually promise a monetary contribution to the projected crusade: Paul II to the Florentine Signoria, 20 Jan. 1465, Sig., Resp., Copiari, 1, fos. 128ʳ–129ʳ.

[32] The Signoria to Tommaso, 22 Dec. 1464, Sig., Leg. e Comm., 15, fos. 132ᵛ–133ʳ. The Signoria also praised Tommaso in its letters of 15 Dec. and 8 Jan. 1465, ibid., fos. 132ʳ⁻ᵛ, 133ʳ.

when he was required to return to Tuscany in January 1465 to take up the position of Captain of Pisa.[33] His assumption of this post meant that he did not return to Florence until the beginning of September 1465. By then the political situation had changed considerably, for after Cosimo de' Medici's death in August 1464 a movement had gradually emerged which combined the two major potential sources of discontent against Medici primacy. On the one hand, resentment against the institutional controls remained widespread in Florence, even within the regime, and was ready to crystallize into effective opposition if influential leaders could be found. This leadership was forthcoming after Cosimo de' Medici's death, as prominent citizens, jealous of Medici power, finally determined to take a stand against the family's growing supremacy. The principal figures in this movement were some of Cosimo's closest collaborators, such as Luca Pitti, Agnolo Acciaiuoli, and Dietisalvi Neroni. Although they had previously deferred to Cosimo's personal authority and influence, they had repeatedly vindicated their right to independent action, and did not regard Medici ascendancy as a permanent or irrevocable element of the city's political life. In particular, they were not prepared to see Cosimo's position of *primus inter pares* assumed by his son Piero, who was much younger and less experienced than they, and who could not command the respect accorded to his father. While they recognized the importance of Medici wealth, contacts, and influence for the regime, they wanted Piero to be content with a position of equality with themselves. However, from Piero's point of view a decline in his authority would have meant the beginning of the end—the destruction of the basis of his wealth, his influence, and even his political security. Consequently, as the other principal citizens proceeded increasingly to neglect his wishes and pursue their own policies, Piero felt compelled to struggle to retain his ascendancy, and a battle for power developed which eventually pitted him

---

[33] Tratte, 68, fo. 3ʳ. Although supposed to begin in July 1464, it was delayed for 6 months because of plague, and then for another month because of Tommaso's duties at Rome.

and a few of his remaining friends against a large, if loose, coalition of opponents.

As the conflict took shape, Piero's rivals tended towards an alliance with those citizens who had for years been hoping for a return to a more liberal political system. They too began to view the developments of the preceding thirty years not as a move towards government by the best, as they had maintained in 1458, but towards the tyranny which Giovanni Cavalcanti had denounced. Soon they began to adopt the slogans of popular liberty which were guaranteed to win them a large following among citizens already hoping for political change.[34] Their decision proved extremely successful, as the various currents of anti-Medici sentiment united in demanding a restoration of the pre-1434 system of government.

By the autumn of 1465, when Tommaso returned to Florence, this anti-Medici tide was reaching full flood.[35] Initially, he was probably unable to gauge the level of resistance to Medici ascendancy and to institutional controls, and his comments in the *Pratiche* reflect the hesitancy of someone still feeling the ground. However, apparently without any wavering of loyalty, Tommaso rapidly emerged as the leading spokesman on Piero's side, and his experience of the Florentine political system stood him in good stead in the subsequent year's struggle between the reforming current and the small group which remained committed to Piero. Yet he succeeded in furthering Medici interests while appearing to assume a moderate, objective stand which both made his partisanship more effective and won him respect and further influence within the inner circle of the regime.

---

[34] Dietisalvi Neroni to the Duke of Milan, 4 Sept. 1465, Milan, Bibl. Ambros., MS Z.247. Sup., fo. 143: 'the citizen body wants more liberty and a wider government'; the Duke to Luca Pitti, 22 Sept. 1465, ibid., fo. 145: the Duke recognizes that what affects all cannot be decided by a few. Cf. Giovanni di Carlo, 'De temporibus suis', fo. 80ʳ; Parenti, 'Ricordi politici', 2, 35; Rubinstein, *Government*, 140–1.

[35] On this factional conflict, cf. Parenti, 'Ricordi politici', 1–2; Ammanati, *Commentariorum liber tertius*, fos. 356ᵛ–357ʳ; Giovanni di Carlo, 'De temporibus suis', which is an apology for the Medici side; Pampaloni, 'Fermenti', 11–62, 241–81; Municchi, *La fazione*; Rubinstein, *Government*, 136–41.

Tommaso's first clash with the emerging liberalizing current occurred over the issue of the special powers which had frequently been granted to the magistracy responsible for state security, the *Otto di Guardia*. As this additional authority was designed to facilitate repression of opposition to the regime, it now aroused growing resistance. In June 1465, the *Cento* had refused to prolong the *Otto*'s special powers, and the inner circle had immediately split over the issue. Whereas Piero insisted that the *Otto*'s authority needed strengthening, the nascent opposition, represented for example by Agnolo Acciaiuoli, had argued that the *Otto*'s ordinary powers were quite sufficient for their needs.

When this matter and financial questions came up for discussion again in early September, hostility towards the restrictive regime of the recent past had become much more widespread and vocal. In these meetings, the questions of taxation or the *Otto*'s authority became springboards for denunciations of the style of government which had grown up under Medici leadership. On 3 September, for example, Dietisalvi Neroni described the existing political system as corrupt and repressive, able to perpetuate itself only because citizens were afraid to speak their minds. Other citizens sympathized with his views, while some, including Agnolo Acciaiuoli, called on the Signoria to consult a wider section of the citizen body than had hitherto been the norm.[36]

While not responding to the general criticism, Tommaso was prepared to spring to the defence of a particular instrument which had helped to defend the Medici group's ascendancy. Unlike Agnolo Acciaiuoli, Dietisalvi's brother and Luca Pitti's son, Tommaso strongly supported the granting of special powers to the *Otto*. He even defended the use of the word '*balìa*' to describe the *Otto*'s authority, despite its critics' assertion that the term was by now universally hated. Still believing it possible to convince his hearers to accept a compromise, he suggested that special powers be granted only to the *Otto* then in office; authority to extend these for a further year could be delegated to the Signoria and Colleges. However, Tommaso had clearly miscalculated the

---

[36] CP, 58, fos. 20ᵛ–22ᵛ. Cf also the *Pratica* of 4 Sept., ibid., fos. 22ᵛ–24ᵛ.

temper of his audience. Even this moderate proposal was rejected by the citizens of the *Pratica* and the idea of extending the *Otto*'s *balìa* had to be abandoned.[37]

Tommaso must have received an even ruder awakening on 10 September, when the critics of the existing political system turned their attack against one of the foundations of Medici authority—elections *a mano* of the Signoria. Although himself an *accoppiatore*, Manno Temperani led the assault by declaring, in terms typical of the recurrent criticism of the Medici regime, that power was concentrated in too few hands. In particular, he asserted, the *accoppiatori* 'have everything in their power', and he therefore recommended that they resign. Whereas most of those present followed Manno's lead, Tommaso again supported the old controls, thereby marking himself as one of the die-hards of the Medici group. But even he felt compelled to bow to public opinion by admitting that the citizens' all-too-evident discontent was caused by their desire for the abolition of elections *a mano*. However, at the same time he argued that elections *a mano* had been useful in the past, presumably in achieving a high quality of Signorie, and urged a restoration of harmony, by which he undoubtedly meant abandoning the present controversial proposals.[38]

Almost alone in his commitment to restrictive controls, Tommaso could do nothing to stem the flow of opinion in favour of sortition. On the following day, he was forced to acquiesce in the now general view that the *accoppiatori* should resign and elections *a mano* be abolished.[39] Understandably, this proposal was carried with large majorities in the legislative councils, and this success further fuelled the movement against the restrictive system of the past. The closing of the election bags of the Signoria, carried out by

---

[37] Ibid. Tommaso repeated his suggestion on 5 Sept. when he added the old spectres of famine and plague as a justification: ibid., fos. 27ʳ–28ᵛ. Tommaso's defence of the term *balìa* occurred on 10 Sept.: ibid., fo. 29ᵛ.

[38] Ibid., 10 Sept. 1465, fos. 28ᵛ–31ʳ. Cf. Rubinstein, *Government*, 141, and Agnolo Acciaiuoli to his son Jacopo, 21 Oct. 1465, published in Strozzi, *Lettere*, 484.

[39] *Pratiche* of 11 Sept. 1465, CP, 58, fos. 31ʳ–33ᵛ.

the *accoppiatori* immediately thereafter, indicated how different the situation in 1465 was from 1449 or 1455. On those previous occasions the *accoppiatori* had united in a last-ditch effort to strengthen the number of friends of the regime with names in the election bags. Now, with several of Piero's principal enemies among the *accoppiatori*, the procedure merely undermined the Medici position yet further. According to Agnolo Acciaiuoli, the names of almost all citizens who had been declared eligible for the *Tre Maggiori* since 1434 were included in the bags, and, although this was clearly an exaggeration, many Florentines who had previously lost their qualifications because they were suspect to the Medici group, now recovered them.[40]

The composition of the first Signoria appointed by lot for November–December 1465 indicated what could be expected from the altered method of selection. The most powerful figure in the new magistracy, the Standardbearer, was none other than Niccolò Soderini, now claiming a place at the head of government after an absence from the Signoria of almost fifteen years. By now Niccolò was generally known as a man of popular sympathies and a declared enemy of the Medici family. According to Alessandra Strozzi, the Medici even feared that Niccolò might use his new power to exile them from Florence.[41] Conversely, ordinary citizens had high expectations that Niccolò would attend to their interests as opposed to those of a narrower circle at the apex of the regime.[42] Although Piero's principal opponents apparently had no close connections with Niccolò at the time of his taking office, they quickly recognized that he would prove a

[40] Agnolo's comment is in his letter to Jacopo (see n. 38). On the popularity of the closure of the bags and the boost it gave to the anti-Medici current, see also Parenti, 'Ricordi politici', 33; Morelli, *Cronaca*, 180–1; Rubinstein, *Government*, 143.

[41] Alessandra Strozzi to her son Filippo, 25 Jan. 1466, *Lettere*, 556, confirmed by Agnolo Acciaiuoli to the Duke of Milan, 22 Dec. 1465, Milan, Bibl. Ambros., MS Z.247 Sup., fo. 349, and Parenti, 'Ricordi politici', 36. For Niccolò's appointment as Standardbearer: Tratte, 202, fo. 26ᵛ.

[42] On Niccolò's reputation for justice and devotion to 'the people's' interest, cf. Giovanni di Carlo, 'De temporibus suis', fos. 80ʳ, 82ᵛ–83ʳ; the introduction, presumably by the recording notary, to the first *Pratica* which Niccolò held, in Pampaloni, 'Fermenti', 242; Parenti, 'Ricordi politici', 35–6; Alessandra Strozzi to Filippo, 2, 22 Nov. 1465, *Lettere*, 506, 519–20.

useful ally in their struggle against Piero. As a contemporary wrote, they tried to win him to their side, but, despite their common purpose, Niccolò retained his own independent ideas of what he wanted to accomplish in office. His object-ives, as this contemporary pointed out, remained very differ-ent from the aims of either the Medici or of their leading opponents.[43]

Initially, however, these tensions within the reforming movement were submerged by the vast popularity which Niccolò enjoyed when he entered office on 1 November 1465. Capitalizing on this surge of public opinion, the Standardbearer turned with confidence to those areas which he felt most needed change. In his first *Pratica*, on 3 Nov-ember, he made his position clear by roundly condemning the system of government which had developed under Medici ascendancy. Offices, he complained, were allocated accord-ing to wealth rather than merit; the legal system had become venal; laws were despised; and both city and countryside were being ruined by excessive taxation motivated only by the avarice of the leading citizens. All this had been possible in the past, he asserted, because citizens had not dared to voice their real views. Now, this should no longer be the case, and those present should feel free to give whatever advice they felt would be of use to the government. The reaction he was expecting was suggested by his final appeal, in which he exhorted them to show by their response whether they intended in future 'to rule or to be ruled'.[44]

Although a thoroughgoing criticism of the policies of the Medici group, this speech was less radical than some Medici supporters had feared; it did not, for example, suggest direct action against the city's leading family. This moderation, according to the Milanese ambassador, was due to Tom-maso, who had spoken to his brother in advance and dissuaded him from extreme measures.[45] However, the ambassador's report was undoubtedly influenced by the

---

[43] Parenti, 'Ricordi politici', 35.
[44] The *Pratica* of 3 Nov. 1465, published by Pampaloni, 'Fermenti', 242–51. Cf. Rubinstein, *Government*, 144–5.
[45] Nicodemo Tranchedini to the Duke of Milan, 5 Nov. 1465, ASMi, SPE, Firenze, 272.

desire of Piero and his circle to prove that they retained some control over what was happening in Florence. While Tommaso may well have tried to moderate his brother's approach, Niccolò had clearly sided with the opposition. Sharing the general desire for wider consultation, he had thrown open the door to free comment and suggestion, while also summoning an unusually large number of citizens to the *Pratica* in the expectation that the existing climate of opinion would lead to the expression of radical anti-Medici views.

However, Niccolò's expectations were rapidly disappointed. While his hearers almost universally praised his speech, they recommended only very moderate means of reforming the widespread political corruption which Niccolò had described. Even some of Piero's principal opponents were reluctant to join him in criticizing past political developments, to which they had contributed so much. Ultimately, widespread approval within the *Pratica* was extended only to such relatively innocuous proposals as the extension of sortition to offices still appointed by election, and the vague goal of tax relief. For Tommaso, who, like the rest of Piero's remaining friends, had decided to bend before Niccolò's popularity rather than oppose him, the failure of the *Pratica* to decide on radical measures undoubtedly made it easier to assume an attitude of judicious statesmanship. He concluded one debate, for example, by urging that whatever the citizens of the *Pratica* decided should be put into effect[46]—a suggestion probably based on a growing conviction that the motley group of citizens whom Niccolò had collected together would not agree on very much.

Since the citizens of the *Pratica* failed to come forward with a method of reforming the government, Niccolò finally decided, on 13 November, to propose his own form of constitutional change. However, the programme which he suggested aroused considerable controversy.[47] On the one hand, it involved a new scrutiny, which, since it would offer

[46] This description includes the *Pratica* of 4 Nov. as well as of 3 Nov. 1465. The former was also published by Pampaloni, 'Fermenti', 251–5.

[47] The *Pratica* of 13 Nov. 1465, Pampaloni, 'Fermenti', 256–61. Cf. Rubinstein, *Government*, 145–7.

citizens an opportunity to acquire political qualifications, was bound to be popular. At the same time, it would also serve as a partisan instrument, for, given the composition of the Signoria, the scrutiny council was bound to be broader than those of the recent past, and the results likely to strengthen the liberalizing tendencies within the ruling group. The response to Niccolò's suggestion was consequently divided, even among Piero's rivals, who were apparently torn between a desire to increase the number of non-Medici partisans in office, and fear that opening up political power to a wider body of citizens might threaten their own influence within the governing group.[48]

Ultimately, a scrutiny was agreed on, primarily because of popular pressure in its favour.[49] However, the same was not true of the second part of Niccolò's programme of 13 November. This proposed that all citizens who had been eligible for office since 1444 should retain their qualifications permanently—a radical departure from the Florentine tradition of regular redistribution of political rights. While Niccolò justified the idea on the grounds that it would reduce the conflicts over power which had repeatedly divided the ruling group, his objectives in making such a radical proposal were undoubtedly both partisan and self-interested. Adoption of the plan would mean that citizens who had recently fallen foul of the Medici group would recover their political rights, while those, like himself, who might fear to lose their qualifications in future would be reassured. Thus, both citizens' independence and the strength of the anti-Medici current would be guaranteed.[50] Apart from these obvious advantages, the scheme also embodied Niccolò's old ideal of a more permanent but equal ruling group. While it did not disallow the entry of new citizens into the city's political

---

[48] Cf. the comments on the scrutiny, and the decreasing enthusiasm for it within the *Pratiche* of 13–15 Nov. 1465: Pampaloni, 'Fermenti', 256–67.

[49] Cf. the *Pratica* of 15 Nov. 1465, ibid.: The citizens generally agreed that, since word of the proposed scrutiny had got out, enthusiasm for it was so high that it had better be carried out.

[50] According to Marco Parenti, even the scrutiny proposal had a self-interested motive in that Niccolò wanted his favourite son, who had recently left clerical life, to gain qualifications for public office: 'Ricordi politici', 37–8.

class, the plan would have accepted the existing regime as permanent and thus have been a step towards stability along Venetian lines.

For the citizens of the *Pratica* this guarantee of qualifications was much more controversial than the scrutiny. Many praised the fact that it would reduce the recurrent and dangerous conflict over public offices. Tommaso in particular welcomed the idea as a means of reducing the frequency of contentious scrutinies. On the other hand, several citizens pointed out that the impossibility of losing political rights would remove the incentive for citizens to behave with honesty and rectitude in public office, while the major criticism centred round the oligarchic implications of the proposal. As one of the leading proponents of the liberalization of government pointed out, the result would be rule by an effective upper class—the *optimates*—rather than Florence's more popular form of government, in which mobility had been an essential element. Thus, the speakers complained, Niccolò's plan would make the Florentine political system resemble more closely the more aristocratic one of Venice. This was, of course, precisely what Niccolò had been hoping for from the Medici regime since the 1430s, but, despite the admiration for the Venetian constitution among certain patricians, his goal now proved too oligarchic for the majority to stomach.[51]

In the end it was Niccolò who was most affected by his radical proposal, for, although it never reached the legislative stage, the long discussions it inspired meant that other, more beneficial legislation was neglected. Moreover, divisions within the ruling group were exacerbated, while the Standardbearer and his objective of reform lost some of the credit which they had possessed at the beginning of the month. The advent of the scrutiny had the same effect, as even more agitated lobbying than usual occurred, and the long sessions of voting for candidates diverted the Signoria from other legislative endeavours. Even the composition of the scrutiny council became a subject for debate, as many prominent

---

[51] Cf. e.g. the comments of Manno Temperani on 14 Nov. and of Carlo Pandolfini and Franco Sacchetti on 15 Nov., Pampaloni, 'Fermenti', 261, 263, 265.

citizens began to fear its deliberations, because of its large size, and the fact that it included an abnormally large number of lower guildsmen.

By late November, Niccolò was noticeably losing the wide support which he had enjoyed at the beginning of his term. On 22 November, the ever-perceptive Alessandra Strozzi wrote that 'the people' now feared that they would be worse rather than better off as a result of Niccolò's term of office.[52] Moreover, the prominent citizens who had hoped to use Niccolò against Piero de' Medici saw their opportunity slipping away, and became angry with the Standardbearer's stubborn pursuit of impractical goals. Writing to the Duke of Milan in mid-December, Agnolo Acciaiuoli complained that Niccolò was an imprudent citizen, who 'knows nothing on his own and won't listen to anyone else'.[53] In turn, as Niccolò saw his support fading, he lost the courage of his earlier convictions, and abandoned even his initial efforts to improve the lot of the ordinary citizen.[54]

Later it was said that such proposals as the scrutiny had been made in order to deflect Niccolò from potentially more dangerous anti-Medici schemes.[55] Whether or not this was true, Tommaso had certainly been attempting to influence his brother in directions beneficial to the small circle still

[52] Alessandra Strozzi to Filippo, 22 Nov. 1465, *Lettere*, 520.
[53] Agnolo to the Duke, 17 Dec. 1465, ASMi, SPE, Firenze, 272. On 22 Dec. Agnolo wrote that Niccolò 'by himself would be worth nothing and could do nothing', Milan, Bibl. Ambros. MS Z.247 Sup., fo. 349.
[54] Cf. Alessandra to Filippo, 11 Jan. 1466, *Lettere*, 550, and Giovanni di Carlo, 'De temporibus suis', fos. 89ʳ–90ᵛ. The view that Niccolò wasted his time in impractical ideas and lost his opportunity to do great things became a commonplace with Machiavelli (*Istorie*, 167) and Ammirato (*Istorie*, v. 362–3). Niccolò did succeed in accomplishing some things for 'the people', such as lowering the wine tax: Landucci, *Diario fiorentino*, 5. Cf. Benedetto Dei's comment that Niccolò *'die' assai benefizio e ufizio al popolo . . .'*, *Cronica*, fo. 22ʳ.
[55] The theory that Niccolò had been deliberately deflected from measures dangerous to the Medici group—by Tommaso in particular—became part of official Florentine historiography; cf. e.g. Ammirato, *Istorie*, v. 362–3; Machiavelli, *Istorie*, 167; Nerli, *Commentari*, i. 85–6. It originated in Piero de' Medici's efforts to convince the Milanese that he had let the scrutiny go ahead for this reason: Nicodemo Tranchedini to the Duke, 25 Nov. 1465, ASMi, SPE, Firenze, 272. Tommaso's encouragement of Niccolò's constitutional proposal might seem to give weight to this theory, but his opposition to the scrutiny proves that his principal goal was not to divert his brother to time-consuming legislation.

loyal to Piero. For example, in late November, when he learned that Niccolò and Piero's other leading rivals were intending to hire soldiers who might be hostile to the Medici, he went to remonstrate with his brother, arguing that whereas Niccolò had promised to relieve the Florentines of expense, he was now planning to increase it.[56] Moreover, Tommaso informed Piero of the supposedly secret discussions of the *Pratiche*, and was probably involved in organizing some of the pressure groups to which both sides were resorting by late November.[57]

In late November, Tommaso also undertook an independent initiative to try and win Piero's principal opponent back to the Medici fold. He visited Luca Pitti, who, of all Piero's opponents, retained the most sympathy for his erstwhile Medici friend. Taking advantage of the growing disillusionment with Niccolò's policies, Tommaso tried to persuade Luca to agree to a reconciliation with Piero, reminding him of his earlier loyalty to the Medici family, and warning him that he would eventually repent if he continued to oppose Piero. According to the Milanese ambassador, Luca listened carefully to what Tommaso said because, as brother of the Standardbearer and confidant of Piero, he was in a position, or so it was apparently believed, to know what was going on in both camps.[58] Tommaso's overture probably contributed towards the tenuous accord which was patched up among the warring *principali* at the end of the month.[59] Certainly his role as mediator, and the guise of moderation which he assumed, led to the rise in his reputation which the Milanese ambassador noted towards the end of the month. As Nicodemo Tranchedini then wrote, Tommaso had 'made great strides as a result of these rivalries, although he has been very esteemed for quite a while because he is a good person and a good Medici man'.[60]

---

[56] Tranchedini to the Duke, 29 Nov. 1465, ASMi, SPE, Firenze, 272.

[57] Ibid. On the secret engagements being made at the time, see Parenti, 'Ricordi politici', 36–7; Giovanni di Carlo, 'De temporibus suis', fos. 80ᵛ, 81bᵛ–82ʳ; Rubinstein, *Government*, 150.

[58] Tranchedini to the Duke, 23 Nov. 1465, ASMi, SPE, Firenze, 272.

[59] Tommaso mentioned that he himself had been present at discussion of an accord: *Pratica* of 29 Nov. 1465, in Pampaloni, 'Fermenti', 277.

[60] Tranchedini to the Duke, 23 Nov. 1465, cit.: Tommaso had '*factossi molto*

Since his own authority was growing, Tommaso was well placed, after Niccolò left office in disgrace at the end of December 1465, to lead the counterattack from the Medici side.[61] Together with Piero, his first objective was to terminate the scrutiny which Niccolò had begun, and to cancel the results of the part already completed in December. One of the most outspoken critics of the scrutiny from the start, Tommaso now joined with other citizens in condemning the large size and the composition of his brother's scrutiny council. The reviewing body should, he agreed, be dissolved, while the results of the completed first phase—that of the *Tre Maggiori*—should be annulled. In the apocalyptic language he reserved for political crises, Tommaso insisted that the scrutiny had merely exacerbated political unrest; if nothing were done to end it, the city would be totally destroyed.[62] Evidently, it was widely known that Tommaso, Piero de' Medici, and a few other Medici partisans were leading the anti-scrutiny campaign, trying to 'annihilate the scrutiny', as one observer put it.[63] To achieve this goal, Tommaso must have been using all his eloquence, for, as Alessandra Strozzi graphically described him, he was going about the city in late January with 'honey in his mouth and a knife at his belt'.[64]

The pains taken by Tommaso and his collaborators were rewarded when, at the end of January, the legislative councils agreed that, although the scrutiny results completed so far would stand, the composition of the reviewing body would be altered for the second stage of the scrutiny. Although this represented only a partial success, it still meant victory and

---

inanti per queste loro gharre, licet sia stato bon pezzo fa assai extimato perche è bona persona et bon Cosmiano'.

[61] When Niccolò left office, bonfires were lit to celebrate, and graffiti appeared proclaiming that 'nine fools', i.e. the Signoria, had left office: Alessandra Strozzi to Filippo, 4 Jan. 1466, *Lettere*, 540. Earlier, Tommaso had prophesied that although Niccolò had 'come in like a lion' he would 'go out like a lamb': 11 Jan. 1466, ibid., 550.

[62] Cf. the *Pratiche* of 30 Nov. 1465 and 2, 3 Jan. 1466, Pampaloni, 'Fermenti', 280, and 'Nuovi tentativi', 526, 528–9.

[63] Alessandra to Filippo, 30 Jan. 1466, *Lettere*, 565.

[64] Alessandra to Filippo, 31 Jan. 1466, ibid., 566.

an increase in the reputation of the Medici group. Tommaso in particular, as one of the most vocal opponents of the scrutiny, saw his reputation rise as a result of the legislation; as Alessandra Strozzi put it, he now possessed 'greater authority than ever'.[65]

Despite this partial Medici victory, the political conflict was no closer to resolution. From February to August 1466 the battle continued over issues of both internal and foreign policy. In March the death of Francesco Sforza and his successor's request for a loan led to a long political wrangle, for the Sforza were recognized as special friends of the Medici, and Piero's rivals would not agree to grant them a subsidy unless the Sforza recognized it as a favour from themselves. On that occasion Piero's rivals won, for resistance in the *Pratica* eventually forced the Florentine government into the embarrassing position of having to refuse the loan.[66] On the other hand, an effort undertaken in July to abolish the permanent special council, the *Cento*, ended in victory for the Medici supporters. According to leading figures of the anti-Medici current, such as Agnolo Acciaiuoli, the *Cento* provided a vehicle for those who wished to 'tyrannize' the city, while other critics of the *Cento*, including Niccolò Soderini, inveighed against the élite nature of the assembly. He argued that lesser guildsmen were inadequately represented while past Standardbearers of Justice held too great a sway. Niccolò, like Agnolo, claimed that the *Cento* was used by leading citizens to dominate the less powerful, and, in a demagogic moment, called on the Signoria to convoke the 'people' in order to discover the real views of the citizen body.[67]

---

[65] Ibid. This letter and that of the preceding day testify to the increased prestige which the passage of the bill brought to Piero and his supporters. On the scrutiny legislation of this month, cf. Rubinstein, *Government*, 151–2.

[66] On this issue of the loan, see Parenti, 'Ricordi politici', 39–40; Giovanni di Carlo, 'De temporibus suis', fos. 81ᵛ–81bᵛ; Rinuccini, *Ricordi storici*, p. xcix; Guicciardini, *Memorie di famiglia*, 20–1; Rubinstein, *Government*, 155–6. Naturally, Tommaso was heartily in favour of the loan (cf. the *Pratiche* of 7, 9, 14 Apr. 1466, CP, 58, fos. 127ᵛ–128ʳ, 130ᵛ–131ʳ, 143ʳ), while Niccolò just as firmly opposed it: *Pratica* of 2 May 1466, in Pampaloni, 'Nuovi tentativi', 552–3.

[67] Cf. the *Pratiche* of 6, 8 July and the undated one between 8 July and 1 Aug. 1466, Pampaloni, ibid., 562, 567, 570, 572. On this dispute over the *Cento*, cf. also Rinuccini, *Ricordi storici*, p. c; Rubinstein, *Government*, 159–60.

Niccolò's appeal was a response to citizens like his brother, who insisted that since the *Cento* had been established by the *parlamento* of 1458, it was a manifestation of the people's will, and could not be changed by the normal legislative process! He also justified the high proportion of Standard-bearers in the assembly on the grounds that they contributed to a better quality of election. Moreover, in an effort to turn the tables on his opponents, he stigmatized the movement against the *Cento* as partisan and disruptive as well as illegal. Instead of such radical projects, he advocated restoring harmony and tranquillity among the citizens and seeing that the laws were observed, all with a view to devoting attention to more important issues such as the city's trade.[68]

Many citizens must have agreed with Tommaso that reform had gone far enough, for the project of dissolving the *Cento* was soon abandoned. By this time, however, the conflict had become so serious that the Signoria felt it necessary to intervene. In May 1466 the Signoria demanded that all citizens of the regime swear to forget the errors and injuries of the past, and to renounce the secret engagements into which so many of them had entered. Moreover, it tried to satisfy some of the grievances of the anti-Medici current, as the signatories promised that all government business would be transacted in the Signoria's seat (rather than in the Medici palace), and that in future justice would be administered impartially.[69]

This oath achieved very little, however, for it could not in itself guarantee security to either side or fulfil the still unsatisfied objectives of both factions. Indeed, later in the same month, over four hundred advocates of wider government felt it necessary to band together in a private defence of their political goals. Concerned about the pacts and secret agreements still being made by the opposite side, they pledged themselves to uphold the existing 'just and popular government', mentioning sortition of the Signoria as a

---

[68] Cf. Tommaso's contribution to the same three *Pratiche* of 6, 8 July and the undated one, 1466: Pampaloni, 'Nuovi tentativi', 562, 566, 572–3.

[69] Cf. the *Pratica* of 4 May 1466, ibid., 555. The oath has been published by Municchi, *La fazione*, App., 116–17. On the oath and the conflicts which gave rise to it, see Pampaloni, 'Il giuramento', 212–25.

cornerstone of the new regime. They also specifically committed themselves to preserve freedom of speech and counsel,
to prevent citizens from being subjected to illegal pressures,
and, in short, to defend that permanent ideal of Florentine
political life—'the great, golden word, liberty'. Among the
signatories was, as we might expect, Niccolò Soderini, while
his brother Tommaso was conspicuously absent.[70]

With even government initiatives ineffective in the factional conflict, a violent resolution seemed increasingly likely
by the summer of 1466. Tempers had been raised to fever
pitch by the battle over the *Cento* in July, and in the
aftermath citizens began to collect arms and plan their
personal defence.[71] In these circumstances, external allies
became of extreme importance and Piero de' Medici was the
one who could count on foreign forces nearest at hand.
Pressured by both Tommaso and the Milanese ambassador,
who had steadfastly supported the Medici throughout the
conflict, Piero may have arranged for Milanese troops sta-
tioned around Bologna to come to his aid if necessary.[72]
Meanwhile, the leading anti-Mediceans were seriously considering an alliance with Venice, and, afraid that Piero might
resort to violence, eventually accepted an offer of assistance
from a Venetian adherent, Marquis Borso d'Este of Ferrara.[73]
In fact, Borso precipitated the final crisis of late August 1466,
as, apparently without informing his friends in Florence, he
sent his soldiers towards the Florentine frontier, where they
could be ready for action.[74] News of their approach awakened fear of an attack in Florence, and panic ensued as both
sides strove to prepare for their defence.

[70] This pact has been published and commented on by Pampaloni, ibid., 226–38.
Cf. Rubinstein, *Government*, 156–8.

[71] Cf. Parenti, 'Ricordi politici', fos. 63ᵛ–64ʳ; Giovanni di Carlo, 'De temporibus
suis', fo. 89ʳ; Rubinstein, *Government*, 160–2.

[72] Cf. Parenti and Giovanni di Carlo, op. cit. Tommaso was meanwhile
providing for every eventuality by transferring his property to his sons: Notarile
Antecos., P130, fos. 45ʳ–48ʳ, 15 Aug. 1466.

[73] Borso had plans for major political changes in Italy, i.e. the Angevins would
recover Naples with the support of the Venetians and of Florence, once it was
purged of the pro-Milanese Medici group; Gherardo Colli to the Duke of Milan,
18 Aug. 1466 and 26 Dec. 1467, ASMi, SPE, Venezia, 353; *Cronaca di anonimo
veronese*, 239–40; *Storia di Milano*, vii. 234.

[74] Cf. especially Rubinstein, 'La confessione', 373–87.

In this confusion, the only person really eager to resort to force was Niccolò Soderini, who, after gathering together some two hundred men from his quarter, went to Luca Pitti's house to urge him and the other leading anti-Mediceans to attack Piero while they still had a chance of success. Luca and the others were, however, less bold or less desperate than Niccolò, while they also hesitated to initiate violence which they might prove unable to control.[75] Moreover, they were unwilling to put themselves in the wrong by taking action against a legally constituted government, and therefore chose instead to trust to the peace initiatives immediately undertaken by citizens on both sides with the blessing of the government. With Tommaso Soderini acting as Piero's spokesman, it was soon agreed that the heads of the two factions would meet in the Palace of the Signoria in order to guarantee that peace would be kept and no citizen harmed. Once this was done, and all soldiers had been ordered out of the city, the brief crisis had apparently come to an end.[76]

However, during the crisis Piero had gained a military advantage, for he had called up supporters from the countryside, and Milanese troops had moved south in his defence. Meanwhile, his opponents were placed at a moral disadvantage, as they were suspected of having intended to attack Piero and the Signoria. The political advantage also moved in Piero's direction as the new Signoria selected on 28 August was composed of citizens more favourable to him than to his opponents.[77] As a result, it was easier for Piero and his supporters to persuade the more wavering of their opponents to desert to their side. Luca Pitti had already proved susceptible to appeals to his old loyalty to the Medici, and now, in return for a promise of specific favours, he agreed to rejoin Piero.[78] With his defection, the coalition ranged against the

[75] On this incident, cf. Dei, *Cronica*, fos. 23ᵛ–24ʳ; Giovanni di Carlo, 'De temporibus suis', fos. 93ʳ–94ʳ; Ammanati, *Commentariorum liber tertius*, fo. 358ʳ; Parenti, 'Ricordi politici', fo. 66ʳ.

[76] Cf. an undated *Pratica*, apparently of late Aug. 1466, in Pampaloni, 'Nuovi tentativi', 577; Rubinstein, 'La confessione', 384–5. Many citizens were attempting to make peace during this crisis: Giovanni di Carlo 'De temporibus suis', fo. 94ʳ⁻ᵛ.

[77] Cf. Rubinstein, *Government*, 162–3.

[78] It was widely rumoured that Luca promised his support to Piero in return for his own appointment as *accoppiatore*, his brother's as one of the *Otto di Guardia*,

Medici disintegrated, as its leading members rushed to make their peace with Piero for fear of repressive measures which might follow.[79] Indeed, some sought the honour of proposing a political reorganization which would re-establish the unity of the leading citizens as well as the authority of the Medici and their friends. In the end, it was Luca Pitti who performed this task, as on 2 September he made the key address to a *Pratica* held, not in the Palace of the Signoria, but in the Medici house. Luca's principal proposal was that, as in 1458, a *parlamento* be summoned, and the plan was unanimously approved.[80]

In fact, the *parlamento* took place that very day, and, with Medici troops drawn up in the public square, the citizens who assembled made no objection to the legislation which was then read to them. As in 1458, this involved the creation of a short-term special council with full legislative powers. Following the precedent of the *Cento*, this *Balìa* included the upper echelons of the post-1434 regime—i.e. all those whose names had been drawn for the post of Standardbearer of Justice and a number of those qualified for the *Tre Maggiori* since 1434, the latter to be selected by the Signoria and Colleges.[81] Therefore, once again, many recent enemies of the Medici were included in the very group formed to reassert Piero's authority, and considerable moderation was shown in punishing those who had joined the recent anti-Medici movement. Soon after the *parlamento* had been held, a new

and his daughter's marriage to a member of the Medici family. He received all but the last, as his daughter was married to Giovanni Tornabuoni: Parenti, 'Ricordi politici', fos. 68ʳ⁻ᵛ, 73ᵛ; Giovanni di Carlo, 'De temporibus suis', fo. 94ᵛ. In fact, a Medici–Pitti marriage had been under discussion for some time, promoted by the Pope: Agostino Rossi to the Duke and Duchess of Milan, 11 May, 11, 24 June 1466, ASMi, SPE, Roma, 59. Later, Rossi and Giovaniacomo Ricci reported that discussion now involved a Tornabuoni–Pitti marriage.

[79] Among those who went to Piero were Niccolò Soderini and Tommaso's son Lorenzo who had quarrelled with his father and joined the anti-Medici side: cf. Nicodemo Tranchedini to the Duke, 31 Aug. 1466, ASMi, SPE, Firenze, 272; Piero to Pigello Portinari, 2 Sept. 1466, copy in ASMa, Lettere della Signoria di Firenze e dei Medici ai Gonzaga, 1085.

[80] *Pratica* of 2 Sept. 1466, in Pampaloni, 'Nuovi tentativi', 578–80. Cf. Parenti, 'Ricordi politici', fos. 67ᵛ, 69ʳ; Rubinstein, *Government*, 163–4.

[81] On the creation and powers of this *Balìa*, cf. Parenti, 'Ricordi politici', fos. 69ʳ⁻ᵛ; Rubinstein, *Government*, 164, 166 ff.

Otto di Guardia was elected by the *Balìa*, and its members proved devoted partisans of the Medici. Among their first acts was to issue warrants for the arrest of a number of the outstanding figures of the recent opposition, including Dietisalvi Neroni, Agnolo Acciaiuoli, and Niccolò Soderini. However, these citizens, aware of their danger, had either already fled or else did so immediately, leaving it to the Florentine judiciary to exile them *in absentia*. Along with them, a limited number of citizens who had participated in the anti-Medici movement were either exiled or deprived of their political rights.[82]

While no real innovations were introduced, the system of government in force before September 1465 was reinstated, with one major exception. Presumably as a concession to public opinion, the *accoppiatori* placed in charge of screening the members of the Signoria were not the same officials as had resigned their post the previous September. Instead, the *accoppiatori* were in future to be elected annually by the Signoria and *Cento*, and their selection was thus given a regular basis within the new permanent institutions of the Medici regime.

The changed method of selecting the *accoppiatori* meant that, for the first time since 1444, the institution of elections *a mano* did not give Tommaso a share in these officials' power and patronage. Nevertheless, his political position by no means suffered as a result. Now that Piero's supremacy had been reaffirmed and strengthened, the citizens closest to him, like Tommaso, could be sure that their own authority would benefit accordingly. Tommaso's reward came in the years following 1466, when Piero, appreciating his loyalty and ability, relied on him as confidant, collaborator, and adviser.

While Tommaso was thus gradually to climb to a position of authority second only to Piero's, his brother had joined the legion of the political has-beens of Florence. Although he

---

[82] On these punishments, see in particular Otto di Guardia, periodo repubblicano, 224, fos. 12ʳ–14ʳ, and Rubinstein, *Government*, 165–6. In spirit, if not in letter, these condemnations contravened the promises made by the factions' leaders at the end of August.

attempted for years afterwards to return, his flight in 1466 signalled the end of his life in his native city, and his family's decline from the position of prominence which he had won. Just as previous political vicissitudes had caused Francesco Soderini's line to give way to that of Lorenzo di Messer Tommaso, so now a new factional struggle meant that Niccolò Soderini's family succumbed to Tommaso's, who would monopolize the clan's illustrious tradition during the rest of the fifteenth century.

4. The Soderini Brothers' Economic World

As has frequently been pointed out, political influence and wealth did not necessarily coincide in fifteenth-century Florence. While some degree of political authority was generally necessary to preserve a family's patrimony, and politics could help increase a citizen's fortune, great wealth was not essential for a political career. The Soderini brothers provide an example of patricians who gained political success despite their limited financial resources. Yet, at the same time their careers indicate how political activity could provide direct and indirect opportunities for monetary gain, and how a citizen's personal financial situation could affect his views on political questions. In fact, Niccolò's and Tommaso's finances closely followed their political careers, with Tommaso eventually increasing his meagre fortune, while Niccolò found himself in economic difficulties even before the crisis of 1466 threw his financial affairs into complete disorder.

From the start, the Soderini brothers' financial careers illustrated the different alternatives available to Florentine patricians. Their father Lorenzo had left them a fairly typical patrimony, in that their assets were invested in such diverse enterprises as commerce, the state debt, and property. However, these investments could have brought the brothers only a modest income, for they comprised only one farm, with some additional pieces of land just south-west of Florence on the River Arno, something over 1,000 florins in credits in the *Monte* or public funded debt, and a small commercial investment made with a supplement added to Ghilla's dowry.[1]

In addition to its modest start in life, this Soderini family was economically handicapped by Lorenzo's early death. As the contemporary Giovanni Morelli pointed out, the patrimony of widows and orphans was more likely to decline than increase, for, without a father's protective hand, possessions were only too vulnerable to misappropriation. Not only would creditors, real and fraudulent, come forward to make demands on the defenceless estate, Morelli wrote, even the children's guardians would seek to line their pockets from the money passing through their hands.[2] For the Soderini, this might not have been the worst problem, for they were subject to the added disadvantage of being under the wardship of the *Ufficiali dei Pupilli*, a state magistracy created to administer the estates of heirs left without legal guardians. Lorenzo's widow, Ghilla Cambi, decided to renounce the custody of her children to this board, apparently because of the vindictiveness of the guardians of Messer Tommaso Soderini's legitimate heirs. After Lorenzo's death they had brought a suit for 2,000 florins in damages against his estate, and, as an alternative to financial disaster, Ghilla had sought the protection of the state. As public officials, she must have thought, the *Ufficiali dei Pupilli* would be better placed than she was to defend her children's patrimony. These officials did succeed in quashing the claim for damages, but they clearly did not give the infants' estate the care that a father would have done. Records of their administration suggest considerable carelessness, while Tommaso himself was clearly convinced that it proved detrimental to his own financial prospects. When drawing up his will in 1462, he insisted that his own children should never for any

---

[1] Cf. the inventory of Lorenzo Soderini's possessions in Pupilli, 17, fos. 66ᵛ–67ʳ, 69ʳ; Acquisto Soderini, 27 July 1414. On the Florentines' belief in the importance of diversifying their holdings cf. Rucellai, *Il Zibaldone*, 8–9; Goldthwaite, *Private Wealth*, 192–3, 236. In 1427, Niccolò and Tommaso came 131st in the list of the highest taxpayers of S. Spirito: Martines, *Social World*, 378. Cf. also Cambi, *Istorie*, in *Delizie*, xxi. 194: Tommaso, when young, had been a 'povero gientilomo'.

[2] For Morelli's comments, cf. his *Ricordi*, 202 ff.

reason be placed under the jurisdiction of the *Ufficiali dei Pupilli*.[3]

Understandably, then, the Soderini brothers' financial position showed no sign of improvement until they themselves grew up and began to manage their own affairs. By that time they had acquired a new source of income, for both had matriculated in the trade of manufacturing silk cloth. Of all Florence's industries, silk cloth manufacture experienced the greatest growth during the fifteenth century,[4] and Niccolò and Tommaso appear initially to have prospered in their trade. In the early 1420s they were in business with a member of the Rucellai family, one of the more prominent commercial clans of the quarter in which the brothers were then living.[5] The Rucellai may have invested most of the capital required by the firm, while Niccolò and Tommaso probably worked as factors or managers, investing in addition what capital they could. Thereby they must have accumulated sufficient means to found their own firm which, by 1427, was exporting silk products at least as far afield as Catalonia.[6] By that stage, moreover, the brothers had apparently made enough money to invest in a second farm near their father's original property at Marliano.[7]

Meanwhile, Niccolò and Tommaso had been seizing every opportunity to add to their meagre sources of wealth. One such occasion occurred during the later 1420s, when a long war against Milan raised the level of taxation to astronomical proportions. In order to find the cash to pay their taxes, many citizens were compelled to sell their credits in the public funded debt, and with many credits coming on to the

[3] Notarile Antecos., M570, fo. 90ᵛ. An incident which occurred in 1410 suggests that *Monte* credits belonging to Lorenzo's heirs had been cashed and the money collected without the *Ufficiali dei Pupilli* learning about it for some 4 years: Pupilli, 20, fos. 60ᵛ–61ʳ.

[4] On the flourishing silk trade with the Levant, cf. e.g. Ashtor, 'L'exportation', especially pp. 363, 371–4.

[5] i.e. S. Maria Novella. References to the silk company with Piero Rucellai are in Cat., 25, fo. 457ʳ (1427); 345, fo. 687ʳ (1430); 347, fo. 320ʳ (1433).

[6] In their tax return of 1427, Niccolò and Tommaso mention having shipped silk cloth to a Florentine company in Barcelona: Cat., 25, fo. 457ʳ⁻ᵛ.

[7] Ibid., fo. 456ʳ⁻ᵛ. This, however, cannot be certain, as the inventories of Lorenzo's possessions may be incomplete.

market, their price rapidly fell. Citizens with the money to purchase them could therefore do so at a reduced rate, hoping either to sell them when the market improved or, by collecting interest on the original value of the credits, obtain double or even triple the normal interest rate. Perhaps lacking cash for the latter, Niccolò and Tommaso took the former course, effectively gambling on the futures market by buying credits with a down payment and attempting to sell them rapidly. However, their hopes for quick profits proved illusory, for, since the war continued, the market price continued to fall and the city proved unable to keep pace with the interest payments on its loans. Therefore, the brothers were forced to sell the credits at a disadvantage, and, at least according to their tax return of 1427, they lost a considerable amount of money in this deal.[8]

The late 1420s and early 1430s were years of financial difficulty in Florence as war demanded high taxes which bit into citizens' patrimonies and created obstacles to trade. The Soderini brothers suffered as did the others; at one point, Tommaso chose to lose his precious right to public office rather than keep abreast of the sums demanded.[9] Niccolò, on the other hand, could claim debits greater than his assets, and thereby come to a mutually acceptable agreement with the tax officials regarding how much he should pay.[10] Moreover, in a moment of unfilial desperation, the brothers decided in 1430 to refuse to be responsible any longer for their mother's taxes, forcing her to pay them from the proceeds of the limited property which she herself possessed.[11]

Nevertheless, when they wished the Soderini could still find the cash for essential purchases. For example, at the end

---

[8] Cat., 25, fo. 457[r-v]. On the economic situation of these years, cf. Molho, *Public Finances*, especially pp. 153–82. Speculation in *Monte* credits was nothing new. For a 14th-c. example, cf. Sapori, 'Case e botteghe a Firenze nel Trecento', in *Studi*, i. 347–52.

[9] Tratte, 155, fo. 152[r]. On the large number of citizens prohibited from office by failure to pay their taxes at this time, cf. Klapisch-Zuber and Herlihy, *Les Toscans*, 45–6.

[10] Niccolò was paying taxes '*per composizione*' by 31 March 1433, Cat., 347, fo. 298[v].

[11] Cf. Ghilla's tax return of 31 Jan. 1431, Cat., 362, fo. 613[r-v].

of 1431, while the war was in full swing, Niccolò, Tommaso, and their mother Ghilla decided to buy a house, or rather two houses on one property, in the S. Spirito district of Florence.[12] In large part, their purchase must have been motivated by the desire to get out of the rented accommodation in the S. Maria Novella quarter in which they had been living. As Tommaso pointed out in about 1447, a Florentine who did not possess his own house hardly seemed a citizen, and for these patricians, who were beginning to make a name for themselves in politics, the lack of their own residence was particularly galling.[13] If they were to move, Niccolò and Tommaso must have been determined to gain a suitable house in the quarter of S. Spirito, in which they were still officially registered for administrative purposes. Residence in S. Spirito would give them a better opportunity to exert influence within the district, where meetings of local inhabitants helped to decide such major issues as scrutiny lists and how the district's tax burden should be divided among its households. Returning to the area where their clan had traditionally lived would also allow the brothers to benefit from a closer identification with the Soderini's illustrious tradition.

Hence, undoubtedly, their decision to seize the opportunity offered in 1431 by the death of a prominent banker of S. Spirito to purchase a suitable property on the south side of the Arno.[14] From Niccolò's and even Ghilla's point of view, the purchase proved a great success, for they not only took up residence on the property, but Niccolò could thereafter buy adjacent property to create his own enclave close to that of his ancestors.[15] From Tommaso's point of view, however, the deal proved less than satisfactory, for he not only did not

[12] Diplomatico, Acquisto Soderini, 8 Dec. 1431. The larger residence cost the considerable sum of 500 florins.

[13] Tommaso wrote, '*chi non a chasa non pare citadino, ed io lo pruovo ed o provato asaï*': Cat., 655, fo. 839ʳ.

[14] The purchase may have been facilitated by the fact that Tommaso had claims on the estate of this banker, Agnolo d'Isau Martellini: Cat., 347, fo. 620ᵛ.

[15] In 1447, Niccolò bought a house next to his own property from Francesco and Tanai Nerli: Notarile Antecos., P128, fo. 347ᵛ (4 Jan. 1447). He also appears to have acquired further adjacent property from the same family, as the name Nerli, originally included in the description of the confines of this house, subsequently

move to S. Spirito, but was not even reimbursed for his contribution to the transaction. As he later wrote in his tax return, he possessed a share in the house which Niccolò was occupying, but in order to obtain his due he would probably have to take his brother to court. Niccolò had apparently even refused to abide by arbitration, and this was by no means the first time that Tommaso had been driven to seek outside assistance to obtain a reckoning with Niccolò.[16] Most probably, this incident provides an example of one source of that personal animosity which, according to Marco Parenti, had by 1465 made Niccolò and Tommaso enemies in their private as well as in political affairs.[17]

It was during the early 1430s, after the brothers had already separated their households, that their commercial careers also began to go their separate ways. At this time, their co-operation in the silk industry was abruptly halted, as Niccolò apparently abandoned activity in the trade. The immediate reason for this decision was probably the political crisis of 1429 to 1434, which preoccupied his energies and at one point threatened to expel him from Florence. It could have left him little time to devote to business matters, for there is no record that he engaged in any commercial enterprises during these years. Tommaso, on the other hand, went on to form a new company with other partners, such as the Berardi, and although he too may briefly have abandoned the industry in the early 1430s, he nevertheless remained active as a silk merchant until the 1450s.[18]

Unlike Tommaso, Niccolò's break with silk manufacturing proved permanent. When he returned to the business world

disappears. Niccolò's name replaces it in part in e.g. his lease of the house on 24 Feb. 1463, ibid., P129.

[16] Cf. Tommaso's tax return of 1433: Cat., 347, fos. 620ʳ, 621ᵛ. There had by then been four cases of arbitration between the brothers.

[17] Parenti, 'Ricordi politici', 35.

[18] Tommaso mentioned the company involving the Berardi in his tax return of 1430: Cat., 345, fo. 686ᵛ. Although he listed no silk company in his return of 1433 (Cat., 347, fos. 620ʳ–622ʳ), he maintained close relations with the Berardi, and must have been in business with them long before he mentioned another silk partnership with them in 1451: Cat., 692, fo. 369ʳ. The extremely fragmentary information on the brothers' financial careers makes anything but very general conclusions impossible.

in the late 1430s, he did so not as a member of the silk guild of Por S. Maria but as a matriculant in a more traditional Soderini guild, the Calimala.[19] Although he subsequently joined with Tommaso in at least one partnership under the auspices of the silk guild,[20] he had by 1438 definitely selected the Calimala as his principal trade association. However, Niccolò does not seem to have become heavily involved even in the pursuits of Calimala merchants, which consisted in finishing imported woollen cloth and in general international trade. Although once, in 1444, he went as a merchant with the Florentine galleys to England, the only other business investment of which Niccolò left any trace after 1430 was a deposit of 100 florins with a tradesman making *oricello*, a chemical substance used in the dyeing of textiles.[21] Thus, Niccolò's transfer to the Calimala seems to represent less a change in commercial interests than a declining interest in business as a whole. In fact, although he may never have completely abandoned commerce, from the 1430s he seems to have become increasingly committed to the 'safer' form of investment, in property.

During these years, Niccolò was both acquiring property in the Oltrarno, and building up large landed estates. Besides adding to the farm he had inherited at Marliano, just down the Arno from Florence, his term as *Podestà* of Barbialla-Gambassi in 1433–4 led to his purchasing agricultural land in that area.[22] Gradually he acquired other property in the Tuscan countryside, but by the later 1430s his primary interest had concentrated on the pasturelands to the south

[19] Although both brothers had matriculated in the Calimala (Arti, Calimala, 13, fo. 1ᵛ), it was only in 1438 that Niccolò began to be drawn as its Consul rather than the Arte di Por S. Maria's: ibid., 8, fo. 86ᵛ. Florentines could be elected officials of only one of the guilds to which they belonged, which thereby became their principal association: *Statuta*, ii. 159.
[20] This was a company *d'oro filato*, i.e. which produced the gold thread used in embroidering cloth; see Cat., 795, fo. 8ᵛ.
[21] For his trip to England: Niccolò's will of 9 Oct. 1444, Diplomatico, Acquisto Soderini, 19 Oct. 1444. On the activities of the Calimala and ultimate repression of its original occupation, see Filippi, *Calimala*. For Niccolò's *accomanda* with the local tradesman 'per fare oricello': Mercanzia, 10831, fo. 24ʳ. On the use of *oricello*, cf. Battaglia, *Grande Dizionario della lingua italiana*, xii, Turin, 1984.
[22] Cf. Niccolò's tax report of 1442: Cat., 613, fos. 282ʳ–283ʳ. For his appointment as *Podestà* of Barbialla-Gambassi, see Tratte, 67, fo. 60ʳ.

and west of Florence. Niccolò's interest in these pastures may have dated from his long tenure as *Podestà* of Castiglione della Pescaia in about 1435, for although his first acquisitions are undated, by 1439 he had obtained a half-share in the pasture of Donoratico in the Tuscan Maremma, to which he soon added shares in the surrounding pastures of Castioncello and Uliveto, Bolgheri and Montemassimo.[23] From the early 1440s he was also renting pastures near Pisa, where he took advantage of the opportunity to lease relatively inexpensive property from one of the town's ecclesiastical institutions.[24] Moreover, he bought large amounts of land—much of this, however, cultivated—near the southern coastal town of Vada.[25] By 1444 he thus possessed large tracts of land in locations stretching from the Pisan hinterland to Grosseto, at the southern boundary of Florentine territory. His interests in these areas were such that he purchased houses in both Pisa and Vada, and maintained a permanent agent in the latter town.

Presumably in an effort to spread the financial burden, Niccolò associated relatives and friends in his rental schemes. His brother Tommaso, Niccolò Bartolini, and Filippo Manetti, for example, all took turns in leasing the pastures around Pisa, while Niccolò's brother-in-law, Carlo Macinghi, eventually acquired the section of the pasture of Donoratico which was not in Niccolò's control.[26] Most of these individuals were apparently interested in the land for the pasturing of the animals which they kept on their farms in the Tuscan countryside. This, for example, was the origin of Tommaso's involvement in the pastures near Pisa, which lasted for several decades.[27] However, Niccolò rented and

---

[23] Cf. Notarile Antecos., G693, fo. 254ᵛ, 9 Oct. 1439; Cat., 613, fos. 283ᵛ–284ʳ (1442); Niccolò's will, Diplomatico, Acquisto Soderini, 19 Oct. 1444.

[24] i.e. the Domus Misericordia of Pisa: Notarile Antecos., G693, fo. 17ʳ. On the manner in which Florentines tended to take over the property of ecclesiastical institutions in the Pisano, cf. Luzzati, 'Contratti agrari', 581–4.

[25] On Niccolò's rentals in the Pisano, purchases in the area of Vada, and his houses at Pisa and Empoli (the latter used to store fodder): Notarile Antecos., P128, fos. 81ʳ⁻ᵛ, 86ʳ, 103ᵛ, 104ʳ⁻ᵛ, 107ʳ–111ᵛ, 116ʳ⁻ᵛ; ibid., G693, fo. 6ʳ⁻ᵛ.

[26] On the lands near Pisa, ibid., fo. 103ᵛ. For Carlo Macinghi's purchase of half the pasture of Donoratico, Notarile Antecos., G693, fo. 133ʳ, 27 July 1444.

[27] Tommaso was still renting pastures in the Pisano in 1474, when the Signoria

purchased far more land than was necessary for this purpose. He must, from the start, have been employing his property consciously as a commercial investment which could return a profit in two ways. Quite frequently, contrary to what he told the tax officials, he rented his large pastures in the Tuscan Maremma to inhabitants of the Florentine district, presumably individuals interested in raising animals commercially.[28] In addition, Niccolò kept herds of cattle as well as some buffaloes and horses on part of his land.[29] Thus, opting increasingly for the life of a *rentier*, Niccolò was following the example of other Tuscan families who chose to invest in relatively lucrative stock-raising rather than confining themselves to the profits of ordinary agriculture.[30]

Niccolò's emphasis on the acquisition of landed property rather than participation in commerce or manufacturing marks him as a representative of the 'return to the land' which has been said to characterize the Florentine Renaissance. It is now generally argued that the fifteenth century did not witness a major return to the land, but that this was an alternative available to, and taken by, Florentines at every epoch of the city's history. Nevertheless, as the city's dominion expanded during the fourteenth and fifteenth centuries, investment in property became an increasingly available option. That it was the one on which Niccolò concentrated was undoubtedly the result of a complex of factors. His break with the silk industry in the 1430s may have left him with little capital for further commercial investments. Instead, his constant political activity probably offered him cheaper, easier opportunities for income and acquisitions. In the later 1430s he was actively trying to use his political contacts to obtain prestigious and lucrative positions as

decided to restrict the pasturing of animals in this area because of the damage it did to agriculture. Tommaso must have exerted his influence on this occasion, for he and his partners were granted an exemption from the rent which they owed: Sig., Miss., 2a Canc., 6, fo. 119^{r-v}. Cf. Mallett, 'Pisa and Florence', 429.

[28] Cf. the rentals in Notarile Antecos., P128, fos. 142^r (31 Oct. 1442), 79^r (13 Nov. 1445).

[29] Cf. Cat., 693, fo. 460^r. There is, however, no indication of the contractual arrangements by which Niccolò thus participated in stock-raising.

[30] Cf. Jones, 'Florentine Families', 202.

Podestà in towns outside Florentine territory.[31] Moreover, as already suggested, his postings in the Florentine dominion opened up attractive opportunities in the property market, as could the political vicissitudes of his own home town. For example, the pastureland in the Maremma which Niccolò's brother-in-law bought in 1444 had been owned by members of the Peruzzi family, but had been confiscated after their exile in 1434 in order to pay taxes owing to the government, while parts of Niccolò's pastures had apparently also been confiscated.[32]

The opportunity to acquire property through citizens' political difficulties also occurred because of the shift in power in Niccolò's own clan. Although not sentenced to any specific punishment in 1434, Francesco Soderini remained suspect to the Medici regime and, possibly as a result, his tax assessments continued to be extremely high after 1434. Eventually he was forced to turn for financial assistance to his nephews,[33] who, during the mid-1430s, paid out large amounts on Francesco's behalf. While the terms of these loans are not recorded, it is possible that they were made on the security of Francesco's property, for when they demanded a reckoning with their uncle in 1438, Niccolò and Tommaso were awarded property of Francesco's both in and outside Florence.[34] This the brothers held jointly for several years until, in 1443, a division was made which gave Niccolò a house with several adjacent shops near his residence. By helping to make him a major landowner in S. Spirito, this acquisition must have increased his local prestige as well as his tendency to try to live from the proceeds of his urban and rural property.[35]

While this picture accords with the old image of the grasping Florentine snapping up property at the expense of

---

[31] e.g. in 1438 Niccolò was appealing to Francesco Sforza and others for a *podesteria* at Todi or elsewhere: Niccolò Soderini to Agnolo degli Strozzi, 19, 27 May 1438, Carte Strozz., ser. 3, 130, fos. 239, 246.

[32] Cf. Notarile Antecos., G693, fo. 133ʳ (27 July 1444). Niccolò bought some of his pastureland from the *Monte* and Sales Officials: Diplomatico, Acquisto Soderini, 19 Oct. 1444.

[33] On Francesco's situation, cf. Kent and Kent, *Neighbours*, 64–5.

[34] Notarile Antecos., G695, 16 June 1438; Diplomatico, Acquisto Soderini, 6 June 1438.

[35] The division is recorded in Notarile Antecos., G693, fos. 47ʳ–48ᵛ.

the disadvantaged, the result for Niccolò was by no means financial ease. Apart from the fact that the return on property was lower than that on commercial investments, the rents he could obtain for his pastures fluctuated considerably. During the later 1440s and early 1450s, for example, he could have obtained almost nothing for his southern property, as it was occupied by Aragonese forces. Most probably, then, this concentration on landed property helped to keep Niccolò's income relatively low, despite the large size of his possessions. Consequently, it must have contributed to that disorder which the contemporary Marco Parenti felt characterized Niccolò's private affairs. In the early 1450s Niccolò, who was most probably living beyond his means, contracted large loans not only with relatives and friends but from bankers, who charged him considerable interest rates.[36] This undoubtedly underlay Niccolò's enthusiasm, noted again by Marco Parenti, to pursue every opportunity for gain, whether it involved property, *Monte* credits, or any other asset. Both Parenti and Alessandra Strozzi mentioned Niccolò's litigiousness in these matters, and Alessandra added that Nicolò's 'force', presumably his force of character and personal influence, brought him frequent victory in his suits.[37]

As Parenti pointed out, Niccolò's private financial problems had a direct influence on his public stand regarding such issues as taxation and the city's expenditure. We have seen that during the later 1450s Niccolò assumed a 'popular' approach regarding taxation, complaining that the existing incidence was unjust, and championing the cause of the less wealthy citizens whom he held were paying an unfair share.

[36] Cf. Niccolò's tax return of 1442: Cat., 613, fos. 283ᵛ, 286ʳ. In 1451, Niccolò claimed debts of over 2,400 florins, and stated that he had been forced to sell some of his property in order to meet his obligations: Cat., 693, fos. 459ʳ, 460ʳ. Tommaso confirmed that Niccolò owed him a large sum of money, and that he had obligated himself to many people on his brother's behalf: Cat., 795, fo. 8ᵛ (1458); Notarile Antecos., P128, fo. 272ᵛ (13 May 1457). On the confusion in Niccolò's financial affairs, cf. Parenti, 'Ricordi politici', 35–6.

[37] Alessandra Strozzi to her son Lorenzo, 27 Feb. 1452, *Lettere*, 126. On one occasion Niccolò even bought the legal claims of a fellow citizen, presumably believing that he was in a better position to win a favourable verdict: Notarile Antecos., M568, fos. 312ʳ–313ᵛ, 17 June 1443. It is notable that when Parenti described Niccolò's search for acquisitions, he made no mention of his seeking profits in manufacturing or commerce.

Niccolò probably saw himself as one of those who were contributing more than their financial situation would allow. Possibly because his assets were more visible, he was, for example, paying taxes twice as high as his brother during the 1450s.[38] Niccolò's enthusiasm, once he became Standard-bearer of Justice in 1465, to reduce taxes and expenditures, ostensibly directed towards improving the lot of the ordinary citizen, was thus probably related to his own economic situation. Moreover, the fact that by this stage he was himself little involved in commerce undoubtedly influenced his decision while Standardbearer to save government money by cancelling the commercial projects undertaken in 1458—i.e. to stimulate trade through the construction of the canal in the Arno and improvements in the ports of Pisa and Livorno.[39] In addition, Niccolò's other financial reforms, such as those regarding the *Monte*, may well, as Parenti suggested, have been motivated by self-interest.[40] Thus, Niccolò was undoubtedly using his public authority for his private interests no less than were the members of the preceding administration whom he so condemned.

Niccolò's assault on the interests of the merchants and manufacturers who predominated within the ruling group undoubtedly contributed to his loss of popularity in late November and December 1465. In fact, as soon as he left office his legislation regarding the canal and the ports was rescinded, even while the leading citizens, recognizing the unpopularity of the canal tax, decided not to reinstate it.[41] Thus, Niccolò generally failed in his efforts to reverse the economic priorities of the ruling group, just as he failed in

[38] In 1451 Tommaso's assessment was about 25 florins, while Niccolò paid twice that: Cat., 694, pt. 1, fo. 300ʳ; ibid., pt. 2, fo. 907ʳ. In 1458/9, Tommaso's *catasto* assessment was a little over 3, and Niccolò's over 6, florins: Cat., 834, fos. 145ʳ, 133ʳ. It is tempting to suspect that political discrimination may have caused this difference, but there is no documentary basis for such a supposition.

[39] Niccolò started criticizing the special tax levied for the canal project in his speech of 3 Nov. 1465, and he subsequently introduced legislation to terminate work on the canal and eventually to abolish the tax: Provv., 156, fos. 217ʳ–218ᵛ.

[40] For this legislation, cf. ibid., fos. 213ʳ–266ʳ.

[41] Criticism of Niccolò's legislation was expressed in the *Pratiche* of 3, 4 Jan. 1466 (Pampaloni, 'Nuovi tentativi', 526, 528–9, 531–2), and work on the canal was resumed in April, Balìe, 32, fos. 1ʳ–3ʳ, 6ʳ, 11ʳ–14ʳ, 16ʳ–18ᵛ. Cf. Baruchello, *Livorno*, 69–70.

his plan for constitutional reform. Moreover, his economic and political failure were further intertwined in that political defeat meant financial decline for himself and his family. Since he failed to observe the sentence of exile imposed on him in 1466, he was declared a rebel the following year, and, as such, all his property was forfeit to the state.[42] Although his wife managed to recover enough to repay her dowry of 1,400 florins, the rest was either used to reimburse Niccolò's many creditors or was entrusted to the care of the appropriate communal officials.[43] As for Niccolò, he was forced to appeal to the charity of foreign powers who wished to preserve him as a potential weapon against the Medici regime. He obtained, for example, a small pension from the Venetian government, and possibly something from the Emperor Frederick III, by whom he was knighted in 1468.[44] Meanwhile, his sons, who were forced to follow him into exile, managed to gain university educations which opened up positions in the Church. Nevertheless, the political penalties inflicted on them condemned them to relative poverty by comparison with the branch of the family which remained in Florence.

In the financial world as in the political world, then, Tommaso offers an example of success which directly contrasts with the misfortune of his brother. Nevertheless, Tommaso followed the same pattern as Niccolò in gradually abandoning direct activity in industry. While his motives for this are not clear, his decision was probably affected by his growing political involvement, and by setbacks suffered by his silk company during the 1450s. During these years, he continued his partnership with the Berardi, but left the running of the shop increasingly to them, as he apparently did in the case of other companies in which he invested. For example, he could only have supplied capital as his share in a

[42] Otto di Guardia, periodo repubblicano, 224, fo. 128ᵛ, 15 Jan. 1467.
[43] Information regarding Niccolò's confiscated property is in Capitani di Parte, numeri rossi, 74. Some of it was eventually acquired by Tommaso's sons, possibly in repayment of what Niccolò had still owed his brother at his exile.
[44] For the pension from Venice: Diplomatico, Acquisto Soderini, 16 Oct. 1474. On his knighthood, cf. e.g. Baldovinetti, Sepoltuario, Florence, Bibl. Moreniana, MS 339.

pharmacy owned by his distant relatives and sometime political colleagues, the Palmieri.[45] By the later 1450s Tommaso also held deposits in the Baroncelli-Rucellai bank, a major firm with an important branch in Rome. Although the terms on which Tommaso was investing are unrecorded, he must have been either supplying funds at a guaranteed rate of interest or leaving it to his bankers to use the money as they saw fit.[46]

Tommaso's continuing, if less direct, interest in commerce also had political ramifications, as it was during the later 1450s that he was giving serious attention to the promotion of Florentine trade, particularly as one of the Five Governors of Pisa. Indeed, his desire to improve the conditions for Florentine commerce took on a directly personal note, for by the early 1450s his profits from the silk company were falling off considerably, primarily because the long war over the Milanese succession seriously disrupted Florence's trade. Tommaso's silk firm must have suffered particularly from the war, for it was probably exporting to areas under the control of Florence's principal enemy, the King of Naples and Aragon, and now found this trade obstructed. By 1451 the company was doing so badly that both Tommaso and the Berardi were forced to borrow large sums to keep it afloat, and the firm finally went bankrupt sometime before 1458.[47]

According to a near contemporary, Tommaso's bankruptcy left him so vulnerable to his creditors that he dared

[45] Cat., 692, fo. 369ᵛ (1451) and 795, fo. 8ᵛ (1458). Early in the century, Francesco d'Antonio Palmieri had married Tommaso's aunt, Dada Cambi: Diplomatico, Acquisto Soderini, 27 July 1414. On Tommaso's investment in the Palmieri pharmacy, cf. Molho, 'The Florentine "Tassa"', 110.

[46] In 1458, Tommaso reported that he was owed nearly 700 florins by Francesco Baroncelli, Guglielmo Rucellai, and company, although he gave no particulars regarding the origin of this debt: Cat., 795, fo. 8ʳ. Tommaso also had a personal connection with the Baroncelli, in that in 1451 his daughter Margherita married Francesco Baroncelli: Monte Comune, 3734, fo. 104ʳ, and Carte Ancisa, EE, 352, fo. 156ᵛ.

[47] Cf. Tommaso's tax returns of 1451 and 1458, Cat., 692, fo. 369ʳ and 795, fo. 8ᵛ. In the former declaration Tommaso referred to the problems created for the company by 'le nave rubate nella pacie del Re d'Araghona e debitori cattivi di là', adding that 'siamo in grandi impacci di qua per queste nostre faciende di Lisbona . . .'.

not leave his house for fear of being arrested for debt. That he nevertheless emerged from this crisis with both his reputation and his finances intact was attributed by the same author to assistance from the Medici,[48] and, although no other evidence on the incident exists, it is likely that Cosimo was prepared to aid Tommaso as he did other merchants who found themselves in similar difficulties.[49] However, if the Medici did bail Tommaso out of this crisis, they apparently made no immediate effort to tie him further to their interests by making him a partner in their banking network. Instead, Tommaso's response was to follow a path similar to his brother's some two decades earlier. Like Niccolò, Tommaso abandoned the silk industry, and chose the Calimala as his principal trade association.[50] However, again like Niccolò, his commitment to the Calimala remained primarily formal. For Tommaso as well, this change in guild allegiance was tantamount to retirement from active commercial life. Presumably, once active involvement in the guild had terminated, the Calimala offered prestige and political advantages which could be useful to Florentines of Niccolò's and Tommaso's stature.[51]

Although in his case too set-backs led to his abandoning the silk trade, Tommaso did not totally desert commerce for investment in assets such as property or *Monte* shares. Instead, he remained involved in commerce, concentrating on the kind of investment which he had begun with the Baroncelli–Rucellai bank. Apart from this company, in which Tommaso remained a partner until its final dissolution

[48] Il minutario di Goro Gheri, i, fos. 231ᵛ–232ʳ: '... *Messer Thommaso Soderini fu già tempo che non passava el Ponte Vecchio per paura de' buri, che, a dirla come è, era fallito, et dalla casa de' Medici fu facto et nello stato et nelle facultà el primo homo di questa città.*' I am grateful to Kate Lowe for bringing this document to my attention.

[49] Cf. e.g. Parenti, 'Ricordi politici', 16–17.

[50] Tommaso's name began to be drawn for the post of Consul of the Calimala from 1461 (Calimala, 8), while Niccolò apparently did not fill the post between 1457 and 1466: ibid. and Carte Strozz., ser. 2, 66. Thus, Tommaso seems to have replaced him within the guild hierarchy as he did within communal politics, thereby undoubtedly fuelling Niccolò's resentment of him.

[51] The Calimala provided access to at least one office, the Lords of the Mint, who were drawn from only the Calimala and the Cambio guilds. On the greater prestige attributed to the Calimala, cf. Filippi, *Calimala*, 184–5.

in the 1480s,[52] he invested in other banks, such as the firm of Luigi and Giovanni Quaratesi, of which he was a partner from at least 1462 to 1470, when it, like so many banking firms of the later fifteenth century, declared bankruptcy.[53] Tommaso's prior experience probably stood him in good stead on this occasion, for, in an effort to salvage his investment, he took control of the assets of the whole firm and undertook to sell them in order to reimburse the bank's creditors. However, according to Tommaso, the Pazzi War of 1478–80 created a decline in the property market, and the Quaratesi property consequently remained in his hands.[54] How he satisfied the creditors is far from clear, but it is possible that his action prevented his incurring much of a loss in the liquidation.

Apart from these investments, by the mid-1470s Tommaso also possessed deposits with an Inghirami company operating in Venice and with the Medici branch in the same city. Presumably, his frequent visits to his admired Venice had convinced Tommaso of the buoyancy of the city's trade, and of the opportunities of making money there. Moreover, he possessed a good friend in the manager of the Medici bank, Giovanni Lanfredini, who could be relied on to take special care with Tommaso's account. In fact, when the Inghirami company went into liquidation in 1477, Tommaso turned over his deposits in it to the Medici firm for use both in exchange dealings (i.e. loans) and in trade. Apart from Tommaso's transfer of 920 gold ducats to Florence, he left a total of some 6,000 ducats in Lanfredini's hands. These the banker seems to have invested skilfully,[55] as during the

[52] In Oct. 1467, Tommaso appointed procurators to participate on his behalf in a periodic settlement of the Baroncelli partnership: Notarile Antecos., M570, fo. 649[r]. By 1483, he was trying to collect the money owed to him as a member of the then defunct company of Matteo Baroncelli, Guglielmo Rucellai, and company, ibid., M565, fos. 168[r-v], 255[r]–256[r].

[53] Arti, Cambio, 15, fos. 7[v], 10[r], 12[v], 15[r], 20[v], 23[v], 26[v], 29[v]. On the decline in Florentine banking during this period, cf. de Roover, *Rise and Decline*, 16.

[54] Cf. Tommaso's tax return of 1480, Cat., 1001, pt. 2, fo. 357[v]. When Tommaso passed on this property to his heirs, it was evaluated much more highly than in his tax declaration: cf. a division of property by his sons in 1486, Capitani di Parte, numeri rossi, 75, fos. 54[r]–57[v].

[55] Cf. Giovanni Lanfredini to Tommaso, 23 Jan. 1478 and 28 Feb. 1478, BNF, ii, v, 16, fos. 18[v], 23[r].

following year Tommaso earned the considerable interest rate of 11 per cent on his deposit.[56]

Although Tommaso's commitment to Venice thus proved profitable, political events intervened to separate his finances, like his city, from the alliance of 1474. During the Pazzi War the Medici bank in Venice was liquidated, and Tommaso's lucrative investment must have been transferred elsewhere.[57] Although the history of Tommaso's finances in his later years becomes increasingly obscure, it is possible that some of his Venetian deposit resurfaced in the sums which he invested in Naples and Bruges and was attempting to recover in the mid-1480s. In Naples Tommaso and his son Piero had lent some 300 florins to the King and his son, the Duke of Calabria, although through whom and for what purpose remains unclear. Ultimately, Tommaso did recover the loan, primarily because his political influence allowed him and his son to bring pressure on both the King of Naples and the Florentine ambassador, Tommaso's old friend, Giovanni Lanfredini.[58] Tommaso also persuaded Lorenzo de' Medici to take his side, and it was eventually Lorenzo's intervention with the Duke of Calabria which ensured that Tommaso and his son were paid some interest as well as the original capital—an arrangement which aroused considerable resentment among other Florentine creditors of the Neapolitan court who did not receive such a favourable settlement.[59]

Obscurity also surrounds the Soderini deposit in Bruges. References to it exist in 1487, when Tommaso's sons were

[56] On 5 July 1479, Lorenzo de' Medici and company informed Tommaso that he had earned 700 florins on the deposit of 6,000 florins which Lanfredini had reported on 23 Jan. 1478: ibid., fo. 90ᵛ. There is no indication of how long Tommaso had been investing with Lanfredini nor of the origin of this relatively large sum. He may, ironically, have been investing the money received from the Duke of Milan in Venice. On Tommaso's pension from Milan, see Chap. 7.

[57] On the fate of the Medici bank in Venice, see de Roover, *Rise and Decline*, 240–53.

[58] Cf. Tommaso to Giovanni, 11 June, 19 Oct. 1484, BNF, ii, v, 12, fos. 86ʳ, 220ʳ, and Piero Soderini to Giovanni, 16 June, 17, 31 July, 10 Aug., 2, 14 Oct., 8 Nov., 24 Dec. 1484, and 29 Jan. 1485, ibid., fos. 94ʳ, 137ʳ, 149ʳ, 164, 212, 216, 248, 285, 305.

[59] Lorenzo de' Medici to Niccolò Michelozzi, 1 Aug. 1484, BNF, Ginori Conti, 29, 125 *bis*, and Piero Soderini to Giovanni, 16 June, 31 July, 2 Oct. 1484, BNF, ii, v, 12.

attempting to recover 4,200 florins formerly placed with the firm of Tommaso Portinari.[60] This money may have been invested before 1480, while Portinari was directing the Medici bank in Bruges, or after he had been forced by the Medici to assume sole responsibility for the company, distinguished as it was by risky ventures and bad debts. Certainly, the fact that Tommaso's granddaughter had married Portinari in 1469[61] gave Tommaso a personal reason for sending his money north. However, the investment proved a poor choice, for Portinari lost the money and tried to avoid repayment by insisting that it had been given to him not *a discrezione* but as capital invested at the risk of the depositor. It is therefore possible that Portinari won the case and Tommaso's heirs received back little of their family's investment.

Such investments indicate that Tommaso was spreading his risks among many firms and, like other Florentine investors, diversifying his commercial holdings. Like the Medici, he was, for example, eager to take advantage of the opportunities offered by mining ventures, which required only a minimal capital outlay and left the operations of the firm to those with technical skill. This was the kind of arrangement set up in the early 1470s when Tommaso joined a company mining for copper in the hinterland of Volterra. Although Tommaso purchased a quarter of the company's shares, he insisted that it possessed no permanent capital and returned no regular profit. Although profits may have been irregular, the company must have been lucrative, for Tommaso's share in it was estimated at some 800 florins in 1480.[62] Later, this company tried to expand its operations by leasing additional mines near S. Maria Impruneta,[63] while Tommaso became

[60] On this deposit, see Gilliodts van Severen, *Cartulaire*, ii. 260; de Roover, *Rise and Decline*, 105. On Portinari's management of the Medici bank in Bruges and his forced settlement with the Medici, ibid., 346–57.

[61] Monte Comune, 3737, fo. 59ᵛ; Ammirato, *Della famiglia de' Baroncelli*, 232. The girl in question was the daughter of Francesco Baroncelli and, although the mother's name was not given in this statement of the transfer of part of the dowry, she was presumably the daughter of Francesco's wife, Margherita Soderini.

[62] Cat., 1001, pt. 2, fo. 357ᵛ. On Lorenzo de' Medici's mining interests at this time, cf. Uzielli, *Toscanelli*, 481–2; Fiumi, *L'impresa*, 63–4.

[63] Notarile Antecos., P130, fo. 90ᵛ, 17 Apr. 1471.

involved in smelting operations by acquiring the rights to woods providing the necessary charcoal.[64]

It is notable that in his search for lucrative investments Tommaso rarely opted for credits in the public-funded debt. Although, according to Marco Parenti, Niccolò eagerly sought out *Monte* credits as well as other assets, after the apparent fiasco of their speculation of the late 1420s, Tommaso seems for a while to have lost interest in government shares. For particular objectives where a secure investment was necessary, such as dowries for his daughters, Tommaso was prepared to accumulate holdings in the *Monte Comune* as well as in the *Monte delle doti*, which had been established precisely in order to provide dowries for Florentine girls. Moreover, the payment of his taxes, which were quite high by the later years of his life, automatically brought him *Monte* credits, of which he could generally dispose only at a loss. Therefore Tommaso registered considerable holdings in various *Monti* in his later years, but they were never as large as his other investments.[65] Indeed, the return on credits in the state debt was at best uncertain, and rarely as great as could be obtained from commercial, or even at times from landed, wealth.[66]

Tommaso also differed from Niccolò in that investment in land remained for him of secondary interest. During his early years he seems to have purchased property only when it was necessary for particular purposes. When his and Niccolò's division of their household in about 1429 left him with only one small farm just down the Arno from Florence, Tommaso immediately purchased two more farms close by.[67] These he undoubtedly needed to support the family which he had just begun, and to supply it with a summer residence, as the Soderini family's villa had just gone to Niccolò. It was not

[64] Notarile Antecos., M563, 18 July 1471.

[65] In 1469–70 Tommaso possessed only some 300 florins in the *Monte Comune*, although his eldest son Paolantonio held some 1,900 florins: Monte Comune, 195, fos. 132ʳ, 133ᵛ, 15ᵛ. In 1479–80 Tommaso had 1,200 florins in the same *Monte* (ibid., 205, fo. 134ʳ), and by the time of his death 2,565 florins (ibid., 206, fo. 134ʳ).

[66] Cf. Goldthwaite, *Private Wealth*, 244–5.

[67] Cat., 345, fo. 686ʳ. In the marginal annotations to Tommaso's return of 1458, the value of the farms was reckoned as nearly 800 florins in 1427: Cat., 795, fo. 6ᵛ.

until after the death of his first wife, Maria Torrigiani, that Tommaso made any sizeable additions to his rural holdings. Then he, like Niccolò, took advantage of the opportunities offered by the partisan conflicts in Florence to acquire a huge amount of property a short distance down the Arno from his other farms.[68] All this property had previously belonged to Messer Palla Strozzi, but had been confiscated in order to pay his creditors, including the Florentine tax officials. According to Palla, he had been deliberately saddled with excessive taxes, and his property sequestered and sold for unduly low rates.[69] The information regarding Tommaso's purchases suggests that this was correct, for although he originally paid about 1,760 florins for the property, and later asserted that flooding by the Arno had decreased its value, when he eventually sold it, it was evaluated at 2,300 florins.[70] Tommaso's objective in acquiring the land was probably to repay to Maria Torrigiani's sons the dowry which was due them as her heirs, and to provide security for the dowries of his daughters. At least, he bought the property in his children's names, although his own financial difficulties in the 1450s meant that they never received it.[71]

The relatively low priority which Tommaso attached to property in his early years was evident in his approach to his own accommodation. He and his family remained in rented accommodation until the 1450s, much later than Niccolò and long after Tommaso had achieved political prominence

[68] In 1441 Tommaso bought land worth 575 florins near Empoli, to which he added another farm worth 85 florins in 1442, and another worth 1,100 florins in 1444: Notarile Antecos., M568, fos. 224^r–225^v; M569, fos. 196^r–197^r; M572, fo. 157^r; Cat., 816, pt. 2a, fo. 558^{r-v}; Cat., 655, fos. 840^r–841^v.

[69] Cf. Kent and Kent, *Neighbours*, 145; Palla's wills of 24 Aug. 1447 and 6 May 1462, ASFe, Archivio Bentivoglio d'Aragona, serie partimoniale, buste 4/2 and 6/34. Tommaso acquired the land from Palla's son-in-law, Giovanni Rucellai, from Piero Minerbetti, the *Monte* Officials, and the Sales Officials. The documents cited in n. 68 declare its ultimate provenance from Palla.

[70] After selling one section of the land for 200 florins and retaining another worth 400 (Cat., 655, fo. 840^v; 795, fos. 7^r–8^r), Tommaso sold the rest to the Hospital of S. Gallo for 1,700 florins—a price determined by Piero de' Medici and Antonio Martelli: Notarile Antecos., M569, fos. 201^r–203^r, 6 Sept. 1457. For Tommaso's declaration of the decline in the land's value see ibid., M568, fo. 197^{r-v}, 29 Sept. 1447.

[71] See Chap. 5.

as an intimate of the Medici. Although he probably envisaged acquiring a residence in the traditional Soderini district from the 1430s, his steps in this direction were very slow. When he and Niccolò acquired property from Francesco Soderini in 1438, included in it were several houses close to Francesco's own home in Via S. Spirito. It was not until 1443, however, that the division of this property assigned these houses to Tommaso, along with another residence in the present-day Via de' Serragli and a farm just outside Florence. In the following years Tommaso spent considerable time and money refurbishing the three small contiguous houses in the Via S. Spirito, enlarging them to create a residence worthy of a prominent Florentine patrician.[72]

However, even while he was working on the remodelling, greater things were being prepared for him. In 1438 Francesco Soderini was arrested on a charge of sending information to an enemy of the city, and, after several years' confinement in the notorious prison, the Stinche, he was finally exiled to Venetian territory in 1444.[73] Once again, Tommaso, and this time apparently he alone, stepped forward to assist Francesco with his taxes, eventually winning as his reward Francesco's own residence in S. Spirito. By 1451 Tommaso had obtained the right to occupy this house, and when it was subsequently confiscated for non-payment of taxes, Tommaso's wife, Dianora Tornabuoni, used her own money to purchase it for her sons.[74] Although he had now gained his ancestral home, Tommaso lacked either the money or the will to replace it with a new Renaissance palace after the model of the Medici. Instead, he invested a relatively large sum of money in renovation. Besides building a loggia, he purchased and demolished some adjacent houses in the Via Maffia in order to create a garden, and to make the house more comfortable and grander than his uncle's had

[72] Cf. Tommaso's tax reports of 1447, 1451, and 1458: Cat., 655, fo. 839ʳ; 692, fo. 369ʳ; 795, fo. 6ʳ.
[73] Otto di Guardia, periodo repubblicano, 224, fos. 72ᵛ–73ʳ; Boninsegni, *Storie*, 68; Cavalcanti, *Istorie*, i. 352–3; Guicciardini, *Le cose fiorentine*, 233, 266.
[74] Cf. Francesco's and Tommaso's tax returns of 1451, Cat., 693, fo. 476, and 692, fo. 670ʳ, and Tommaso's will of 10 Mar. 1462, Notarile Antecos. M570, fo. 89ʳ⁻ᵛ.

been.[75] Thus, with Tommaso's acquisition of Francesco's residence in addition to the brothers' assumption of his other property, a radical transformation had been brought about in the district of Drago, S. Spirito. Visibly, the legitimate branch of Messer Tommaso's family, allied with the defeated Albizzi faction, had lost out to the illegitimate but rising branch affiliated with the Medici. While Francesco and his family sank from wealth and prominence to obscurity, exile, and poverty, the brilliant inheritance of the clan was being assumed by Niccolò and Tommaso, who were becoming major landowners as well as the leading political force in the area. In fact, the designation of the square leading to the Ponte alla Carraia as the Piazza Soderini seems to date from this period, as Niccolò and Tommaso's accumulation of property around it allowed them to dominate the square.[76]

Although acquiring property was not Tommaso's first concern, he nevertheless regarded it as a secure investment to which to add as opportunity offered. He also sought to increase the value of his property by improvements, such as planting vines and olives. Both acquisitions and improvements enabled him to raise the value of his land in the Marliano area to some 2,400 florins by 1466.[77] By 1475 he had also created a scattered estate, worth approximately 2,000 florins, around Empoli.[78] The only new area in which

[75] In a statement of 1466, Tommaso asserted that he had made these alterations at a cost of some 800 florins: Notarile Antecos., P130, fo. 54ʳ, 3 Sept. 1466.

[76] In 1443 the property which Niccolò acquired from his uncle was described as in the Piazza de' Nerli. A year earlier Niccolò had bought a house from Francesco Nerli and in 1449 Niccolò's son Geri purchased two houses next to his father's by the Ponte alla Carraia: Notarile Antecos., P128, fos. 347ᵛ, 442ʳ⁻ᵛ. By 1455, the local notary recording these transactions was describing Niccolò's property as '*sulla piazza de' Soderini*': e.g. ibid., fos. 155ᵛ, 176ʳ. In later maps of the city, the square on the Oltrarno side of this bridge is in fact called the 'Piazza Soderini': e.g. *Stradario storico*, 129.

[77] For Tommaso's acquisitions of small plots of land, see the *protocolli* of Ser Piero Migliorelli and Ser Paolo di Lorenzo di Paolo, Notarile Antecos., M568–M570 and P128–P130. On his efforts to improve productivity: Cat., 655, fo. 839ᵛ (cf. Jones, 'Florentine Families', 200–2 on the general tendency of Florentine landowners to do this). Tommaso's estimate of 1466 is in Notarile Antecos., P130 (1466–73), fo. 45ʳ⁻ᵛ. However, by 1475 sales had reduced the value to *c.* 2,000 florins: ibid., B726, fos. 198ʳ, 199ʳ.

[78] Ibid. Tommaso even purchased houses in Empoli to store his harvests and to house a factor who looked after his land in the area: Tommaso's tax return of 1458 Cat., 795, fo. 7ᵛ and his will of 10 Mar. 1462, Notarile Antecos., M570, fo. 87ʳ.

he made major acquisitions was in the Arno Valley near Pisa—an area open to Florentine penetration after the city's acquisition of Pisa in 1406, and one whose marshy nature made land relatively inexpensive and in need of the infusion of Florentine capital for maintenance and improvements. Although Tommaso first became involved in the Pisano through his brother's rental schemes, it was through just this sort of land improvement that he began to own property there. According to Tommaso, he helped some friends in Pontedera better the land which they had bought from the Cathedral Works of Pisa, and, in repayment, they turned over half the land to him.[79] As it happened, they also had need of Tommaso's political influence, for the original owners demanded a higher price to match the land's increased value, and Tommaso had to intervene with Piero de' Medici to ask that the original agreement be observed.[80] Tommaso's mutually beneficial connection with these friends continued, with his purchasing more property from them and joining them in additional leases.[81]

Medici influence was obviously important in Tommaso's acquisition of land in the Pisano. Along with many other Florentine families, the Medici were increasingly interested in the area, and they obviously carried much weight in determining who obtained available property there.[82] A veritable scramble for possessions in the Pisano seems to have been taking place in the early 1460s, when Tommaso had to appeal directly to Piero to stop interference in his property by two Florentines who claimed to be acting on Piero's behalf.[83] On yet a further occasion in the early 1460s,

[79] This type of payment was apparently a custom, if a rare one, in the Pisano: Luzzati, 'Contratti agrari', 573.

[80] Tommaso to Piero, undated, MAP, cxxxvii, 878, apparently written just before another letter dated 29 Feb. 1464, MAP, xvii, 382.

[81] Notarile Antecos., M570, fo. 550ʳ, 22 July 1466. These inhabitants of Pontedera were leasing pastures with Tommaso and his son-in-law in 1474.

[82] On the interest of the Medici and other Florentine families in the Pisano, see Mallett, 'Pisa and Florence', 409, 432–41; Rochon, *La Jeunesse*, 263. Rochon and Picotti (*La giovinezza*, 237) agree that property in the Pisano could often be had for relatively low prices.

[83] Tommaso to Ormanno Foraboschi and Domenico Nucci, 10 June 1463, MAP, lxvii, 58. Apparently, a letter to Foraboschi from Giovanni de' Medici put an

Tommaso asked Piero that 'of certain lands in the Val di Serchio I be satisfied on a par with anyone else, whether Florentine or Pisan'. As Tommaso then pointed out, 'since I became your relative, I don't think you ever heard that I took advantage of anything pertaining to the government, or before, except for the usual; and, although I had many opportunities, if I had wanted to attend to them, for possessions and things in that district [the Pisano], I never paid any attention to them'. Now, however, his attitude had clearly changed, not least because he felt the need to establish a patrimony for his sons. He also felt that his loyalty to Piero gave him a right to Medici support, for he justified his request on the grounds that 'as regards faith towards your house, I don't think anyone precedes me'.[84]

Although this appeal to Piero went unsatisfied, Tommaso still possessed independent opportunities to acquire Pisan property. When, for example, he served as Captain of Pisa in 1465, he was able to lease a large stretch of land from a Pisan hospital in perpetuity for the negligible rent of under 5 florins a year.[85] By this and other means he must gradually have acquired considerable property in the area, to which his sons later added. When, for example, Tommaso's son Francesco was a student at the University of Pisa, he bought more land in the same area, while some of Tommaso's other sons later did the same.[86] Although no complete record exists of the family's possessions in the Pisano, they must eventually have reached the proportions of Tommaso's other estates.[87] Certainly, they constituted the major part of the inheritance he left to one of his sons.[88]

---

end to this interference: Ormanno Foraboschi to Giovanni de' Medici, 22 June 1463, MAP, x, 516.

[84] Cf. Tommaso's undated letter to Piero, MAP, cxxxvii, 878.

[85] Diplomatico, Acquisto Soderini, 14 June 1465.

[86] Cf. Verde, *Lo studio fiorentino*, iii. 316–18. On the Soderini family's holdings in the Pisano, cf. Mallett, 'Pisa and Florence', 437.

[87] At least some of Tommaso's holdings in the Pisano in 1481 are recorded in ASPisa, Fiumi e Fossi, 1579, fos. 184, 421, 424^v, 429, 574, 580^v, 624, 771, 851, 861; and those of his sons in 1496, ibid., Comune, 123, fos. 22, 33^v, 62, 67. On the incompleteness of these records, however, cf. Mallett, 'Pisa and Florence', 433–4.

[88] Tommaso's possessions in the Pisano formed the nucleus of the portion of his estate which he assigned first to Francesco in 1475 and, after Francesco had left

As Tommaso became older, his financial affairs came increasingly under the management of his sons, who were old enough by the 1470s to start their own enterprises. In the case of the churchmen and lawyers in Tommaso's family, these consisted primarily of purchasing property, but for the others commercial ventures continued to be important. Paolantonio and Piero, for example, maintained the tradition of diversity of investment by becoming involved in mining, in their father's earlier occupation of silk manufacturing, and also in banking and the wool trade.[89] Although Tommaso might gradually disengage himself from commerce, he clearly expected that during their youth, at least, his sons should be involved in those traditional occupations on which Florence's wealth had been based.

Already in 1472 Benedetto Dei had listed Tommaso as one of Florence's wealthier citizens,[90] and Tommaso and his sons added considerably to their assets after 1472. By 1475, a decade before his death, Tommaso himself estimated the total value of his property as 8,000 florins.[91] If his commercial investments, conservatively estimated at 7,000 florins, are added, Tommaso's personal value must have been well over 15,000 florins. Although these holdings by no means put him in the same league as the Medici or the Strozzi, they represented a success of no small magnitude for someone who had started out with taxable assets of less than 1,000 florins in 1427. Nevertheless, Tommaso did not feel that his financial progress was adequate. Late in life he was still concerned about his large expenditures and high taxes,[92] and his need for additional funds lay behind his growing tendency

Pisa to become Bishop of Volterra, to his and Dianora's fourth son Giovanvettorio.

[89] By 1471 Paolantonio was a partner in a bank: Notarile Antecos., M563, 5 Feb. 1474. By 1485 he and Piero had formed a company which, among other things, was selling copper to the *Dieci di Balìa*: Dieci, Condotte e Stanziamenti, 29, fo. 11ᵛ. On their trading in wool and silk cloth: Richards, *Florentine Merchants*, 141–3, 152–4, 168, 183; Cooper, 'L'elezione', 168.

[90] *Cronica*, fo. 34ʳ.

[91] Cf. his division of property of that date, Notarile Antecos., B726, fos. 197ᵛ–199ʳ.

[92] Tommaso to Giovanni Lanfredini, 11 June 1484, BNF, ii, v, 12, fo. 86.

to accept bribes and misappropriate government money. As Agnolo degli Strozzi pointed out in 1471, Tommaso's well-known greed was occasioned by the huge expenses caused by his 'large family of children'.[93] Agnolo was aware that Tommaso repeatedly had to finance not only the weddings of his daughters, all of whom received large dowries, but also his sons' education and their participation in ostentatious social events such as the elaborate joust organized by Lorenzo de' Medici in 1469 or the trip to Rome to collect Lorenzo's bride.[94] Family obligations and pride also required expenditures on chapels or works of art, lavish houses and furnishings, and elaborate clothes. The fact that during the fifteenth century the level of expenditure in these areas was rising meant that ever greater sums had to be spent on conspicuous consumption, for a patrician's sense of his own and his family's honour would not permit him to live in a style unbefitting his rank.[95] Thus, despite his relative economic success, life remained for Tommaso a permanent struggle to find the means to support his family in a patrician style.

While Tommaso's history helps to explain the financial pressures which led to his corruption, it also demonstrates Florentines' enduring dedication to commerce and the continuing possibilities of making money in it even in the second half of the fifteenth century. On the other hand, Tommaso's career, as well as that of Niccolò, suggests that economic opportunities within the city were in decline. That both Tommaso and Niccolò should have deserted the most promising of Florentine industries indicates not only the pressures of public life but the difficulties which had to be overcome, and the energy necessary to take advantage of the possibilities

[93] Sacramoro to the Duke of Milan, 9 Jan. 1471, ASMi, SPE, Firenze, 281.

[94] On Paolantonio's trip to Rome to bring back Clarice Orsini, cf. the letters of a 'B' and Giovanni de' Nobili in Rome to Filippo Strozzi, 6, 11, 16 May 1469, Carte Strozz., ser. 1, 325, fos. 92, 94, 95; Filippo to the Duke, 27 Apr. 1469, ASMi, SPE, Firenze, 276; Rochon, *La Jeunesse*, 99. On Paolantonio's participation in the joust of 1469, and Tommaso's function as a judge, cf. Pulci, *La giostra*.

[95] On the importance of honour to a Florentine patrician, cf. Kirschner, 'Pursuing Honor', and Sacramoro's letter to the Duke, 9 Jan. 1471, ASMi, SPE, Firenze, 281, which mentions Tommaso's *grande reputatione* as another of his explanations for his constant need for money.

of profit offered even by this promising trade. From one perspective, it was natural for Tommaso to move from less lucrative manufacturing to what had always been the more profitable sectors of banking and general international trade. However, that he tended increasingly to look outside his own city for business opportunities, whether in Naples, Venice, or even further afield in northern Europe, implies a less thriving economy at home. Moreover, the fact that Tommaso's money was being removed from the area where it could most benefit his fellow Florentines suggests that his economic choices were helping to undermine the very economy in which he lived. In these tendencies, Tommaso may also have been typical of his time, as there seems to have been a growing trend for Florentines to seek their fortunes in more promising fields abroad.[96]

Finally, it must be pointed out how important political factors were in Tommaso's financial success. The political influence which he gained brought him direct profit through the pensions he acquired from Milan and possibly Naples, along with the opportunity to use government funds surreptitiously. Positions such as *Monte* Official drew him into the state lending apparatus, which could be profitable for those with large sums to invest. Political influence could be exerted for his financial interests, whether to regain his money from Naples in 1484 or, if Rinuccini is correct, to alter the tax system in 1480. Most importantly, Tommaso's connection with the Medici, which arose from primarily political motives, proved extremely important to Tommaso financially, whether in acquiring and protecting property or in avoiding the consequences of bankruptcy. Indeed, his political status affected his opportunities in every field, even in finding wives with relatively large dowries for himself and

---

[96] Cf. Marks, 'The Development of the Institutions of Public Finance in Florence During the Last Sixty Years of the Republic, *c.*1470–1530', unpublished Ph.D. thesis in the University of Oxford, 1954, pp. 10–15: Marks feels that as trade conditions turned against the Florentines they sometimes sought more profitable fields for investment in commercial enterprises outside the city. However, he also believes that they turned to the land as an alternative form of investment, while his predominantly pessimistic picture of the Florentine economy in this period is disputed by such historians as Goldthwaite, *Renaissance Florence*, 29–66.

his sons. Niccolò also used his influence for his private interests, whether in lawsuits or in his legislation of 1465, but his exclusion from the successful power circle in Florence may have meant that he was unable to protect his finances from taxation. While the brothers' personal decisions, particularly whether to concentrate their investments in land or commerce, were obviously of major importance in creating the differences in their financial positions, politics nevertheless had a role to play in bringing about their economic success or failure in Medicean Florence. Indeed, their careers suggest not only that politics could make a great difference to citizens' chances of economic success, but that, as contemporaries asserted, the search by Florentines for political prominence was motivated in part by the knowledge of the opportunities it provided for economic gain.[97]

[97] For a statement to this effect from a person hostile to the Medici group: Francesco Naselli to Borso d'Este, 17 Dec. 1467, ASMo, Carteggio degli ambasc., Firenze, 1. Cf. also, however, statements by Sacramoro, e.g. that Medici friends wanted a scrutiny in order to reduce the number of people seeking public office and the '*utili che cavano dal loro stato*': Sacramoro to the Duke, 1 Dec, 1468, ASMi, SPE, Firenze, 275.

5. Parenti, Amici, Vicini

One of the more salient and perhaps surprising facts which emerge from the preceding pages is that Niccolò and Tommaso Soderini took such different political paths despite being brothers. However, as has often been recognized, the close bonds which existed among family members could create grounds for conflict as well as co-operation, and several generations of the Soderini family are examples of this. In the case of Niccolò and Tommaso, fraternal rivalry must have played a role in the development of their political enmity, as jealousy developed over political success and the acquisition of positions and power. Financial obligations also created strains, and these were compounded by differences over political principle and alignment, leading eventually to a permanent rift.

Yet their lives were not characterized solely by conflict. Initially, the two enjoyed close relations, as they lived together and started their business careers in tandem. Even during their quarrels over money and politics they continued to co-operate in business matters and to come to each other's assistance. In 1431, for example, they and their mother collectively purchased a house in the S. Spirito district, and although this was a source of financial conflict, it by no means ended the brothers' co-operative efforts. They continued to share family responsibilities, such as the renovations in their family chapel, while the fact that they both eventually established themselves in close proximity in S. Spirito meant that they remained in frequent contact. When Niccolò was in financial difficulties Tommaso agreed to lend him money, even though (he asserted), he had little immediate hope of recovering it.[1] In the political sphere, Tommaso again did his best to assist Niccolò, using his post as *accoppiatore* to give his brother an advantage in the election bags, and, apparently, saving him from political disaster in 1458. As we have seen, the bonds between them were still sufficiently strong in 1465 for Tommaso's special relationship with his brother to be recognized by both the Milanese ambassador and by the leading figures of the anti-Medici group.

It was apparently this crisis of 1465–6 which brought about the final break between the brothers. There is no indication that Tommaso tried to save Niccolò from the banishment to which he was condemned in September 1466, and although Tommaso encountered several of the exiles during his subsequent missions as ambassador, apparently Niccolò was never among them. For his part, once he had been exiled, Niccolò directed much of the resentment for his fate against his brother, who had certainly done his best to undermine Niccolò's efforts towards reform, and who represented everything Niccolò had fought against. Before 1465, conflicts within Tommaso's own family had already brought Lorenzo, the only surviving son of Tommaso and Maria Torrigiani, on to the anti-Medici side, and after 1466 Niccolò tried to take revenge against his brother by entangling Lorenzo in further plots against the regime. This at least is what Tommaso thought, for after Niccolò had drawn Lorenzo into yet another anti-Medici conspiracy in 1468, Tommaso wrote to Piero de' Medici, with some bitterness, that Niccolò was doing this merely to spite him.[2]

Although the resentment between the brothers thus lived on, Tommaso was still fond enough of Niccolò to be deeply saddened by his death in 1474.[3] Moreover, Niccolò's death seems to have encouraged Tommaso's natural inclination to

---

[1] Cf. Tommaso's *catasto* of 1458, Cat., 795, fo. 8ᵛ. Tommaso and Niccolò also repeatedly served as procurators or arbiters for each other, while in 1463 Niccolò appointed Tommaso to help determine the dowry of one of his daughters: Notarile Antecos., M570, fo. 235ʳ.

[2] Tommaso to Piero de' Medici, 19 Mar. 1468, MAP, xvii, 539.

[3] Zaccaria Saggio to Lodovico Gonzaga, 7 Oct. 1474, ASMa, Carteggio degli inviati, Milano, 1624.

come to the assistance of his brother's family. Although he had apparently done little since his brother's exile to help his nephews and nieces, he now proceeded to further their careers, in part filling the role which Niccolò would have played if he had lived.[4] Nevertheless, he was not prepared to forget that Niccolò had owed him money, or to renounce his claims on his brother's estate.[5] Even after Niccolò's sons, who were forced to join their father in exile once they reached maturity, had gained permission to return to Florence in 1484, they had to seek arbitration with their cousins, possibly in order to recover some of their father's former property.[6]

Tommaso's history of conflict with Niccolò repeated itself within his own family, as his relations with his eldest son followed the same pattern of personal conflict with repercussions in the political sphere. According to Tommaso, Lorenzo was merely a disobedient and wayward son, who at the age of twenty had already behaved so badly towards his father and his stepmother, Dianora Tornabuoni, that Tommaso had removed him to a separate residence next door.[7] However, from Lorenzo's perspective, Tommaso's second marriage may have seemed a betrayal of himself and his siblings, as it drew his father's attention towards both a new family and more powerful connections. Moreover, although Tommaso purchased land with which to repay Lorenzo the dowry due to Maria's heirs,[8] he later reclaimed the land and sold it, without (Lorenzo wrote) ever reimbursing him.[9] Tommaso's

---

[4] On Tommaso's efforts to obtain benefices for Niccolò's sons, cf. Giovanni Lanfredini to Tommaso, Mar. 1478, BNF, ii, v, 16, fo. 26ᵛ; Antonio Montecatini to Ercole d'Este, 26 June, 22 July 1480, ASMo, Careggio degli ambasc., Firenze, 2. Tommaso was also involved in determining the dowry of one of Niccolò's daughters, cf. Ginevra Macinghi-Soderini's tax return of 1480 in Cat., 1000, pt. 1, fo. 63ʳ.

[5] In 1468 Tommaso claimed that Niccolò still owed him 800 florins: Capitani di Parte, numeri rossi, 74, fo. 15ᵛ.

[6] Notarile Antecos., M565, fos. 183ʳ⁻ᵛ, 3 Jan. 1487.

[7] Cf. Tommaso's will of 10 Mar. 1462, Notarile Antecos., M570, fos. 88ᵛ–89ʳ.

[8] Tommaso purchased a great deal of property in the names of his and Maria's children, and, perhaps to reduce his own taxes, filed it as a separate return in Lorenzo's name in 1447, when Lorenzo could have been no more than 14. Cf. above, Chap. 4.

[9] Cf. Lorenzo's tax report of 1458, Cat., 795, fo. 163ʳ. Arbitration over this

financial difficulties of the early 1450s had probably motivated this action, and as they worsened, Tommaso went
further. He even used a legal quibble to deprive Lorenzo of
part of his inheritance, claiming that he himself was the heir
of Maria's dead sons and therefore their shares of the dowry
belonged to him rather than to Lorenzo![10]
This conflict with Tommaso may have created a bond of
sympathy between Lorenzo and his uncle Niccolò, whose
own relations with Tommaso must have degenerated as
badly by the later 1450s. Certainly, once the anti-Medici
movement broke out in 1465, Lorenzo sided with the Pitti
group, but when the Medici recovered the upper hand in
September 1466 Tommaso must have exerted his influence
on Lorenzo's behalf. Although Lorenzo was summoned by
the pro-Medici *Otto di Guardia*, he was not among those
punished.[11] Instead, Tommaso sought a reconciliation with
his erring son, obtaining new property for him from the
Archbishop of Florence, and submitting their quarrel over
Maria Torrigiani's dowry to arbitration.[12]
Nevertheless, the situation did not change, as Tommaso
failed to fulfil the terms of the ensuing accord, and Lorenzo
continued his career of political opposition. Drawn on by the
blandishments of his uncle, he became involved in further
plots against the regime. When one of these was discovered
in 1468,[13] Piero de' Medici did Tommaso the courtesy of
asking his opinion regarding a fitting penalty for his son, but
Tommaso, following republican tradition, refused in such a

issue had already occurred between Lorenzo and his father in 1447: Notarile
Antecos., G693, fo. 268[r].

[10] Notarile Antecos., P128, 23 Mar. 1457. Tommaso continued to insist on this
argument until 1466, when arbiters appointed between him and Lorenzo declared
him in the wrong.
[11] Cf. the summons of 7 Sept. 1466, in Atti del Capitano del Popolo, 3984,
fo. 23[r], and Pampaloni, 'Fermenti', 56.
[12] Notarile Antecos., P130, fos. 61[r]–65[v]; M570, fos. 574[v]–575[v], both of 25 Sept.
1466. This agreement also involved Lorenzo's emancipation, which was commonly
included in the settlement of old family conflicts: Kuehn, *Emancipation*, 72.
[13] On this plot, cf. Nicodemo Tranchedini to the Duke of Milan, 9 Feb. 1468,
ASMi, SPE, Firenze, 274; Niccolò de' Roberti to Borso d'Este, 19, 29 Feb. 1468,
ASMo, Carteggio degli ambasc., Firenze, 1; Piero de' Medici to Otto Niccolini,
20 Feb. 1468, published in Niccolini, *Chronicles*, 350; Ammirato, *Istorie*, v. 376.

case to place family interests before those of the city. If Lorenzo were still in Florence, Tommaso replied, he would like him to be punished physically. However, as he had fled, he recommended that he be exiled outside Florence for ten years, with the possibility of a reduction of this term for good behaviour. It is a testimony to Piero's consideration for Tommaso that this was the sentence which Lorenzo subsequently received.[14] It may equally have been due to Piero's intervention that this sentence was soon rescinded and Lorenzo was sent by his father to stay with relatives in Milan, where he would be removed from further contact with his uncle. Even this lesson did not, however, persuade Lorenzo to disassociate himself from the exiles and their plots. After his return to Florence a year or two later, he again engaged in conspiracies against the regime, although these were never again serious enough to warrant punishment.[15] They may nevertheless have contributed to Tommaso's apparent despair of ever recovering his eldest son's loyalty. He never bothered to fulfil the terms of the earlier award, and, although he provided Lorenzo's family with the money they needed, he seems to have wanted little to do with them. After the death of Lorenzo's wife in the early 1470s, he had his granddaughters raised in a convent rather than take them into his own house, and although he eventually settled the dowry question with his grandson Tommaso after Lorenzo's own death in about 1479, he agreed to give him little beyond the amount strictly due.[16]

In the light of Tommaso's repeated experience of family conflict, it is hardly surprising that his own ideal of family life should centre round the currently widespread concept of harmony. He expressed this view in 1475, when he divided

[14] Tommaso to Piero, 19 Mar. 1468, MAP, xvii, 539; Otto di Guardia, periodo repubblicano, 224, fo. 159ʳ⁻ᵛ. However, this sentence was lifted in Oct. 1468, apparently on the understanding that Lorenzo would go into exile outside Florentine territory: CP, 60, fo. 38ᵛ; Libri fab., 68, fos. 138ᵛ, 139ʳ, 140ʳ. Tommaso and Piero then decided that it would be best for Lorenzo to go to Milan: Tommaso to the Duke, 8 Nov. 1468, ASMi, SPE, Venezia, 354, but 9 Nov. in Sig., Dieci, Otto, 63, fo. 121ʳ.
[15] Cf. Sacramoro to the Duke, 29 Oct. 1470, ASMi, SPE, Firenze, 280.
[16] Cf. the codicils to Tommaso's will added 7 Mar. 1474: Notarile Antecos., M571, fos. 90ᵛ–91ʳ, and Tommaso di Lorenzo's tax report of 1480, Cat., 1001, pt. 2, fo. 351ᵛ.

his patrimony among his and Dianora Tornabuoni's four surviving sons. His reason for doing so, he implied, was to ensure that his sons' own division of their inheritance did not lead to the quarrels which could destroy a house; having brought up these sons to live in harmony, he wrote, he wanted them to continue to do so.[17] Harmony also seems to have underlain Tommaso's rather traditional ideal of a large family living under one roof and working together for the wellbeing of the whole. At the most basic level, Tommaso placed much emphasis on marriage and on family life. Unlike Niccolò, he married earlier than was normal for his time, never remained widowed for long, and ensured that his six daughters and all but one of his five surviving legitimate sons married rather than entering religious life. The story that he encouraged Botticelli to marry, if it is not apocryphal, suggests his conviction regarding the value of the married state and of the humanizing influence of family life.[18] Tommaso's goal of harmonious co-operation among members of a household was suggested by his tendency to keep his children together in his home even after the sons had married, while he also subscribed to the widely held views that daughters should be allowed to return to the paternal home during their widowhood, and that widows should remain with their young children rather than remarrying.[19] Finally, Tommaso's construction of a loggia in his residence in S. Spirito suggests a desire for a focal point where his large family could congregate with neighbours and friends to discuss personal matters or the latest issues of the day, at the same time spreading Soderini contacts and influence in the area.[20] Tommaso's attitudes were also traditional in his

[17] Notarile Antecos., B726, fos. 197ᵛ–199ʳ, 16 Oct. 1475. Cf. Marsilio Ficini's comment on the value of fraternal harmony cited in Kent, *Household and Lineage*, 62.

[18] For this story, cf. Lightbown, *Sandro Botticelli*, i. 32.

[19] Cf. Tommaso's will of 10 Mar. 1462 and the codicils of 7 Mar. 1474, Notarile Antecos., M570, fos. 85ʳ–90ᵛ and M571, fos. 90ʳ–91ᵛ. Tommaso followed the advice of contemporaries such as Morelli in making his potential widow one of the principal guardians of his children and executors of his estate, presumably with the intention of discouraging her from remarrying: cf. Morelli, *Ricordi*, 213–18.

[20] On the significance of a loggia for a family, cf. Rucellai, *Il Zibaldone*, 20, and Heers, *Family Clans*, 160.

approach to his illegitimate son and daughter, the offspring of household slaves. They were not consistently raised in his household, and Tommaso ensured, like his grandfather before him, that neither made substantial inroads into the patrimony which he intended to leave to his legitimate heirs. The dowry of Tommaso's illegitimate daughter was noticeably less than those of his legitimate offspring, while his illegitimate son went into monastic life, whence he would make no further claims on the family property beyond the limited amount which Tommaso had provided for him.[21]

In contrast to Tommaso, Niccolò seems to have overturned the normal order of family life. He did not marry until the age of 37 and by then he already had an illegitimate son who continued, even after the birth of his other children, to take first place in his affections. This son, Geri, also took the normal course of a bastard by entering the Church, but Niccolò put unusual efforts into winning him a successful ecclesiastical career, and into making him a figure of importance, with property and influence in the quarter of S. Spirito. Eventually, in about 1460, Geri left the priesthood, and Niccolò then exerted himself to see that he enjoyed a successful lay career. As was mentioned earlier, Marco Parenti claimed that Niccolò's extraordinary love for this child influenced his decision in 1465 to press for a scrutiny, in order that the defrocked Geri could gain qualifications for public office. In fact, Niccolò did have the communal councils declare Geri eligible to hold public posts, and legitimate, so that he could inherit from his father, but, according to Parenti, Geri then failed to gain a majority in the scrutiny.[22] Given this strong affection between father and son, it is

[21] Tommaso's illegitimate daughter was raised by Soldo del Soldato for some unspecified length of time: Tommaso's codicils of 21 Oct. 1467, Notarile Antecos., M570, fo. 652ᵛ. Tommaso created a dowry for her in the *Monte Comune*, and directed his heirs to increase this to 700 florins: codicils of 7 Mar. 1474, Notarile Antecos., M571, fo. 90ᵛ. Meanwhile, Tommaso had purchased 1,000 florins in the *Monte Comune* as a nest-egg for his illegitimate son Giovangualberto: Tommaso's will of 10 Mar. 1462, Notarile Antecos., M570, fo. 87ᵛ.

[22] Provv., Registri, 156, fos. 231ʳ–232ᵛ; Parenti, 'Ricordi politici', 37–8. Geri renounced a canonry in the Florentine cathedral, as well as benefices at Barbialla and Castratole, and the Priory of S. Candida just outside Florence. In some of these cases, Niccolò possessed a share in the appointment.

hardly surprising that Geri joined Niccolò in the anti-Medici movement of 1465–6, and was exiled with him in 1466. Thereafter, he shared in his father's plots to return to Florence, and, after being declared a rebel in 1467 and seeing his property confiscated by the state, he, like Niccolò, was forced to remain permanently in exile.[23]

Such, then, was the importance of family bonds in producing both political co-operation and political conflict in fifteenth-century Florence. Such also were the differing attitudes regarding the family which the Soderini brothers displayed. On the other hand, both seem to have shared the assumption that the closest bonds they possessed in the family lay within their direct line of descent. Although commitments to collateral branches continued to be felt in the fifteenth century,[24] Niccolò and Tommaso demonstrated a relative aloofness from other Soderini families which must have originated in their early separation from the main branches of their clan. This does not mean that they ignored their responsibility towards their kinsmen, for they did at times assist them financially and in their personal affairs.[25] Nevertheless, given their connection with the Medici group, Niccolò and Tommaso probably appeared as rivals rather than allies of certain branches of their clan. To their uncle Francesco and to Luigi di Giovanni, who had sided with the Albizzi faction, they must have represented a definite threat, for after 1434 Niccolò and Tommaso assumed political positions which would otherwise have gone to Soderini who lost their political qualifications after 1434. Tommaso may

[23] Cf. Otto di Guardia, periodo repubblicano, 224, fos. 127ᵛ–128ʳ.

[24] That such bonds were fading in this period has been suggested by Goldthwaite, *Private Wealth*, 267–8, and *Renaissance Florence*, 62–5. Cf., however, Kent, *Household and Lineage*, and the review of this work by L. Martines in *The Renaissance Quarterly*, 31 (1978), 198–9.

[25] e.g. Niccolò and Tommaso lent money to their poor relative, Soderino Soderini. Although they claimed the money was lost, Soderino pointed out that they were charging him 8% interest: Cat., 345, fos. 391ʳ, 653ʳ, 679ʳ. Tommaso also lent some 2,000 florins to Giovanni Soderini: Notarile Antecos., M570, fo. 651ʳ, 21 Oct. 1467. In 1461 Tommaso intervened with Piero de' Medici to see that a daughter of Guccio Soderini received her dowry in land so that her spendthrift husband could not waste it: MAP, cxxxvii, 792. In 1446 Tommaso had acted as procurator for the same Guccio Soderini, as he did for Guccio's son in 1459: Notarile Antecos., P128, fos., 309ʳ, 336ʳ.

even have directly contributed to this shift in political power within the clan, for he apparently did not oppose his fellow *accoppiatori*'s decision in 1455 to deprive Luigi Soderini of his political rights.[26] Moreover, Niccolò and Tommaso clearly took advantage of their uncle Francesco's high taxes and financial difficulties to win much of his property from him, while there is no indication that they came to his defence when he was imprisoned and then exiled in the late 1430s and 1440s.

Despite their relative distance from the other branches of their father's family, Niccolò and Tommaso were anxious to associate themselves with the distinguished tradition of the Soderini clan. Apart from returning to the Soderini area of S. Spirito, Tommaso managed to acquire what was apparently his grandfather's house, which, by making it his own residence, declared him the true ancestor of the most distinguished figure of his line.[27] Similarly, he and Niccolò assumed the patronage of the family chapel in the neighbouring church of the Carmine, where they insisted they should be buried among the tombs of their ancestors.[28] Tommaso's acquisition of the patronage of his parish church of S. Frediano during his embassy to the Pope in 1464 was undoubtedly intended not merely as a statement of his personal power in the district or another means for his family to acquire ecclesiastical income, but a further effort to assume the mantle of the Soderini clan. One of the arguments he used when requesting this favour from the Pope was that the Soderini had previously possessed the patronage and had been benefactors of this church for generations.[29] In both the

[26] Cf. Rubinstein, *Government*, 45 n. 1.

[27] Cf. Chap. 4. Cambi (*Istorie*, in *Delizie*, xxi. 194) suggests that Tommaso's houses had not traditionally belonged to the Soderini. He may have been referring to the other houses which Tommaso bought, for his principal residence was certainly that previously owned by his uncle Francesco.

[28] Cf. Niccolò's will of 19 Oct. 1444, Diplomatico, Acquisto Soderini, and Tommaso's will of 10 Mar. 1462, Notarile Antecos., M570, fo. 85ʳ.

[29] In the petition to the Pope Tommaso stated that he, his grandfather, and other Soderini had helped to decorate S. Frediano and that some Soderini had been buried there: Notarile Antecos., M570, fo. 446ᵛ. According to Litta, *Celebri famiglie*, disp. 141, tables 1 and 2, the Soderini had founded the monastery of S. Frediano and possessed the right to appoint its Prior in the mid-14th c. Cf. also Richa, *Notizie*

Carmine and S. Frediano, the Soderini brothers undertook
building and endowments, which were intended to glorify
both themselves and their clan. Whether in chapels previously owned by the family or in edifices which they acquired
or constructed, they commissioned altars or devotional paint-
ings, or renovated older structures in need of repair. In the
family's traditional church of the Carmine, Tommaso even
decided to install an organ and to construct a library, the
latter clearly reflecting his interest in the literary developments of his time. At the same time as he was following the
contemporary tendency to found libraries, he also adopted
the old custom of ensuring that the Soderini coat of arms
was sculpted prominently on his monuments in order to
immortalize both his own achievements and his family
name.[30]

If Niccolò and Tommaso could with pride identify themselves with their earlier Soderini ancestors, their father's
history represented a potential source of shame. Nevertheless, Lorenzo's widow appears to have preserved a strong
commitment to his memory and a determination to clear his
name from the slur which she evidently felt was the result of
persecution by the legitimate Soderini and their friends.[31] It
must have been she and her sons who, for example, sought
partially to clear Lorenzo's name through a legal judgment
stating that the *Podestà* had exceeded his powers in condemning Lorenzo to death.[32] In addition, Niccolò, at least,
attempted assassination in the traditional manner of aveng-
ing the family's honour through a blood vendetta. Although
this attempt failed, it does testify to the need felt by the

storiche, ix. 170–1. Tommaso used his powers of patronage to appoint another
Soderini, Messer Bartolomeo di Matteo, as Prior of S. Frediano.

[30] On Tommaso's decoration of the Carmine and of S. Frediano, cf. his codicils
of 7 Mar. 1474, Notarile Antecos., M571, fos. 90ʳ–91ʳ; Neri di Bicci, *Le ricordanze*,
241–2, 332–3, 382–5, 397–8. The project to place a new window in the main
chapel of the Carmine dated back to the 1440s: Niccolò's will of 19 Oct. 1444,
Diplomatico, Acquisto Soderini.

[31] Giovanni di Carlo has left a colourful but probably completely fanciful
description of how Ghilla kept her husband's bloody shirt, which she used in a long
oration inciting her sons to revenge: 'De temporibus suis', fos. 22ᵛ–23ᵛ.

[32] Cf. Carte Strozz., ser. 1, 352, fos. 29ʳ–39ᵛ, undated.

family to remove a stain which, even if it had few practical ramifications, evidently seemed to them a blot on their patrician origins and honour.[33]

The emphasis placed by Niccolò and Tommaso on their direct line of descent is further indicated by their concern to enhance their children's prospects in all spheres and to ensure that their sons were left in a position to preserve and build on their own achievements. Tommaso's desire that his own line receive permanent affirmation was demonstrated by the manner in which he tried to guarantee that his property remained in his descendants' hands forever, even while he gave his sons a degree of economic independence by seeing that they received their shares of his patrimony at a relatively early age.[34] Their concern to provide for their children was an ever-present motive in the brothers' political and financial decisions. Tommaso used his position as *accoppiatore*, for example, to see that his sons obtained a favourable start in their political careers, while he took his elder sons with him during his embassies in order to give them political experience abroad.[35] Similarly, he gained prestigious positions for them when possible, and in the case of his third son, Francesco, he used all his political influence to further his career within the Church. Apparently, it was the attraction of a bishopric which caused Tommaso to direct this son towards an ecclesiastical career, in which he could call on both Medici and Sforza assistance to advance Francesco to the highest ranks of the hierarchy.[36] Tommaso's ambition

[33] e.g. Giovanni Morelli warned his sons not to form connections with citizens tainted by the stain of illegitimacy or crime: *Ricordi*, 208.

[34] Tommaso divided his property among his sons in both 1466 and 1475: Notarile Antecos., P130, fos. 45ʳ–48ʳ; B726, fos. 197ᵛ–199ᵛ. On the latter occasion he insisted that his sons should not alienate this property to anyone but themselves or their descendants. On Florentines' tendency to divide their property for their sons' benefit before their death, cf. Herlihy, 'Family and Property', 16–17, 23–4.

[35] For the early dates at which Tommaso's sons were *veduti ai Tre Maggiori*, cf. Tratte, 5. Tommaso took his sons Lorenzo, Piero, and Paolantonio with him on embassies and obtained for Paolantonio the post of *Podestà* of Milan: cf. Tommaso to the Duke, 28 Feb. 1475, and Paolantonio's refusal of the post, 16 Jan. 1476, ASMi, SPE, Firenze, 286, 289.

[36] On the circumstances of Francesco's entry into the priesthood, cf. Matteo Strozzi's memoirs in Carte Strozz., ser. 3, 138, fo. 47ʳ⁻ᵛ. I am grateful to Dr Kate Lowe for drawing my attention to this source.

would have made Francesco an Archbishop when he was only 25, but obstacles, not least rival Medici ambition, stood in his way.[37] Nevertheless, Francesco did eventually rise to the illustrious position of Cardinal, whence, as Tommaso had originally been planning, he could not only add lustre to the Soderini name, but also advance the fortunes and influence of his family.[38]

As Francesco's case suggests, education was an important element in preparing sons for successful careers, and, despite their own limited educations, Niccolò and Tommaso were careful to give their children the best preparation possible for their future lives. A clear emphasis was placed on the value of degrees in law, which could prove valuable politically, could further careers in the Church, or could lead to prestigious professional posts. Not only were Niccolò's son Geri and Francesco di Tommaso doctors of law, but also Francesco's brother Giovanvettorio was for many years a professor of law in the University of Pisa. While in Tommaso's family the legal profession does not appear to have provided an alternative for a fading interest in commerce, in Niccolò's case, it may have done. More immediately, however, it provided a means of income for individuals whose other sources of revenue had been confiscated by the state, for Niccolò's two legitimate sons as well as Geri acquired university degrees in law and sought at least part of their income through the Church.[39]

[37] Presumably, Tommaso's influence was behind the Milanese suggestion in 1478 that the position of the defunct Archbishop of Pisa should go to Francesco Soderini. Although the Duke and Duchess believed that Tommaso's son would prove completely loyal to the Medici, Lorenzo preferred to promote the candidacy of his old tutor Gentile Becchi. Cf. Medici, *Lettere*, iii. 15–16.

[38] On Francesco, see K. J. P. Lowe, 'Francesco Soderini (1453–1524), Florentine Patrician and Cardinal', unpublished Ph.D. thesis in the University of London, 1985. Tommaso also sought benefices for his and Dianora's fourth son, Giovanvettorio: Tommaso to the Duke of Milan, 28 Feb., 11 Mar., 7, 25 Oct. 1475: ASMi, SPE, Firenze, 286, 290.

[39] Cf. Litta, *Famiglie*, disp. 141, table 8; Verde, *Lo studio*, e.g. ii. 406–11; Picotti, *Scritti*, 33; Passerini, 'Sigillo del cardinale Francesco', 299–300. That Florentine families may have taken to the legal profession as an alternative to commercial activity was suggested by Goldthwaite, *Private Wealth*, 134. On the contrast between Tommaso's and Niccolò's commitments to commerce, see Chap. 4.

Naturally, for children of patrician families growing up in fifteenth-century Florence, humanist learning held great attractions, while, from the more pragmatic point of view, it served as a means of gaining respect and reputation with one's peers. Since Tommaso seems to have taken a rather late interest in classical literature and humanism, it is hardly surprising that several of his sons became active figures within humanist circles and within the co-called 'Platonic Academy' which grew up around Ficino and the Medici. By doing so, they reinforced their intimacy with such important citizens as Lorenzo de' Medici, and undoubtedly enhanced their social and even their political standing.[40]

One of the principal ways in which Niccolò and Tommaso could further their children's prospects—and affect their own standing in the city—was through their choice of marriage partners for their families. For Florentine patricians, marriage implied the alliance of families and the creation of mutual obligations which could function in practically all fields. Consequently, the selection of marriage partners became the subject of careful consideration, in which many factors were taken into account. From the brothers' selection of *parenti* or in-laws, it would seem that they shared contemporary attitudes as expressed by the diarist Giovanni Morelli. According to Giovanni, the ideal in-law should be 'a merchant, rich, of an old Florentine family, Guelf, in the ruling group, loved by all and loving and good in every act'.[41] Understandably, however, this ideal was not always easy to attain, especially by patricians of cadet branches with limited financial resources. As a result, particularly for Tommaso, who married at a younger age than Niccolò, marriage contracts must initially have represented a compromise between what he desired in his in-laws and what he could hope to attract. At the start, Tommaso could offer an old name and promising political prospects, while what he principally needed was a boost to his finances. It is therefore understandable that wealth formed one of his principal criteria in selecting *parenti*, and that he preferred

---

[40] Cf. Della Torre, *La storia*, 82, 624–5, 719–21, 726–7, 772–4, 792, 805–8.
[41] Morelli, *Ricordi*, 264.

it, when a choice was necessary, to social distinction. Tommaso's own first marriage, for example, was into a family apparently lacking a political tradition and high social standing in Florence, but who were evidently wealthy. The Torrigiani seem to have been successful merchants with interests in Bologna, and the large dowry of 1,450 florins which Tommaso received suggests that they were willing to pay for a connection with a Florentine of such distinguished ancestry.[42] Similarly, when Tommaso contracted the first marriage for his children in the early 1440s, his prospective in-laws were not among the old patrician clans of Florence. Rather, the most notable characteristic of his son-in-law, Piero Banchi, was the huge fortune which his father Andrea was accumulating in the silk industry.[43] The match would therefore bring Tommaso a useful contact within his own industry as well as a wealthy friend. Moreover, the fact that Andrea had begun to be appointed to the Signoria offered the prospect of contacts in the political sphere, and a rise in the Banchi family's social status.

As time went on, Tommaso could expect to win in-laws with high social status as well as wealth. In part, this was because of his own marriage with Dianora Tornabuoni, which emphasized his connection with the Medici and must, along with his growing political authority, have raised his value in the marriage market. In particular, citizens who were suspect to the regime or did not themselves have access to Medici patronage might see in Tommaso a valuable ally and advocate. This factor may have influenced certain marriages which his children contracted in the 1450s. In 1451, for

---

[42] On the Torrigiani's financial standing, see Giuliano's tax return of 1427, Cat., 78, fo. 113^(r–v). There is no evidence to connect this family with the more politically successful Torrigiani of S. Croce, while the Torrigiani who were wine merchants of S. Spirito and who later rose into the nobility were evidently an altogether different family. The size of Maria's dowry is given e.g. in her son Lorenzo's tax return of 1446–7, ibid., 655, fos. 840^(r)–841^(r).

[43] On Andrea Banchi, cf. Edler de Roover, 'Andrea Banchi'. For the betrothal between Lisabetta Soderini and Piero Banchi, Notarile Antecos., G693, fos. 83^(v)–84^(r), 14 Dec. 1443. For the transfer of part of her dowry, Monte Comune, 3733, fo. 117^(r). However, Lisabetta must soon have died, for Piero Banchi went on to marry a daughter of Luigi Ridolfi: Edler de Roover, 'Andrea Banchi', 230 n. 26.

example, Tommaso's daughter Margherita wedded Francesco di Jacopo Baroncelli, a member of a very distinguished and wealthy family, who was a partner in a successful banking operation with a major branch in Rome. However, the Baroncelli had been associated with the Albizzi faction, and after 1434 they continued to be regarded as potential enemies by the Medici group. In 1444 Jacopo and his sons were deprived of their political rights, while in 1458 they were ordered to their villas so as not to obstruct the leading citizens' plans for a *parlamento*.[44] Thus for Tommaso, the Baroncelli connection, politically, could only have been a liability, but this was evidently more than compensated by their wealth and social standing. Very soon, in fact, he began to take advantage of his son-in-law's commercial activities, investing in the Baroncelli bank, from which he derived considerable profit for many years.[45]

If in turn the Baroncelli were looking to Tommaso to serve as their advocate within the Medici group they were not disappointed, for Tommaso did use his influence in their favour. In 1459, for example, he wrote to Piero de' Medici thanking him for his role in negotiating a marriage for Francesco's brother Carlo. He then reassured Piero that Carlo and his father and brothers 'would act in everything as Cosimo and the rest of you want', and therefore recommended the whole family to Piero 'in everything'.[46] Clearly, Tommaso was serving as a link between the Baroncelli and the Medici, and not only Piero's involvement in Carlo's marriage but also the fact that Francesco and his brothers recovered their political rights in 1466 suggests that Tommaso's intervention may gradually have had some effect.[47]

---

[44] Rubinstein, *Government*, 18 n. 5, and 103 n. 6. On the Baroncelli's connection with the Albizzi faction, cf. Kent, *Rise*, 141, 237, 248, 317, 319. On the Baroncelli, cf. Ammirato, *Della famiglia de' Baroncelli*, 200–34.

[45] Cf. Chap. 4.

[46] Tommaso to Piero, 21 Dec. 1459, MAP, xvi, 276. Carlo Baroncelli married into a family related to the Medici, the Bardi counts of Vernio, Ammirato, *Della famiglia de' Baroncelli*, 234.

[47] For the Baroncelli's pardon: Balìe, 30, fos. 20ᵛ–22ʳ. On 13 Nov. 1466, Tommaso and Jacopo Guicciardini also expressed to Piero de' Medici their pleasure at a *parentado* made between the Baroncelli and Niccolò Tornabuoni, in which the Medici may again have been involved: MAP, xvi, 212.

The goal of winning an influential friend within the Medici group may also have motivated Bernardo d'Andrea Bardi's wedding to Tommaso's daughter Caterina in 1454. Although previously business partners of the Medici, Andrea's family had fallen out of favour in about 1434, probably because of their failure to support the Medici during the crisis of those years. They may consequently have wanted a connection on the right side of the political fence, while for Tommaso the fame of the Bardi name and its banking tradition must have made the family a welcome connection.[48]

Tommaso's marriage with Dianora, apart from making him an attractive *parente* to families out of favour with the Medici group, undoubtedly also meant that the Medici took a considerable interest in his family's marriage connections. By finding his children good partners they could reinforce Soderini gratitude and loyalty to them. On the other hand, they might hope to use Tommaso's family to establish links with other families, just as the Tornabuoni had apparently earlier been used to cement the tie between themselves and Tommaso. Certainly, the Medici were involved in even the first marriage of a child of Tommaso, as Cosimo was appointed to determine the dowry which Lisabetta Soderini brought Piero Banchi. While it is unclear whether the Medici played a further role in this match, it is possible that they encouraged it with a view to bringing the rising Banchi family into closer contact with themselves.

The Medici were also involved in one of the more brilliant matches which Tommaso's family made during the 1450s, although possibly with a different motive. Again, Cosimo was asked to determine the dowry which Lorenzo Soderini received when he wedded a daughter of the wealthy banker of Milanese origins, Paolo da Castagnuolo. Cosimo was undoubtedly chosen because he was a friend not only of Tommaso but also of Paolo, whose company was a correspondent of the Medici bank.[49] Although in the end Cosimo

[48] For Caterina's marriage, Notarile Antecos., P128, fo. 145^v. On the Bardi, cf. e.g. Tiribilli-Giuliani, *Sommario*, i. On the possible failure of this branch to support the Medici, cf. Kent, *Rise*, 73–4.

[49] Cf. Paolo da Castagnuolo to Piero de' Medici, 3 May 1458, MAP, xii, 288. In Parma on papal business, Paolo writes that he has found an expert on gout, and,

merely named the sum already invested in the *Monte delle Doti* on behalf of the future bride,[50] his contribution to such a lucrative match may have helped to demonstrate to the Soderini the value of Medici friendship, while Paolo must have been pleased to gain a good political and social connection—one which he may have seen as an indirect bond with the Medici. On the other hand, it is unlikely that this marriage was intended to reinforce the Medici's position in Florence.

That the Medici nevertheless at times became involved in the *parentadi* of Tommaso's family for primarily political motives was indicated in the later 1450s when Tommaso's daughter Caterina married for a second time, to Maso degli Albizzi. Maso's family was of particular importance to the Medici, not merely because they were prominent and influential, but because other branches of the clan had led the opposition against them in the 1420s and early 1430s. Maso's father, Luca degli Albizzi, had then deserted his brother Rinaldo to side with Cosimo, and subsequently the Medici remained very anxious to maintain his valuable support. Luca's own political commitment had earlier been reinforced by his marriage to a Medici lady, and, according to Scipione Ammirato, his son Maso had also initially been wedded to a Medici in order to help cement this loyalty. Ammirato also asserted that Maso's second marriage, to Caterina Soderini, was arranged by Cosimo and Luca Pitti, and the implication was that it too was intended to help keep him loyal to the Medici.[51]

Moreover, the most exalted alliance which Tommaso ever made—his son Piero's betrothal in 1469 to a daughter of Marquis Gabriele Malaspina of Fosdinovo—was undoubtedly negotiated with at least the consent of the Medici.[52] Not

---

'*come vostro*', is having him write to Piero about the possibility of a cure. On the Medici bank's dealings with the Da Castagnuolo firm: de Roover, *Rise and Decline*, 90–91, 128.

[50] After this marriage had been contracted in 1451, Paolo apparently experienced financial difficulties. Yet Cosimo insisted he pay the original 4,000 florins: Notarile Antecos., B1182 (1434–56), fo. 115ʳ, 7 Apr. 1456; Monte Comune, 3734, fos. 287ʳ, 328ʳ.

[51] Ammirato, *Delle famiglie*, pt. 1, 41.

[52] For this marriage and its dowry of 4,000 florins: cf. Capitani di Parte, numeri rossi, 75, fos. 58ᵛ–63ʳ. On its political significance see also Chap. 6.

only did the Malaspina have close relations with the Medici, but the political significance of the Malaspina–Soderini match was such as to ensure that it would not be discussed, or possibly even considered, without Medici approval. For Gabriele was one of Florence's principal friends in the Lunigiana (the coastal area north of Tuscany), and the Soderini marriage meant a reinforcement of the regime's commitment to her clients and her sphere of influence there. This presumably represented Medici policy, and the selection of Tommaso's daughter for the connection with the Malaspina meant not only an enhancement of the social and political position of Tommaso's family but possibly also an indirect indication of Medici backing for Gabriele.

It is difficult to know how many of Tommaso's family's *parentadi* felt the effect of Medici interest. It may, for example, have influenced the second marriage of Tommaso's daughter Margherita to Gerozzo Pigli in about 1462.[53] Tommaso's new son-in-law had not only dedicated his life to trade and banking in London, but had been head of the Medici bank there from 1446 to the early 1450s. From Tommaso's perspective, the match could have been only moderately attractive politically, for, while Gerozzo was appointed to some political posts after his return to Florence,[54] he did not emerge as a really authoritative member of the ruling group. Moreover, according to Gerozzo, his service to the Medici had not resulted in riches, as the branches of the bank with which he was involved experienced severe losses for which he was partially responsible. Nevertheless, he could offer the correct credentials of mercantile activity and antiquity of family, for the Pigli were descended from an old feudal clan. He must also have been a competent individual, to judge from Tommaso's readiness to employ him in delicate family affairs.[55] Thus Gerozzo's birth, his

[53] For this marriage, see Carte Ancisa, EE 352, fo. 156^v, and BNF, Magl., xxvi, 141, p. 315. On Gerozzo himself, de Roover, *Rise and Decline*, especially pp. 321–5, 328–30.

[54] e.g. he was appointed to the *Balìa* of 1458: Rubinstein, *Government*, 288.

[55] e.g. Gerozzo acted, along with two other of Tommaso's sons-in-law, Lorenzo Lenzi and Maso degli Albizzi, as arbiters between Tommaso and his son Lorenzo: Notarile Antecos., P130, fos. 61^r–66^v.

banking career, and his personal ability must have seemed to Tommaso sufficient reason for the attachment with his family, while the match may also have been promoted by the Medici with the goal of finding a good connection not only for Tommaso but also for one of their partners.

With time the Medici may have taken a greater interest in their fellow patricians' marriage connections;[56] indeed one of Tommaso's letters suggests that by the later 1470s it was wise for prominent individuals to follow Medici will in such matters. In 1478 Tommaso asked Lorenzo to think about 'giving' a second wife to his son Paolantonio,[57] as though he intended to leave the decision totally to him. Paolantonio's second wife, Margherita di Strozza di Messer Marcello Strozzi, may therefore have been chosen by Lorenzo, although the reasons are not completely clear. Although Messer Marcello had proved untypical of his family in supporting the Medici in the early 1430s, his son Strozza had been regarded as a Medici enemy when appointed to the Signoria in 1471.[58] Although Lorenzo was being warned in 1476 that Paolantonio was also his enemy, by 1478 he may have had sufficient trust in both the Soderini and the Strozzi to feel that the marriage would reinforce rather than undermine Medici support in the city.[59]

Yet, despite this growing involvement of the Medici, the Soderini continued to form alliances independently. There is, for example, no indication that the Medici played any role in Tommaso's own third marriage, to Oretta di Simone Altoviti, while his fourth wife, Alessandra di Lando degli Albizzi, was

[56] Cf. Lorenzo's involvement in the many marriages recorded by his secretary, Niccolò Michelozzi: Klapisch-Zuber, 'Zacharie', 1225; Cohn, *The Labouring Classes*, 53.

[57] Tommaso to Lorenzo de' Medici, 19 Feb. 1478, MAP, xxxiv, 56. Paolantonio's first wife, Lisabetta Spinelli, had recently died.

[58] Sacramoro to the Duke of Milan, 1 May 1471, ASMi, SPE, Firenze, 281. On Messer Marcello's loyalty to the Medici, see H. Gregory, 'A Florentine Family in Crisis: The Strozzi in the Fifteenth Century', unpublished Ph.D. thesis in the University of London, 1981, pp. 141, 154, 160–1, 166. Paolantonio's marriage to Margherita is recorded in Carte Ancisa, EE, 352, and BNF, Poligrafo Gargani, 1900.

[59] Strozza was included in the *Balìa* of 1480, as his father had been in those of 1434 and 1438: Rubinstein, *Government*, 313, 251, 262. On Paolantonio's being an enemy of Lorenzo, see Chap. 8 below.

undoubtedly chosen because her father was a business partner of Tommaso's.[60] The same absence of Medici involvement seems true for the first marriage of Paolantonio di
Tommaso to a daughter of Tommaso Spinelli, and there is
no reference to the Medici in the marriage of another of
Tommaso's daughters to Lorenzo d'Anfrione Lenzi in the
early 1460s.[61] While all these families represented distinguished mercantile clans, of the branches to which Tommaso associated himself, only the Altoviti and the Lenzi seem
to have been particularly active in politics.

There is, then, no clear pattern behind these *parentadi*
apart from the general orientation suggested by Morelli and
a desire to connect the Soderini with distinguished Florentine
clans. Yet there is a suggestion, in Tommaso's later years, of
the emergence of a different direction in his family's marriage
policy. In Florence, it was normal to look for *parenti* within
one's neighbourhood or *gonfalone*; indeed, Morelli recommended it as a means of gaining a useful local friend.[62]
However, neither Niccolò nor Tommaso showed much interest in seeking their in-laws locally, perhaps because they were
already sufficiently influential in their *gonfalone* not to feel
the need for such attachments, or because there were few
suitable candidates in their relatively undistinguished district.
In fact, prior to 1469 the only local marriage contracted by
either of the brothers was between one of Niccolò's daughters and a member of one of the few Serragli families to
escape proscription as an enemy of the Medici group.[63] If
this seems to indicate a commitment on Niccolò's part to

[60] For the Altoviti marriage: Notarile Antecos., M570, fos. 89ᵛ–90ʳ, 10 Mar.
1462. On the Albizzi marriage: ibid., fo. 265ᵛ, 13 Oct. 1463. Tommaso had been
in business with Lando from at least 1 Dec. 1462: ibid., M131, fo. 149ʳ, 25 Apr.
1465.

[61] On the Spinelli marriage: Litta, *Famiglie*, disp. 141, table 8 and Tommaso's
tax return of 1469, Cat., 910, fo. 535ᵛ. Maria di Tommaso Soderini and Lorenzo
d'Anfrione Lenzi exchanged rings on 12 Sept. 1462, Notarile Antecos., P128.

[62] Morelli, *Ricordi*, 263.

[63] According to Litta, *Famiglie*, disp. 141, table 3, in 1456 Niccolò's daughter
Alessandra married Angelo di Piero Serragli. However, the date given in Carte
Ancisa, EE 352, fo. 161ʳ, is 1452. On the Serragli's connections with the Albizzi
group, see Kent, *Rise*, 137–8, 155, 166, 188, 291. The Serragli were deprived of
political rights in 1444, although an exception was made for Giorgio di Piero
Serragli, and his sons and brothers: Rubinstein, *Government*, 18.

anti-Medici circles, the fact remains that the Serragli apparently did not support Niccolò in his anti-Medici stand, and that Niccolò later formed connections with figures as close to the Medici as Roberto Martelli, who served for many years as the manager of the Medici bank in Rome.[64] Indeed, Niccolò seems to have shared Tommaso's general desire for connections with prominent commercial families, as his other sons-in-law came from such clans as the Alessandri, Davizzi, and Gerini.[65] Clearly, Niccolò's degenerating relations with the Medici did not reduce his attraction as a potential father-in-law, and at the time of the Serragli marriage he may, in fact, have seemed a valuable contact within the ruling group.

Apart from the Serragli–Soderini match, the only other local connection formed by the brothers was made in about 1469, when at nearly the same time two of Tommaso's daughters married two residents of Tommaso's *gonfalone*. The families of both his new sons-in-law (Francesco Antinori and Giovambattista Corbinelli) possessed political influence in Florence, as both had frequently filled the highest posts of the republic, and by carrying on this tradition Francesco and Giovambattista promised to supply the Soderini with relatives potentially useful in the political sphere.[66] Both, then, represented good candidates, close to home, from families with whom Tommaso was already on good terms.[67] Moreover, by consolidating his relationship with these prominent

---

[64] On Roberto, see de Roover, *Rise and Decline*, especially pp. 65–6, 198, 211. The marriage between Roberto and Maria Soderini is mentioned in Notarile Antecos., G694, fos. 225ʳ–226ʳ, 11 Jan. 1463.

[65] According to Litta, *Famiglie*, disp. 141, table 3, Nanna Soderini married Ugo di Bartolomeo Alessandri in 1455. For the Davizzi marriage, see Notarile Antecos., M570, fo. 439, 14 May 1465. For the Gerini connection, ibid., fo. 235ʳ, 16 July 1463, and P129, 6 Oct. 1463.

[66] Although the Antinori did not enter the Signoria until 1351 and had no representatives in it between 1373 and 1431, they were afterwards more active at this highest government level: see e.g. the Priorista in the British Library, MSS Egerton, 1170, p. 208. On the Corbinelli's political activities in the late 1420s and early 1430s, see Kent, *Rise*, 5–53, 197 n. 17, 333. For Francesca and Giovanna Soderini's marriages to these men, Carte Ancisa, EE 352, fo. 156ᵛ, and BNF, Poligrafo Gargani, 1897.

[67] The Antinori properties bordered on Tommaso's, and Tommaso had recommended Giovambattista Corbinelli to Piero de' Medici as early as 13 Nov. 1466: MAP, xvi, 212.

families, these marriages served to strengthen Soderini influence in their *gonfalone*. By 1469 Tommaso and his sons may have had a specific reason for doing this, for Piero de' Medici was in poor health and the possibility existed that his death might lead to another large-scale conflict of the sort which had followed Cosimo's demise. In the event of a Medici defeat, Tommaso's family would need all the local support they could muster in order to defend their patrimony against the victorious group. As has been illustrated, local connections could serve just this function, and thus these two exceptional *parentadi* may have been intended in part as a sort of insurance policy against the vissicitudes of Florentine politics.[68] Even so, the fact remains that this policy came well after that of consolidating personal connections with families important in the city-wide sphere, and thus at most can represent only a secondary goal on the part of the Soderini.

In fact, such local marriage connections could at best have reinforced the authority which Tommaso already possessed in his local district. On the basis of the Soderini tradition, both he and Niccolò had almost automatically played a prominent role in their *gonfalone*, particularly as they began to assert themselves as property owners in the area. From at least the 1440s, they were accepted as active participants in the meetings of the inhabitants of the *gonfalone*, and were sufficiently prominent to be selected as its representatives for such special duties as confiscating or selling the property of tax delinquents.[69] Moreover, both brothers frequently served as *gonfaloniere*, while, as already noted, their acquisition of Soderini property and their gradual emergence as the clan's leading figures meant that they could assume the strong voice in local politics which the Soderini had always possessed. The fact that Tommaso gained the patronage of the parish church where the *gonfalone*'s meetings were held probably gave him an additional element of authority over the citizens

---

[68] Cf. Kent and Kent, *Neighbours, passim*. Later, Tommaso's son Giovanvettorio strengthened this local connection by marrying into the Nerli family.

[69] Tommaso was elected as syndic of Drago in 1446 and 1453, and Niccolò was present at the earlier meeting at least: Notarile Antecos., P128 (1439–50), fo. 286ʳ⁻ᵛ, ibid. (1451–61), fo. 75ʳ⁻ᵛ.

who gathered there.[70] Moreover, the friendships which they rapidly made with such families as the Del Pugliese, Bonsi, Del Soldato, and with Filippo Manetti meant that, even without local *parentadi*, citizens who were important and served in offices at a local level were often on close terms with them.

It might be argued that this influence which Tommaso wielded in his *gonfalone* arose principally from his ability to mediate Medici patronage. Certainly, Tommaso did act as intercessor with the Medici for inhabitants of S. Spirito; the Piero Tazzi whom he recommended to Lorenzo for a post on the *Otto di Guardia* was, for example, a resident of Tommaso's *gonfalone*.[71] Yet surviving examples of such patronage are rare, while it is clear that Tommaso's and Niccolò's local influence also depended on other factors. As we have seen, family tradition was fundamental in winning local authority, as it was also in gaining prominence within the city's government, which in turn implied importance at the local level. Moreover, personal contacts, a family's reputation, and its financial position all played a role in creating enduring ties with its neighbours. The fact that the Soderini owned the shops or residences in which local inhabitants lived and worked, and that they spent money in the district, contributed to their local ascendancy. These factors were undoubtedly of great importance in gaining them that respect which caused both prominent families and tradesmen of S. Spirito to call on them to settle their personal disputes.[72] While such respect may have been based in part on patronage, whether business, artistic, or political, it was certainly in large part independent of the Medici. This is particularly clear from the manner in which, in late August 1466, Niccolò turned his local influence against the Medici, leading some

[70] Meetings of the men of Drago, S. Spirito, were held in S. Frediano: Kent and Kent, *Neighbours*, 96 n. 3.

[71] Tommaso to Lorenzo, 14 July 1477, MAP, xxxv, 620.

[72] In 1445 two obscure inhabitants of the parish of S. Felice in Piazza appointed Niccolò and Tommaso arbiters between them: Notarile Antecos., G693, fo. 199ʳ. A saddle maker of S. Frediano similarly selected Tommaso as an arbiter in a dispute with relatives over a house in the district: ibid., P129, 7 Feb. 1465. Tommaso was also appointed arbiter by two of the Bonsi family: ibid., M570, fo. 417ʳ, 18 Feb. 1465.

200 men, apparently local workers or artisans, to Luca Pitti's house in an effort to rouse the anti-Medici group to action.[73] Most probably these men not only knew Niccolò well but enthusiastically supported his popular political stand, and may have been inspired by his demagogic rhetoric. Indeed, Niccolò's continuing influence within his district and within the ruling group in general is sufficient proof that political authority did not depend primarily on distributing patronage which originated with the city's leading family.

To a degree, contacts at the local level overlapped with the last of the major categories in the Soderini's social world— their friends. If the brothers did not form many *parentadi* locally, they certainly came to know and were on good terms with many people in the two principal districts in which they lived. Their enduring friendship with Agnolo di Messer Palla Novello Strozzi probably dates from the period when they, like Agnolo, were residents of the S. Maria Novella quarter, and, once the brothers moved to S. Spirito, they quickly created friendships there. Tommaso's connections with the Del Soldato, Bonsi, and other families of his *gonfalone* have already been mentioned, while Niccolò's friendship with Filippo Manetti, the brother of the famous humanist Giannozzo, presumably dates from his return to the S. Frediano area, where Filippo also lived.[74] Other friendships, although they originated in common political activity, may have felt the strength of neighbourhood ties. Nastagio Guiducci, for example, was a resident of the S. Maria Novella quarter, while Tommaso Barbadori and Tommaso's friend Giovanni Lanfredini were inhabitants of S. Spirito.

Naturally, the other activities and relationships of the Soderini brothers' lives also led to the formation of friendships. Business associations undoubtedly did so, and Tommaso's selection of Antonio da Rabatta, Bernardo Cambi, and Jacopo Torelli as executors of his will probably attests

---

[73] According to Ammanati (*Commentariorum liber tertius*, fo. 358ʳ), Niccolò led 300 'Germans' from the neighbouring weaving shops. Benedetto Dei asserted that Niccolò collected '*il popolo al ponte alla Charaia*' and went to Luca's house with '*suoi masnadieri e sateliti*': Cronica, fo. 24ʳ.

[74] Filippo began to participate in Niccolò's private affairs in 1435 (as procurator): Notarile Antecos., G695, 11 Jan. 1435.

to common business activities, even if these have left no traces in Tommaso's papers.[75] Finally, marriage connections could give rise to friendships, as may have been the case with Bernardo Cambi, and most probably was with Matteo Palmieri, who was sufficiently close to Tommaso to be appointed by him to help look after his illegitimate son in the event of his death.[76] Presumably, apart from collaboration in the political and economic spheres, this friendship was the result of the old connection between the Palmieri and Tommaso's maternal grandfather, Tommaso Cambi, which had been reinforced early in the century by a *parentado*.[77]

Like their marriage connections, the Soderini brothers' friendships tended to cross political lines. This is particularly evident in the case of Agnolo Strozzi, who remained a life-long friend of Tommaso and was initially, at least, a close friend of Niccolò. Their friendship went back to at least the 1430s, despite the fact that Agnolo was a member of a family closely associated with the Albizzi faction. In 1434 he and his father did not, however, support the Albizzi party, possibly in part because of the influence of Medici friends such as Niccolò. Nevertheless, they suffered proscription after 1434; in 1436 Agnolo was designated a magnate, which effectively deprived him of political rights. Despite this, Niccolò and Tommaso remained on the best of terms with both father and son, contributing their efforts to overcome the disabilities under which both were placed. In 1438, for example, they were lending their support to a private petition of Agnolo's by which he may have sought the cancellation of his magnate status.[78] Although their efforts on that occasion failed, they must have continued to try to assist Agnolo politically. Tommaso may have influenced the fact that, although Agnolo did not obtain a majority in the scrutiny of

[75] Tommaso's will of 10 Mar. 1462, Notarile Antecos. M570, fo. 90ᵛ.
[76] Ibid., fo. 87ᵛ.
[77] Francesco d'Antonio Palmieri had married Tommaso's aunt, Dada Cambi: Diplomatico, Acquisto Soderini, 27 July 1414.
[78] Cf. Niccolò Soderini to Agnolo Strozzi, 1, 19 May, and 6, 15, 20 June 1438, Carte Strozz., ser. 3, 130, fos. 240ʳ, 244ʳ, 261ʳ, 262ʳ. Agnolo's magnate status was finally revoked in Feb. 1441: Provv., 131, fos. 306ᵛ–307ᵛ.

1458, the *accoppiatori* restored his name to the election bags, allowing him later to become Prior.[79] As Agnolo did not join in the anti-Medici movement of 1465–6, he must have raised his political capital with Tommaso and other members of the Medici circle, and he was subsequently elected as a member of the *Balìa* of that year. As we shall see, in 1471 he again provided political assistance to the Medici, as he helped to effect a reconciliation between Tommaso and Lorenzo di Piero. This must have won him Lorenzo's gratitude, which may in turn have contributed to his inclusion in the *Balìa* created after this conflict had been resolved in July, 1471.[80]

In this case, the influence of the Soderini brothers helped to win Agnolo acceptance into the post-1434 regime. In other cases as well, Tommaso and Niccolò must have furthered their friends' careers, whether by recommending them to the Medici, as Tommaso repeatedly did, or by using their own opportunities to fulfil what was recognized as a mutual obligation of assistance among friends. The Del Cittadino and Ceffini, for example, undoubtedly benefited from Tommaso's support, and they may have owed their success at gaining posts in leading magistracies to him as well as to their other friends within the Medici group.[81] Indeed, both Tommaso and Niccolò possessed many opportunities for independent patronage, when serving as *accoppiatore*, Standardbearers of Justice or of the Company, as members of the communal councils which voted on all legislation, and as members of the scrutiny councils which determined citizens' eligibility for office. As Tommaso used his position as

---

[79] Rubinstein, *Government*, 124 n. 2.

[80] On Agnolo's role as mediator see Chap. 7. For his membership in the *Balìe*, Rubinstein, *Government*, 298, 307. Agnolo's father had been included in the *Balìa* of 1434, but not again until 1452, when he received ex officio membership as a knight: ibid. 251, 277.

[81] Tommaso's friendship with the Ceffini family was already well established when he urged Giovanni de' Medici to see that Mauro Ceffini was appointed as *Podestà* of Città di Castello: Tommaso to Giovanni, 5 Mar. 1450, MAP, viii, 203. By the 1470s Tommaso was also investing in Salvestro Ceffini's firm: Sig., Min., 10, fo. 183ʳ, 5 Nov. 1474. The Ceffini were repeatedly present in the *Balìe* of the 15th c., as were the Del Cittadino, as artisans, from 1466. Writing to Lorenzo de' Medici in Aug. 1479, Tommaso's son Paolantonio mentioned that 'we are very obligated' to Simone del Cittadino: MAP, xxxvii, 630.

accoppiatore to benefit his immediate family, so he presumably took advantage of this and other opportunities to advance the interests of *parenti* and friends. Indeed, he was expected at times to use his political position in the interests of a much wider circle than his immediate relatives and friends. For example, in 1454 a confraternity to which Tommaso belonged—the Jesù Pellegrino company—decided that their members who were 'weak in the scrutiny' should be helped by the more prominent confrères. Tommaso, who was serving in the scrutiny council at the time, was among those who were expected to lend their aid.[82] Thus the incident shows not only how confraternities could become political pressure groups, but how even less immediate personal ties could create obligations and loyalties extending widely within the ruling group.

By giving assistance to those connected to him, so Tommaso could expect to receive it in return, and this was true in the political as in the private sphere. Perhaps the clearest illustration is offered by Tommaso's relations with one of the most distinguished of his sons-in-law, Maso degli Albizzi. After the *parentado* with Maso, Tommaso tried to promote his political career, successfully urging Piero de' Medici in 1459, for example, to see that Maso was appointed to the Signoria.[83] In 1470, as we shall see, Tommaso was able to appeal to Maso, as to others of his friends, to see that action was taken which temporarily removed two of his rivals from Florence at a critical moment in an internal struggle for power.[84]

Apart from such concrete instances of support, relatives and friends within the ruling circle could be useful by serving as a natural group within which a Florentine could lobby for his policies, as they were undoubtedly more susceptible to arguments voiced repeatedly and privately by those close to them. When the Milanese ambassador asserted in 1470 that Tommaso argued for his policy 'with those whom he could trust', he may have meant friends and relatives, as well as

---

[82] Domenico Pollini, 'Ricordanze', BNF, Magl., viii, 1282, fo. 45ʳ.
[83] Tommaso to Piero, 21 Dec. 1459, MAP, xvi, 276.
[84] See Chap. 7.

those of a similar political slant.[85] The repeated political
collaboration between Tommaso and Giovanni Lanfredini
must also have depended on the close friendship between
them, for, as Sacramoro wrote on another occasion, Giovanni
was Tommaso's 'body and soul'.[86] Moreover, the fact that
various *parenti* of Niccolò Soderini—Paolo Gerini, Gherardo
Davizzi, and Giovanni Macinghi—were all punished after
the anti-Medici movement of 1465–6 may well be a result
not only of the tendency for citizens to rally to the defence of
their *parenti* but also of susceptibility to the arguments of a
relative as eloquent and impassioned as was Niccolò.[87] The
political value of relatives and friends undoubtedly contributed to the Florentines' desire to promote their careers
through scrutiny councils and, in the case of citizens as
exalted as Tommaso, to act as *accoppiatori* for the scrutiny.
As we shall see, Tommaso was so anxious to be present for
the scrutiny of 1471 that he returned in haste from an
embassy abroad, and part of his motivation was undoubtedly
to secure the presence of those close to him within important
magistracies at a time when his own political position was
insecure.[88]

Yet, while this kind of co-operation was evidently important to a Florentine's career, the political aid which relatives
and friends could give possessed certain limitations. In
Tommaso's case, some of these were of his own making,
for, by serving as a vehicle whereby suspect families could
improve their relations with the Medici or the Medici
consolidate their connections with other families, he was
furthering other's interests more than his own. Of this he
was undoubtedly fully aware, and when he was on a good
footing with the Medici he was happy to further their
connections knowing that this would ultimately serve his
own ends. Indeed, he himself implied as much when he

[85] Cf. below, Chap. 7.
[86] Sacramoro to the Duke, 12 Aug. 1471, ASMi, SPE, Firenze, 283. However,
this friendship in turn was undoubtedly based on the fact that Giovanni, like
Tommaso, was a great admirer of Venice: Sacramoro to the Duke, 9 Feb. 1472, ibid.
[87] They were either exiled or deprived of political rights: Otto di Guardia,
periodo repubblicano, 224, fos. 137ᵛ–138ʳ, 159ʳ⁻ᵛ, 162.
[88] See Chap. 7.

appealed to Piero de' Medici to see that Maso degli Albizzi was included in the Signoria. Referring to the noted partisanship which Maso's father Luca had displayed for the Medici cause, Tommaso justified his request on the grounds that 'just as Luca was always your man, his children will be the same'. Therefore, Tommaso went on, 'it is in the interest of us, your true friends, to advance him'.[89] As Maso was duly appointed Prior, he probably recognized a lesser obligation to Tommaso than to Piero, the real author of his appointment. Consequently, while Tommaso might rely on Maso for aid in certain matters, it is unlikely that he could do so where Medici interests were concerned. In fact there is, for example, no indication that Maso followed Tommaso into anti-Medici activities in 1470–1.

Apart from the implications of Tommaso's relationship with the Medici, there were other limitations to the assistance which might be offered the Soderini by those close to them. On the one hand, they could not always rely on having *parenti* and *amici* in key offices, while personal obligations must at times have overlapped and contradicted one another in a manner which prevented them from being clear guides to political behaviour. More importantly, the political loyalty of even those closest to them was insufficiently reliable to serve as a permanent basis of support. Citizens active in the political process had their own agendas to consider when making political decisions, whether these involved obligations to other powerful figures within or outside Florence, the effects of their action on themselves or their families, or the welfare of the city as a whole. Any of these might prove a more powerful motive than a personal connection with the Soderini. It is, for example, undoubtedly significant that despite his friendship for both Soderini brothers, Agnolo degli Strozzi followed neither of them into their anti-Medici stand, evidently concluding that his best interests lay in avoiding such risky political enterprises.

[89] Tommaso to Piero, 21 Dec. 1459, MAP, xvi, 276. Although Tommaso was himself one of the *accoppiatori*, he explicitly stated that he wanted Piero to be responsible for Maso's appointment, as though anxious to advance Piero's interests as well as recognizing that Medici influence would be much more effective than his own.

Indeed, as we have already seen, if Tommaso or Niccolò really wished to guide Florence's political destinies, they needed more than personal bonds with powerful citizens. Rather, they had to convince their fellow citizens that the policy which they advocated was in their or the city's best interest. Here it was the brothers' intelligence, and in particular their eloquence, which served to win them political notability and a sizeable following. We have already seen how in 1454 Tommaso's defence of the status quo rested principally on his convincing the Standardbearer of Justice that his best interest lay in continuing the existing interrelation between the '*borse, Balìe* and *catasto*'. Again, in 1465, persuasion was the method he used both to convince Luca Pitti to be reconciled with Piero de' Medici, and to dissuade his brother from measures which might further injure the Medici group. Similarly, the moments of Niccolò Soderini's major political success—in the early 1450s and 1465—depended not primarily on personal bonds within the ruling group but rather on his particular political stand and on the energy and conviction which he displayed in carrying out his objectives. The same qualities were undoubtedly important in winning him the support of even those relatives who were exiled with him in 1466, and may have helped create the following which made Cosimo de' Medici treat him with such caution in the early 1450s.

If in contrast it seems that Tommaso's political success was determined by his personal connection with the Medici, the fact remains that the bond between Tommaso and the Medici was based not merely on friendship or on the marriage tie but on a community of interests and political objectives. As we shall see, when these interests and objectives altered, the personal bond and the advantages to be derived from it were insufficient to ensure continuing co-operation in the political sphere. Moreover, when Tommaso moved into opposition to the Medici, he succeeded in putting together an effective political group in whose formation personal ties could have had only minimal importance by comparison with the common political interests uniting those involved. Then, it was Tommaso's political stand and his capacities of persuasion and manipulation, not just through relatives and friends but through the city's complex political system, which made him such a formidable enemy, as he could equally prove such a valuable friend.[90]

[90] For these incidents, see Chap. 7.

6. Tommaso at the Pinnacle of Power

During the last years of Piero de' Medici's life—1466 to 1469—the careers of Niccolò and Tommaso Soderini demonstrated what the political winners and losers could expect in Medicean Florence. While Tommaso benefited from the reconfirmed authority of the inner circle and from Piero de' Medici's unchallenged leadership of the regime to increase his political status, Niccolò gradually saw his hopes of returning in triumph to Florence disappear. Instead of his dream of a more stable patrician republic, he saw his native city becoming increasingly subject to personal Medici rule, under which citizens like his brother dominated the political scene.

After his departure from Florence, Niccolò did his best to alter his city's destiny by trying to construct a coalition of forces to overthrow the Medici regime and restore the exiles to Florence. To this end he visited not only Borso d'Este of Ferrara, but the Signoria of Venice and the Venetian Captain, Bartolomeo Colleoni, who was a military power in his own right.[1] Meanwhile other exiles were also trying to drum up support for an attack on Florence, arguing that there remained in the city many supporters of the traditional constitution who were merely waiting for an opportunity to

[1] On the exiles' movements, see Malipiero, *Annali veneti*, 210–11; Belotti, *Colleoni*, 357 ff; Romanin, *Storia di Venezia*, iv. 326–7; *Cronaca di anonimo veronese*, 241. On Niccolò Soderini's movements in particular, see Municchi, *La fazione*, 139–40, 142–3, 152; Nicodemo Tranchedini to Bianca Maria and Galeazzo Maria Sforza, 23 Sept., 13 Oct. 1466, ASMi, SPE, Firenze, 272; ASV, Sen. Secr., 23, fos. 7ᵛ–8ʳ, 11ʳ⁻ᵛ.

rise again against the Medici regime. This threat from the Florentine exiles was sufficiently serious to call forth a response from the restored Medici circle. Late in 1466 they launched a propaganda campaign designed to prove that they possessed the confidence and support of the entire citizen body. The defeated faction, they maintained, represented merely a self-interested and misguided handful of dissidents, who had been expelled by popular will and who could therefore expect no further backing in Florence.[2] In order to spread this message, and, more importantly, to gauge the reaction of the major Italian powers to the exiles' claims, the Florentine government also dispatched ambassadors to all the principal states in Italy. It was an indication of the degree of Medici control in Florence, and of the continuing, if latent, resentment towards Piero's ascendancy, that the citizens chosen for this task were not merely those 'experienced in state affairs', but, as Piero wrote to the rulers of Milan, 'my own very trusted friends'.[3] Among these pro-Medici ambassadors was Tommaso Soderini, who was appointed along with Jacopo Guicciardini as envoy to both Venice and Milan.[4]

From the start, the Florentines were concerned as to how the Venetians would respond to their embassy, for the latter had clearly listened, at least, to the exiles' plans. Niccolò Soderini, for example, was received by the Venetian Signoria, and although he was sent away with only a tiny subsidy, the Venetians did relay his proposals to their Captain, Bartolomeo Colleoni.[5] Moreover, once Tommaso and Jacopo arrived, the Venetians adopted an intransigent position,

---

[2] Cf. the Florentine Signoria's letter to the King of France, 23 Sept. 1466, in e.g. Municchi, *La fazione*, App., 133–5; and to the Signoria of Venice, Sig., *1a* Canc., 45, fos. 105ᵛ–106ʳ; Palmieri, *Annales*, 184; Parenti, 'Ricordi politici', fo. 73ʳ.

[3] Piero de' Medici to Bianca Maria and Galeazzo Maria Sforza, 27 Sept. 1466, Milan, Bibl. Ambros., MS Z.247. Sup., fo. 223.

[4] For Tommaso and Jacopo's instructions see Sig., Leg. e Comm., 16, fos. 41ʳ–44ʳ. On the embassy, cf. Palmieri, *Annales*, 184; Belotti, *Colleoni*, 364.

[5] Cf. ASV, Sen. Secr., 23, fos. 7ᵛ–8ʳ and 11ʳ⁻ᵛ, 9, 17 Oct. 1466; *Cronaca di anonimo veronese*, 241; Belotti, *Colleoni*, 360–3. The Venetians were really none too anxious for war, but were pressured by their Captain, Bartolomeo Colleoni, into supporting him: cf. also Romanin, *Storia di Venezia*, iv. 326–7.

refusing either to expel the Florentine exiles from Venetian territory or to promise that Colleoni would not undertake an expedition against Florence.[6] After receiving this reply and hearing from the Milanese ambassador of the comings and goings between the ducal palace and Colleoni's seat, Tommaso and Jacopo must have reported that the Venetians were definitely intending to support the Florentine exiles, for they were directed by their government to proceed immediately to the second part of their mission, at Milan. This they did, after warning the Venetians that the Florentines would be ready for any action being planned against them.[7]

On arriving in Milan the Florentine ambassadors tried to persuade the young Duke, Galeazzo Maria Sforza, to prepare for war, as only this, they argued, would convince the Venetians to abandon their belligerent intentions. Setting the example themselves, they presented a Florentine request to be allowed to hire some 600 Milanese men-at-arms, and although the Duke seemed in no hurry to prepare his own men, he was happy for the Florentines to assume some of their salaries. In fact, he argued that 600 men-at-arms were too few for Florence in the threatening circumstances, and Tommaso and Jacopo needed little persuasion to agree. On 13 November they wrote privately to Piero de' Medici, reporting the Duke's suggestion and adding their own advice that authority be granted to a group of high officials to hire a much larger number of soldiers and to impose the taxes necessary for their pay. However, they asked Piero to keep their advice secret, as they did not want other citizens to know that they had written their opinion so freely to him.[8] Clearly, despite the recent confirmation of Piero's primacy,

[6] Cf. the Venetian Senate's replies to Tommaso and Jacopo, 21, 25 Oct. 1466, ASV, Sen. Secr., 23, fo. 12r–v.

[7] ASV, Cons. dei Dieci, Misti, 17, fo. 47r (8 Nov. 1466); Guicciardini, *Memorie di famiglia*, 31–2. The ambassadors were given permission to leave Venice on 27 Oct. 1466, Sig., Leg. e Comm., 16, fos. 50v–51r.

[8] Tommaso and Jacopo to Piero, 13 Nov. 1466, MAP, xvi, 212. By the time the ambassadors had written, the Florentine government had already taken action similar to that which they suggested: Balìe, 30, fos. 59v–62r, 7–8 Nov. 1466. On the Duke's reluctance to prepare his own troops and eagerness to persuade the Florentines to hire them, cf. Marsilio Andreasi to Lodovico Gonzaga, 10, 14, 17, 20 Nov. 1466, ASMa, Carteggio degli inviati, Milano, 1623.

he was still regarded very much as a private citizen; acknow-
ledgement of his real but unofficial public influence had to
be concealed for fear of giving offence to citizens unwilling
to abandon traditional government procedures and ideals.
Nevertheless, at the same time, Tommaso and Jacopo were
acting as spokesmen for Medici policy. This was evident in
their response regarding the captain of the troops whom they
had been authorized to hire. Since Piero's survival in Florence
might depend on the political allegiance of the city's soldiers,
the ambassadors were prepared to allow him the final word
on the question. When the Duke of Milan generously allowed
the Florentine ambassadors to select whichever captain they
wished, they opted for Roberto da Sanseverino on the
grounds that he was Piero's choice, even though Roberto
was unpopular at Florence.[9]

This military issue provided a further instance of the
personal nature of the Milanese–Medici connection, and the
manner in which the ambassadors furthered it. The Duke
hoped that, as a preparation for war, the Florentines would
grant him an annual subsidy of some 30,000 ducats in return
for his promise to supply the city with 2,000 cavalry whenever she should need them. Anxious for the cash, he suggested that Piero de' Medici should advance the money and
recover it later from funds allocated for the purpose by the
Florentine government.[10] Whether the plan went into effect
is unclear, for although the subsidy was apparently approved
by the Florentine councils in January or February 1467, the
method of payment was not recorded.[11] However, such
instances of the Medici's making payments on the city's

---

[9] Marsilio to Lodovico, 14, 19, 21, 24, 26, 27 Nov. 1466, ASMa, Carteggio
degli inviati, Milano, 1623.

[10] No formal statement of this proposal exists. However, it was mentioned in
some form in: Sig., Min., 7, fos. 58ᵛ–59ʳ (mid-Jan. 1467, instructions for the
Florentine orators to Milan); Marsilio to Lodovico, 11 Dec. 1466, ASMa, Carteggio
degli inviati, Milano, 1623; Nicodemo Tranchedini to the Duke of Milan, 3 Jan.
1467, ASMi, SPE, Firenze, 273; Guicciardini, *Memorie di famiglia*, 32.

[11] Although no legislation on the subject is extant in the Provvisioni, it was
referred to not only in Sig., Min., 7, fos. 58ᵛ–59ʳ, but by Parenti, 'Ricordi politici',
fo. 75ʳ, and F. L. Marks, 'The Development of the Institutions of Public Finance at
Florence During the Last Sixty Years of the Republic, unpublished Ph.D. thesis,
University of Oxford, 1954, p. 39.

behalf were quite normal, both because the Medici served as one of the city's principal contacts with powers abroad, and because of the convenience offered by their bank for transferring money. Yet this function, which depended on the leading citizens' ratifying repayment to the Medici, gave them a key role in public finance, and ensured that Medici interests were increasingly intertwined with those of the state.

For Tommaso, one of the most important features of his embassies was the opportunity which they provided to make contacts abroad. In Medicean Florence the most significant foreign power after 1450 was always Milan, and Tommaso, like many other prominent citizens, tried to use his position as ambassador to establish his own special relationship with the Duke. This ambition was the more easily realizable in Tommaso's case because several of the Sforza's closest friends in Florence had recently been exiled, and Galeazzo Maria must have been anxious to create a bond with other authoritative citizens. He certainly gave Tommaso and Jacopo a warm welcome and treated them graciously while they were with him.[12] After his return to Florence in early December 1466, Tommaso was careful to build on this initial goodwill, letting the Duke know that he was acting in his interests. When, for example, the question of the Duke's subsidy came before the Florentine councils in January 1467 and, like so many financial bills, encountered serious resistance, Tommaso went before the assemblies to assure them of the sincerity of the Duke's promises of aid. He himself later reminded the Duke of his support on this occasion,[13] while the Milanese ambassador, Nicodemo Tranchedini, reported, on the basis of what Tommaso and others had told him, that Soderini 'eagerly favours what is in your honour and benefit', and that he was among those who 'are sincerely on our side'.[14]

---

[12] On the Duke's treatment of the Florentine ambassadors, cf. Marsilio Andreasi to Lodovico Gonzaga, 11, 12, 16, 20 Nov. 1466, ASMa, Carteggio degli inviati, Milano, 1623. It was normal for princes to seek the goodwill of foreign ambassadors by giving them money or other gifts: Maulde-La-Clavière, *La Diplomatie*, ii, particularly pp. 388 ff.

[13] Tommaso to the Duke, 16 Nov. 1474, ASMi, SPE, Venezia, 360.

[14] Tranchedini to the Duke, 15 Jan. 1467, and to the Dowager Duchess, 2 June 1467, ASMi, SPE, Firenze, 273.

Although Tommaso might try to win the Duke's goodwill by furthering his objectives in Florence, this goal never took precedence over his commitment to the interests of his native city. Indeed, his emergence as an intermediary between Florence and the Sforza court brought Tommaso increased responsibility for bringing Milanese policy into line with Florence's wishes, even if this seemed to threaten his personal relations with the Milanese ruler. In January 1467, for example, it became obvious that Bartolomeo Colleoni was preparing to attack Florence. In the circumstances, Galeazzo Maria should have been mobilizing his forces for Florence's defence, and the leading Florentines were dismayed that he was taking no action. Tommaso Soderini, Piero de' Medici, and another leading Medici partisan, Otto Niccolini, consequently led what the Milanese ambassador described as a verbal attack on ducal policy. After pointing out Florence's danger, they accused Galeazzo in the strongest terms of merely trying to extract money from the city. Moreover, they warned that they might lose popular support if it seemed, as the exiles had been claiming, that Milan was not really on the side of the restored Medici regime.[15]

This rather bellicose exchange was not typical of Tommaso's contacts with Sforza's representatives in Florence. More normal was the occasion on which Piero de' Medici advised the ambassador to discuss a particular issue with Tommaso, possibly in the expectation that Tommaso would support his own point of view.[16] Alternatively, Tommaso might act formally in presenting the requests of the inner circle of the regime to the Milanese envoy. In January 1467 he and Luigi Guicciardini served as spokesmen for the *Pratica* when they sought an assurance from the Milanese and Neapolitan ambassadors that Agnolo Acciaiuoli would not be allowed to leave his confines in the Kingdom of Naples to join the exiles' planned attack on Florence.[17]

---

[15] On the verbal battle, see Tranchedini to the Duke, 15, 19 Jan. 1467, ibid. During the internal conflict in Florence, the Sforza had been inclined to show some sympathy for Piero's opponents, and therefore the exiles' claims were not without some semblance of reality: cf. e.g. Rubinstein, *Government*, 137.

[16] Tranchedini to the Duke, 31 Dec. 1466, ASMi, SPE, Firenze, 273.

[17] Tranchedini to the Duke and Duchess of Milan, 20 Jan. 1467, ibid.

As this incident suggests, Tommaso was an important figure in Florence's relations not just with Milan but with foreign powers in general. Naples figured largely in his foreign contacts, as the King of Naples emerged during the 1460s as Florence's second major ally. The Aragonese house of Naples had already been connected with the Sforza, both through a marriage alliance arranged in 1455, and, after King Alfonso's death in 1458, by the assistance which Francesco Sforza had given Alfonso's illegitimate son Ferrante in his battle against the Angevin claimants to the Neapolitan throne. Having won control of the southern kingdom, Ferrante remained a friend of the Duke, and Naples and Florence therefore formed a natural block with Milan against Venice, the Venetian Pope, and their minor satellites. Once war with Venice threatened, this connection was consolidated by a formal alliance in January 1467.

Tommaso's importance for Florence's southern ally was indicated shortly thereafter when, in August 1467, King Ferrante's eldest son, the Duke of Calabria, led his father's forces to Florence's defence. He was then instructed by Ferrante to discuss all important issues with certain leading Florentines, one of whom was Tommaso.[18] Other states also recognized the importance of Tommaso's political support in their relations with Florence. In the same month, August 1467, the Ferrarese ambassador sounded out Tommaso along with other prominent citizens about his master's offer to mediate peace between Colleoni and the Florence–Milan–Naples league.[19] Clearly, Tommaso, along with Piero and a few other prominent Florentines, was one of that small but influential group who dealt constantly, if often informally, with major government affairs.

Tommaso's authoritative position was reflected and reinforced by the series of high offices which he occupied during 1467 and 1468. In March 1467 he became one of the *Otto di Guardia*, elected by the *Cento* for a six-month term.

---

[18] The King of Naples to the Duke of Calabria, 30 Aug. 1467, in Trinchera (ed.), *Codice aragonese*, 324.

[19] Francesco Naselli to Borso d'Este, 4 Aug. 1467, ASMo, Carteggio degli ambasc., Firenze, 1.

The role of this *Otto* was particularly crucial for, by the time of their appointment, the exiles' efforts and Colleoni's ambition were coalescing to produce a military threat from abroad and a growing danger of subversion at home. As the magistracy responsible for state security, the *Otto* were the obvious public body to respond to these challenges, at least until the actual outbreak of war required the appointment of the special war magistracy, the *Dieci di Balìa*. Recognizing this, the leading citizens introduced legislation granting the *Otto* special powers over both internal conspiracies and foreign attack.[20] Moreover, once the *Otto* had been elected, the principal Florentines decided that they possessed sufficient personal authority and experience to take on the more extensive powers of the *Dieci* once war was declared.[21]

Before the *Otto* had even begun work, Tommaso had to abandon his colleagues in order to take up the post of Standardbearer of Justice, as the *accoppiatori* included his name among the candidates for the office during the months of March and April 1467.[22] Once he had completed his term as head of the city's executive, he returned to his original duties, which were almost immediately increased by the *Otto*'s promotion on 6 May 1467 to the *Dieci di Balìa*. By then Bartolomeo Colleoni, accompanied by the Florentine exiles and backed by Venetian money and troops, had begun his offensive against Florence. Consequently, the leading citizens acted on their original plan of adding two prominent citizens, including Piero de' Medici, to the *Otto*, and the resultant ten were granted the *Dieci*'s usual powers over the management of the war, foreign affairs, troop hire, and peace negotiations for the duration of their six-month term.[23] Subsequently, these *Dieci* were confirmed in office for a second term, on the grounds not only that they were experienced, wise, and competent but that their direction of the

---

[20] Provv., 157, fo. 191^{r-v}, 14 Jan. 1467. The appointment of the *Otto* is recorded in Tratte, 81, fo. 6^r.

[21] Tranchedini to the Duke and Duchess of Milan, 30 Jan. 1467, ASMi, SPE, Firenze, 273.

[22] Tratte, 202, fo. 50^r.

[23] On the creation of the *Dieci*, see Tratte, 81, fo. 6^v; Rinuccini, *Ricordi storici*, p. cvii; Provv., 158, fos. 48^v–51^v.

city's war effort during their first term had been 'diligent and praiseworthy'.[24] Thus, Tommaso and his colleagues were permitted to exercise their extraordinary powers for a full year.

As a member of the *Dieci*, Tommaso made further contacts with the foreign power of which he had become such a partisan—the Sforza Duke of Milan. In late May the Duke decided on the unusual step of leading his troops personally to Florence's defence, and Tommaso was sent as the city's delegate not only to deal with military matters but also to express their immense gratitude for this indication of support.[25] However, as Galeazzo later argued, he had come south only to fend off Colleoni until sufficient Florentine and Neapolitan forces had been gathered, and he had therefore barely arrived in the war zone in the Romagna before he was announcing his imminent return to Lombardy. The Florentines, on the other hand, were hoping that he would remain to lead their combined armies to a decisive victory, and did their best to persuade him to stay. Galeazzo's decision to visit Florence in late July 1467 was motivated in large part by this problem, as he hoped to convince the Florentines that they would have to grant him additional funds if he was to remain in the field beyond mid-August. On this occasion Tommaso was one of twelve citizens appointed to meet with the Duke,[26] and the talks between the two sides rapidly became acrimonious. In pressing for further financing, the young Duke apparently acted in an arrogant and objectionable fashion, for the Milanese ambassador, horrified at the

[24] Ibid., fos. 131ᵛ–133ᵛ; Cento, 1, fo. 65ʳ. Cf. the *Pratica* of 23 Sept. 1467, CP, 60, fos. 1ʳ–2ʳ. In Mar. 1468, under Piero's influence, it was decided to create a new *Dieci* rather than try to confirm the existing magistrates for a third term: Medici, *Lettere*, i. 31–2. On the *Dieci*, see in particular Pampaloni, 'Gli organi', 270 ff.

[25] Cf. the *Dieci* to the Duke, 25 May 1467, ASMi, SPE, Firenze, 273; the *Dieci* to Tommaso, 26, 29, 30 May 1467, Dieci, Miss., 3, fos. 46ᵛ–47ʳ, 48ʳ⁻ᵛ. When the *Dieci* recalled Tommaso on 30 May, they wrote that they wished him to return '*che per la prudentia et auctorità vostra desideriamo la vostra presenza*': ibid.

[26] Galeazzo Maria Sforza (24 July 1467) and Tranchedini (29 July 1467) to the Dowager Duchess of Milan, ASMi, SPE, Firenze, 273. On Galeazzo's visit to Florence, cf. also Francesco Naselli to Borso d'Este, 23 July 1467, ASMo, Carteggio degli ambasc., Firenze, 1; Parenti, 'Ricordi politici', fos. 77ᵛ–79ʳ; Dei, 'Cronica', fo. 26ʳ; Rinuccini, *Ricordi storici*, p. cvii; Belotti, *Colleoni*, 384–5, *Storia di Milano*, vii. 240–1.

damage being done to Milanese—Florentine relations, felt it necessary to intervene. He begged the principal Sforza partisans, including Piero de' Medici and Tommaso Soderini, to make allowances for the Duke's lack of his father's 'dexterity and tact', citing the Duke's youth and the long friendship between the two states as reasons for them to overlook his offensive behaviour. This the citizens agreed to do, for the sake of maintaining what they regarded as a necessary friendship between Florence and the Sforza house. However, they made it clear that, while they would tolerate Galeazzo's behaviour, they placed little reliance on either his wisdom or his ability.[27]

The leading Florentines' opinion of Galeazzo must further have declined in mid-August, when, despite a promise of extra subsidies, he acted on his previous threat and left for home, taking most of his soldiers with him. His decision infuriated the *Dieci*, for they felt he had capriciously deprived them of their opportunity to bring the war to a rapid and successful close. Although mollified in part by the explanations of Galeazzo's mother, the Dowager Duchess Bianca, they remained extremely angry at the young Duke's wilful behaviour. It had, they wrote to the Duchess, not only endangered the remaining allied forces but had brought into question the friendship between the two states.[28] Indeed, although the close relationship between the two governments remained intact, Galeazzo's reputation had suffered in the eyes of the Florentines, and their faith in Milan's reliability was undermined.[29]

The departure of the Duke, with its implications of a costly

---

[27] Tranchedini to the Duchess of Milan, 29 July 1467, ASMi, SPE, Firenze, 273.

[28] The *Dieci* to the Duchess, 18 Aug. 1467; Tranchedini to the Duke, 23 Aug. 1467; Tranchedini and Sacramoro to the Duke, Sept. [no day] 1467; all ibid. The official explanation for Galeazzo's departure was his fear of an attack from Savoy, which remained hostile to the Sforza and sympathetic to Venice during this Colleoni War.

[29] Cf. the comments rife in Florence that Galeazzo left the allied camp 'through fear' (Rinuccini, *Ricordi storici*, p. cvii) and that his presence there had merely been a nuisance to his commanders (Ammirato, *Istorie*, v. 372). Tommaso himself must have questioned his earlier judgement that Galeazzo would prove a good ruler: Tommaso and Jacopo Guicciardini to Piero de' Medici, 13 Nov. 1466, MAP, xvi, 212.

and lengthy war, increased the Florentines' desire for a mediated settlement. As the *Dieci* were aware, Florence could not for long maintain the huge expenditure occasioned by the war, while the heavy tax burden was encouraging discontent with a government which many already viewed as repressive and oligarchic.[30] Although various peace negotiations had been underway since the beginning of the conflict, none had made any real progress, one of the major obstacles being that Florence's principal opponent, Venice, had never officially entered the war.[31] Already in conflict with the Turks, they had chosen to maintain a superficial neutrality in Italy, while surreptitiously supplying Colleoni with money and troops. However, as the war dragged on without Colleoni's gaining any clear hope of victory, the Venetians became less enthusiastic to maintain even this indirect participation, and the *Dieci* began to hope that a direct appeal to them might produce peace. Therefore when an opportunity arose, in the early autumn of 1467, to send an ambassador to Venice, the *Dieci* seized on the occasion as a chance to sound out the Venetians on the essential issue of peace.

As in 1463, the Florentine overture to Venice arose from the latter's efforts to prevent other Italian powers profiting from the trade with Constantinople. In 1467 they were interfering forcibly with other cities' traffic to the East, using the justification that ships sailing to the Turkish capital were carrying arms and ammunition to their enemies. It was on these grounds that, in the late summer of 1467, the Venetian fleet captured four vessels returning to Ancona from Constantinople, aboard which were several Florentine merchants with their goods. When these were summarily arrested by the Venetians, the Florentine Signoria not only wrote in protest to its Venetian counterpart, but also contemplated sending an ambassador to press for the release of the men and merchandise.[32] At this point Piero de' Medici, acting in

[30] On Florentines' desire for peace and for an extreme statement of the discontent occasioned in Florence by the war, cf. Francesco Naselli to Borso d'Este, 3, 4 Aug. and 17 Dec. 1467, ASMo, Carteggio degli ambasc., Firenze, 1.

[31] On these peace negotiations, see Belotti, *Colleoni*, 378, 381–2, 395 ff.; Maliperio, *Annali veneti*, 214, 228 ff.; Niccolini, 'Lettere', 36–8.

[32] On this incident, cf. Rubinstein, 'Michelozzo, 218–28; Malipiero, *Annali veneti*, 212; Belotti, *Colleoni*, 401–2; Palmieri, *Annales*, 187.

a semi-private capacity, had his bank manager at Venice sound out how the government would react if the ambassador were also to raise the question of peace. Although carefully non-committal, the Venetian reply did indicate that they would not refuse to listen,[33] and with this limited encouragement, Piero and the other leading citizens decided to go ahead. The citizen chosen for this delicate mission was Tommaso Soderini, and the reason for his appointment was probably connected with the Medici. Piero must have wanted someone in Venice with whom he could work closely, for he remained in complete control of Florence's participation in the peace negotiations. He personally handled all the correspondence relating to this aspect of Tommaso's mission, leaving only the commercial issue and minor matters for the *Dieci*'s official letters.

Although he began with high hopes, Tommaso's mission to Venice was not a success, and the reasons were manifold. On the one hand, Florence's allies were suspicious of the unilateral overture, which also threatened to offend the other powers conducting peace negotiations, particularly the Pope. Moreover, the *Dieci* realized that the Florentine populace might refuse the taxes necessary for war if they learned that serious peace talks were underway.[34] They therefore decided to keep the more important object of Tommaso's mission secret, and give him no formal commission in its regard. As Tommaso himself explained to some very suspicious Milanese ambassadors, his goal was merely to recover the Florentine goods; if the Venetians raised the question of peace, he was to reply that he had no commission to discuss it and was to write to Florence for directions.[35]

This was not, however, the approach which Tommaso took once he arrived in Venice in early November 1467.

[33] ASV, Sen. Secr., 23, fo. 73ᵛ, 12 Sept. 1467: Vittore Soranzo should reply to Giovanni Lanfredini that the Collegio have replied to his communication 'as lovers of peace . . . [who] are excellently disposed towards [Florence]. If [Florence] sends an ambassador, he will be welcomed and honoured . . .'

[34] This was the reason given by Piero de' Medici for the secrecy surrounding the mission: Tranchedini to the Duke, 3 Jan. 1468, ASMi, SPE, Firenze, 274.

[35] Giustiniano Cavitelli to the Duke, 4 Nov. 1467, ibid. 273. Although Tommaso's explanation fooled no one, it is impossible to determine exactly what his instructions were, as his commission is, perhaps significantly, not extant.

Instead of waiting for the Venetians to suggest terms, he himself took the initiative, and he presumably did so on instructions from the *Dieci*. In his first audience with the Venetian Signoria on 5 November 1467, he accused the Venetians of contravening the old friendship between the two states by aiding Colleoni and by seizing the Florentine merchants and their goods. After demanding the release of the latter, he broached the question of peace by assuring the Venetians that, although he spoke only in a private capacity, he was nevertheless sure that they could obtain a settlement if they wished. He therefore urged them to indicate whether or not they wanted to pursue the issue, as he would do his best to further a negotiation.[36] The Venetian response was fairly encouraging, for the Senate indicated its willingness to listen if Tommaso wished to go into further detail regarding peace, and also promised that the question of the Florentine goods would be settled equitably.[37] Meanwhile, Tommaso's report must have been favourable, for on the basis of what he wrote Piero undertook to send both the Milanese and Neapolitan ambassadors in person to their masters in order to obtain their agreement to participate in peace talks.

Although Tommaso was correct that the Venetians wanted peace, he was probably unaware that they were less than satisfied with his overture. According to the Milanese ambassador, they had been hoping for a Florentine envoy less close to Piero, so that they might, through his reports, try to influence the Florentines in the exiles' favour. Moreover, the

[36] This reconstruction of Tommaso's speech is drawn from the dispatch of the Milanese ambassador in Venice, Gherardo Colli, and from the preface to the Venetian Senate's reply to Tommaso: Gherardo Colli to the Duke and Duchess, 6 Nov. 1467, ASMi, SPE, Venezia, 353; 9 Nov. 1467, ASV, Sen. Secr., 23, fo. 85^{r-v}. Cf. Malipiero, *Annali veneti*, 218–19, 225–8, whose account is based on Venetian documents, but is not completely accurate.

[37] Tommaso had to make his presentation to the Signoria twice before he obtained a reply, and then the Senate had to choose between differing responses, of which they opted for the more cautious: reply of 9 Nov. ASV, Sen. Secr., 23, fo. 85^{r-v}. The Florentines felt that the Venetian response concerning their merchants' goods would indicate their position regarding peace, e.g. Piero de' Medici to Tommaso, 14 Nov. 1467, Carte Strozz., ser., 1, 352, fo. 1; Tommaso to the Duke and Duchess, 17 Nov. 1467, ASMi, SPE, Venezia, 353. According to Malipiero, *Annali veneti*, 225, the Venetians did intend to restore the goods only if peace were made.

ducal agent felt, they lost enthusiasm for Tommaso's mission
once they learned that he did not bear an official mandate to
make peace.[38] Presumably the Venetians were hoping that
the Florentine envoy would offer terms giving some satisfaction to the Florentine exiles and some compensation to
Colleoni for his efforts in the war. These hopes were disappointed when Tommaso made it clear in unofficial discussions that the allies would agree to neither of these terms. At
the same time it rapidly became doubtful whether Milan and
Naples would agree to the Venetians' desire for the talks to
be held at Venice. Although Tommaso assured the Doge that
this would be done, both the King and the Duke were
reluctant to send their mandates to Venice. Moreover, the
Duke even tried to disrupt the Florentine overture by offering
to the Venetians to negotiate peace on the league's behalf,
provided the talks were held in Milan![39]

In the light of this dissension among the allies, it is
understandable that by early December 1467 the Venetians
had decided to look elsewhere for a means of ending the
war. In particular, since the Pope was Venetian, they hoped
to persuade him to conclude the peace negotiations (which
he had been conducting desultorily for months) in a manner
favourable to Colleoni. To this end, they promised that
Colleoni would modify his demands and that they themselves
would end their resistance and join in the peace as a
principal.[40] In order to gain time for this negotiation with
the Pope without losing the possibility of concluding peace
with the Florentines, they kept this new development secret
from Tommaso. In fact, they succeeded in convincing Tommaso that they were sincerely interested in his overture, and
that the obstacles to it came from the allies' side. Thus, in
mid-December Tommaso wrote despondently to Piero de'
Medici, lamenting the allies' delay in sending their mandates
to Venice and attributing the Venetians' reluctance to discuss

[38] Gherardo Colli to the Duke, 6 Nov. 1467, ASMi, SPE, Venezia, 353.
[39] On this incident, cf. Gherardo to the Duke and a separate letter to the
Duchess, both of 25 Nov. 1467, ibid.; Malipieri, *Annali veneti*, 215–18, 221–4;
Belotti, *Colleoni*, 402–3.
[40] 8 Dec. 1467, ASV, Sen. Secr., 23, fo. 91ʳ. On the negotiations between Venice
and the Pope, cf. Belotti, *Colleoni*, 364, 378, 400–1, 403–4.

terms to the frantic attempts of the Florentine exiles to break
up a negotiation which they feared might go against them.
However, as Piero indicated in his reply, if the Venetians
wanted a conclusion along lines acceptable to the league, it
was there for the taking. The Venetians must, Piero wrote,
be insincere, and therefore Tommaso should consider breaking off the negotiations and proceeding to Milan, where a
conference to plan for the spring campaign was taking
place.[41]

However, Piero's advice was unofficial, and Tommaso did
not act on it. Undoubtedly, he agreed with Piero that peace
was essential, and hoped to obtain for himself the glory of
ending the war. In contrast, by the end of December most of
his colleagues had concluded that the overture to Venice had
proved a failure, and of the members of the *Dieci*, apparently
only Piero defended his decision to remain. Piero argued that
Tommaso's mission might prove the only road to peace, but
his colleagues and the Duke of Milan increasingly condemned Tommaso's remaining in Venice fruitlessly, and
urged that he move on to the second stage of his embassy, at
Milan. The Duke of Milan in particular saw Tommaso's
presence at Venice as a hindrance to the allies' war effort,
and many of Tommaso's fellow citizens agreed that by now
his mission was merely embarrassing and humiliating for the
league.[42] As criticism of the mission mounted, both Tommaso and his protector Piero found themselves in an awkward position, and this turned into extreme embarrassment
when, in late December, the Venetians finally announced
that they had transferred the peace talks to Rome. Their
gambit to the Pope had succeeded, and now they felt it safe
to inform the allies that peace would have to be sought
elsewhere.[43]

---

[41] Piero to Tommaso, 21 Dec. 1467, Carte Strozz., ser. 1, 352, fo. 7ʳ.

[42] From 21 Dec. 1467, pressed by Milan, Piero repeatedly warned Tommaso
that if he remained fruitlessly at Venice, both of them would be blamed: ibid. Cf.
also a later, unsigned, undated letter apparently from Piero to Tommaso: ibid.,
fo. 15.

[43] 22, 28 Dec. 1467, ASV, Sen. Secr., 23, fo. 92ʳ⁻ᵛ; Nicodemo Tranchedini to
the Duke, 1 Jan. 1467, ASMi, SPE, Firenze, 274. Cf. also Gherardo Colli to the
Duke, 28 Dec. 1468 (but actually referring to 1467), 31 Dec., ibid., Venezia, 354,
353; Malipiero, *Annali veneti*, 225–8, who states wrongly that this reply was given
to Tommaso early in December.

Tommaso's disillusionment and indignation on receiving this news can well be imagined, and in his response he must have threatened that, after this display of duplicity, the allies would no longer be interested in the peace negotiations at all. Afraid, therefore, that peace might elude them, the Venetians began publicly and privately to encourage Tommaso not to leave, promising that if the negotiation at Rome failed, they might still reach a settlement with him.[44] Tommaso's anxiety to come to a conclusion was such that, despite his experience of the Venetians' unreliability, he decided to remain, and once again Piero de' Medici supported him. Piero felt that if the talks at Rome should fail, the appeal to Venice would prove the only alternative to war, while the rest of the *Dieci* and the Milanese ambassador argued that this latest news was merely proof that the Venetians had no intention of reaching a conclusion.[45] However, Piero's will again prevailed, and the *Dieci* left it to Tommaso to decide whether he should remain for a few more days.[46] With this permission, Tommaso stayed on at Venice, apparently until the Duke threatened to withhold military support from Florence if the negotiations at Venice were not terminated. Only then, on 22 January 1468, did the *Dieci* decisively order Tommaso to leave Venice[47]—an order which by then he had already executed.

On his departure, Tommaso declared to the Milanese ambassador that he was now convinced that the Milanese had been right: the Venetians had merely been deceiving him

[44] In addition, the Senate hinted that the issue of the Florentine goods, on which they had been delaying for months, would now be settled: cf. the Senate's reply to Tommaso of 28 Dec. 1467, ASV, Sen. Secr., 23, fo. 92ᵛ. Cf. also Tranchedini to the Duke, 1 Jan. 1468, ASMi, SPE, Firenze, 274.

[45] Tranchedini to the Duke, 1 Jan. 1468, ibid.

[46] The *Dieci* to Tommaso, 2 Jan. 1468, Dieci, Miss., 3, fo. 163ᵛ, and 1 Jan. 1468 in Carte Strozz., ser 1, 352, fo. 6.

[47] The *Dieci* to Tommaso, 22 Jan. 1468, and, to Antonio Ridolfi, 23 Jan. 1468, Dieci, Miss., 3, fos. 169ᵛ–71ʳ; Piero to the Duke, 23 Jan. 1468, ASMi, SPE, Firenze, 274. On the Duke's attitude, cf. e.g. Pigello Portinari to Tommaso, 30 Dec. 1467, Carte Strozz., ser. 1, 352, fo. 9; the Duke to Gherardo Colli, 15 Jan. 1468, ASMi, SPE, Venezia, 354; Ugoletto Facino to Borso d'Este, 10 Jan. 1468, ASMo, Carteggio degli ambasc., Milano, 1. Shortly after Tommaso left Venice, the Venetians did restore the Florentine merchants' goods, hoping thereby to facilitate the conclusion of peace: e.g. Malipiero, *Annali veneti*, 229–30.

and had never had any intention of making peace.[48] His remark may have represented the first of his efforts to appease the Duke of Milan's wrath over his long and fruitless appeal to Venice. For months, Galeazzo Maria had been charging that Tommaso's presence had merely encouraged the Venetians in their obstinacy, and now it seemed that he had been proven correct. Besides exacerbating divisions within the league, Tommaso's negotiation at Venice was being blamed for undermining the work of the allied conference which had been called at Milan to concert plans for the following season's campaign. Although another delegate had been sent in Tommaso's place, Tommaso's remaining at Venice left the conference members unsure whether to plan for peace or war.[49] After Tommaso had arrived at Milan in late January, then, he had to face the Duke's anger, and his feelings towards Galeazzo could hardly have improved. Nevertheless, astute politician that he was, he must have devoted his attention both to restoring his own reputation and to repairing Florence's relations with the Duke of Milan.[50] As it happened, he received extra time in which to fulfil this objective, for various issues arose to require the presence of a Florentine representative at the ducal court, and, despite an early notice of recall, Tommaso, rather than his replacement, was eventually instructed to remain.[51]

The principal issue which kept Tommaso in Milan was the peace settlement which the Pope finally proposed in February 1468. Since the terms were favourable to Colleoni, the triple

---

[48] Gherardo Colli to the Duke, 15 Jan. 1468, ASMi, SPE, Venezia, 354.

[49] Cf. e.g. the *Dieci* to Tommaso, 22 Jan. 1468, Dieci, Miss., 3, fos. 169ᵛ–170ʳ.

[50] That this was necessary is suggested not only by the frantic efforts at self-justification of Piero and the *Dieci* (Piero to the Duke, and the *Dieci* to Antonio Ridolfi, 23 Jan. 1468, ibid., fos. 170ʳ–171ʳ, and ASMi, SPE, Firenze, 274), but by the recriminations between the Duke and Tommaso's replacement at Milan, Antonio Ridolfi: cf. Ugoletto Facino to Borso d'Este, 10 Jan. 1468, ASMo, Carteggio degli ambasc., Milano, 1. According to Ammirato, *Istorie*, v. 374, Tommaso also took part in these recriminations.

[51] Tommaso was initially ordered to return to Florence on 20 Feb. 1468: the *Dieci* to Tommaso and Antonio Ridolfi, 20 Feb. 1468, Dieci, Miss., 3, fo. 181ᵛ. However, this order must have been countermanded, for, on 21 April 1468, Antonio was ordered to return and Tommaso to stay: the *Dieci* to Tommaso and Antonio, 21 Apr. 1468, ibid., fo. 202ᵛ. No explanation was offered for this change in policy.

alliance rejected the accord, and further preparations for war had to be made before Paul II, pressed by the Venetians, would agree to the allies' terms.[52] According to the settlement finally concluded in April 1468, neither Colleoni nor the Florentine exiles obtained any concessions, and thus, for Niccolò Soderini, it marked the defeat of his hopes of overthrowing the Medici regime with Venetian backing. Although he continued to plot against the Florentine government, his conspiracies were no more than foredoomed attacks. With their failure, Niccolò was forced to retire into Venetian territory, where he received a small pension from the government, and was left free to seek what advantage he could from the shifting circumstances of Italian politics. Although he eventually gained a knighthood and, after his death, a tomb in Ravenna, these could have provided only an inadequate compensation for the loss of the power and the prestige which he had enjoyed in Florence.[53]

Meanwhile, Tommaso saw his efforts to regain the Duke's favour gradually succeed. By June 1468 Galeazzo Maria was feeling sufficiently warmly towards him to ask the Florentine authorities that his term in Milan be again extended so that he could act as the city's representative at the Duke's approaching wedding with Bona of Savoy.[54] Since permission was granted, Tommaso did not return to Florence until late July 1468, when he again proceeded to reinforce the Duke's goodwill by furthering his interests there. However, his relations with the Duke were never to regain quite the same footing as they had possessed in the autumn of 1466. Since

[52] Cf. Malipiero, *Annali veneti*, 230–6; Ammirato, *Istorie*, v. 374–6; Niccolini, 'Lettere', 38; Belotti, *Colleoni*, 404–9; Medici, *Lettere*, i. 30.

[53] On Niccolò's plot of 1468, see above, Chap. 5. On another of 1471 against Lorenzo de' Medici, see Sacramoro to the Duke of Milan, 1 Oct. 1471, ASMi, SPE, Firenze, 282 and 283. In 1468 Niccolò was knighted by the visiting Emperor Frederick III, while he was apparently granted a life-long pension from Venice: cf. e.g. Belotti, *Colleoni*, 409; Baldovinetti, Bibl. Moreniana, MS 339; Sacramoro to the Duke, 13 May 1469, ASMi, SPE, Firenze, 276.

[54] The Duke of Milan to Nicodemo Tranchedini, 4 June 1468, ASMi, SPE, Firenze, 274: The Duke stated in his request that Tommaso was 'very welcome and acceptable to us'. An example of Tommaso's protestations of loyalty to the Duke was provided in his letter of 2 June 1468, in which he asserted that in all things he attempted to gratify Galeazzo Maria, and that in this he acted '*bono animo, sincera fide, summa integritate, et toto posse*': ibid.

then Galeazzo's erratic behaviour, the Florentines' loss of
confidence in him, and the recurring recriminations during
the Colleoni War had driven a wedge between the Medici
circle and the Sforza court.[55].

The Florentines' changed attitude was evident in a series
of events of late 1468, in which Piero de' Medici and
Tommaso Soderini together continued to play the major role
in Florentine foreign policy. Earlier in 1468 Galeazzo Maria
had agreed with the King of France to subjugate Savoy to
their joint influence, and had persuaded his Italian allies to
promise to assist him if the Venetians should choose this
moment to attack his eastern flank.[56] At the end of July the
planned invasion of Savoy seemed imminent, and Galeazzo
was pressing his allies to fulfil their pledge. However, the idea
of becoming involved in another costly war for Galeazzo's
advantage was very unpopular in Florence, and the Duke's
requests that the city retain some Neapolitan troops in her
territory and send an ambassador to Venice to express
solidarity with him, aroused considerable resistance even
among Galeazzo's friends. In certain circles more sympathy
was evident for Venice than for Milan, and some Florentines
were even going so far as to consider breaking with Milan
completely in favour of a closer relationship with Venice.
During the course of the autumn even Piero de' Medici was
suspected by the Milanese of favouring this policy, and while
Piero's position is unclear, the threat of a potential alliance
with Venice was a useful weapon in his relations with the
Duke. Piero must have been fully aware that the Venetians
were interested in an alliance with Florence, not least because
during Tommaso's embassy of 1467 they had raised the
subject with him informally.[57]

---

[55] Apart from Galeazzo's actions mentioned above, he had made attempts to
hire Colleoni himself, and, while criticizing Florence's efforts to gain peace, had
himself been offering the Venetians peace in terms almost traitorous to the league:
Belotti, *Colleoni*, 368–9; Malipiero, *Annali veneti*, 215 ff.

[56] On this incident, cf. *Storia di Milano*, vii. 250–7; Perret, *Relations*, i.
494–511; Medici, *Lettere*, i. 90 n. 7, 154 n. 5, 541; Vaesen and Charavay, *Lettres
de Louis XI*, iii. 253–5, 259–60, 275–6.

[57] A Venetian patrician had mentioned the subject to Tommaso while he was on
his way to an official audience: Gherardo Colli to the Duke, 6 Nov. 1467, ASMi,
SPE, Venezia, 353. On the Milanese suspicions, cf. Medici, *Lettere*, i. 41, 46–50.

Nevertheless, during this crisis over Savoy the leading Florentines remained loyal to Milan, and Piero and Tommaso in particular did their best to see that the commitment to Galeazzo was fulfilled. Together they privately asked the Duke of Calabria to have his troops remain in Florentine territory, and Tommaso spoke in support of Galeazzo's demands in a *Pratica* called on the subject.[58] Moreover, Tommaso was an important figure in another *Pratica*, arranged specially by Piero and composed almost entirely of Sforza partisans, which recommended acceptance of the Milanese requests. On these occasions Tommaso's advocacy of the Duke's wishes was of considerable importance, and the Milanese ambassadors gave him full credit for his contribution to Florence's eventual acceptance of the Duke's requests.[59]

Given the widespread resistance in Florence to ducal policy, the Milanese were understandably concerned about who would be selected as ambassador to Venice to express Florence's solidarity with the Duke. As the Milanese wanted someone close to Piero and therefore likely to be on their side,[60] their views may have had an influence on the selection of Tommaso for the post. However, to his fellow citizens Tommaso's diplomatic experience at Venice may have been a more important reason for his election.[61] Indeed, despite the hopes of the Milanese, Tommaso and the other leading Florentines intended to pursue their own city's interests during the embassy, and these by no means completely coincided with the Duke's. Whereas Galeazzo Maria was anxious for war in order to increase his influence in Europe,

[58] Sacramoro to the Duke, 31 July 1468, ASMi, SPE, Firenze, 275; 5 Aug. 1468, CP, 60, fo. 30ʳ. Tommaso took the opportunity to express his devotion to the Duke's interests in this as in other issues: Tommaso to the Duke, 10 Sept. 1468, ASMi, SPE, Firenze, 275.
[59] 12 Sept. 1468, CP, 60, fos. 35ʳ⁻ᵛ; 13 Sept. 1468, ibid. 36ʳ⁻ᵛ; Nicodemo Tranchedini and Sacramoro to the Duke, 13 Sept. 1468, ASMi, SPE, Firenze, 275. On 9 Aug. the same ambassadors had described Tommaso as one of those who '*vanno a bon giocho*' regarding Milanese policy, while they again expressed their appreciation of Tommaso's assistance on 14 Sept.: ibid.
[60] e.g. in his instructions to Sacramoro the Duke specified that this ambassador should be '*amico et afficionato d'esso Piero*': 31 Aug. 1468, ASMi, SPE, Firenze, 275. Cf. also Tranchedini and Sacramoro to the Duke, 14 Sept. 1468, ibid.
[61] Cf. Agnolo della Stufa to the Duke, 4 Oct. 1468, ibid.

the Florentines were more concerned to see that peace was kept in Italy. It was an appeal for peace which was uppermost in Tommaso's instructions and in the message which he delivered once he arrived at Venice in late October 1468.[62]

As it happened, the Florentines obtained their wish, for the King of France soon decided against the planned attack on Savoy, and the threat of war dissipated.[63] Nevertheless, the incident had demonstrated how easily Italy might slip into another armed conflict, and statesmen were therefore increasingly anxious to find some means whereby these recurrent crises could be avoided. Ever since 1466 the idea of renewing the general Italian league of 1455 had been under discussion, but the Venetians had always resisted the idea in order to maintain a free hand against their enemies in Italy.[64] Now that the ambassadors of the various powers were gathered at Venice in an effort to avert another flare-up, they began again to discuss the possibility of reviving the Italian alliance,[65] but apparently no action was taken until most of them had left Venice in late November. Then, after Piero de' Medici had learned that the Venetians might now be more sympathetic to a general league, Tommaso must have been instructed to raise the issue with the Venetian government.[66] However, when Tommaso made the proposal, again only in a private capacity, the Venetians once again rejected it. Instead they hinted, as they had to Tommaso on previous occasions, at a preference for a separate alliance

[62] For Tommaso's emphasis on peace, cf. Giovaniacomo Riccio and Gherardo Colli to the Duke, 9 Nov. 1468; Tommaso to the Duke, 4 Nov. 1468, ASMi, SPE, Venezia, 354; Tommaso's contribution to the *Pratica* of 5 Aug. 1468, CP, 60, fo. 30ʳ. On Piero de' Medici's concern for peace, cf. his letter to Pigello Portinari, 10 Sept. 1468, ASMi, SPE, Firenze, 275. Tommaso's instructions of 4 Oct. 1468 are in Sig., Leg. e Comm., 16, fo. 173ʳ⁻ᵛ.

[63] Louis XI to Galeazzo Maria Sforza, 28 Sept., 13 Oct. 1468, in Vaesen and Charavay, *Lettres de Louis XI*, iii. 284–5; *Storia di Milano*, vii. 256–7.

[64] Cf. e.g. Gherardo Colli to the Duke and Duchess, 22 Sept. 1466, ASMi, SPE, Venezia, 353; Palmieri, *Annales*, 184–5; Belotti, *Colleoni*, 360; Malipiero, *Annali veneti*, 234.

[65] On their discussions, cf. Giovanni Lodovico Marchesio to Borso d'Este, 18 Nov. 1468, ASMo, Carteggio degli ambasc., Venezia, 1. Cf. also Malipiero, *Annali veneti*, 237.

[66] Cf. Sacramoro to the Duke, 12 Nov. 1468, re a letter to Piero from Giovanfrancesco Strozzi, ASMi, SPE, Firenze, 275.

with Florence.[67] Yet once again Tommaso apparently rejected the suggestion, which was not even mentioned in his official letters to Florence.

During the autumn of 1468 Galeazzo Maria Sforza probably felt that he was struggling against Venice for the Florentines' support, and this, possibly combined with a desire to know what had really been discussed at Venice, undoubtedly lay behind his invitation to Tommaso to visit him at Milan.[68] From Tommaso's point of view, the invitation was both an honour and an opportunity to strengthen his diplomatic position. Happy to accept, he nevertheless recognized that he required permission from his government to do so while their representative abroad. Although Tommaso buttressed his request with an appeal to Piero and letters of support from the Milanese ambassadors in Venice, the Duke's invitation so aroused the envy of Tommaso's peers that they obstructed every effort to prolong his legation. Florentine patricians were always resentful of any special favour shown to any of them; the previous year there had, for example, been resistance to the repeated renewals of Tommaso's mandate as ambassador to Milan. On that occasion Tommaso had even felt it necessary to write to Piero to vindicate himself against some slanders made by one of the *Dieci*, and Piero had in reply implied that Tommaso's 'credit, benevolence and reputation' in Florence were strong enough to overcome the ill will aroused by his political success.[69] In November 1468, however, the resistance of Tommaso's enemies was apparently too strong to be overcome. As Sacramoro wrote, they claimed that Tommaso had sought the invitation from the Duke himself, and this was adequate to ensure that his request was refused and another ambassador appointed to Milan for whatever purpose the Duke had in mind.[70]

[67] 22 Nov. 1468, ASV, Sen. Secr., 23, fos. 148ᵛ–149ʳ.

[68] Galeazzo may also have wanted to be sure that the ambassadors had not discussed anything beyond their commissions. Cf. his insistence that they leave Venice as soon as they had delivered their message: the Duke to Angelo Gerardini and Tommaso, 7 Nov. 1468, ASMi, SPE, Venezia, 354.

[69] Piero to Tommaso, 4 June 1468, ASMi, SPE, Firenze, 274.

[70] Sacramoro to the Duke, 21 Nov. 1468, ibid., 275; the Signoria to Tommaso,

Despite Tommaso's loyalty to the Sforza, his prolonged stay in Venice gave him time to pursue an amelioration of relations with Venice which the Duke's invitation may have been intended in part to prevent. Tommaso's objectives were evident in the same speech with which he proposed the idea of the general league to the Venetian Signoria. He then stated that his motives in suggesting it were not only his desire for peace but his personal regard for the Venetian state. This was not merely a rhetorical flourish, for Tommaso's repeated visits to Venice, possibly combined with a prior sympathy for Venice as a sister republic and for its patrician government, had aroused in him considerable respect for the city. In turn, the Venetians welcomed Tommaso's declaration of goodwill; in reply, the Senate asserted that his devotion deserved their regard and benevolence in return.[71] Again, this was not merely a formal declaration, for the Venetians were undoubtedly anxious to win partisans within the Medici group, which had hitherto proved generally pro-Sforza. Tommaso was particularly important to them, for his official visits had demonstrated his eloquence and political astuteness,[72] while the leading Venetians were fully aware of his influence in Florence, especially with Piero. Thus, during the rest of Tommaso's stay, they tried to reinforce his affection for their city. When, for example, Tommaso was prostrated with fever, the Signoria sent three prominent physicians to care for him, and provided him with generous quantities of sweets and wine.[73] They even paid him the unusual honour of visiting him during his illness, and showed their respect for him to such a degree as to win comment from a Milanese observer.[74]

---

19 Nov. 1468, Sig., Leg. e Comm., 16, fo. 173ᵛ. Sacramoro added in his letter, 'et così se trattano l'uno l'altro in simile cose sebene al stato tireno ad uno segno'.

[71] The Venetian Senate's reply to Tommaso, 22 Nov. 1468, in ASV, Sen. Secr., 23, fos. 148ᵛ–149ʳ.

[72] Cf. Favilla, 'De origine', fo. 52ʳ⁻ᵛ, in Razzi, *Vita di Piero Soderini*, 165–6; Giovanni Lanfredini to Lorenzo de' Medici, 24 Feb. 1470, MAP, xxi, 125: 'M. Tommaxo è molto acetto a costoro e fannone oggi grande hopinione e annolo in riverenza di bontà, sapientia e ogn'altra cosa . . .'

[73] Michele Colli to the Duke, 9 Dec. 1468, ASMi, SPE, Venezia, 354.

[74] Ibid.

Possibly, the Venetians' efforts had some effect, and this may have influenced Piero de' Medici's position late in 1468. Certainly, Tommaso's overture for a *rapprochement* with Venice was undertaken within the context of Medici interests. In the same audience in which he raised the subject of the general league, Tommaso reminded the Venetians of the assistance which they had given to Cosimo de' Medici during his exile in 1433–4, and he urged the Signoria to look on Cosimo's son Piero with the same affection and goodwill. While nothing immediately resulted from this overture, Tommaso had at least begun to lay the groundwork for better Medici–Venetian relations and potentially for a shift in Florence's foreign policy.

Delayed in Venice by illness, Tommaso did not finally return to Florence until December 1468, when he resumed his role as Piero's principal counsellor and confidant. By this stage, Tommaso was clearly the second citizen of Florence—Piero's right-hand man and a political power in his own right. As the Milanese ambassador testified in the spring of 1468, not only were Tommaso's intelligence and eloquence highly valued in Florence; he had become particularly skilled in manipulating political procedures to achieve his political goals. As a result, he had gained a personal ascendancy within the inner circle which was surpassed only by that of Piero de' Medici.[75] Tommaso's exalted political position was given social expression in the spring of 1469, when a marriage was contracted between his son Piero and a daughter of the Marquis of Fosdinovo, Gabriele Malaspina. The betrothal aroused considerable comment in Florence, where it was unusual for a Florentine to marry into an aristocratic foreign family. Only the most eminent and powerful citizens aspired to such connections, the most recent example being that of Piero de' Medici's eldest son Lorenzo, whose wedding with a girl of the powerful Orsini family of Rome was celebrated with great splendour in June 1469.[76] Like the

[75] Sacramoro to the Duke, 1 May, 3 June 1469, ibid., Firenze, 276.
[76] For comments on the Medici–Orsini marriage, cf. Sacramoro to the Duke, 10, 12 Dec, 1468, ibid., 275, and 16 Mar. 1469, ibid., 276. See also Giovanni di Carlo, 'De temporibus suis', fo. 83ʳ; Parenti, 'Ricordi politici', fo. 73ᵛ. On Gabriele's position in the Lunigiana, cf. Branchi, *Lunigiana*, iii. 566–75.

Orsini wedding, the Soderini–Malaspina connection possessed political implications, for the Marquis of Fosdinovo had for many years been under Florentine protection. He repeatedly acted for Florentine interests in the coastal area to the north-west, the Lunigiana, where he was their agent, soldier, and informant. This meant that Gabriele was frequently, along with Florence herself, in minor conflicts with Milan, for while the Florentines tended to enlarge their jurisdiction northwards, the Duke of Milan was similarly extending his influence south.[77] Marrying into the Soderini family represented a strengthening of Gabriele's commitment to Florence and Florence's to Gabriele and to expansion in the coastal area, and therefore aroused further antagonism between Sforza and his supposed partisans in Florence.

In fact, the announcement of the Soderini–Malaspina betrothal created a temporary breach between Tommaso and the Duke, which deeply worried the former. Since his authority depended in part on Galeazzo's friendship, Tommaso was concerned that his standing would suffer if relations between them were disturbed. At the same time the Milanese ambassador, Sacramoro de' Mengozzi da Rimini, was equally worried about a rift between his master and Tommaso, particularly as Florentine sympathies for the Duke were noticeably declining and affection for Venice was on the increase. Florentine–Milanese relations were further endangered by the ill health of Piero de' Medici, who, for all his doubts about Sforza, had remained the Duke's most committed partisan. If Piero should die, as it seemed he might from late 1468, Milanese influence in Florence could, Sacramoro feared, receive a blow from which it might never recover. He therefore pressed his master to mend relations with Tommaso, pointing out that he was too powerful and respected a citizen to alienate, and that his support might prove crucial in the years ahead.[78] Finally, after nursing his grudge for months, Galeazzo Maria gave way, and in October 1469

---

[77] Tommaso was himself a firm advocate of Florence's expansion in the Lunigiana, e.g. he had strongly favoured Florence's buying the territories of Lodovico and Tommasino da Campofregoso, even though the Duke also wanted them: cf. Giustiniano Cavitelli to the Duke, 29 Oct. 1467, ASMi, SPE, Firenze, 273.

[78] Sacramoro to the Duke, 1 May 1469, ibid., 276.

sent a much-delayed congratulatory note to Tommaso, who received it with relieved and extravagant protestations of gratitude and loyalty.[79]

Apart from reinforcing Tommaso's connection with Milan, Sacramoro was anxious, in the prevailing circumstances, to ensure that Piero's heir, Lorenzo, became more fully committed to the Milanese alliance than his father had recently seemed. Once convinced of Lorenzo's reliability, he exerted himself to reinforce the leading Florentines' loyalty to the Medici house, for he was aware of the strong, if latent, resentment against Piero prevalent within even the highest circles of the regime. Concerned that this might surface on Piero's death, Sacramoro sponsored an effort by certain citizens 'with intelligence and loyalty' to instruct Lorenzo in the delicate art of political management. As one of its finest practitioners, the principal Medici supporter in Florence, and Lorenzo's uncle into the bargain, Tommaso was most probably within this group.[80] Certainly, Lorenzo, whose political education had in fact begun long before, was an able and willing student. With Sacramoro's encouragement, and undoubtedly that of Piero too, he set about trying to win the commitment of the leading citizens, and by the beginning of December 1469 had had such success that he was able to reassure the Milanese ambassador that he had so 'arranged and stabilized his position . . . with these leading citizens that he felt securely in the saddle'.[81] These preparations were taken none too soon, for Piero, having suffered increasingly from various illnesses, died somewhat suddenly on 2 December 1469. Once again the Medici faced that delicate moment of transition in which, with their leadership temporarily weakened, the opportunity arose for their opponents to try and undermine their supremacy in Florence.

[79] The Duke to Sacramoro, 16 Oct. 1469; Tommaso Soderini to the Duke, 25 Oct. 1469; Sacramoro to the Duke, 25 Oct. 1469, all ibid., 277.
[80] Sacramoro to the Duke, 20 Mar. 1469, ibid., 276, and cf. also 1 May 1469, ibid.; Medici, *Lettere*, i. 49–50.
[81] Sacramoro to the Duke, 1 Dec. 1469, ASMi, SPE, Firenze, 277.

7. Conflict with Lorenzo

Despite all his efforts to unite the foremost Florentines under Medici leadership, Sacramoro Mengozzi remained aware that Piero's death might cause any of them to try to unseat the young Lorenzo de' Medici. On 1 December 1469, when it was obvious that Piero had only a few hours to live, he anxiously reviewed the chances which each might have of success. The first to whom he turned his attention was Tommaso Soderini, for, as the most influential Florentine after Piero, he was now the one whose attitude was most crucial. After some consideration, Sacramoro dismissed the idea that Tommaso would turn against Lorenzo, for, although he possessed the intelligence to aspire to Piero's place, Tommaso lacked the popularity. 'The common people', the ambassador wrote, 'don't believe he is so good as he is clever, and therefore I don't think that he can expect all the spices to be sold at his house.'[1] Sacramoro's assessment of Tommaso's position was essentially accurate, for by devoting himself to pursuing his own interests and those of the other leading citizens by fair means or foul, Tommaso had forfeited the goodwill of the wider citizen body. Sacramoro might have added that, by committing himself to the Medici, Tommaso had failed to build up a large following of his own, while, conversely, Piero's death offered him the opportunity to make himself Lorenzo's mentor and thereby indirectly to exercise effective political power.

---

[1] Sacramoro Mengozzi to the Duke of Milan, 1 Dec. 1469, ASMi, SPE, Firenze, 277. Cf. also his letter to the Duke of 3 June 1469, ibid., 276: 'se l'havesse de luy [i.e. Tommaso] tanta oppinione de bontà in questo popolo quanto se ha che'l sia savio, seria bon per luy'.

It was presumably for these reasons that, as Sacramoro had prophesied, Tommaso did decide to throw his support behind Lorenzo in the crucial days of Piero's last illness. He was, for example, one of the prime movers behind the large gathering of about 500 members of the regime held in the monastery of S. Antonio on the eve of Piero's death. The meeting was comparable to a large *Pratica* called in a moment of crisis, and, as in previous *Pratiche*, Tommaso was the principal and most influential speaker. His contribution proved vital in achieving a consensus that the unity of the regime should be maintained under the guidance of Piero's sons. This was the first time that the principle of Medici succession had been accepted by a representative section of the regime, and it provided Lorenzo with a legitimacy which his predecessors had not possessed.[2]

Moreover, Tommaso joined with Lorenzo in several measures designed to ensure the security of the Medici and their friends. Together they appealed to the Duke of Milan to send additional troops to Tuscany, and suggested that he dispatch a distinguished embassy to demonstrate his support for the regime. Despite his rivalry with Luigi Guicciardini, Tommaso urged him to return from his embassy in Milan in order to strengthen the now vulnerable regime. Tommaso even discussed with Lorenzo the possibility of taking action against suspected enemies of the Medici group, but they decided against this idea both because it seemed unnecessary and because they feared that the Standardbearer of Justice, Piero Nasi, was not sufficiently committed to the regime to want to sponsor such an unpopular measure.[3]

While these precautions ensured that the regime's enemies remained quiet and the transition from father to son proceeded smoothly, they by no means removed the potential

---

[2] The fullest accounts of this meeting are those of Bernardo Corbinelli to Otto Niccolini, 9 Dec. 1469, in Niccolini, *Chronicles*, 299–301; Sacramoro to the Duke, 2 Dec. 1469, ASMi, SPE, Firenze, 277; Marco Parenti to Filippo Strozzi, 3 Dec. 1469, in Strozzi, *Lettere*, 607–10; Niccolò de' Roberti to Borso d'Este, 4 Dec. 1469, ASMo, Carteggio degli ambasc., Firenze, 1. Cf. also Fabroni, *Laurentii . . . vita*, i. 24–5, and Rubinstein, *Government*, 174–5.

[3] Sacramoro to the Duke, 2 Dec. 1469, ASMi. SPE, Firenze, 277; Bernardo Corbinelli to Otto Niccolini, 9 Dec. 1469, in Niccolini, *Chronicles*, 309. On the precautions following Piero's death, cf. Medici, *Lettere*, i. 53, 55.

threat to Lorenzo. Just as after Cosimo's death in 1464 an anti-Medici current had gradually strengthened within the highest ranks of the regime, so after Piero's demise a movement of opposition to Medici supremacy eventually emerged among the citizens who had been closest to Piero. Again, the problem lay with rivalry for power, and with the leading citizens' dissatisfaction with the ascendancy of one family over their own. However, these rifts within the inner circle of the regime emerged only gradually, as its members first sought to secure and advance their own authority by furthering Lorenzo's. It was only as differences of opinion among them arose, as an opportunity to shift the internal balance of power presented itself, and as Lorenzo indicated that he intended to steer public policy himself, that an opposition developed against him—one which, as in 1466, found ample support among dissatisfied elements throughout the regime.

The challenge to Lorenzo originated in issues of foreign policy, in particular in the serious and permanent antagonism which had developed between Florence's principal allies, the Duke of Milan and King Ferrante of Naples. In particular, Galeazzo's close connection with France increased Ferrante's fear of a French-backed Angevin expedition which might expel him from his kingdom. Consequently, he sought closer connections with enemies of the King of France, with Venice, and with the Pope, thereby potentially threatening Galeazzo's security in Milan. Moreover, both rulers were ambitious, seeking connections with lesser powers who could further their expansionist schemes, with the result that minor incidents could become the cause of major controversies in which the Florentines were left in the uncomfortable position of having to mediate between their allies, often at the risk of alienating both.

Such was the case in the Rimini crisis which developed in the autumn of 1468 following the death of the city's ruler, Sigismondo Malatesta.[4] Referring to an earlier agreement with Sigismondo, Rimini's nominal overlord Pope Paul II

---

[4] On this issue, see Tommasoli, *Momenti e figure*; Fossati, 'Documenti', 423–72; Jones, *Malatesta*, 245–8; *Storia di Milano*, vii. 259–63; Medici, *Lettere*, i. 44–50, 67–76, 81–93, 99–101, 543–6.

tried to recover the town, but Sigismondo's illegitimate son Roberto succeeded in gaining control there, assisted by the Count of Urbino and the Naples–Milan–Florence league. However, the league rapidly became divided on the issue, for Galeazzo Maria Sforza, concerned at the possibility of hostile action from across the Alps, became increasingly anxious to maintain peace in Italy and to conciliate the Pope. He therefore insisted on a peaceful solution, even if it meant that Roberto must give up Rimini. In contrast, King Ferrante had adopted an aggressive stance towards Paul II in the hope of forcing a settlement of his own conflicts with the papacy. He was therefore eager to support Roberto, even at the risk of war with the Holy See, while he also saw in the Rimini controversy a means of driving a wedge between Milan and Florence and attaching the latter more closely to himself. In fact the Florentines, annoyed at the Duke's narrow-minded policy, inclined increasingly in the late summer and autumn of 1469 to side with Ferrante—or did so until Piero de' Medici's death. Then, members of the inner circle, in particular Lorenzo de' Medici, became more interested in peace, in order both to secure Milanese support and to consolidate the regime at home.

Finally, in late December 1469 the allies determined to hold a conference in Florence, where a common policy regarding Rimini could be worked out. From the Florentines' point of view the meeting promised to be problematic, for while they were eager to support Roberto in order to keep the strategic town of Rimini faithful to the triple league, they recognized how important Sforza support was. Personal partisanship for either Milan or Naples, based on favours received or expected, also influenced the Florentines' views, and was rapidly taken advantage of by both the city's allies. When Luigi Guicciardini returned from Milan, for example, he was well primed to serve as a spokesman for Sforza interests, while Antonio Ridolfi, who was similarly sent back from his embassy in Naples, was known to be no less committed to the views of the King.[5] Finally, the Florentines

---

[5] On Luigi Guicciardini, cf. Sacramoro to the Duke, 6, 13 Dec. 1469, ASMi, SPE, Firenze, 277; Guicciardini, *Memorie di famiglia*, 18, 23. On Antonio Ridolfi,

184 *Conflict with Lorenzo*

were aware that, in disgust at his allies' behaviour, King Ferrante had begun negotiating seriously for an alliance with Venice. If Florence failed to support him, he might abandon his existing alliance for one with Venice and possibly with the Pope, leaving Florence and Milan on the lighter side of the Italian balance of power.

The Florentines' solution to this dilemma was to play safe—that is, to try to repair relations between the King and the Duke, while making sure that they alienated neither side. This policy, as well as their own divisions on the issue, was evident in their selection of their own five delegates to the conference, and in the attitude of these representatives during the discussions. Included among the five Florentine delegates were both Luigi Guicciardini, the Milanese partisan, and Antonio Ridolfi, the King's spokesman. Subsequently, this delegation tried to adopt a completely neutral stand. When their spokesman, Tommaso Soderini, was urged by the Milanese and Neapolitan representatives to state Florence's position, he replied that the Florentines would be content with any conclusion reached in harmony by their allies.[6] When forced to be more specific, Tommaso responded, after consultation, that the Florentines would prefer that the league begin by presenting the Pope with terms favourable to Roberto Malatesta; if these were rejected, however, they should be reduced until a compromise was reached by peaceful means.[7]

This determined impartiality was, however, merely a façade behind which all five delegates were privately lobbying for their personal views. As Luigi Guicciardini explained to the Milanese representatives at the end of December 1469, he himself, Lorenzo de' Medici, and Jacopo Pazzi supported

Sacramoro to the Duke, 18, 21 Nov., 13 Dec. 1469, ASMi, SPE, Firenze, 277. The relationship between Ridolfi and the King was, however, much older: King Ferrante to the Florentine Signoria, 22 Apr., 12 June 1467, Sig., Resp., Copiari, 1, fos. 157ᵛ–158ʳ, 164.

[6] Giovanni Arcimboldi, Lorenzo Terenzi, and Sacramoro to the Duke, 8, 10 Jan. 1470, ASMi, SPE, Firenze, 278. Cf. also Vespasiano da Bisticci, *Vite*, ii. 319–20.

[7] Arcimboldi, Terenzi, and Sacramoro to the Duke, 11, 14 Jan. 1470, ASMi, SPE, Firenze, 278.

the Duke's policy of a peaceful settlement regarding Rimini.[8] Antonio Ridolfi naturally sided with the Neapolitans in advocating war on Roberto's behalf, but the position of the fifth delegate, Tommaso Soderini, was to Luigi unfathomable. Only gradually did the Sforza ambassadors discover the reason why Tommaso concealed his point of view. Although theoretically a Milanese partisan, he really wanted war, not, Sacramoro wrote, because of partiality towards the King, but because he felt it would increase his own authority in Florence. Tommaso knew, according to Sacramoro, that because he was unpopular, he did less well during peace than in times of war, when 'the offices and affairs . . . must be entrusted to a smaller number in order to be kept more secret'.[9] As his recent experience during the Colleoni war had shown, Tommaso could expect to be one of the small number of prominent citizens appointed to manage the city's most important affairs in any emergency. Moreover, Sacramoro pointed out, Tommaso knew that Lorenzo would be more dependent on his experience and advice during war, and therefore would be compelled to yield more to Tommaso's wishes. For these reasons, Sacramoro concluded, 'with those he can trust, [Tommaso] cites the strongest arguments . . . showing that peace is the ruin of the *grandi*'—and war, by implication, to their advantage.[10]

Sacramoro's conclusion is probably accurate, not only because it may have been based on information from someone within Tommaso's household,[11] but also because it coincides with Tommaso's constant desire to advance his own interests and those of the upper stratum of the regime.

[8] Arcimboldi and Terenzi to the Duke, 30 Dec. 1469, ibid., 277. Cf. also Soranzo, 'Lorenzo il Magnifico', 50–4.
[9] Sacramoro to the ducal Chancellor, Cecco Simonetta, 12 Feb. 1470, ASMi, SPE, Firenze, 278.
[10] Ibid. Cf. also Arcimboldi, Terenzi, and Sacramoro to the Duke, 5, 9 Feb. 1470, and Sacramoro to Cecco Simonetta, 1 Feb. 1470, ibid.; Soranzo, 'Lorenzo il Magnifico', 57. This, of course, supports the repeated claims of contemporaries that great citizens sought war for their own advantage: cf. Cavalcanti, *Istorie*, i. 22–3.
[11] Sacramoro to the Duke, 1 May 1469, ASMi, SPE, Firenze, 276. Cf. Soranzo, 'Lorenzo il Magnifico', 54. Sacramoro had also built up a relationship of considerable trust with Tommaso: Sacramoro to Cecco Simonetta, 1 Feb. 1470, ASMi, SPE, Firenze, 278.

However, it represented only one aspect of Tommaso's thinking, for while he was undoubtedly profoundly influenced by the internal situation in Florence, he was also deeply concerned for his city's position in Italy. During the autumn of 1469 Tommaso had strongly supported a firm stand on Roberto's behalf, and like most Florentines he wanted to preserve Rimini as a dependency of the triple league.[12] By now advocating war, he could steer his fellow citizens and his city's allies in a direction which would bring benefit, as he saw it, not only to Florence, but also to himself.

Throughout January and February the conference continued its sessions, with little result beyond a hardening of the powers' original positions. During this time, Tommaso managed to rally considerable support for his point of view, among both the King's partisans in Florence and others similarly hoping to improve their standing through war.[13] Moreover, Tommaso's influence within the inner circle was strengthened by means of the political manipulation at which he was a past master. By March 1470 the rivalry for Lorenzo's favour, particularly among Tommaso, Luigi Guicciardini, and Antonio Ridolfi, had reached serious proportions. Therefore Tommaso's enemies determined to discredit him by creating a scandal regarding certain public income which he was enjoying without the government's knowledge. Forced to renounce these funds, Tommaso decided to take revenge. Through relatives and friends in the *Otto di Guardia* he arranged that a regulation be introduced whereby citizens with posts in the Dominion could come to Florence only with the *Otto*'s unanimous consent. Thereby, both Luigi and Antonio Ridolfi, who had been appointed to positions in the Dominion, were forced to leave Florence, leaving Lorenzo and the inner circle in general more exposed to Tommaso's influence.[14]

This was the more important as the conflict over the Rimini issue was rapidly coming to a head. By late February

[12] Cf. e.g. the *Pratiche* of 2, 4 Sept. 1469, CP, 60, fos. 83ᵛ–85ᵛ.
[13] Cf. Sacramoro to Cecco Simonetta, 12 Feb. 1470, ASMi, SPE, Firenze, 278.
[14] Cf. Sacramoro to the Duke and to Arcimboldi and Terenzi, 29 Mar. 1470, ibid. Luigi realized that Lorenzo had greater faith in Tommaso's judgement than in his own, cf. Sacramoro to Cecco Simonetta, 1 Feb. 1470, ibid.

King Ferrante was openly threatening to desert his allies for Venice, while the Duke was complaining in the frankest terms of his many grievances against the King.[15] A climax was reached when, on 18 March 1470, Galeazzo Maria Sforza recalled his delegates from the conference, a decision which not only left the Rimini issue unresolved but seemed to herald the dissolution of the triple alliance. Desperately anxious to avoid a total rupture, the Florentines decided to intervene, and it was undoubtedly under Tommaso's influence that they suggested that they try to resolve the Rimini question by an appeal to Venice. Presumably with Lorenzo's consent, Tommaso had already made an overture to the Venetian government through the manager of the Medici bank in Venice, Giovanni Lanfredini. Availing himself of the good opinion which he had acquired among the Venetians and of Lanfredini's friendship, Tommaso had proposed that he come as ambasssador in order to conclude peace between the two opposing power blocs. The reply of the Venetian Senate was essentially favourable, for they praised Tommaso's suggestion and promised that he would find them well disposed to peace.[16]

Later Sacramoro decided that Tommaso's proposal of an overture to Venice had been intended to bring about a closer understanding between the two republics, towards which some Florentines were inclining as a rupture between their own allies seemed increasingly imminent.[17] Yet it is unlikely that he expected his fellow citizens to agree to a Venetian alliance, particularly as Lorenzo de' Medici disapproved.[18] Rather, Tommaso's motives were undoubtedly to resolve Florence's dilemma and forestall the threatened alliance between Venice and Naples, while a success for his initiative would have meant the growth of his own reputation and the

[15] Medici, *Lettere*, i. 100, 104–7; the Duke to Arcimboldi, Terenzi, and Sacramoro, 3 Mar. 1470; Arcimboldi, Terenzi, and Sacramoro to the Duke, 10 Mar. 1470, ASMi, SPE, Firenze, 278.

[16] 3 Mar. 1470, ASV, Sen. Secr., 24, fo. 95^r; Medici, *Lettere*, i. 103, 114. On the Florentine response to the Duke's decision, cf. Vespasiano da Bisticci, *Vite*, ii. 320; Medici, *Lettere*, i. 107, 113–16.

[17] Cf. e.g. Sacramoro to the Duke, 30 June 1470, ASMi, SPE, Firenze, 279; Medici, *Lettere*, i. 103.

[18] Cf. Sacramoro to the Duke, 13 Apr. 1470, ASMi, SPE, Firenze, 278.

greater reliance of Lorenzo and the other *principali* on his leadership. However, his plan failed, as the Florentine suggestion was vetoed by the Duke of Milan, who was undoubtedly reluctant to lose control of the situation or to agree to anything which might allow his allies to improve their relations with Venice.[19] Thus there was no means of avoiding a confrontation when King Ferrante responded to the Milanese action by recalling his own ambassadors from both Milan and Florence. To the Florentines this seemed a realization of their worst fears, that the King would withdraw from the triple league, and they were correspondingly relieved that Ferrante left a ray of hope by insisting that he still wanted to maintain good relations with the city.[20] Therefore, the principal difficulty seemed to lie with the Duke, and annoyance with him surfaced in the critical *Pratica* held on 11 April 1470 to determine how to respond to the crisis.

In this meeting, the first and most influential speaker was again Tommaso Soderini, whose long-term sympathy for Ferrante's position, annoyance with the Duke, and self-interest all combined to lead him finally to take an open stand in favour of Naples. He argued that the King was justified in complaining that his allies were neglecting their obligations to Roberto Malatesta, and recommended that Florence satisfy the King by joining with him in hiring the Count of Urbino for Roberto's defence, even if the Duke persisted, as he had throughout the conference, in refusing to do so.[21] Thus, Tommaso was essentially proposing that Florence side with Ferrante without even consulting the Duke, and his views received wide support. As Sacramoro had to admit, many Florentines felt not only that their city would be in constant danger without the King's friendship, but also that Ferrante had proved the more reliable and less costly ally.[22] Even such Sforza partisans as Luigi Guicciardini

[19] The Duke to Sacramoro, 30 Mar. 1470, ibid.; Medici, *Lettere*, i. 119, 121.
[20] Sacramoro to the Duke, 11 Apr. 1470, ASMi, SPE, Firenze, 278. Cf. Vespasiano da Bisticci, *Vite*, ii. 320; Medici, *Lettere*, i. 126.
[21] CP, 60, fos. 101ᵛ–102ʳ. Cf. Medici, *Lettere*, i. 121.
[22] Cf. Sacramoro to the Duke, 13 Apr., 6 May, 1470, ASMi, SPE, Firenze, 278, 279.

and Lorenzo de' Medici endorsed Tommaso's recommendation, evidently convinced that it was essential to preserve the connection with Ferrante in order to renew the triple league. Indeed at this point this was undoubtedly also Tommaso's aim, for he was equally concerned over the threatened dissolution of the triple league, and his action was surely motivated by the desire to prevent the loss to the Venetians of the ally whom he evidently regarded as the more important.

However, Tommaso's goal of satisfying Ferrante was not immediately successful, as the Neapolitan envoy, Antonio Cicinello, insisted that he had to carry out the order to leave Florence. Subsequently, in a rather more agitated *Pratica*, the proposal was made that ambassadors be sent to both the King and the Duke to smooth over the rift between them, and Tommaso urged that this be done with speed. By now, however, Lorenzo de' Medici was evidently becoming concerned that the Duke was being ignored in the rush to satisfy Ferrante, and urged that an effort first be made to mollify the King with letters. Nevertheless, in an indication of the greater importance placed on maintaining friendship with the King, the Florentine ambassador in Rome, Otto Niccolini, was ordered post-haste to Naples, to try to repair relations.[23]

Thus it was evident that opinion among the leading citizens supported Tommaso and the others who advocated preserving the King's friendship at all costs. Moreover, with Otto's appointment to Naples Tommaso's influence over policy could only increase, for Otto was his close acquaintance, who regarded Tommaso as the most astute and effective politician in Florence. He therefore tended to write his most complete and confidential reports to Tommaso first, before the head of the Medici house, thus giving Tommaso an advantage in what was emerging as a battle for control over Florentine foreign policy and opinion.[24] Otto's first reports

---

[23] Two *Pratiche* of 12 Apr. 1470, in CP, 60, fos. 102ᵛ–104ʳ. Cf. also Sacramoro to the Duke, 12, 13 Apr. 1470, ASMi, SPE, Firenze, 278; Medici, *Lettere*, i. 126. The ambassador to Milan, Agnolo della Stufa, did not leave until 28 April: ibid., 128.

[24] For Otto's opinion of Tommaso, cf. his letters to him of 27 Apr., 15 May, 4 June 1470, Florence, Archivio Niccolini, Filza 13. I am grateful to Professor

from Naples, which arrived in Florence in early May 1470, precipitated a further crisis. To the Signoria he wrote only a literal account of his interview with the King, indicating that Ferrante regarded the triple league as dissolved but not necessarily beyond resuscitation. To Tommaso, however, he revealed his personal conclusion that Ferrante had agreed on terms with Venice, but was delaying signing an alliance in order to draw Florence, and possibly Milan, into it. Part of the agreement with Venice, Otto thought, was that Roberto Malatesta would be left in possession of Rimini and that a general Italian league would be formed which would not only protect Ferrante from the Angevins but would keep Italy at peace for many years.[25] This package was certainly one to appeal to the Florentines, who were concerned above all with the danger that Italy would find itself in perpetual war if divided into two camps. Moreover, Otto's letter contained a further implication which opened up an alternative possibly not less attractive to its recipient. He suggested that if Florence were now to side whole-heartedly with the King, the result might be an alliance with him and Venice and a break with Sforza Milan. For Tommaso, who was already an admirer of Venice and by now clearly valued Ferrante above the Duke, this alternative must also have seemed a good solution for his city, as it would give her powerful allies as well as potentially furthering a general league. Moreover, astute politician that he was, he must have seen the implications for his personal political position. Already highly thought of by the Venetians, Tommaso's reputation with King Ferrante was growing as a result of Otto's praise and his own political stand.[26] If Florence were now to ally with both these powers, Tommaso might well become Florence's principal liaison with them, thereby

Nicolai Rubinstein for providing me with a copy of these documents from the private Niccolini archive.

[25] Cf. Otto Niccolini to Tommaso Soderini, 27, 28 Apr. 1470, ibid.; Sacramoro to the Duke, 4 May 1470, ASMi, SPE, Firenze, 279.

[26] For Otto's praise and Tommaso's reputation in Naples: Otto to Tommaso, to Lorenzo de' Medici, and to Bernardo Corbinelli, 15 May 1470; Otto to Tommaso, 7, 23, 27 June 1470, Florence, Archivio Niccolini, 13.

greatly increasing his political authority. At the same time, if Florence were separated from Milan, Lorenzo would lose reputation and authority, and the relationship between the two citizens would so alter that Tommaso might become the first instead of the second citizen of Florence.

Thus private as well as public interest urged Tommaso to see that Florence replied with an expression of full solidarity with the King. In fact, according to Sacramoro, as soon as Otto's letter arrived, Tommaso exerted all his powers of manipulation to achieve just this goal, using his influence with the then Gonfalonier of Justice, Carlo Pandolfini, to see that a small *Pratica* consisting solely of the King's partisans was immediately held. Sacramoro wrote that his efforts to see that Luigi Guicciardini was present to voice the Duke's interests failed, while even Lorenzo de' Medici had no influence on the debate, telling Sacramoro that he had arrived too late. As a result, a letter to Otto was deliberated which asserted that the Florentines were prepared to follow his wishes completely, only incidentally adding that they expected the triple league to be renewed.[27]

Unfortunately the minutes of this *Pratica* do not provide a clear picture of what happened in this crucial debate. Certainly, Tommaso did not manipulate it to the degree Sacramoro thought, for its membership was not very different from other debates at the time, while Luigi Guicciardini, despite what he later told Sacramoro, did attend and give his approval to the letter.[28] Nevertheless, Tommaso must have advocated full support for the King, and may have done so on the grounds that it was the only way to preserve the triple league. It must have been this argument which won the approval of Sforza's partisans, who apparently saw little difference between their position and that of Tommaso.

It was only with Sacramoro's intervention that Lorenzo

[27] Sacramoro to the Duke, 6, 8, 9, 11 May 1470, ASMi, SPE, Firenze, 279. Carlo Pandolfini's appointment as Standardbearer had been attributed to Tommaso: Sacramoro to the Duke, 4 June 1470, ibid.; Niccolò de' Roberti to Borso d'Este, 15 May 1470, ASMo, Carteggio degli ambasc., Firenze, 1. Cf. also Piero del Tovaglia to Lodovico Gonzaga, 6 May 1470, ASMa, Carteggio degli inviati, Firenze, 1100; Medici, *Lettere*, i. 131.
[28] CP, 60, fo. 105^v.

and other Florentines realized the danger behind the policy of complete submission to the King. More politically experienced than Lorenzo, Sacramoro immediately saw that the position adopted by the *Pratica* might lead to a break between Florence and Milan. Determined to persuade the leading Florentines not to desert the Duke, he pointed out to the *principali* the disadvantages which they would suffer if they did. In particular, to Lorenzo and Luigi he revealed his suspicions that Tommaso and the others who were advocating complete solidarity with the King were doing so in order to increase their own authority at the expense of Lorenzo and the Duke's other friends. This idea initially took Lorenzo by surprise; as he later put it, he had such confidence in Tommaso that he felt that anyone on Tommaso's side must be on his side too.[29] Nevertheless, when Sacramoro pointed out the implications of the letter to Otto and the danger which might result from it, Lorenzo became increasingly worried. Eventually, he and Luigi Guicciardini became 'upset and desperate, feeling that they have been reduced to an extremity, as they see their reputation has been placed in serious danger'. Despite Sacramoro's arguments, however, Lorenzo was apparently still not totally convinced of Tommaso's malevolence, while he continued to believe that it was essential to conciliate Ferrante in order to prevent him from concluding the alliance with the Venetians. Therefore, he advised the Duke to follow the same policy of submission to Ferrante, while he promised Sacramoro that if a plot were afoot to break the Florence–Milan connection, he would assert his influence to ensure that he and the Duke retained the upper hand.[30]

To Tommaso as well Sacramoro complained of the little regard which the leading citizens were showing his master. However, from Tommaso he received only fervent expressions of constant loyalty both to the Duke and to Lorenzo, for, even if by now he was hoping to connect Florence with Naples and Venice, he was not prepared to

[29] Sacramoro to the Duke of Milan, 4 June 1470, ASMi, SPE, Firenze, 279.
[30] Cf. on all this, Sacramoro's letters of early May, ibid. Cf. Medici, *Lettere*, i. 131–2.

risk his future on an outcome which was still uncertain. In turn, Sacramoro pretended to believe Tommaso's protestations in order not to alienate him completely from either Lorenzo or the Duke.[31] Yet he remained convinced that Tommaso was prepared to sacrifice both his master's and Lorenzo's interests for the sake of his own power, and events gradually proved that he was correct.

The first evidence came when, in reply to the Florentines' conciliatory letter, Ferrante did not commit himself to the old alliance, but asked instead for open mandates, first from Florence and then from Milan, so that he could, as he put it, show his benevolence to them and bring about peace. Even before it was clear that the Duke had been included in this invitation, Tommaso fully supported agreement with the King's request, insisting on the need to maintain faith and to act with speed. On the other hand, seeing that if the Duke did not send the mandate Florence would be committed to an alliance with the King and Venice, Lorenzo succeeded in delaying the Florentine response until the Duke promised to do as the King had asked. Moreover, he ensured that the Duke advised Florence to do the same, thereby enabling him to recover his position as guide of Florentine policy. Meanwhile he also saw that a rider was added to Otto's instructions saying that the Florentines were expecting the triple alliance to be renewed.[32]

Lorenzo's success in thus imposing his will revealed the nature of the opposition facing him. Seeing that the Duke was recovering his authority in Florence and Lorenzo consequently reinforcing his position, they increased their efforts to convince him and Sacramoro that they were really on the Medici–Milanese side. Tommaso, for example, began to show greater humility towards Lorenzo and a desire for

---

[31] Sacramoro to the Duke, 18, 20 May 1470, ASMi, SPE, Firenze, 279.

[32] CP, 60, fos. 107ʳ–108ᵛ, 1 June 1470; Sacramoro to the Duke, 1 June 1470, ASMi, SPE, Firenze, 279; Niccolò de' Roberti to Borso d'Este, 27 May 1470, ASMo, Carteggio degli ambasc., Firenze, 1; Medici, *Lettere*, i. 133–4, 137–40, 143–9, 152–4. Otto's letters and the King's failure to ask the Duke for a mandate when he asked Florence for one suggests that he was intending to conclude with Venice and Florence, leaving a place for the Duke to enter, if he wished, at a later time.

194   *Conflict with Lorenzo*

greater intimacy with Sacramoro.[33] Nevertheless, by now he had, even if secretly, committed himself to the Neapolitan side. Rumours were circulating by early June that he, along with other Aragonese partisans such as Antonio Ridolfi, was receiving bribes from Naples, while the resident Neapolitan ambassador in the city was seeking out Tommaso as well as Ridolfi to co-ordinate the presentation of his master's demands.[34]

Although prepared to submit once Lorenzo exerted his authority, the group now emerging as a pro-Neapolitan faction in Florence received new life when news arrived that, under pressure from the King, Otto had used the open mandate to agree to sign whatever alliance the King chose—whether with Milan, with Venice, or a general league including both.[35] It was now clear that accepting the King's wishes might mean a break with Milan, but by this point the pro-Neapolitan group had succeeded in convincing their fellow citizens that an alliance with Ferrante was the only way to achieve an Italian settlement which would ensure them permanent peace. Consequently, neglecting Sforza's interests, the citizens of the *Pratica* were so completely in favour of endorsing Otto's action that even Lorenzo, as he told Sacramoro, was forced to agree.[36]

However, by now aware of the danger facing him, Lorenzo proceeded more energetically to counter the lobbying of the King's friends. As Sacramoro wrote, Lorenzo's pressure on his fellow citizens, along with Sacramoro's own arguments, and the Duke's threat to recall his ambassador if Florence made any alliance excluding Milan, had a profound effect.

[33] Sacramoro to the Duke, 1 June 1470, ASMi, SPE, Firenze, 279. Cf. also his letters of 5 June and 18, 20 May 1470, ibid.
[34] Sacramoro to the Duke, 3, 27 June 1470, and Luigi Guicciardini to Sacramoro, 20 May 1470, ibid. Cf. Zanobi Neroni to his father Dietisalvi, 24 Nov. 1470, ibid., 280, and Sacramoro to the Duke, 9 Jan. 1471, ibid., 281, saying that Tommaso had '*pizigato altrove* [i.e. with the King] *ma non molta somma*'.
[35] Otto Niccolini to Lorenzo de' Medici and Tommaso, 18 June 1470, Florence, Archivio Niccolini, 13; Sacramoro to the Duke, 20, 23, 25 June 1470, ASMi, SPE, Firenze, 279. Cf. Medici, *Lettere*, i. 166–8. Sacramoro felt that private letters had urged Otto to do this (30 June, ASMi, SPE, Firenze, 279), but there is no indication that Tommaso was so writing.
[36] Sacramoro to the Duke, 20 June 1470, ibid.

In a final *Pratica* held on 27 June to discuss the response to Otto, the debate centred clearly on the issue of whether Florence should join the King in an alliance with Venice or insist on maintaining the old attachment with Milan. This time, it was not Tommaso but Lorenzo who manipulated the meeting, as he organized some of his friends to argue the Sforza case and stem the tide against an unconditional commitment to the King. Meanwhile, Tommaso and other Aragonese partisans may have been further fortified with money from the King, and their commitment was demonstrated in the strong arguments which they initially made for continued solidarity with Naples. Lorenzo's preparations, however, paid off, for the gradual build up of opinion in favour of the alliance with Milan eventually swayed the *Pratica* in that direction, and, anxious to be on the winning side, even Tommaso and other Neapolitan partisans came round to this point of view. Consequently, Otto Niccolini was ordered not to make any commitment to Venice which excluded the Duke, and, as the Venetians had meanwhile rejected the terms which Ferrante had offered them, the way was opened for the renewal of the triple league on 8 July 1470.[37]

Tommaso and his allies had thus lost the battle over alliances, and their response indicated their recognition of the importance of their defeat. According to Sacramoro, Lorenzo's opponents were 'white' with shock and fear after the decisive *Pratica*, and more than ever eager to convince him of their loyalty.[38] Nevertheless, their resentment of Lorenzo's primacy had merely been increased by his victory, and they were by no means prepared to abandon the nascent struggle for power. In fact, during the conflict over the alliances, a powerful anti-Medici coalition had begun to form within the upper echelons of the regime which made some strange bed-fellows. For example, whereas Antonio

---

[37] Sacramoro to the Duke, 25, 27 June 1470, ibid. Cf. Medici, *Lettere*, i. 170–2. Otto was punished for his temerity by being fined for receiving salaries for 2 offices: Sacramoro to the Duke, 30 June 1470, ASMi, SPE, Firenze, 279.

[38] Sacramoro to the Duke, 27 June 1470, ibid., and cf. 14 July 1470. If Lorenzo had lost this battle, it would have been necessary to revert to an action such as that of 1466: Medici, *Lettere*, i. 172.

Ridolfi and Tommaso had formerly been rivals for Lorenzo's favour, they were now concerting their efforts to promote the Neapolitan cause and were united in their growing resentment towards the Medici. Even Luigi Guicciardini apparently toyed for a while with the idea of joining them before deciding that his best interests lay in supporting the Medici side.[39]

The fact that the anti-Medici coalition included so many of the most prominent citizens meant that it was powerful enough to pose a threat from within the very institutions on which the Medici relied for their political security. This was illustrated in late June when Lorenzo, finally convinced of the need to reassert his authority by institutional means, decided to seek greater control over the composition of the Signoria. Since 1466 the *accoppiatori* had been chosen by the *Cento*, whose members were no longer proving loyal to Lorenzo. Recent Signorie had been more sympathetic to Tommaso and the Neapolitan current than to the Medici, and Lorenzo wanted to change this. However, his method of doing so demonstrated his relative inexperience in the processes of institutional manipulation, or the influence of citizens anxious to use his power for their own purposes. His plan was to create a permanent body of some forty-five citizens from whom the *accoppiatori* would in future be chosen annually. By selecting these forty-five himself, Lorenzo hoped to avoid the danger of future disloyalty. However, as some of his supporters pointed out, his candidates included many of the powerful citizens who were now emerging as his principal opponents. If they decided some day to unite against him, they might be able to take over the government and destroy Medici ascendancy. Indeed, it was undoubtedly because he felt it would further his own authority that Tommaso, for example, heartily supported the scheme, which was ultimately rejected, however, by the *Cento*. Although Lorenzo may thus have been well served by the rebellious council, the defeat of his proposal was yet additional evidence of his lack of effective control over this crucial body.[40]

---

[39] Cf. e.g. Sacramoro to the Duke, 20 July 1470, ASMi, SPE, Firenze, 279.
[40] Cf. Sacramoro to the Duke, 3, 6, 7 July 1470, ibid.; CP, 60, fos. 109ᵛ–110ᵛ,

With citizens so ready to resist Lorenzo's will, Tommaso and his allies had good reason to continue the struggle which they had begun against him. During the summer of 1470 Lorenzo encountered further opposition to his efforts to assert his political authority. His nominees for posts of ambassador or *accoppiatore*, for example, were accepted with great reluctance by the *Cento*, where a body of resistance was centring around the knights. As Sacramoro asserted on 20 July, the issues being discussed by Lorenzo's opponents involved not only Medici supremacy but the '*conditione popolare*', which had won such wide support for the anti-Medici movement of 1466. By August secret meetings were being held by Lorenzo's opponents to organize against him, and one of Ferrante's partisans, in almost a repetition of 1466, even sought the King's assistance for an assault on Lorenzo's supremacy. However, Ferrante, anxious to maintain good relations with Florence, refused so overtly to back the anti-Medici side.[41]

As the strength and determination of the opposition to Lorenzo was revealed, Sacramoro became convinced that some additional stimulus was necessary to bring citizens back to the Medici fold. Aware that the King had been doling out funds to strengthen the commitment of his partisans in Florence, Sacramoro had, with some success, been urging his own master to follow suit.[42] Since Tommaso was the brains behind the anti-Medici current, Sacramoro felt that he in particular should be lured by financial means, for, he wrote, a person of his intelligence could do much in a city containing so many malcontents. The problem was both that

---

2, 3 July 1470; Rinuccini, *Ricordi storici*, p. cxiii; Medici, *Lettere*, i. 206; Rubinstein, *Government*, 177–8. As Sacramoro stated on 3 July, in controlling the appointment of the *accoppiatori* 'consists keeping or losing power'. His letters also indicate that Lorenzo claimed that he had been responsible for the rejection of the proposal, and that since it was unpopular, it had been attributed to others rather than to himself.

[41] Sacramoro to the Duke, 20, 27, 31 July, 11, 17 August 1470, ASMi, SPE, Firenze, 279.

[42] Cf. e.g. the Duke to Sacramoro, 30 June 1470, ibid. Galeazzo intended to send the Florentine Chancellor, Bartolomeo Scala, a present of some sort. Writing to Cecco Simonetta on 14 July, Sacramoro pointed out what a ducal partisan Luigi Guicciardini had been since receiving presents such as a benefice for his son: ibid.

Tommaso's greed was so great and that the Duke was naturally reluctant to reward a Florentine who had proved so disloyal to Milanese interests.[43] Nevertheless, by late August Galeazzo had apparently changed his mind, for on 25 August Sacramoro could finally offer Tommaso 'the necessary food'. Under the influence of this bribe, Tommaso promised yet again to be the true servant of Lorenzo and the Duke and 'to want only what Lorenzo wants'. He even agreed to go in person to talk to Lorenzo, with whom he seems to have effected a reconciliation, for he subsequently assured the Duke that if Lorenzo did not contravene the love and benevolence which now existed between them, he would never do so.[44]

Whether Tommaso was won over by this renewed assurance of Milanese favour, or whether his hope of wresting power from Lorenzo had diminished, this reconciliation of late August did have a short-term effect. In September Tommaso was no longer in the forefront of the anti-Medici opposition, and, without his support, resistance to Lorenzo declined.[45] Nevertheless, Tommaso's political ambitions remained, and if he was going to accept Lorenzo's supremacy, he expected that in return his interests would be served. Recognizing this, Lorenzo ensured that he was promoted to prestigious offices, such as the *Otto di Guardia*, of which Tommaso became a member in mid-September.[46] Tommaso clearly appreciated this mark of favour, particularly as he had not had to ask for it, but membership of the *Otto* was hardly the pinnacle of his ambition. He was, for example, hoping to be appointed as ambassador to Rome after his old friend Otto Niccolini died in that office at the end of September. However, Lorenzo did not feel that he could trust Tommaso in posts of such responsibility; even on Tommaso's appointment to the *Otto*, he had felt it necessary to ensure that the other members of the magistracy were truly loyal to

---

[43] Cf. Sacramoro to the Duke, 27 June, 14 July 1470, and to Cecco Simonetta, 14 July 1470, ibid.

[44] Sacramoro to the Duke, 25 Aug. 1470, and Tommaso to the Duke, 30 Aug. 1470, ibid. Cf. Medici, *Lettere*, i. 207–8.

[45] Cf. Sacramoro to the Duke, 1, 5 Sept. 1470, ASMi, SPE, Firenze, 280.

[46] Sacramoro to the Duke, 15 Sept. 1470, ibid.; Tratte, 81, fo. 7ᵛ.

himself. Tommaso's failure to obtain the appointment at the papal court left him with thwarted ambition and the fear that he no longer possessed the confidence of the leader of the regime.[47] As a result, he remained resentful of Lorenzo and ripe for further insubordination when the occasion offered.

Occasions were not lacking, for although the triple alliance had been renewed, disagreements within it immediately recurred, this time over the question of the general league. King Ferrante remained eager for this alliance, particularly in order to combat the Turks, and in this he possessed the support of the Venetians. The Florentines would have been prepared to agree to a general league, at least if limited to Italy, but the Duke of Milan, anxious to retain the option of attacking his enemies, refused to agree, and Lorenzo obediently tried to bring Florentine policy into line with his desires. When, therefore, in October 1470 a Venetian ambassador arrived in Florence with the goal of persuading the Florentines to agree to the general league and to war against the Turks, he represented a menace to Milanese and Medici policy. While Lorenzo, along with Sacramoro, therefore did his best to thwart the envoy's efforts, Tommaso did everything he could to smooth his path. He first attempted to persuade the Florentine government to show the ambassador special honours, and, when that failed, he visited him privately, giving him advice as to how best to go about his tasks.[48] Thereby he undoubtedly increased his political capital at Venice, even while continuing to protest his loyalty to Milan and Lorenzo. Moreover, he was also indicating to those resentful of Medici leadership that he was discontent with Lorenzo so as to maintain his influence in anti-Medici circles. As Sacramoro wrote at one point, in desperation, Tommaso was 'a wicked wolf', who, while using 'the best words in the world' to himself and Lorenzo, was really doing everything possible in his own political interests.[49]

---

[47] Cf. Sacramoro to the Duke, 3 Oct. 1470, ASMi, SPE, Firenze, 280.

[48] Sacramoro to the Duke, 13, 15, 24, 29 Oct., 8 Nov. 1470, ibid. Cf. Medici, *Lettere*, i. 208–9, 222, 232.

[49] Sacramoro to the Duke, 15 Oct. 1470, ASMi, SPE, Firenze, 280.

Given Tommaso's duplicity, it was particularly disturbing to Lorenzo that, contrary to his own wishes, Tommaso was elected by the *Cento* as ambassador to Naples in late October 1470. The idea of sending an embassy to King Ferrante had been pushed through by the King's partisans, who hoped to strengthen Florence's connection with Naples. Combined with the Venetian overture, it revived Lorenzo's fear that his enemies might carry Florence into the Naples–Venice camp. Therefore he had sponsored his own candidate for the mission, but the *Cento* had again proved rebellious, and even though Tommaso had apparently not pressed for the appointment, he was elected. Thus Lorenzo was left with the prospect of Tommaso's not only encouraging the King to draw Florence into the alliance which Naples and Venice had finally concluded early in the year, but of his having every opportunity to improve his standing in the King's eyes and to convince Ferrante that he rather than Lorenzo had the power to get things done in Florence.[50] The further danger also existed that when passing through Rome Tommaso might encounter the Florentine exiles there, who were evidently hoping to receive a sympathetic hearing from him.[51]

Lorenzo's response to Tommaso's appointment provided the final chapter in this Machiavellian story of intrigue, duplicity, and manipulation. Afraid that it would make Tommaso seem too powerful if he insisted that he refuse the embassy to Naples, Lorenzo decided to pretend instead that he did not care whether Tommaso stayed or went. Meanwhile, however, he indicated that he might take action to reassert his authority in Florence so that Tommaso would think that he wanted him out of the city in order to assert his ascendancy more easily! Lorenzo's plan worked, for Tommaso really began to fear his intentions, and although anxious to go to Naples, he dared not leave the city for fear

[50] Sacramoro to the Duke, 22, 29 Oct. 1470, ibid. Cf. also Medici, *Lettere*, i. 208–9, 222–3.

[51] Cf. Lorenzo Neroni to his brother Zanobi, 12 Nov. 1470; Zanobi to his father Dietisalvi, 13, 24 Nov. 1470, ASMi, SPE, Firenze, 280. Tommaso had for months been corresponding with Giovanni Neroni, the Archbishop of Florence, but this may have been merely about his family's ecclesiastical ambitions.

of losing out in whatever was being planned.[52] In a quandary as to what to do, Tommaso tried to discover what the King wanted by taking into his confidence a prince close to Ferrante, the Count of Urbino. As Tommaso put it to the Count's ambassador, he wanted to go to Naples in order to establish a closer understanding with the King, but he feared that in his absence the Milanese party might gain ground.[53] Tommaso had still not decided what to do when Lorenzo determined to force a decision on him by seeing that he was ordered to leave for Naples almost immediately. Finally convinced that Lorenzo was planning to act, Tommaso determined to refuse the embassy, and went to beg Lorenzo to ensure that he was allowed to remain at home. Feigning surprise at Tommaso's request, Lorenzo promised to do what he could, and Tommaso was, of course, immediately relieved of the mission.[54]

Although Lorenzo had won this round, the apparent ineradicability of the opposition, combined with Milanese pressure, had convinced him by the end of 1470 to try again to take legislative action to reinforce his position. One of the citizens on whom he could best rely in this was Agnolo della Stufa—a prominent Florentine who was, however, by no means as respected as the other *principali* who were leading the opposition against Lorenzo. Agnolo was also a fervent Sforza partisan, and was therefore happy to increase his favour with Lorenzo and the Duke by serving as the vehicle for a reaffirmation of Medici authority.[55] Lorenzo planned to see that Agnolo was made Standardbearer of Justice in January 1471 in order to introduce legislation which would

[52] Sacramoro to the Duke, 2, 4, 8, Nov. 1470, ASMi, SPE, Firenze, 280. In fact, the Duke was encouraging Lorenzo to exile his principal enemies, among whom would, of course, be Tommaso: the Duke to Sacramoro, 2 Nov., 12 Dec. 1470, ibid.

[53] Cf. Gentile Becchi to Lorenzo de' Medici, 23 Nov. 1470, Carte Strozz., ser. 1, 1, fo. 84ʳ⁻ᵛ; Medici, *Lettere*, i. 223. Sacramoro felt that Tommaso also wanted to go for what the King might give him: Sacramoro to the Duke, 29 Oct. 1470, ASMi, SPE, Firenze, 280.

[54] Sacramoro to the Duke, 21 Nov. 1470, ibid.

[55] e.g. Agnolo was one of the Florentines who had received money from Milan: Sacramoro to the Duke, 11 Jan. 1471, ASMi, SPE, Firenze, 281. He had also, on urging from Florence, been knighted by the Duke in his recent embassy to Milan.

increase Lorenzo's influence over the *Cento* and the *accop-piatori*. However, Sacramoro and Lorenzo were afraid that his initiative might not succeed if Tommaso decided to rally opposition against it, and, while Lorenzo hesitated to act, Sacramoro concluded that it was imperative to ensure Tommaso's assent before anything could be done.[56]

Sacramoro's solution was again to try and bribe Tommaso. Tommaso's loyalty had to be guaranteed, he was convinced, by 'other than words', and Lorenzo was not only ready to agree but desperate enough to offer to contribute to a Milanese pension for Tommaso, provided, of course, that Tommaso was not told. Once again, then, Sacramoro urged the Duke to buy Tommaso off, arguing that although his avarice was greater than that of other Florentines, his political value was also many times more than theirs. Beyond this appeal, Sacramoro undertook an independent initiative to reconcile Tommaso with Lorenzo. For some time he had taken the precaution of cultivating relations with one of Tommaso's close friends with Sforza connections, Agnolo degli Strozzi. Through Agnolo he now arranged for Tommaso to come to dinner at his house, along with Lorenzo and Agnolo himself. Tommaso was there subjected to some five hours of close argument as to why he should support Lorenzo and recognize the necessity of Florence's connection with Milan. Something of Lorenzo's plan must have been leaked to him, for finally Tommaso yielded, and, 'with terrible oaths', promised in future to subordinate his own interests to those of Lorenzo and the Duke. At this point, once it seemed that Tommaso had really been won over, he was fully informed of Lorenzo's plan, and after a little thought he gave his word to support it.[57]

This oath represented the final turning point in the long conflict between the two leading citizens of Florence. As Tommaso had pointed out at the dinner party, the fact that he was generally the first speaker in the *Pratiche* meant that his support could turn the tide of the discussion, and this

---

[56] Cf. the Duke to Sacramoro, 4 Jan. 1471; Sacramoro to the Duke, 9 Jan. 1471, ibid., 281.

[57] Sacramoro to the Duke, 9 Jan. 1471, ibid.

apparently happened in the debate of 10 January 1471. To Sacramoro's surprise, Tommaso then placed the full weight of his influence behind Lorenzo's plan for altering the method of appointing the *accoppiatori*, and his unexpected support for the measure threw the rest of Lorenzo's opponents into confusion. Thus the measure easily won approval, and the great advantage which it brought Lorenzo was widely recognized. From then on the next *accoppiatori* would be selected by the *accoppiatori* and the Signoria then in office. The *Cento* would merely approve their decision, and this ratification would require only half the council's votes, since that was all Lorenzo could be sure of getting. Real power regarding the selection of the *accoppiatori* was thereby taken out of the *Cento*'s hands and entrusted to a smaller number, among whom Lorenzo's influence would be more effective.[58]

The significance of this legislation lay not just in the power it gave Lorenzo, but also in the effect it had on the opposition. The back of the resistance to his primacy was now broken, while Tommaso's commitment to Medici and Sforza interests was of great importance in shifting the balance of power to Lorenzo's side. For one thing, Tommaso stopped giving aid and advice to the Venetian ambassador in Florence. Moreover, as Sacramoro wrote six months later, it was because of Tommaso's support that 'many things have been guided through wisely and without scandal which, although they may appear minor from the outside, are nevertheless very important, unprecedented, and displeasing to those opposed to the consolidation of their regime.[59] Tommaso's new frame of mind had been reinforced meanwhile by the arrival of the first instalment of the Milanese pension, which the Duke had finally agreed to bestow. As Sacramoro wrote, he presented these 500 ducats to Tommaso with words intended 'to draw him completely from any other inclination', and Tommaso, after an initial demonstration of

[58] On this proposal, besides Sacramoro to the Duke, 9, 11 Jan. 1471, ibid., cf. Rinuccini, *Ricordi storici*, pp. cxiv–cxv; Rubinstein, *Government*, 180–1. Only the preliminary debates on this subject are extant: CP, 60, fo. 116ʳ⁻ᵛ.

[59] Sacramoro to the Duke, 26 July 1471, ASMi, SPE, Firenze, 281. On Tommaso's no longer aiding the Venetian: Sacramoro to the Duke, 13, 25 Jan., 15 Feb. 1471, ibid.

reluctance, accepted them in the full knowledge of what they implied.[60]

Although Tommaso had now definitely returned to the Medici fold, there were still currents beneath the surface calm. He was still irked by Lorenzo's obvious reluctance to trust him in positions of major responsibility,[61] and was haunted by the fear that his recent change of sides might lead to reprisals from those citizens with whom he had previously collaborated against Lorenzo. Paradoxically, this caused him to try yet further to reinforce Lorenzo's control over the Florentine government. In late April 1471 Lorenzo, not wanting to interfere too much in the *accoppiatori*'s business, allowed them to appoint a Signoria whose loyalty to him was suspect. While Lorenzo seemed inclined to accept this with equanimity, Tommaso, Sacramoro, and others felt that they had been subjected to an unnecessary risk. To deal with this situation, Sacramoro organized another working dinner at which he, Tommaso, Agnolo della Stufa, and others subjected Lorenzo to a barrage of advice on the need to be more vigilant, particularly in such crucial matters as the membership of the Signoria. Despite his reluctance to behave in an authoritarian manner, Lorenzo eventually felt forced to yield to the pressure of these friends. In future, he promised, he would act so that 'the security of the regime should outweigh the desire to appear too honourable'.[62] Lorenzo's political education had advanced a stage further.

Lorenzo's efforts to re-establish his authority had not yet ended, as more signs of resistance, combined with pressure from Milan, eventually convinced him that other measures were necessary both to ensure his primacy and to guarantee the Duke that he could give him effective support. However,

---

[60] Sacramoro to the Duke, 25 Jan. 1471; the Duke to Sacramoro, 15 Jan. 1471, ibid. Cf. Medici, *Lettere*, i. 209–10.

[61] e.g. Tommaso wanted to be made Standardbearer of Justice during Mar.–Apr. 1471, and was disappointed when Lorenzo backed another candidate: Sacramoro to the Duke, 30 Jan., 21, 23 Feb. 1471, ASMi, SPE, Firenze, 281.

[62] Sacramoro to the Duke, 1, 5 May 1471, ibid. Tommaso and others obstructed this Signoria's efforts with such success that, according to Rinuccini, a Signoria dedicated to 'the liberty of the people' was prevented from doing many good things: *Ricordi storici*, p. cxvii. Cf. also Sacramoro to the Duke, 5, 23, 28, 30 May 1471, ASMi, SPE, Firenze, 281.

this again raised the possibility of resistance from prominent citizens. As Sacramoro pointed out, Lorenzo's friends of moderate authority were happy for him to increase his influence, hoping to benefit from it themselves. Yet the most eminent citizens, even though they might benefit from a further concentration of power, hesitated to promote changes which would increase Lorenzo's power at the expense of their own.[63] Therefore, both Sacramoro and Lorenzo were suspicious of Tommaso's reaction when he first heard Lorenzo's proposal. He suggested that the changes should be delayed until November, when the Standardbearer of Justice was to be chosen from his quarter of the city. Then he himself could be appointed as head of the Signoria, and could lend all his experience and skill to piloting the legislation to a successful conclusion.[64]

Tommaso's offer was probably sincere, but neither Lorenzo nor Sacramoro was prepared to trust him, or to wait until November. Instead, as soon as a Signoria loyal to him took office at the beginning of July, Lorenzo went ahead with his plan. Clearly the leading citizens, including Tommaso, had decided that their best interests lay in supporting the measure, and in the *Pratiche* of 2 and 3 July no objection was raised to the institutional changes which Lorenzo advocated. Tommaso, in fact, distinguished himself by giving his full and influential support to the proposals, and thereby won Milan's appreciation for his contribution to Lorenzo's continuing political success.[65]

This legislation of July 1471 provided a further variant in the institutional modifications repeatedly introduced by the Medici regime. It provided for the creation of another *Balìa* which was now to be nominated in two stages. First, the Signoria, the retiring *accoppiatori* and the *accoppiatori* for the coming year were to select forty of the most authoritative

[63] Sacramoro to the Duke, 20 June 1471, ibid. Cf. Bonello Uricchio, 'I rapporti', 38. The Milanese had been constantly pressuring Lorenzo to reinforce his position further: Sacramoro to the Duke, 1 Feb., 27 Apr., 16, 23 May 1471; the Duke to Sacramoro, 1, 6, 12 June 1471, ASMi, SPE, Firenze, 281.

[64] Sacramoro to the Duke, 30 May, 16 June 1471, ibid.

[65] CP, 60, fos. 131ᵛ–132ʳ; Sacramoro to the Duke, 5 July 1471, ASMi. SPE, Firenze, 281.

citizens, who then joined with their electors in choosing the remaining 200 members of the special council. According to Sacramoro, these forty citizens were hand picked by Lorenzo, so that, even though they contained some of his recent opponents, including Tommaso, the majority was very much on the Medici side.[66] Lorenzo's primary objective in creating this *Balìa* was to reform the *Cento*, which, despite its recent rebelliousness, he still wanted to use as an instrument of Medici policy. In fact, he was prepared to increase the powers of the *Cento*, provided its composition was altered. Thus, the new *Balìa* granted the *Cento* full power over those areas in which it had previously merely voted before the other councils, that is, finance, constitutional matters and government appointments, the hiring of troops, etc. In all the most important government affairs, then, it now replaced the older, more broadly based councils, which were thereby deprived of any real political power. Meanwhile, the forty citizens selected by Lorenzo were granted permanent membership in the *Cento* and, with the *accoppiatori*, the right to vet a section of the citizens eligible for this council. Athough this again meant that some of Lorenzo's recent rivals were being trusted with considerable responsibility, the fact that most of the forty were his friends would strengthen his own influence within the *Cento*. Even if some enemies should again challenge his leadership, it was now unlikely that they would have much chance of success.

The legislation of July 1471 proved a decisive confirmation of Lorenzo's ascendancy.[67] During the rest of his life he had to face no more major rebellions of the sort which Tommaso had led. Instead, his attention was directed at winning over the citizens who had recently resisted him, and doing his best to maintain his friends. While he attempted to heal old wounds with Tommaso, distrust and sources of animosity

---

[66] Sacramoro to Nicodemo Tranchedini, 5 July 1471, ibid. As he also wrote to the Duke on 9 July, real authority would not be retained by the full *Balìa*, but '*se redurrà*' in the *accoppiatori* and the forty, ibid. On these institutional changes, see Balìe, 31, fos. 9ʳ–17ʳ; Rinuccini, *Ricordi storici*, p. cxvii; Rubinstein, *Government*, 181–5; Medici, *Lettere*, i. 319–20.

[67] On the manner in which the legislation increased Lorenzo's reputation, cf. Sacramoro to Tranchedini and to the Duke, 5 July 1471, ASMi, SPE, Firenze, 281.

nevertheless remained. Tommaso was still annoyed that Lorenzo refused to appoint him to the powerful offices which he wanted, such as the post of *accoppiatore* in 1471–2. As Sacramoro admitted, not only Lorenzo's distrust of Tommaso but also his growing desire to run things himself sometimes caused him to frustrate Tommaso's ambition unnecessarily.[68]

Tommaso was particularly angry at another element in Lorenzo's programme to consolidate his ascendancy in Florence. In mid-July 1471 he was selected as ambassador to Milan, which he rightly regarded as a ploy by Lorenzo to send him out of the city into an 'honourable exile'.[69] To Sacramoro, Tommaso vented his anger over Lorenzo's 'ingratitude' even while he calculated how he might use the appointment to further his own authority at Lorenzo's expense. With Sacramoro's encouragement, he began to hope that if he succeeded in reconciling the King and the Duke, he might improve his declining standing at Naples.[70] Moreover, he must also have been thinking of trying to undermine Lorenzo's reputation with Galeazzo Maria, for he asked Sacramoro whether the Duke would keep secret what he discussed with him, especially where Lorenzo was concerned. To Sacramoro this seemed a good sign, for it indicated Tommaso's willingness to reveal his true feelings to the Duke. He therefore responded that, whereas his master would do anything for Lorenzo, he also realized that his connection with Florence depended on Tommaso's 'counsel and authority', particularly as Tommaso was wiser and more experienced than the young Medici. He also expatiated on Galeazzo Maria's goodwill for Tommaso, implying that Tommaso could build on it through another visit to the

[68] Cf. Sacramoro to the Duke, 8, 12 Aug. 1471, ibid., 283: Sacramoro mentions Lorenzo's 'ambition', which makes him want to have power to himself, and adds that at times he could content Tommaso more. Cf. also Sacramoro to the Duke, 20 June 1471, ibid., 281: since Cosimo's death the Medici have had the reputation of not sharing with others but of wanting to '*tropo riputarsi*'.

[69] Cf. Sacramoro to the Duke, 9, 13, 26 July 1471, ibid. On Florence's sending ambassadors at this time to both Milan and Naples, cf. Medici, *Lettere*, i. 319–23; Bonello Uricchio, 'I rapporti', 39–40.

[70] Cf. Sacramoro to the Duke, 26 July, 14 Aug. 1471, ASMi, SPE, Firenze, 281, 283.

Milanese court.[71] All this appealed to Tommaso, who obviously relished the possibility of having sole access to the Duke's ear. Combined with encouragement from the Neapolitan side,[72] it persuaded him to accept the mission, as it seemed he might gain more abroad than he could gain by annoying Lorenzo and remaining at home.

As for Sacramoro, although he was acting primarily in Lorenzo's interest, he was not being insincere in encouraging Tommaso to establish his own special relationship with the Duke. Although Lorenzo remained the principal Sforza partisan in Florence, it was advantageous for Galeazzo Maria to maintain direct contacts with other prominent citizens whose support he could call on independently. Moreover, especially now that Lorenzo's supremacy had been definitely confirmed, it was wise, Sacramoro felt, not to allow him to feel that he could always have things his own way. By maintaining contacts with his potential opponents, the Duke would always possess a lever by which he could exert force on Lorenzo to remain faithful to Milanese policies.[73] Indeed, Galeazzo Maria recognized the wisdom in his ambassador's arguments, and determined to follow his advice to reconfirm Tommaso's commitment to Milan. 'We will', he wrote to Sacramoro on 15 August, 'use [towards Tommaso] so many warm and gracious acts that we do not doubt that he will reveal his heart to us and return [to Florence] well edified, well satisfied, and well directed.[74]

Despite his defeat by Lorenzo, then, Tommaso had by no means lost his power either within Florence or abroad. His political skill and his caution had combined to preserve him as a prominent member of the regime, with immense value for Florence's allies abroad. Moreover, as his comments to Sacramoro suggest, his challenge to Medici authority was by no means over. Although forced to follow Lorenzo's wishes

[71] Sacramoro to the Duke, 12 Aug. 1471, ibid.

[72] Although the Neapolitan ambassador at Florence seemed unhopeful of any positive result, the Count of Urbino reported that the King was eager for a reconciliation with Galeazzo, and this apparently influenced Tommaso in favour of the mission: Sacramoro to the Duke, 14 Aug. 1471, ibid.

[73] Cf. Sacramoro to the Duke, 8 Aug. 1471, ibid.

[74] Ibid., 282.

and subordinate his interests to those of the Medici, he still possessed sufficient authority to remain a danger to Lorenzo as well as an essential collaborator of his, for many years to come.

8. An Uneasy Truce

Although Galeazzo Maria Sforza must still have been rather wary of Tommaso, he fulfilled his promise to Sacramoro to do his best to confirm the influential Florentine in his commitment to the Sforza house. While Tommaso was at Milan, he treated him graciously, welcoming him warmly and doing him the courtesy of ensuring that he was regularly consulted and kept informed of all major issues. Much more importantly, Galeazzo Maria added the monetary stimulus which had become such a significant factor in cementing Tommaso's loyalty. Although there is no record of his response to Tommaso's complaints about Lorenzo, the effects of his careful treatment were evident in the ambassador's reports to Florence. As Sacramoro wrote, they spoke more affectionately of the Duke than he could express and thereby were very useful in shoring up Galeazzo's standing in Florence.[1]

Nevertheless, while Tommaso did his best to satisfy the Duke's expectations, he was not prepared to subordinate either Florence's interests to Milan's or his own to Lorenzo's. Both these factors contributed to moments of tension during his embassy, in which the Duke's and Lorenzo's suspicions regarding his reliability were revived. On one occasion, for example, Galeazzo was embarrassed by Tommaso's full report to Florence of his response to a French embassy seeking finance for an Angevin campaign against Catalonia.

---

[1] Cf. Tommaso Soderini to the Signoria, 27, 28 Aug. 1471, Sig., Dieci, Otto, 63, fos. 128ᵛ–130ʳ; the Duke of Milan to Sacramoro, 28 Aug. 1471 and to Giovanni Simonetta, 9 Sept. 1471, Sacramoro to the Duke, 3 Sept, 23 Nov. 1471, ASMi, SPE, Firenze, 282.

Since the ruler of Catalonia was King Ferrante's half-brother, any Milanese assistance for the campaign could only provoke further conflict within the league, and set back the Florentines' efforts to effect a Naples–Milan reconciliation. Although Galeazzo finally succumbed to French pressure and agreed to provide a part of the sum requested, he was anxious to hide his decision from his allies, and Tommaso's revelation of the whole affair was therefore extremely embarrassing, particularly as it aroused severe criticism of the Duke in Florence.

Lorenzo was also upset at Tommaso's handling of the issue, as he felt that he could have sent the news to him secretly rather than publicizing it by informing the Signoria. Still suspicious of Tommaso, he feared that the ambassador might have acted from some ulterior motive, presumably that of alienating the Florentines from Milan in order to renew pressure for an alliance with Venice and thereby to undermine the Medici position in Florence.[2] While it is unlikely that Tommaso was seriously attempting to lead another assault against Medici supremacy, it is true that he was determined not to show Lorenzo the same consideration as he had Piero. By serving Florence's interests independently, he could shore up his authority without having to rely on the Medici. It must have been this motive that caused Tommaso to devote himself to fulfilling his formal duty of keeping the Florentine Signoria abreast of political events, despite the fact that it created further problems for Lorenzo and Sacramoro. At times the latter was driven to arrange with the Standardbearer of Justice for Tommaso's reports to be kept secret until Lorenzo could be informed and the ground prepared for the reception of Galeazzo's sometimes unwelcome policies.[3] Moreover, Tommaso was clearly using his

[2] Tommaso to the Signoria, 2, 14 Sept. 1471, Sig. Dieci, Otto, 63, fos. 130ʳ, 131ʳ; Sacramoro to the Duke, 6 Sept. 1471, ASMi, SPE, Firenze, 283. Cf. Bonello Uricchio, 'I rapporti', 43; Perret, *Relations*, 459, 462 ff.

[3] e.g. the Duke communicated important information to both Tommaso and the Neapolitan ambassadors, and Tommaso, much to Lorenzo's annoyance, sent it directly to the Signoria: Sacramoro to the Duke, 25 (PS), 27 Sept. 1471; Sacramoro to Cecco Simonetta, 13–14 Oct. 1471, Lorenzo de' Medici to Sacramoro, 28 Sept., 3 Oct. 1471, ASMi. SPE, Firenze, 282, 283. Cf. Medici, *Lettere*, i. 325–7, 334–7, 344.

position to further his own standing in Florence. For example, when another conflict flared between the Duke and Florence over jurisdiction in the Lunigiana, Tommaso not only reported the incident so frankly as to arouse tempers in Florence against Milan's ambitions, but went so far as to warn his relative, Gabriele Malaspina, that he might be in danger from the Duke because of his support of Florence's interests. Thereby he apparently raised not only Gabriele's but his own reputation in Florence, whereas Lorenzo must have been seen as an advocate of Milanese interests, prepared to sell out to the Duke for the sake of his own supremacy.[4]

Although Tommaso thus acted at times so as to be a thorn in Lorenzo's flesh, the young Medici fully recognized Tommaso's value in Italian diplomacy. When, for example, the Duke was contemplating a trip to Rome to visit the new Pope, Sixtus IV, Lorenzo urged him to take Tommaso along. Since Lorenzo himself was to be a member of the Florentine embassy to the new pontiff and it was likely that Ferrante would also be in Rome, Lorenzo hoped that a meeting between Galeazzo and Ferrante might, through his own and Tommaso's mediation, effect that permanent reconciliation which seemed forever to elude the Florentines.[5]

Apart from his value in Italian diplomacy, Tommaso was also, from the Medici perspective, less dangerous abroad than at home, particularly when internal matters of political importance were to be treated. Such was the case, for example, in October and November 1471, when the time for a new scrutiny was approaching. For a person of Tommaso's standing, it was important to be present during a scrutiny and, particularly, to be *accoppiatore*, in order to influence its outcome, and thereby reinforce his following within the regime. For precisely these reasons, Lorenzo preferred Tommaso to remain away from Florence, and the Duke of Milan furthered Lorenzo's interests by requesting extensions of Tommaso's stay. However, as Tommaso's 'honourable exile'

---

[4] Sacramoro to the Duke, 26, 29 Oct., 5 Nov. 1471, ASMi, SPE, Firenze, 282; Bartolomeo Scala to Tommaso, 15 Oct. 1471, Carte Strozz., ser. 1, 136, fo. 244.

[5] Sacramoro to the Duke, 22 Aug., 11 Sept. 1471, ASMi, SPE, Firenze. 282, 283; Bonello Uricchio, 'I rapporti', 43; Medici, *Lettere*, i. 323.

kept being prolonged, both he, his relatives, and his friends became extremely worried that they were intentionally being kept at a political disadvantage.[6] Their concern reinforced Sacramoro's fear that Tommaso would suspect that the Duke was acting at Lorenzo's behest in keeping him in Milan and that this would undermine the good relations which he and the Duke had re-established with the Florentine statesman. Thus, his voice was added to the other forces which, by late November 1471, had convinced both Lorenzo and the Milanese that Tommaso should finally be allowed to return.[7]

Meanwhile, this was the goal for which Tommaso himself had been pressing, as he had assured the Milanese Chancellor that he had to return to Florence not only to deal with his personal affairs but because of 'certain arrangements which are about to be made'—presumably the scrutiny. Although the Milanese hesitated to let him go before receiving word from Lorenzo, Tommaso insisted that he had to depart, and even delayed forwarding the Duke's request for a further extension of his embassy in the hope that he would be recalled before it reached Florence.[8] Once Tommaso was permitted to return home, Galeazzo Maria tried to remove any remnants of suspicion by appointing him along with Sacramoro as Milan's representative if further negotiations between himself and King Ferrante should occur.[9]

Thus, Tommaso arrived home in time to participate in the last part of the scrutiny, and with his partisanship for Milanese interests intact. According to Sacramoro, Tommaso's report to his government was useful, as it justified the Duke's position and thereby helped to counterbalance the growing opinion in Florence that Galeazzo was primarily responsible for the failure of this further Florentine effort to

[6] Sacramoro to the Duke, 28 Nov. 1471, ASMi, SPE, Firenze, 283. Cf. also Sacramoro to Cecco Simonetta, 13–14 Oct., and to the Duke, 23 Nov. 1471, ibid., 282, and Rubinstein, *Government*, 186–7.
[7] Sacramoro to the Duke, 28 Nov. 1471, ASMi, SPE, Firenze, 283. The Duke had asked Tommaso to remain until the objective of Bartolomeo Colleoni's recent movements became clear: the Duke to Tommaso, 21 Nov. 1471, ibid., 282.
[8] Sacramoro to the Duke, 8 Dec. 1471, and Cecco Simonetta to the Duke, 7 Dec. 1471, ibid.
[9] The Duke to Sacramoro, 1 Dec. 1471, ibid.

214   *An Uneasy Truce*

achieve a reconciliation between their allies.[10] Tommaso's contribution in this regard was particularly valuable not merely because opinion in Florence was running against the Duke, but because King Ferrante, anticipating yet again the dissolution of the triple alliance, had redoubled his efforts to win partisans among the leading Florentines.[11] All the more forcefully, then, Sacramoro urged his master to maintain Tommaso's sympathy by showing his confidence in him in his letters, and by continuing the monetary payments to which Tommaso had become used.[12] Moreover, Sacramoro renewed his own special relationship with Tommaso, reassuring him of the Duke's goodwill, and sympathizing with his complaints about Lorenzo. If he tried to soothe these for the inner circle to function smoothly in its alliance with the Duke, he subtly maintained that modicum of distrust between Tommaso and Lorenzo which, as long as it did not blossom into open conflict, gave his master greater leverage in his dealings with the Florentines.[13]

Thus, distrust and resentment still underlay relations between Tommaso and Lorenzo when, in the spring of 1472, Florence's conflict with her subject town of Volterra reached a climax.[14] The issue at stake was superficially a minor one, involving Volterra's right to rescind a favourable contract granted to a mining company for the exploitation of minerals in the town's hinterland. Beyond this, however, the conflict represented factional differences within Volterra, for some of

[10] Sacramoro to the Duke, 4, 28 Dec. 1471, ibid. and 283.
[11] The King was making overtures especially to Lorenzo and other leading Sforza partisans: Sacramoro to Cecco Simonetta, 13–14 Oct. 1471, ibid., 282; Sacramoro to the Duke, 28 Dec. 1471, ibid. Cf. also Piero del Tovaglia to Lodovico Gonzaga, 5 Jan. 1472, ASMa, Carteggio degli inviati, Firenze, 1100.
[12] Sacramoro to the Duke, 19 Oct. 1471, ASMi. SPE, Firenze, 282. The Duke did communicate directly with Tommaso (e.g. letter of 24 Jan. 1472, ibid., 283), and sent Sacramoro money to give to Tommaso: the Duke to Sacramoro, 6 Jan. 1472, ibid.
[13] Cf. Sacramoro to Cecco Simonetta, 13–14 Oct. 1471, and to the Duke of Milan, 30 Sept. 1472, ibid. On Sacramoro's encouraging Lorenzo's suspicions that Tommaso was seeking an alliance with Venice in order to undermine his position, cf. Sacramoro to the Duke, 28 Jan., 15, 18 Mar. 1472, ibid.
[14] On this incident, cf. in particular Fiumi, *L'impresa*; Roberto Palmarocchi's review of this work in *Rivista storica italiana*, 61 (1949), 289–97; Medici, *Lettere*, i. 363–6, 547–50.

the contractors were among the town's wealthiest and most powerful inhabitants, whose enemies naturally opposed the economic advantage they had gained. This factional conflict was transferred to Florence, where the concessionaires possessed powerful contacts. In particular, they were friends of Lorenzo de' Medici, who may have been indirectly involved in the mining company, and thus may have been serving his own interests by vindicating the concessionaires' claims. In any event, Lorenzo's espousal of the mining company's cause was calculated to enhance his own political power, as it would secure the strength in Volterra of a faction friendly to himself.

Since it was connected with the extension of Medici power, the Volterran conflict reawakened in Florence the old resentment against Lorenzo's authority. According to Sacramoro, those who remained secretly restive under Lorenzo's leadership set out to oppose Medici policy regarding Volterra and to use it to discredit Lorenzo wherever possible. Thus, they not only blamed him for the crisis which had emerged in the subject town (and with some justification), but actually encouraged the anti-Medici faction there to resist Florence's decrees.[15] Their objectives were facilitated by the fact that Lorenzo assumed an extremely aggressive stance in favour of the concessionaires. Whereas many Florentines favoured leniency towards the subject town, Lorenzo seemed determined to force a complete surrender from Volterra. His influence was apparently behind the Florentine government's decision to imprison several envoys sent to reach a settlement with the ruling town, and, eventually, to send an armed Florentine escort to reinstate the rights of the mining concessionaires. When a mob incited by their opponents in Volterra attacked and murdered some members of the returning group, the Florentines used this act of rebellion to insist on unconditional submission, and when this was not immediately forthcoming they launched a military campaign against the town. This action was unpopular in Florence not least because there was a danger of intervention by the Florentine

---

[15] Sacramoro to the Duke of Milan, 7, 27 Feb. 1472, ASMi, SPE, Firenze, 283; Fiumi, *L'impresa*, 88–9; Medici, *Lettere*, i. 364–5, 548, 550–2.

exiles or foreign powers, whether Venice, Naples, or the Pope. Although this did not materialize, the campaign ended unhappily: after a successful attack which brought about Volterra's unconditional surrender, Florence's troops sacked the town for which Lorenzo, in recognition of his influence in Florentine policy, was ultimately blamed.

Although, according to Machiavelli, Tommaso remained one of the principal critics of Medici policy throughout the Volterra incident, his position is not totally clear. Since he was himself involved in mining concessions in the Volterrese, Tommaso took a personal interest in the dispute. While ambassador in Milan in late 1471, he wrote to Lorenzo de' Medici, reminding him of his own interests, and those of his sons, in the case.[16] Although his meaning is obscure, it is possible that he was hoping that the original mining company might be disbanded, giving the one to which he belonged a chance to gain additional lucrative concessions. Therefore, for personal reasons he may have felt anything but sympathy for the company whose interests Lorenzo was championing. Moreover, along with many other Florentines, Tommaso probably disapproved of Lorenzo's handling of the case, for, according to Machiavelli, Tommaso was one of the leading figures who favoured leniency towards the subject town.[17] Although Tommaso was never named as a fomenter of anti-Medici agitation in Volterra, Sacramoro's cryptic comments suggest that during the spring of 1472 he was creating serious problems for Lorenzo. At one point, Sacramoro even wrote that once Volterra was subdued, and, by implication, Lorenzo's authority reconfirmed, covert action would be taken to make Tommaso 'retreat', unless, he added menacingly, worse was not done to the troublesome Florentine.[18]

Whatever Tommaso's personal views, he would not act

---

[16] Tommaso Soderini to Lorenzo, 12 Nov. 1471, MAP, xxvii, 480. Tommaso was a partner in a different company formed to mine copper in the Volterra area: Cat., 1001, pt. 2, fo. 358ʳ; Uzielli, *Paolo dal Pozzo Toscanelli*, 482 ff.

[17] Machiavelli, *Istorie*, 583–5. Machiavelli was used by later writers as the source for Lorenzo's and Tommaso's stands on the Volterra question: cf. Fabroni, *Laurentii . . . vita*, i. 41–2; Roscoe, *Lorenzo de' Medici*, i. 149–50; Fiumi, *L'impresa*, 118.

[18] Sacramoro to the Duke, 25 Mar. 1472, ASMi, SPE, Firenze, 283. Cf. also Sacramoro to the Duke, 7, 27 Feb., 7 Mar. 1472, ibid.

contrary to government policy, and, as the Signoria followed
Medici wishes, he was perfectly prepared to implement them.
When war between Florence and Volterra was imminent in
late April 1472, he was among the Twenty given special
powers to conduct the campaign. As the Twenty's spokesman, he firmly expressed the Florentine position that, since
Volterra had rebelled against Florence, only an unconditional
surrender would be acceptable, and subsequently he helped
conduct the vigorous and successful campaign against the
town.[19]

However, again according to a Machiavellian tradition
which cannot be substantiated, after the war Tommaso
remained critical of Florence's harsh action against Volterra.
He asserted, Machiavelli wrote, that even though Volterra
had been successfully subdued, the military conquest meant
that she would remain a permanent enemy of Florence rather
than a willing subject.[20] As for Lorenzo, he was apparently
content with the victory over Volterra, and had no desire to
disturb the situation in Florence further by taking action
against his enemies. Shortly after the conclusion of the
Volterra compaign, it is true, Tommaso was again appointed
as ambassador to Milan, in yet another Florentine initiative
to improve relations between Galeazzo Maria Sforza and
King Ferrante of Naples. However, there is no indication
that this was intended as an 'honourable exile', and in any
event the Duke's determination to receive no embassy on the
subject meant that Tommaso could remain peaceably at
home.[21]

Despite the tension during the Volterra affair, relations
between Tommaso and Lorenzo gradually improved during
the mid-1470s. After the legislative changes of 1471 and the

---

[19] Tommaso's reply is in Sig., Leg. e Comm., Risposte verbali di oratori, 2, fos.
42ᵛ–43ʳ and Sig., Min., 10, fo. 22ʳ⁻ᵛ. Cf. Medici, *Lettere*, i. 366. For his appointment, Cento, 1, fo. 75ʳ⁻ᵛ; Fiumi, *L'impresa*, 183.
[20] Machiavelli, *Istorie*, 583–5.
[21] Tommaso's appointment is recorded in Sig., Leg. e. Comm., 17, fo. 145ʳ,
20 June 1472. Although Tommaso was reluctant to accept the mission, there is no
evidence that this was because he feared for his position in Florence: Sacramoro to
the Duke 22, 26 June 1472, ASMi, SPE, Firenze, 283. On relations between Naples
and Milan at this time, cf. Bonello Uricchio, 'I rapporti', 46–7.

victory over Volterra in 1472, Lorenzo's position was sufficiently secure that Tommaso no longer posed a real political
threat.[22] Apart from Lorenzo's failure to take action against
him after the Volterra campaign, the fact that in 1473
Tommaso was finally reappointed as *accoppiatore* for the
first time since 1465 suggests that Lorenzo believed he could
now trust him even in the most responsible of positions.[23]
Indeed not only in posts at home but also in those abroad
Lorenzo's greater confidence in Tommaso was evident, for
Tommaso was eventually dispatched on missions not only to
the 'safe' Milan, but also to his favourite city, Venice. In fact
Tommaso's continuing proclivity for a closer connection
with the other major Italian republic became a positive asset,
as Lorenzo, gradually despairing of making the triple league
enduringly viable and aware of the growing hostility felt for
him by King Ferrante and the Pope, reached the conviction
that Venice was Florence's only alternative for a reliable
connection abroad. By that time, however, a Venetian alliance was no longer a pawn in an internal struggle for power,
as Lorenzo had not only secured himself at home but had so
improved his relations with Venice that the new alliance
acted only to reinforce his position.

Although Tommaso had tried to further good Medici–
Venice relations in Piero's time, there is no indication that
he sought to do so for Lorenzo. On the other hand, he played
a part in events which led up to the dramatic shift in
Florence's foreign policy, whereby in 1474 the city's long-
standing connection with Naples was severed in favour of a
triple alliance with Venice and Milan. Tommaso's participation in these events began early in 1474, when the Florentines
made a last desperate effort to reconcile their two constantly
warring allies. This time it was the Duke who was threatening to desert the alliance for Venice, while he was also
working more closely with Pope Sixtus IV in Italian affairs.

---

[22] In fact the Milanese felt that Lorenzo was behaving with too much of a sense
of superiority, but they hesitated to reprove him for fear that he would be angry at
their intervention: Sacramoro to the Duke. 30 Sept. 1472 and the Duke to
Sacramoro, 22 Sept. 1472, ASMi, SPE, Firenze, 283.

[23] For Tommaso's appointment as *accoppiatore* see Rubinstein, *Government*,
241.

Consequently, King Ferrante, who was also seeking the favour of the Pope, was as concerned as were the Florentines about the direction of Milanese policy, and encouraged them to attempt another reconfirmation of the triple league.

In February 1474, then, Tommaso Soderini was once again sent off to Milan, as his statesmanlike qualities and long experience made him seem the citizen best able to achieve the desired reconciliation.[24] However, on this occasion, even Tommaso could get nowhere with the Duke, for rather than being seriously interested in a reconciliation with Ferrante, Galeazzo Sforza was really anxious to use the Florentine overture as a lever in his negotiations with Venice. Alternatively, it would be useful to pressure the Pope into renewing the general Italian league which, given the unsettled relations among the Italian powers, seemed to him a valuable alternative.[25] By June 1474 Tommaso had realized that his chances of success were slight, and had requested permission to return home, when the emergence of a major crisis led to a prolongation of his mission in Milan.[26]

This crisis was precipitated by Pope Sixtus IV who, after repressing rebellions against papal government at Todi and Spoleto, turned his forces against Città di Castello in a continuing campaign to subject the papal states to his effective rule.[27] Although the *de facto* ruler of Città di Castello, Niccolò Vitelli, was under the protection of the triple alliance, the conflicts within the league made decisive intervention difficult. Whereas the Florentines were anxious to prevent the extension of papal authority in the Romagna, both King Ferrante and the Duke of Milan had sent the Pope troops for his campaign, and it rapidly became evident that

---

[24] Cf. Filippo Sacramoro to the Duke, 2, 9, 13, 19 Feb., 7 Mar., and Tommaso's reply to the Duke of 4 Apr. 1474, ASMi, SPE, Firenze, 286. On the deteriorating relations between the Duke and the King, cf. Medici, *Lettere*, ii. 13, 477–9; *Storia di Milano*, vii. 287 ff; Perret, *Relations*, ii. 21; Pontieri, *Per la storia*, 135–8. Tommaso's commission is recorded in Sig., Leg. e Comm., 17, fos. 174ʳ–175ʳ.
[25] Cf. the Duke of Milan to Filippo Sacramoro, 7, 25, 26 Feb. 1474; Filippo to the Duke, 2 May 1474, ASMi, SPE, Firenze, 286.
[26] Zaccaria Saggio to Lodovico Gonzaga, 25 June 1474, ASMa, Carteggio degli inviati, Milano, 1624.
[27] On the attack on Città di Castello, cf. Medici, *Lettere*, ii. 5–8; *Storia di Milano*, vii. 288–90; Rochon, *La Jeunesse*, 204–6; Perret, *Relations*, ii. 28.

Ferrante was prepared to send them against Vitelli rather than sever relations with the Pope. Concerned by Ferrante's decision but unprepared to act alone, the Florentines placed pressure on the Duke of Milan to send forces to Vitelli's aid, but, torn by his desire to satisfy both Florence and the Pope, Galeazzo Maria would offer nothing more than to act as a mediator between Vitelli and the Holy See. On his government's instructions, Tommaso exerted all his energies to convince the Duke to take a firmer stand, and was elated when the Duke's advisers finally succeeded in persuading him not to abandon Florence at this critical juncture. Tommaso was therefore all the more distressed when, on learning that Sixtus IV was prepared to accept his mediation, the Duke reverted to his former decision and countermanded his order to ready his troops. Although convinced, like the other leading Florentines, that the Pope's overture was intended merely to prevent the league from aiding Vitelli, Tommaso could not, for all his eloquence, persuade the Duke to adopt this view.[28]

Like Tommaso, the other leading Florentines were upset by and critical of Galeazzo's response. Some went so far as to say that King Ferrante was now proving the better ally, particularly as he, in an effort to win over the Florentines, was offering to mediate a peace which would have secured Vitelli in Città di Castello.[29] Recalling Tommaso's previous behaviour at the Sforza court, the Milanese began to suspect that he might be responsible for the anti-Sforza sentiment making itself felt in Florence. The ducal Chancellor Cecco Simonetta even directed Filippo Sacramoro to find out whether Tommaso had written anything 'of a bad nature' to the Signoria, while the Duke asked Lorenzo to bypass Tommaso and indicate his real intentions regarding Città di Castello directly to Milan. Although, Galeazzo Maria wrote, Tommaso now seemed to be 'Lorenzo's man', there had been a time when the two had not been able to trust each other, ⁻

---

[28] Zaccaria Saggio to Lodovico Gonzaga, 31 July 1474, ASMa, Carteggio degli inviati, Milano, 1624.

[29] Cf. Filippo Sacramoro to the Duke, 3, 4 Aug. 1474; Gherardo Cerruto to the Duke, 4 Aug. 1474, ASMi, SPE, Firenze, 287; the Signoria to Tommaso Soderini, 6 Aug. 1474, Sig., Leg. e Comm., 18, fos. 45ᵛ–46ʳ.

and therefore, he implied, Tommaso's voice might not accurately reflect Lorenzo's views.[30]

In his response, Lorenzo showed no suspicion that Tommaso might be misrepresenting his policy to the Milanese ruler; nor does it seem that during this embassy Tommaso was attempting in any way to undermine Lorenzo's position. Throughout the whole reconciliation process, he had communicated directly with Lorenzo, accepting his control of the negotiation, and confining to his private letters whatever the Duke had asked.[31] On the other hand, Tommaso was clearly convinced that his city's interests required frank reports of the Duke's actions, and was determined to provide them. Therefore, while he was probably not maliciously encouraging the Florentines' exasperation with Galeazzo, he was undoubtedly contributing indirectly to their growing dissatisfaction with their ally to the north.

Tommaso's opinion of Galeazzo became a factor in further Florence–Milan conflict as the ramifications of the Città di Castello incident unfolded. By mid-July 1474 the Florentines were concerned that they might have to defend themselves against further military action by the Pope, and therefore sought to strengthen their army by obtaining additional soldiers from the Duke. Happy to be able to oblige without offending other powers, Galeazzo not only agreed to supply the soldiers but, much to the Florentines' gratification, even offered to pay for them himself. Nevertheless, Tommaso remained suspicious of Galeazzo's intentions, and when the Duke refused to grant the Florentines certain captains whom they had requested, Tommaso immediately deduced that his offer had been insincere. Galeazzo Maria would, he prophesied to the Mantuan ambassador, refuse Florence the soldiers for fear of annoying the King of Naples, and then, he added ominously, Florence would be forced to join the King and the Pope because of Milan's failure to provide adequate support.[32]

---

[30] The Duke to Filippo, 3 Aug. 1474, and Cecco Simonetta to Filippo, 14 Aug. 1474, ASMi, SPE, Firenze, 287.

[31] Cf. e.g. Filippo to the Duke, 25 June 1474, ibid., 286.

[32] Zaccaria Saggio to Lodovico Gonzaga, 20 Aug. 1474, ASMa, Carteggio degli inviati, Milano, 1624. On this incident, cf. Medici, *Lettere*, ii. 23–30. As the Duke

Tommaso's comment about abandoning the Duke reflected a view widely held in Florence, where annoyance over Galeazzo's behaviour in the Città di Castello incident remained high. It reached a peak when subsequent events seemed to prove Tommaso's suspicions correct. Although Galeazzo did allocate troops for Florence, he selected soldiers who had not seen active service for years. This, Tommaso concluded, meant that the Duke was hoping that the papal campaign would be over before the soldiers were ready, so that he could gain Florence's gratitude without having to offend either the Pope or the King.[33] His frank report of the condition of the soldiers undoubtedly influenced the Florentines to reject the Duke's offer. Some Florentines, in fact, went so far as to say that Galeazzo merely wanted them to equip his troops for him,[34] and, although it is unlikely that Tommaso had included this in his letters, it was quite consistent with his reports. Once again, then, Tommaso was in trouble with his hosts. This time the Duke accused Tommaso directly of having reported badly of him to the Signoria, and even sent Tommaso excerpts from Filippo Sacramoro's dispatches to indicate what was being said in Florence. Tommaso, in his turn, wrote angrily to the Signoria that the Milanese ambassador should never have been informed of what he wrote, while, on the other hand, he assured the Duke that he reported only what was strictly true, and that since coming to Milan he had done only what would further good relations between the two states. In turn, he sent the Duke extracts from his own letters to Florence, which apparently succeeded in mollifying him.[35] Nevertheless, Tommaso's share in the incident could only have

had suggested in 1466, the payment for these troops was to be advanced by the Medici.

[33] Zaccaria Saggio to Lodovico Gonzaga, 30 Aug. 1474, ASMa, Carteggio degli inviati, Milano, 1624. Cf. Tommaso to the Signoria, 27, 28 Aug. 1474; the Duke to Filippo, 27 Aug. 1474, ASMi. SPE, Firenze, 287; Tommaso to the Duke, 24 Aug. 1474, ibid, Carteggio interno, Milano Città, 925; Simonetta, *Diari*, i. 136–7.

[34] Filippo to the Duke, 1 Sept. 1474; Agnolo della Stufa to Cecco Simonetta, 31 Aug. 1474, ASMi, SPE, Firenze, 287; the Signoria to Tommaso, 31 Aug. 1474, Sig., Leg. e Comm., 17, fo. 48ᵛ.

[35] The Signoria to Tommaso, 10 Sept. 1474, ibid., 18, fo. 49ʳ⁻ᵛ; Agnolo della

renewed the suspicions between him and Galeazzo, and must have increased Tommaso's as well as other Florentines' disenchantment with their city's reliance on Milan.

In fact, the whole Città di Castello incident, concluded in late August by Vitelli's complete submission to the Pope, convinced the Florentines that their existing alliance system was inadequate. As Tommaso's comment had suggested, some prominent Florentines were thinking of accepting Ferrante's overtures and deserting Milan for the emerging power bloc of Naples and Rome. However, although Tommaso might use this alternative as a threat to the Milanese, it was probably not the solution which he personally desired. For years Venice had been the foreign power which he most admired, and since at least 1470 he had been contemplating re-establishing the old union between the two republics. While there is no proof that his views influenced Lorenzo, the young Medici leader had also been tending in the same direction. To Lorenzo personally, an alliance with Naples and Rome must have seemed suicidal, for both Sixtus IV and Ferrante had become increasingly convinced that Lorenzo was the principal obstacle to the realization of their political aims in Italy, and had conceived a bitter enmity towards him. Moreover, despite Galeazzo Maria's recent behaviour, deserting the Sforza house was unwise for Lorenzo when his political position was so dependent on its support. Therefore, Lorenzo had gradually opted for the alternative of an alliance with Milan and Venice,[36] and during the spring of 1474, when the situation in Italy was becoming increasingly tense, he had opened secret negotiations with the Venetians, through the manager of his bank in the city, Giovanni Lanfredini. By late July the Venetians were sufficiently concerned about their own position in Italy to accept Lorenzo's

---

Stufa to the Duke, 10 Sept., and Filippo to the Duke, 11 Sept., 1474, ASMi, SPE, Firenze, 287; the Duke to Giovanni Simonetta, 5 Sept., and Tommaso to the Duke, 7, 8 Sept. 1474, ibid., Carteggio interno, Milano Città, 925.

[36] Sacramoro had noted Lorenzo's efforts to win over the Venetians as early as Mar. 1472: Sacramoro to the Duke, 15 Mar. 1472, ASMi, SPE, Firenze, 283. On the subject in general, cf. Medici, *Lettere*, ii, especially pp. 12–15.

proposal of an alliance among the three powers, and at this point, through Tommaso, Lorenzo informed the Duke.

While Tommaso greeted the possibility of a Venetian alliance with enthusiasm, to Galeazzo the idea was by no means welcome. For some time he had been conducting his own negotiations with Venice, and he was annoyed by Venice's obvious preference to work with Florence. Apart from the humiliation of having to accept the republics' lead, the danger existed that, if Lorenzo conducted the negotiation, Milan's interests might be neglected, or that the two republics would form their own alliance if Galeazzo raised objections to the terms. At the least, Galeazzo would offend both the King and the Pope by allying with Venice, and have to abandon his hopes of improving his relations with them. Consequently, although he felt compelled to agree to Lorenzo's suggestion for fear of losing his only reliable ally, he did everything possible to disrupt the negotiation with Venice. This involved both last-ditch efforts to renew his alliance with Ferrante and encouragement to the Venetians to seek not a separate alliance but a reconfirmation of the general Italian league, on the grounds that this might provide them with assistance against the Turks. At the same time, he attempted to convince Lorenzo that a Venetian alliance would merely work to the advantage of his enemies in Florence.[37] Even in late September 1474, after all his efforts to break up the discussions had failed, Galeazzo still prevaricated when the Venetians declared themselves ready to receive a Florentine embassy to conclude. However, Lorenzo, who had consistently rejected Galeazzo's alternative of reconfirming the old triple alliance and the general league, was not prepared to wait any longer. He cut short the Duke's hesitations by informing a *Pratica* of the Venetian request, and once the citizens of the *Pratica* had decided to pursue the Venetian alternative, there was little that the Duke could do.

[37] Cf. the Duke to Filippo Sacramoro, 24 Sept., 1 Oct. 1474, ASMi, SPE, Firenze, 287, 288; Leonardo Botta to the Duke, 5, 8 Sept. 1474, ibid., Venezia, 360; Medici, *Lettere*, ii. 485 ff.

Meanwhile, Tommaso had been doing his best to discourage Galeazzo from his opposition to Medici policy,[38] and must have welcomed with relief the news that the negotiation with Venice had reached a conclusive stage. Moreover, he was ecstatic when the task of finalizing the alliance at Venice was entrusted to him. According to the Mantuan ambassador at Milan, Tommaso was happier about going to Venice for this purpose than he had ever been about anything he had done in his life.[39] As far as Lorenzo was concerned, Tommaso's appointment was meant to save time and to confirm that, despite the Venetians' rejection of the Duke's earlier overtures, the talks were being carried on in his name as well as that of Florence.[40] In addition, the goodwill which Tommaso enjoyed at Venice, and the experience and contacts which he had accumulated there, must have influenced his election. In Florence, the choice of Tommaso as ambassador was taken to mean that he had been involved along with Lorenzo and the Duke of Milan in secretly arranging this shift in foreign policy.[41] While Tommaso had undoubtedly been favouring it, there is no indication that he served as anything more than an agent of Medici policy. Unlike the first years of Lorenzo's primacy, it was Lorenzo rather than Tommaso who made the overtures to Venice, and the negotiation seems to have remained firmly in Lorenzo's hands. At the beginning of September, in fact, Tommaso was so unaware of Lorenzo's intentions that he requested permission to return home, forcing Lorenzo to see that his term at Milan was extended on the generic grounds that it was necessary to see what the various Italian powers were intending.[42]

Galeazzo Maria Sforza's doubts about the Venetian connection continued even after the final process of the negotiation had been set in motion. Even as Tommaso was on his

[38] e.g. when the Duke received a warm letter from the Pope, Tommaso implied he should not be taken in: Tommaso to the Duke, 5 Sept. 1474, ASMi, Carteggio interno, Milano Città, 925.
[39] Zaccaria Saggio to Lodovico Gonzaga, 5, 7 Oct. 1474, ASMa, Carteggio degli inviati, Milano, 1624.
[40] Filippo Sacramoro to the Duke, 12 Sept. 1474, ASMi, SPE, Firenze, 287.
[41] Filippo to the Duke, 4 Oct. 1474, ibid, 288.
[42] Filippo to the Duke, 6 Sept. 1474, 287; Tommaso to the Duke, 5 Sept. 1474, ibid., Carteggio interno, Milano Città, 925.

way to Venice, the Duke was proposing that the conclusion be kept secret until the general league had been finalized at Rome. On the other hand, Galeazzo was afraid that even the Venetian alliance might elude him, for Tommaso's enthusiasm reinforced his suspicions that the Florentines might neglect his interests in the negotiations. To prevent this, he insisted that Tommaso consult with the Milanese ambassador in Venice at every stage, and that the draft terms be sent to Milan as well as to Florence for approval before they were finally signed. Moreover, his inclusion of Tommaso along with the Milanese ambassador as his procurator in the negotiation was undoubtedly intended in part to commit Tommaso to Milan's interests.[43]

Galeazzo's concern about what might happen at Venice was not unreasonable, although the danger lay less with Tommaso than with Florentine policy itself. The Florentines were quite happy to instruct Tommaso to consult with the Milanese ambassador and to send a copy of the terms to Milan, even though, as Giuliano de' Medici pointed out, Tommaso was not a person to act contrary to his commission. However, the Florentines—and particularly Lorenzo— were determined that the Duke's shifting policies should not prevent the conclusion of the accord. Tommaso was specifically instructed that if the Duke's inclusion in the alliance created difficulties or delay, he was to go ahead and conclude without him, leaving him the option of joining, if he wished, at a later date.[44]

All these precautions illustrate the extreme distrust which had developed between the Florentines and the Duke, and which continued to rear its head during the negotiation at Venice. For his part, Tommaso tried to set Galeazzo's suspicions at rest, for after his arrival in Venice on 19 October 1474, he demonstrated such solicitude for Milanese interests as to win favourable comment from the Sforza envoys.[45] As most of the groundwork had already been laid

[43] The Duke to Filippo, 5, 6 Oct. 1474, ibid, 288.
[44] Filippo to the Duke, 10 Oct. 1474, ibid.; the Signoria to Tommaso, 14 Oct. 1474, Sig., Leg. e Comm., 18, fos. 85ʳ–86ʳ, with a copy to the Duke in ASMi, Carteggio interno, Milano Città, 925.
[45] Leonardo Botta and Giovanni de Molo to the Duke, 21 Oct. 1474, ASMi, SPE, Venezia, 360; Tommaso to the Duke, 21, 23, 29 Oct., 2 Nov. 1474, ibid.

during Lorenzo's negotiations, the talks proceeded very smoothly, suffering an interruption only when the Venetians tried to commit their future allies to contribute to a crusade against the Turks. Here Tommaso's experience and his reputation at Venice saved the day, for by convincing his hosts that after the conclusion of the alliance both Florence and Milan would have their new ally's interests at heart, he persuaded them to postpone discussion of what would probably have proven a serious obstacle to the conclusion of the accord.[46] Once this issue had been settled, a draft of the terms could quickly be stipulated and sent for approval, as Galeazzo Maria had requested, to both Florence and Milan. At this point, fears regarding Galeazzo's intentions again surfaced, for Florence's approval of the terms arrived back in Venice days before Milan's, despite the greater distance over which it had to be sent. Aware that Galeazzo had not abandoned negotiations either for an alliance with King Ferrante or for the general league, both Tommaso and the Venetians began to fear that the Milanese ruler had decided to opt for one of those alternatives. As Tommaso said to the Mantuan ambassador at Venice, the Duke might have changed his mind since he had left Milan, and the Milanese envoys testified that Tommaso was consumed with worry over the Duke's delay.[47] On their request, he agreed to postpone announcement of his own city's acceptance of the terms by one day, in the hope that Galeazzo's reply would meanwhile arrive. However, he refused to wait any longer on the grounds that learning the Florentine response would keep the Venetians committed to the alliance.[48] In reality, he was undoubtedly preparing to put into effect his government's instructions to conclude without Milan if difficulties arose. However, to his relief this proved unnecessary, as a

[46] Botta and de Molo to the Duke, and Tommaso to the Duke, 21 Oct. 1474, ibid.; ASV, Sen. Secr., 26, fo. 157ʳ, 22 Oct. 1474. The Florentines did eventually contribute to the crusade: Filippo to the Duke, 28 Apr. 1474, ASMi, SPE, Firenze, 289.
[47] Botta and de Molo to the Duke, 31 Oct. 1474, ibid., Venezia, 360; Jacopo del Palagio to Lodovico Gonzaga, 31 Oct. 1474, ASMa, Carteggio degli inviati, Venezia, 1431.
[48] Botta and de Molo to the Duke, 31 Oct. 1474, ASMi, SPE, Venezia, 360.

positive reply arrived from Milan almost immediately, and on 2 November 1474 the new triple alliance could finally be concluded, severing Florence and Milan's long and conflict-ridden relationship with King Ferrante.[49]

Although the Florentines, and especially Lorenzo de' Medici, could now rest easier in the knowledge that they were relatively secure in Italy, they could not ignore the distrust which remained in this, as in their previous, triple alliance. Tommaso as well as the Florentine Signoria attempted to alleviate this potential threat to the new alliance, writing to urge the Duke to forget his past quarrels with Venice and to live amicably with his new ally.[50] He also offered Galeazzo advice on how not to offend the Venetians' susceptibilities—advice which the Duke, typically, failed to follow.[51]

Indeed, given his continuing admiration and affection for Venice, Tommaso could be relied on to do everything in his power to make the alliance work, and it was undoubtedly for this reason that the Florentines apparently offered him the option of remaining as resident ambassador in Venice. According to Filippo Sacramoro, the Venetians wanted Florence to maintain a permanent ambassador with them, and the Florentines felt that the Venetians might prefer Tommaso, because of his authority as well as his affection for their city. However, several factors acted to prevent Tommaso from accepting the offer. On the one hand, as Sacramoro was aware, he was anxious to return home right away, both because of his appointment to the prestigious and lucrative position of Captain of Pisa, and in order to look

[49] Tommaso to the Duke, 2, 3 Nov. 1474, de Molo to the Duke, 3 Nov. 1474, ibid.; Simonetta, *Diari*, i. 146; Medici, *Lettere*, ii. 489–90; Perret, *Relations*, ii. 30–1; *Cronaca di anonimo veronese*, 306.

[50] Tommaso to the Duke, 3 Nov. 1474, ASMi, SPE, Venezia, 360; the Signoria to the Duke, 10 Nov. 1474, Sig., Min., 10, fo. 184ʳ⁻ᵛ. Cf. Medici, *Lettere*, ii. 47.

[51] This involved the exchange of congratulatory embassies between Milan and Venice, in which Tommaso felt the Duke should accept the measures already taken by Venice despite his displeasure with them. However, his advice merely brought him under suspicion of betraying Milanese interests: the Duke to Tommaso, 8 Nov. 1474, and to Leonardo Botta, 17, 20 Nov. 1474; Botta to the Duke, 20, 24 Nov., 1 Dec. 1474, and to Cecco Simonetta, 26 Nov. 1474; Simonetta to Botta, 21 Nov. 1474; Tommaso to the Duke, 16 Nov. 1474, all in ASMi, SPE, Venezia, 360.

after his private affairs.[52] Quite possibly, he also feared for his authority in Florence if he remained too long abroad, while his sons' political prospects could be better promoted if he were in Florence. Finally, the Florentines themselves apparently decided that it would be better to recall Tommaso, as his behaviour suggested that he might prove too complaisant towards the Venetians to represent Florence's interests effectively.[53]

Thus, late in December 1474 Tommaso returned to Florence, where he felt his pro-Venetian proclivities could now more safely be expressed. They were immediately evident in the extremely favourable reports which he made of the Venetians—much more favourable than his comments regarding the Duke.[54] Tommaso also distinguished himself by fervently urging that the congratulatory Venetian embassy due to arrive in Florence be shown special honour, apparently neglecting the claims of the similar embassy about to be sent by Milan. To Lorenzo, such tendencies raised the spectre that Tommaso might be trying to use the Venetian connection in his own interests, and he responded quickly to quash any such expectations. On this occasion, for example, he saw that the Milanese envoys received equal honours with the Venetians.[55] As this incident suggests, Tommaso's favouritism for Venice continued to create problems in his relations with the Duke. Aware of Tommaso's pro-Venetian sympathies, Galeazzo ensured, for example, that when he sent information to Florence which he did not want the Venetians to know, Tommaso and the other *marcheschi* were not informed of it.[56] While there is no indication that Tommaso

---

[52] Filippo Sacramoro to the Duke 17 Nov. 1474, ibid., Firenze, 288.

[53] This suspicion arose in particular over Tommaso's failure to point out to the Venetians that the deadline for inviting the other Italian powers to join the triple alliance had expired before they had decided to act. Basically, the Venetians wanted a general league and the Florentines did not. Cf. Filippo Sacramoro to the Duke, 29 Nov., 4 Dec. 1474, ibid. Cf. Medici, *Lettere*, ii. 48–9, 82–9, and Pintor, 'Le due ambascerie', 786.

[54] Cf. Filippo to the Duke, 1, 5 Jan. 1475, ASMi, SPE, Firenze, 289.

[55] Ibid.

[56] Cf. the Duke to Filippo Sacramoro and Branda da Castiglione, 8 Jan. 1475, ibid.

ever did leak information to the Venetians, Galeazzo's distrust meant that he remained at the disadvantage of not being fully aware of Milanese policy—a disability obviously not shared by Lorenzo.

Despite the fears of Lorenzo and the Duke, Tommaso was not prepared to carry his pro-Venetian proclivities to dangerous lengths. Rather, he tried to demonstrate to the Duke his complete devotion to Sforza interests,[57] while Galeazzo Maria responded by treating Tommaso as his partisan, at least where Venetian susceptibilities were not involved. In any event, Tommaso's considerable influence in Florentine politics ensured that Galeazzo took appropriate consideration of him.[58] As far as Lorenzo was concerned, Tommaso had long ago decided that his only real option was to accept Lorenzo's leadership, and this he continued to do, emphasizing frequently in his letters his readiness to follow Lorenzo's wishes in all matters.[59] Nevertheless, subordinating his views and interests to Lorenzo's remained difficult, and occasionally, his old resentment of Lorenzo's primacy resurfaced.

One such incident occurred early in 1476, when Filippo Sacramoro approached Tommaso for information regarding Florence's secret purchase of lands in the Lunigiana which the Duke had also been trying to obtain. In order to obtain the news he sought, Filippo flattered Tommaso by emphasizing how greatly Galeazzo Maria relied on him in such matters, and, anxious to prove his worth, Tommaso responded by satisfying Filippo's request. Moreover, he re-emphasized his commitment to Milan by claiming that he had been the only citizen to oppose the purchase, and that he had done so through concern for the Duke's interests. Thereupon he went on to strike a blow against the Milanese government's confidence in Lorenzo by asserting that similar

---

[57] Cf. Tommaso to the Duke, 28 Feb., 11 Mar., 7, 25 Oct. 1475, ibid., 286, 290.

[58] e.g. Galeazzo was ready to grant Tommaso's requests for a wealthy benefice or important office for his sons: Tommaso to the Duke, 28 Feb., 11 Mar. 7, 25 Oct. 1475, ibid., 286, 290.

[59] Cf. e.g. Tommaso to Lorenzo de' Medici, 12 Nov. 1471, MAP, xxvii, 480. Tommaso also carried out Lorenzo's personal financial business while he was ambassador: Tommaso to Lorenzo, 8 Apr. 1477, MAP xlviii, 11; and 30 June 1477, MAP, xxxii, 113.

poor decisions, as he phrased it, had been made in the past
because no one dared to tell Lorenzo the truth. He himself,
he emphasized, would always express his true opinion when
consulted; if Lorenzo did not want to hear the truth, he
should not ask Tommaso what he thought![60] Clearly, there
had been occasions when Lorenzo had spurned Tommaso's
advice, and this evidently rankled with Tommaso. Moreover,
his patrician pride was apparently offended by the manner in
which citizens of the inner circle were abdicating their
political responsibilities, and allowing decision-making to
become increasingly a Medici purview. Apart from the
consequences for his own position, this suggests that Tommaso may also have begun to feel that the concentration of
such power in one individual was having detrimental effects
on the city's government.

If Tommaso's attitude towards Lorenzo remained tinged
with residual resentment, Lorenzo's towards Tommaso also
contained an element of ambivalence. Although Lorenzo had
successfully thwarted Tommaso's bid for supremacy and
subsequently won him over by signs of confidence and the
delegation of authority, he must have been aware that he
could not trust him unreservedly. As some of Lorenzo's
friends kept reminding him, Tommaso and his eldest son
were among his most dangerous enemies,[61] even while they
were some of his closest collaborators. The same was
undoubtedly true of members of other prominent patrician
families, and therefore it is hardly surprising that Lorenzo
had begun to look for his most intimate advisers among less
powerful individuals who were not so likely to pose an
insidious threat to his authority.[62] On the other hand,

[60] Filippo Sacramoro to the Duke, 23 Jan., 5 Feb. 1476, ASMi, SPE, Firenze,
291. That Lorenzo did not want to hear what did not please him was confirmed by
Sacramoro, to the Duke, 30 Sept. 1472, ibid., 283.

[61] Filippo Sacramoro to the Duke, 6 Sept. 1475, ibid., 290.

[62] Cf. Simonetta, *Diari*, i. 136, (27 Aug. 1474): those with whom Lorenzo *'se
stringe più in secreto'* were Bernardo Bongirolami, Girolamo Morelli, Roberto
Leoni, Bernardo del Nero, Ser Niccolò Dini, and Francesco Nori. While several of
these citizens were prominent in politics, none belonged to old, powerful, patrician
families. Francesco Nori was undoubtedly that employee of the Medici bank whom
Lorenzo employed in several personal missions and who was eventually killed in
the Pazzi conspiracy: de Roover, *Rise and Decline*, 238–9, 288; Medici, *Lettere*, i.
71, n. 1.

Lorenzo was aware that as long as he satisfied Tommaso's ambitions, the latter would give him no cause for concern, but would rather place his political skill in the service of Medici and Florentine interests. Consequently, at about the same time as Tommaso was criticizing Lorenzo to Filippo Sacramoro, Lorenzo was assuring the Milanese ambassador that although Tommaso had once wavered in his loyalty to the Medici, he had by now 'so well directed him that he knew he could trust him freely'. In fact, he went on, Tommaso was one of the citizens to whom he would first turn for advice, as he was not only one of 'the most prudent and wisest' of Florentines, but possessed the added virtue of 'taciturnity'.[63] So despite the continuing conflict in personal interests, in affairs of state Tommaso's close working relationship with the Medici had been restored to its old footing. In the last few years of Tommaso's life, it was this effective working relationship between him and Lorenzo which was most evident. Although at times they disagreed on policy, they collaborated effectively in the interests of the city and of the regime, while, since Lorenzo continued to satisfy Tommaso's ambition for the most powerful positions at home and abroad, no serious clashes of interests occurred.

[63] Filippo Sacramoro to the Duke, 4 May 1476, Paris, Bibl. Nat., MSS italiens, 1592, fo. 74ᵛ. Cf. Rochon, *La Jeunesse*, 119, 223–4 and Medici, *Lettere*, ii. 172.

9. The Final Equilibrium

The last ten years of Tommaso's life demonstrate the fruitful
collaboration finally established between Lorenzo and the
other leading figures of the Florentine regime. While Lorenzo's will predominated, Tommaso and the rest of the
maggiori exercised a measure of discretion which allowed
full scope to their skill and experience. Lorenzo was meanwhile careful to satisfy their ambitions and not offend their
susceptibilities. Similarly, Tommaso, aware how far he could
assume an independent role, always ultimately accepted
Lorenzo's wishes even while freely expressing his own views
and pressing for his own policies. Thus the constitutional
balance, which had to a degree been forced on the principal
citizens, did work effectively to the mutual advantage of both
sides, and both were prepared to accept and consolidate it,
despite an element of latent resentment and distrust.

An indication of how Lorenzo relied on Tommaso was
provided at the end of 1476, when the assassination of the
Duke of Milan created a serious crisis throughout Italy. The
Duke's death was of great concern to Florence and especially
to Lorenzo, whose personal political position remained
closely connected to Sforza support. With Galeazzo's death
the Florence–Milan connection was called into question, for
the new Duke, Giangaleazzo Sforza, was too young to
assume control of the government, and the power vacuum
thus created threatened a shift in Milanese policy. At the
least, a struggle for power seemed likely to ensue, for
although the Dowager Duchess Bona of Savoy was quickly
declared Regent, the late Duke's brothers were anxious to
seize control. In an effort to reinforce their position, either
they or the Duchess might seek the support of King Ferrante

of Naples, who had never become reconciled to the Milan–Venice–Florence alliance of 1474, and would undoubtedly be prepared to use the occasion to re-establish his old connection with Milan. In fact, immediately after Galeazzo Maria's death, he began to put pressure on the Milanese government to renew the earlier alliance, thereby threatening the triple alliance and Lorenzo's special relationship with Milan. At this dangerous moment, not even the Venetians seemed totally reliable, for it was feared that their ambition to dominate northern Italy might cause them to forget their recent alliance and to opt instead to enlarge their dominion at Milan's expense.[1]

In these circumstances, the Florentines were naturally anxious to have authoritative ambassadors at the Sforza court. The two selected as soon as news of the Duke's death arrived were Tommaso Soderini and Luigi Guicciardini, both old and influential Sforza partisans and close collaborators with Lorenzo.[2] Of the two, Lorenzo was particularly anxious for Tommaso to represent Florence in Milan. As Tommaso later wrote to him, at the advanced age of 73 and in the midst of winter storms, 'I would never have come if you had not said what you did; I came to please you.'[3] As Luigi had been aware in 1471, although he possessed valuable contacts and credit at the Sforza court, Lorenzo placed greater faith in Tommaso's judgement and ability. This was evident throughout this embassy from the manner in which Lorenzo wrote separately and more fully to Tommaso. As he declared in one letter, he felt he 'could not err in telling [Tommaso] everything', while he in turn looked forward to receiving Tommaso's views, in which, he wrote at one point, 'I have great faith'.[4] Lorenzo's opinion regarding the relative value of Luigi and Tommaso in Italian diplomacy was shared by

[1] On the political situation at this time, cf. Ilardi, 'Assassination', 72–103; Casanova, 'L'uccisione', 299–332; Pontieri, *Per la storia*, 141–53; Medici, *Lettere*, ii. 247–50, 523–35.

[2] Cf. in particular, Filippo Sacramoro to the Duchess of Milan, 29 Dec. 1476, ASMi, SPE, Firenze, 291, and the ambassadors' instructions, in Casanova, 'L'uccisione', 316–18.

[3] Tommaso Soderini to Lorenzo de' Medici, 30 June 1477, MAP, xxxii, 113.

[4] Lorenzo to Tommaso, 2 Mar. (*da parte*), and 10 Mar. 1477, in Medici, *Lettere*, ii. 318–19, 327–37.

the other leading Florentines. In March 1477, when the
Florentine Signoria decided to recall one of their ambassadors from Milan, they chose Luigi, and Luigi's own great-
nephew, Francesco Guicciardini, testified that the decision
had been made because Tommaso was of more authority
and wiser.[5]

Tommaso's value to Florence, Lorenzo, and the Milanese
was evident throughout his long mission, which extended
from December 1476 to June 1478. From the start, the
Milanese were anxiously awaiting the Florentines' arrival,
hoping that they would lend authority and dignity to their
insecure regime. In particular, the late Duke's Chancellor,
Cecco Simonetta, was eager for Florentine support in order
to secure the position he had carved out for himself as the
principal figure in the Milanese administration. Since he had
earlier been one of the leading advocates of Florentine–Milanese friendship, he was confident that the Florentines would help to preserve his ascendancy in Milan, and he
was therefore eager to employ Tommaso and Luigi in even
the most delicate affairs. Immediately after their arrival in
Milan on 10 January 1477 the Florentine ambassadors were
included in the meetings of the Duchess's principal advisory
body, the Secret Council, where they discussed not only
questions affecting Milanese–Florentine relations but also
matters directly concerning the Duchy's security.[6]

Cecco was essentially correct that Florentine influence
would be exerted in his favour. Tommaso and Luigi had
been instructed to recommend Cecco to the Duchess, and
although this was unnecessary, they worked closely with him
in the interests of the Milanese government. As Tommaso
later wrote, he did everything he could for the preservation
of the regime, and the Duchess and her advisers testified to
this by their very real appreciation. Again according to

[5] Guicciardini, *Memorie di famiglia*, 24–5.
[6] e.g. Tommaso was present in the Secret Council on 3 Feb. 1477: *Acta in
consilio secreto*, vol. 1, p. xvi. The dispatches of Marsilio Andreasi to Barbara of
Brandenburg, wife of Lodovico Gonzaga, also attest to his and Luigi's frequent
presence, cf. 2, 11 Mar. 1477, ASMa, Carteggio degli inviati, Milano, 1626. On the
Secret Council during this period, see also Fubini, 'Osservazioni e documenti',
47–103.

Tommaso, they showed the two Florentines 'so much trust and love that I would not have believed the half', and, convinced that Luigi and Tommaso were sincerely concerned for their welfare, they communicated everything with them.[7] Before Luigi left for Florence in March, both he and Tommaso received the unusual honour of appointment to the Secret Council, while the regular payments which they received at Milan were undoubtedly intended as both a recompense for their dedication and an inducement to continued loyalty to the existing regime.[8]

Their involvement in Milan's internal affairs meant that Tommaso and Luigi also had to deal with the claims of the late Duke's brothers, who found their hopes of gaining a more influential role in government repeatedly thwarted by Cecco and his collaborators. As a serious conflict gradually developed between the Sforza brothers, backed by the *condottiero* Roberto da Sanseverino and the faction surrounding Cecco, the Florentines became increasingly worried about its effects on the efficacy and the policies of the Milanese government. Anxious to resolve the problem, they welcomed Cecco's decision to invite the Lieutenant-General of the Duchy, Marquis Lodovico Gonzaga of Mantua, to Milan to serve as mediator and neutral head of government. Whenever this proposal was raised, Tommaso and Luigi enthusiastically encouraged the idea,[9] and once Lodovico arrived at the Sforza court in early February 1477, they joined him in mediating between the Duchess and the Sforza brothers. In this negotiation, the ambassadors sincerely tried to satisfy the Sforza brothers' claims. As Tommaso later revealed, he felt that the brothers should be granted a more important political role, but it was obvious that the Duchess, influenced by Cecco, would not satisfy their ambitions. The best the

---

[7] Tommaso to Lorenzo, 30 June 1477, MAP, xxxii, 113; the Duke and Duchess to Filippo Sacramoro, 29 Apr. 1477, ASMi, SPE, Firenze, 292, and to Marco Trotti, 4 Mar. 1477, ASMi, Potenze sovrane, 1464.

[8] For the appointment of Tommaso and Luigi to the Secret Council: Santoro, *Gli uffizi*, 14–15. On the lucrative nature of the embassy, see Guicciardini, *Memorie di famiglia*, 24–5.

[9] On this issue, cf. Medici, *Lettere*, ii. 251–3, 281–2; Ilardi, 'Assassination', 81–3; Piero del Tovaglia to Lodovico Gonzaga, 30 Dec. 1476, ASMa, Carteggio degli inviati, Firenze, 1101.

mediators could do was to obtain the right for two of the brothers to be admitted to the Secret Council. Cecco would not even allow any of them to reside within the court, as this would threaten both his security and his influence.

Thus, the terms of the accord worked out by Lodovico and the Florentine ambassadors represented a victory for Cecco, and although the Sforza brothers were forced to accept it, the danger remained that they might eventually strike a blow against the hated Chancellor. Anxious therefore to ensure that the accord was observed, Cecco turned once again to the power which seemed most ready to secure his ascendancy in Milan. Secretly, he appealed to Lorenzo de' Medici to arrange for the ambassadors, as Florence's representatives, to act as guarantors of the agreement, but Lorenzo was uncertain how to reply. Although anxious to satisfy Cecco and achieve a resolution at Milan, he was reluctant to commit Florence to Cecco for fear it might encourage the Sforza brothers to accept Neapolitan backing for a coup against the Chancellor. Consequently, he arranged for Tommaso and Luigi to be instructed to do everything possible to favour the Milanese government, while he privately warned them to be very careful as to how they used this authority. Although they should consult Cecco, he wrote, they should decide themselves, on the basis of their own judgement, whether Florence should guarantee the terms. It is, he added, only 'the faith I have in your prudence' which had caused them to be given such wide powers in a matter which might prove crucial to the Florentine regime.[10]

On the basis of these instructions, Tommaso and Luigi must have concluded that Cecco's administration was not sufficiently stable for Florence to do as the Chancellor had asked. The final version of the accord between the Duchess and the Sforza brothers stated that the terms had been reached in accord with the 'judgement and opinion' of the Florentine ambassadors, who were not, however, cited as the

---

[10] Cf. Lorenzo to Tommaso and Luigi Guicciardini, 17 Feb. 1477, MAP, lxxii, 306, edited in Medici, *Lettere*, ii. 285–93. Cf. also the Signoria to Tommaso and Luigi, 17 Feb. 1477, in Casanova, 'L'uccisione', 326–7.

agreement's guarantors.[11] Indeed, despite the Florentine's determination to support Cecco, Tommaso, like Lodovico Gonzaga, was convinced that the Milanese administration would have been stronger and more secure if the Duchess's brothers-in-law were included. Although unable to press for this without alienating Cecco, he could at least prevent his government from allying itself too closely with what he regarded as a weak regime.[12]

In this situation, Lorenzo had effectively delegated decision-making to the Florentine ambassadors, and on other occasions during this embassy he similarly deferred to their judgement. One such instance occurred when Cecco, anxious to get his enemies out of Milan, proposed that Florence offer military contracts, or *condotte*, to both Lodovico Sforza and Roberto da Sanseverino. Happy to do anything to reduce tension in the Lombard capital, Lorenzo proceeded to open negotiations with both, employing the two ambassadors as advisers as well as spokesmen for Florentine policy. For example, when the Milanese suggested that Florence concentrate on hiring Lodovico Sforza, Lorenzo informed Tommaso and Luigi of the suggestion, explaining that since he had not been able to discuss it with anyone else, they should follow his advice only if they agreed with it: he wanted them, he wrote, to act not merely as ambassadors, but as citizens of the *Pratica*.[13] By the time the letter arrived, Luigi had left Milan, and consequently, Tommaso alone responded with his opinion that Florence should not rush the negotiation, but allow him to conduct it unofficially in order to obtain the best possible deal for his city.[14] Lorenzo appears to have had sufficient confidence in Tommaso to agree to this suggestion, for Tommaso did eventually make Lodovico Sforza an offer which was,

[11] Cf. the settlement, in ASMi, Potenze sovrane, 1464; Medici, *Lettere*, ii. 314–15; Ilardi, 'Assassination', 83–4.

[12] Tommaso to Lorenzo, 30 June 1477, MAP, xxxii, 113, in which Tommaso revealed that he had reserved judgement on Cecco's administration from the start because of the 'contradictions' which it contained.

[13] Tommaso to Lorenzo, 29 Mar. 1477, MAP, xiv, 211.

[14] Cf. Tommaso to Lorenzo, 30 June, 1477, MAP xxxii, 113; Filippo Sacramoro to the Duke and Duchess, 27 Apr. 1477, ASMi, SPE, Firenze, 292.

however, refused. As Tommaso later concluded, the Sforza brothers must by then have decided to stake everything on winning political power at home.[15]

Although Lorenzo was prepared to reveal his full thoughts to Tommaso and to follow his opinions, he by no means relied solely on Tommaso as his agent. In the case of the *condotte*, he also employed informal representatives who, since they were his close friends, could be relied on to keep the negotiation secret, and, as private and relatively obscure individuals, would not attract public attention or imply any commitment on Florence's part. In Luigi Pulci, a literary friend who knew Roberto da Sanseverino well, and Andrea Petrini, the cashier of the Medici bank in Milan, Lorenzo seemed to possess the ideal instruments for this personal diplomacy. To them he entrusted special, secret missions to Roberto and Lodovico, which, while intended to further the policies being implemented by the city's ambassadors, resulted in some confusion between them and the officially designated representatives of the city. Petrini in particular seems to have created problems, for on one occasion he sent Lorenzo information conflicting with what he told the ambassadors, while on another he upstaged the latter by reporting Lorenzo's response to Cecco before they did. Lorenzo, fully alive to the delicacy of the situation, was upset that his personal agents might have offended the ambassadors. Besides rebuking Petrini for both errors, he felt it necessary to apologize to Tommaso and Luigi for Petrini's conduct, reassuring them that his cashier was not a person to whom he would reveal his complete thoughts.[16] While this may well have been the case, Tommaso and Luigi were nevertheless being given what may have been a sobering lesson about the consequences of Medici ascendancy. Indeed,

[15] Cf. Lorenzo to Tommaso '*da parte*', 2 Mar. 1477, MAP, lxxxix, 317, edited in Medici, *Lettere*, ii. 318–19. The willingness of the Sforza brothers and Roberto to accept these *condotte* was, of course, generally taken as a sign of their future political intentions.

[16] Cf. Lorenzo to Tommaso and Luigi Guicciardini, and to Andrea Petrini, 17 Feb. 1477, in Medici, *Lettere*, ii. 285–98. On these negotiations, ibid., 281, 316, 320, 324–8, 330–1, 338–40. On Luigi Pulci's friendship with Roberto da Sanseverino, Volpe, 'Luigi Pulci', 1–64. On Andrea Petrini, de Roover, *Rise and Decline*, 271; Medici, *Lettere*, i. 488.

Tommaso's effort to gain control of the negotiation with Lodovico may have been intended in part to assert his authority in the face of Petrini's intervention.

As Tommaso suspected, both Roberto and Lodovico were less interested in the *condotte* than in trying to seize power in Milan. By May 1477 the Sforza brothers, along with Roberto da Sanseverino, had hatched a plot to kill Cecco and take over the government, but their plans were revealed to the Duchess in advance. When she had one of the conspirators arrested, the rest tried unsuccessfully to raise Milan to rebellion, and then sought the intervention of Tommaso and the newly arrived Neapolitan ambassador to restore them to the government's good graces. Tommaso was anxious to restore stability in Milan, and certainly did not intend to allow the Neapolitan ambassador to get the credit for achieving a reconciliation. Together, then, he and Antonio Cicinello went back and forth between the Sforza castle and the brothers' stronghold, trying to convince the conspirators to accept the Duchess's offer of their personal safety in return for laying down their arms.[17] Although Roberto da Sanseverino eventually fled, the Sforza brothers agreed to these terms, and while left unharmed, were given sentences of permanent exile.

Once this crisis had been settled, the conflict between Cecco's faction and the Sforza brothers seemed finally resolved, and to Tommaso this brought great relief. Despite his conviction that the late Duke's brothers should have been included in the administration, he now felt, he wrote to Lorenzo, that with their disappearance the Milanese government would prove more united and more effective. Nor would he agree with Lorenzo that since Cecco was now more secure, he might forget his old allies and seek to buttress his

[17] On this incident, cf. Zaccaria Saggio to Lodovico Gonzaga, 26, 28, 30 May, 1 June, 1477, ASMa, Carteggio degli inviati, Milano, 1626; Niccolo de' Roberti and Bonifazio Bevilacqua to Ercole d'Este, 27, 28, 30 May 1477, ASMo, Carteggio degli ambasc., Milano, 1; the accusation and sentence against Roberto da Sanseverino and the Sforza brothers, 1 June 1477, ASMi, Potenze sovrane, 1464; an anonymous 'Storia di Milano', 1191–1549, Milan, Bibl. Ambros., MS 0.240. Sup., fos. 431ʳ–432ʳ. Cf. Medici, *Lettere*, ii. 358–61; *Storia di Milano*, vii. 316.

regime with Neapolitan support. Cecco would not, Tommaso wrote, abandon the Venetians unless they gave him good cause, and therefore the triple alliance seemed to him secure.[18]

Naturally, as ambassador in Milan, part of Tommaso's task was to ensure that Cecco did remain committed to the triple league. He had already been attempting to achieve this goal, undoubtedly stimulated by his personal commitment to Venice. Although it is not clear what action Tommaso had been taking, when a Venetian ambassador stopped briefly at Milan in May 1477, Tommaso assured him not only that the Milanese government was sincere in its determination to maintain the alliance of 1474, but that he had helped personally to foil King Ferrante's attempts to renew his earlier friendship with Milan.[19] While he was probably exaggerating his role in order to increase his credit in Venice, there must have been some basis for his claim. Certainly later, when Lorenzo's fears that Cecco might try to strengthen his connections with Naples proved correct, Tommaso did his best to dissuade the Milanese from anything which might undermine their friendship with Venice.

Cecco's plan was to create an indirect bond with Naples through Ercole d'Este, Duke of Ferrara, who was closely related to King Ferrante. Not only would the Milanese government offer Ercole a *condotta* and employ him as their principal military commander; a marriage between a daughter of the late Duke of Milan and Ercole's eldest son would further cement the relationship between the two houses. Tommaso was horrified when he learned of these plans, for Ercole was not only close to Ferrante but the ruler of a city with a long history of enmity with Venice. Consequently, when informed of the planned marriage alliance between the Sforza and Este houses, he became thoroughly alarmed, and urged that Venice as well as Florence be consulted before

[18] Tommaso to Lorenzo, 30 June 1477, MAP, xxxii, 113.
[19] Alberto Cortese to Ercole d'Este, 20 May 1477, ASMo, Carteggio degli ambasc., Venezia, 2; Zaccaria Saggio to Lodovico Gonzaga, 9 May 1477, ASMa, Carteggio degli inviati, Milano, 1626. On the efforts of Milan and Florence to remove the Venetians' fears that their allies might desert them, cf. Medici, *Lettere*, ii. 263–4, 362–6.

anything was concluded.[20] Similarly, when Cecco suggested a joint Milan–Florence *condotta* for Ercole, Tommaso was less than enthusiastic. Before he had consulted his own government, he recommended that Venice's opinion be obtained, while he pointed out that Florence really needed a commander of lesser rank, whom they could employ in day-to-day military affairs.[21] In the end, the Sforza–Este marriage did go forward, although Ercole's *condotta* did not, and Cecco's original plans for closer Milan–Ferrara ties by no means fully materialized. Quite possibly, Tommaso's intervention contributed to this result, and he could therefore congratulate himself on both helping to preserve the triple alliance and, at the same time, increasing the Venetians' appreciation of his support.[22]

All this Tommaso achieved while maintaining the impression at Milan that he was completely devoted to the administration's interests. Their appreciation of him became obvious in June 1477, when Tommaso sought permission to return home in order to take up a post to which he had been appointed in the Florentine dominion.[23] The Duchess was determined that Tommaso should not leave, and wrote emphatically to her ambassador in Florence that she needed a Florentine representative constantly at her court in order to discuss all issues which arose. No one, she asserted, could better satisfy this need than Tommaso, who was 'very prudent, and of great experience, integrity and reputation'. Moreover, Tommaso had always proved 'loving and affectionate to us and our government', while 'his discussions and

<hr/>

[20] Niccolò de' Roberti and Bonifazio Bevilacqua to Ercole d' Este, 24 May 1477, ASMo, Carteggio degli ambasc., Milano, 1. The Florentines agreed with Tommaso, for he was ordered secretly to warn the Milanese to reconsider the plan: Filippo Sacramoro to the Duke and Duchess of Milan, 30 May 1477, ASMi, SPE, Firenze, 293. Cecco was hoping that Ercole would improve Milan's relations with Ferrante: Niccolò de' Roberti to Ercole d'Este, 12 May 1477, ASMo, Carteggio degli ambasc., Milano, 1. Ercole was to replace Lodovico Gonzaga, who had lost favour in Milan: cf. Medici, *Lettere*, ii. 339–40, 425.

[21] Niccolò de' Roberti to Paolantonio Trotti, 1 June 1477, and to Ercole d'Este, 27 June 1477, ASMo, Carteggio degli ambasc., Milano, 1.

[22] On the Venetians' appreciation, cf. Filippo to the Duke and Duchess of Milan, 11 June 1477, ASMi, SPE, Firenze, 292, but cf. also Alberto Cortese to Ercole d'Este, 20 May 1477, ASMo, Carteggio degli ambasc., Venezia, 2.

[23] As Vicar of the Mugello: Tratte, 69, fo. 16ʳ.

conversation could not please us more'. In short, Florence could send no replacement with all Tommaso's 'good parts', or who could so please the Milanese rulers.[24]

As the Mantuan ambassador at Milan confirmed, the Milanese were truly loath to see Tommaso go, for his presence was very much 'in their interest'.[25] Moreover, Lorenzo de' Medici was eager for Tommaso to remain, as through him he could continue his close understanding with the Sforza government.[26] However, gaining a further extension of Tommaso's legation from the Florentines was not easy, for the proposal awakened the old envy felt by Tommaso's peers for any mark of special favour which he received. Lorenzo's intervention was necessary before due permission was obtained, and Tommaso's duties in Tuscany were delayed so that he could fulfil his more urgent responsibilities in Milan.[27]

A similar crisis over Tommaso's recall occurred in September 1477, when he was accused of failing adequately to represent Florence's point of view in a dispute between Lucca and Genoa over the possession of Pietrasanta. Most probably, envy again helped to motivate the suggestion made in the *Pratica* that Tommaso was proving so inadequate an advocate of Florentine policy that he should be recalled. Tommaso's response to this attack was indicative of both his *savoir-faire* and his political importance.[28] In outraged indignation, he immediately wrote to Lorenzo to exculpate himself, and offered to resign his position if Lorenzo or the Signoria felt that he should.[29] He must also have informed

[24] The Duke and Duchess to Filippo, 26 June, 9 July 1477, ASMi, SPE, Firenze, 292.
[25] Marsilio Andreasi to Lodovico Gonzaga, 15 July 1477, ASMa, Carteggio degli inviati, Milano, 1626.
[26] Marsilio Andreasi to Lodovico Gonzaga, 12 July 1477, ibid.
[27] Filippo to the Duke and Duchess, 1, 8 July 1477, ASMi, SPE, Firenze, 292. Meanwhile, Tommaso's post in the Mugello was first postponed and later filled, on Tommaso's nomination, by his son Paolantonio: Tratte, 69, fo. 16ʳ. That the Florentines still possessed a proprietary attitude to public office is very appropriately suggested by Witt, *Hercules*, 119.
[28] Filippo to the Duke and Duchess, 9 Sept. 1477, ASMi, SPE, Firenze, 293. On this conflict over Pietrasanta, cf. Medici, *Lettere*, ii. 402–10.
[29] Tommaso to Lorenzo, 18 Sept. 1477, MAP, xx, 703.

the Duchess of the incident, for she again intervened, ordering her ambassador to inform Lorenzo that 'it would hurt us to the quick to be deprived of [Tommaso's] very prudent and loving counsel'. In particular, testifying to Tommaso's efforts on behalf of the Venetian alliance, she pointed out that his 'authority in Venice' was very valuable, as 'through his letters he can resolve many things'.[30] Presumably Lorenzo agreed, for once again his intervention ensured that Tommaso remained in Milan. As for Tommaso, he had made his point to his detractors, and seemed content to accept an extension of his lucrative post, resigning himself to the fact that this additional mark of favour would expose him to yet further jealousy at home.[31]

Tommaso did not finally return from Milan until his city was thrown into its own political crisis. Having failed in his efforts to dissolve the Milan–Venice–Florence alliance, King Ferrante had concentrated instead on extending his authority in central Italy, creating increasing concern in the city which he had come to regard as his greatest enemy in Italy— Florence. In particular, it was Lorenzo de Medici whom he blamed for thwarting his political objectives, and he eventually decided that only by getting rid of him could he achieve success. By January 1478 he had established contacts with the Florentine exiles, who were plotting to kill Lorenzo, as Tommaso informed him.[32] At that stage, the threat of assassination was closing in on Lorenzo from all sides, for Girolamo Riario, the nephew of Pope Sixtus IV, also blamed Lorenzo for foiling his plans to establish his own state in the Romagna, and was plotting to have him removed.[33] Finally, disaffected elements within Florence itself were planning action against Lorenzo. These included the ambitious Pazzi family and Francesco Salviati, whom Lorenzo had tried to

[30] The Duke and Duchess to Filippo, 14 Oct. 1477, and cf. also 23 Oct. 1477, ASMi, SPE, Firenze, 292.
[31] Tommaso to Lorenzo, 27 Oct. 1477, MAP, xxxiv, 403; Filippo to the Duke and Duchess, 24 Oct. 1477, ASMi, SPE, Firenze, 292; the Signoria to Tommaso, 23 Oct. 1477, Sig., Leg. e Comm., 19, fo. 126ʳ.
[32] Tommaso to Lorenzo, 21 Jan. 1478, MAP, xxxiv, 281. Cf. Ilardi, 'Assassination', 100–1; Medici, *Lettere*, ii. 468.
[33] On Ferrante's and the papal Curia's attitude towards Lorenzo, cf. Medici, *Lettere*, ii. 411–24.

deprive of the prestigious Archbishopric of Pisa. It is an indication of how thoroughly the Medici had succeeded in imposing their authority in Florence that all these groups believed their objectives would succeed if only Lorenzo and his brother Giuliano were killed.

In the end, it was the plot hatched by Riario, Salviati, and the Pazzi which was actually carried out on 16 April 1478, while the Medici brothers were attending a formal High Mass in the Florentine Cathedral.[34] The attack was unsuccessful, for although Giuliano was killed, Lorenzo escaped, and the Pazzi's efforts to rouse Florence by the traditional appeal to popular liberty met with no response. Nevertheless, prepared to accept any excuse for attacking Lorenzo, both the Pope and the King of Naples declared war on Florence, and by the summer of 1478 the city was engaged in a major conflict of the sort it had not seen for over a decade.

Hearing of these events while in Milan, Tommaso was extremely concerned, and immediately requested permission to return home. This could no longer be refused him, and the Dukes let him go with a eulogistic description of how valuable his presence had been.[35] Meanwhile, war again proved beneficial to Tommaso's authority, for he was one of the *Dieci di Balìa* appointed on 13 June 1478. In a striking example of how continuity in office and concentration of authority was being promoted by the Medici regime, the term of this *Dieci* was renewed for two more six-month periods, allowing Tommaso and his colleagues to remain effectively at the head of Florence's government for a full year and a half.[36]

Tommaso found his long term as a member of the *Dieci* fraught with anxiety and disappointment, for despite Florence's apparent military advantage, the war went against her from the start. Not the least of the reasons was that, under Milanese pressure, Florence had agreed to hire as her captain

[34] On this Pazzi conspiracy and the sources regarding it, cf. Rubinstein, *Government*, 195–6; Medici, *Lettere*, ii. 412–13; Simonetta, *Diari*, i. 237–9. On the diplomatic aftermath, cf. Zimolo, 'Relazioni', 403–34; Arici, *Bona*, 103–17.
[35] The Duke and Duchess to Giovanangelo Talenti and Filippo, 28 May 1478, ASMi, SPE, Firenze, 294.
[36] Cf. Cento, 2, fos. 43ʳ–44ʳ; Medici *Lettere*, iii. 67.

Ercole d'Este, whose close ties with King Ferrante meant that his loyalties were divided. Although Tommaso had praised the suggestion when it was made to him in Milan, once he was responsible for the war Ercole's obvious reluctance to lead a vigorous attack caused Tommaso to change his mind. As he grumbled to the Milanese ambassador, he had expected to have to restrain the youthful Ercole's military ardour, but instead the captain was acting as a restraining influence on them![37] The second major problem for the Florentines lay in the fact that their allies proved much less supportive than the *Dieci* had hoped. In particular, the Venetians failed to provide adequate assistance, for, engaged in the war with the Turks, they were reluctant to offend the only power who might launch a crusade.[38] Consequently, once the loss of Monte San Savino early in November 1478 heralded the end of a disastrous campaign, the *Dieci* decided that pressure should be put on Venice by embassies from both Florence and Milan to ensure that more effective support was forthcoming for the following year.

Once again, Tommaso was Florence's choice for this mission to Venice. As Lorenzo de' Medici, himself one of the *Dieci*, expressed it, 'we have no more suitable person for this duty'.[39] Tommaso, however, initially refused the embassy on the grounds of his advanced age and the winter season. According to the Milanese ambassador, he even went before the *Cento* to ask that he be allowed to remain at home to die in his own house.[40] Eventually pressure from his colleagues persuaded him to change his mind, and he finally left for Venice on 7 December 1478. Anxious as ever to use his political authority to strengthen his connections abroad, he assured the Milanese government that he would do everything possible to further their wishes in Venice, and received

[37] Undated PS of Filippo Sacramoro, in ASMi, SPE, Firenze, 306. On the suspicions regarding Ercole's loyalty, cf. Medici, *Lettere*, iii. 95, 158, 166–7, 234.

[38] Cf. ibid., 61, 166–7, 220, 222, 301, 339; Morandini, 'Il conflitto' 119–20, 132–3; Zimolo, 'Relazioni', 409–10; Pintor, 'Le due ambascerie', 796 ff.

[39] Lorenzo to Giovaniacomo Simonetta, 21 Nov. 1478, edited in Medici, *Lettere*, iii. 297–9; Filippo to the Duke and Duchess, 15 Nov. 1478, ASMi, SPE, Firenze, 296; Tommaso's instructions in Sig., Leg. e Comm., 20, fos. 48ʳ–50ᵛ.

[40] Filippo to the Duke and Duchess, 15 Nov. 1478, ASMi, SPE, Firenze, 296.

the gratifying reply that the Duchess regarded him as Milan's 'creature', in whom she had the fullest confidence.[41]

Tommaso's mission to Venice proved long, arduous, and discouraging. On his arrival, it became only too obvious that the Venetians really wanted peace, and were prepared to accept almost any means of gaining it. Tommaso nevertheless exerted himself to persuade them to commit themselves to concrete plans for the next season's campaign, concentrating in particular on Florence's proposal of joint *condotte* for Roberto Malatesta and Costanzo Sforza. Tommaso was relieved when his first appeal on the subject seemed successful,[42] but frustration immediately followed, when the Milanese refused to pay their share of these captains' salaries. On learning this, the Venetians also retracted their offer, and Tommaso, desperate to reach a conclusion, decided to intervene directly with Milan to get them to change their minds. In a letter to the Duchess, he argued that Milan's refusal to participate in the *condotte* might result in the league's losing these valuable commanders to the enemy.[43] However, his appeal had no success, and Lorenzo, who was dealing with the *condotte* for Florence, was forced to commit his city to paying the salaries of both Roberto and Costanzo.

Disappointed on this issue, Tommaso had to face further difficulties and delays when he tried to persuade the Venetians to specify the troops which they would provide Florence in the spring. By late January 1479 his failure to obtain any definite reply subjected him to complaints and pressure from his colleagues at home. Tommaso had, they pointed out at the end of the month, been at Venice for nearly two months without obtaining more than 'good words'. He knew why he had been sent, and it was up to him to see that any failure was Venice's fault and not the result of his own lack of

[41] Filippo to the Duke and Duchess, 4 Dec. 1478, ASMi, SPE, Firenze, 296; the Duke and Duchess to Tommaso, 8 Dec. 1478, ibid., Venezia, 367.
[42] Cf. Gherardo Colli and Leonardo Botta to the Duke and Duchess, 8, 13 Jan. 1479, ibid., 368. On the negotiations for the hiring of Costanzo Sforza and Roberto Malatesta, cf. in particular, Medici, *Lettere*. iii. 399, iv. 9–12.
[43] On the refusal of the Duke and Duchess, and Tommaso's letter, cf. *Acta in consilio secreto*, iii. 42, 51. On Tommaso's disappointment at the Venetians' response, Gherardo Colli and Leonardo Botta to the Duke and Duchess, 28 Jan., 12 Feb. 1479, ASMi, SPE, Venezia, 368.

diligence! At the same time, however, the *Dieci* demonstrated their confidence in him by reminding him that his commission had been given only for form's sake; he was to do anything which occurred to him to obtain some good result at Venice.[44]

Whatever private strings Tommaso may have pulled, he was able soon thereafter to inform the *Dieci* that his hosts had agreed to supply some 1,500 foot and 2,000 horse in the spring. However, since this number fell far short of what Florence had been hoping for, he was forced to continue his solicitations for troops.[45] Meanwhile, the Venetians had raised yet further difficulties over taking the territories of Roberto Malatesta and Costanzo Sforza under their protection, and Tommaso was compelled to go through yet more tortuous negotiations in order to obtain a resolution acceptable to all concerned. In the end he must have agreed with the Milanese ambassador that this had been one of the most complicated and difficult negotiations in which he had ever been engaged.[46]

Given all the problems which the Venetians raised, it was hardly surprising that by early February 1479 Lorenzo de' Medici was openly criticizing them for their cold attitude which, he claimed, was undermining Florence's chances of winning the war.[47] Tommaso, on the other hand, retained some hope that they would eventually rally to Florence's support. In particular, after in February 1479 the Venetians announced the conclusion of peace with the Turks, he expected that his hosts would divert more men and money to the Italian front. He was therefore bitterly disappointed to find that, despite his entreaties, the Venetians refused to promise Florence more than the troops already named. According to the Milanese ambassador, Tommaso was so

[44] The *Dieci* to Tommaso, 23, 26 Jan. 1479, Dieci, Miss., 7, fos. 107ᵛ–108ᵛ, 114ᵛ–117ʳ.

[45] Cf. the *Dieci* to Tommaso, 3 Feb. 1479, ibid. fos. 132ʳ–133ᵛ; Medici, *Lettere*, iii. 398.

[46] Leonardo Botta to the Duke and Duchess, 20 Mar. 1479, ASMi, SPE, Venezia, 368. The agreement on this protection was finally concluded on 22 Mar.: Medici, *Lettere*, iv. 21.

[47] Lorenzo to Girolamo Morelli, 1 Feb. 1479, edited in Medici *Lettere*, iii. 396–7.

disillusioned by this response that he 'has completely lost the devotion which he had in them'.[48] However, this was clearly an exaggeration, for once the Venetians were persuaded to promise their full forces to Florence if the peace talks being held at Rome should fail, he was once again convinced of their fundamental goodwill. The problem lay, Tommaso concluded, with a few powerful individuals who were preventing Florence's demands from being presented to the Senate. If only someone could be found to undertake this task, he felt sure that they would be granted.[49]

However, Tommaso's faith in the Venetians proved to be unfounded, for it was only after the peace negotiations at Rome had definitely failed that, in early June 1479, they would send Florence even the full complement of soldiers that they had earlier promised.[50] By this time it seemed likely that no further Venetian assistance would be forthcoming for this campaign, and Tommaso sought permission to return home. Before he did so, Florence had suffered further military disasters, while the overthrow of Cecco Simonetta's administration early in September 1479 threatened the loss of her only reliable ally.[51] Once Lodovico Sforza and Roberto da Sanseverino finally succeeded in returning to Milan, with King Ferrante's backing, and gained control of the Milanese government, a Milan–Naples alliance seemed inevitable. To Tommaso, his city's situation looked hopeless, and even though these new developments required further discussions between Venice and Florence, he insisted that he be allowed to return home.[52]

---

[48] Leonardo Botta to the Duke and Duchess, 8 Mar. 1479, ASMi, SPE, Venezia, 368. On this peace, see Setton, *The Papacy and the Levant*, ii. 328. On the allies' hopes that it would benefit them, Medici, *Lettere*, iv. 15–16; Pintor, 'Le due ambascerie', 803.

[49] Undated PS of Filippo to the Duke and Duchess, ASMi, SPE, Firenze, 306.

[50] The *Dieci* to Tommaso, 2, 15 June 1479, Dieci, Miss., 9, fos. 19ʳ–20ʳ, 51ᵛ; and the Venetian Senate's deliberation of 21 June 1479, ASV, Sen. Secr., 29, fo. 32ᵛ.

[51] On events in Milan, cf. Medici, *Lettere*, iv. 189–91, 200–16, 227–8; Piva, 'Origine e conclusione', 51–54; Morandini, 'Il conflitto', 145–7; Pontieri, *Per la storia*, 151–3.

[52] Tommaso's departure may have been hastened by news that he might be appointed Standardbearer of Justice for November–December 1479. Although he had originally intended to wait for his successor, he abruptly informed the Milanese

The news with which Tommaso returned regarding the Venetians' future intentions was immensely important to the Florentines, for with Milan's intentions still unclear, continued resistance depended entirely on the aid which the Venetians would supply. It was undoubtedly to discuss this crucial problem that Lorenzo de' Medici arranged for Tommaso to spend a day with him at the Medici villa of Careggi before entering Florence late in October 1479.[53] In these discussions, Tommaso may well have reported favourably of the Venetians, for according to the manager of the Medici bank in Venice, he had left his hosts 'very eager to do every good'.[54] On the other hand, many Florentines had lost hope of any effective support from Venice, and some, including Lorenzo de' Medici, were beginning to be convinced of the necessity of making peace at almost any price. Since this would probably mean allying with King Ferrante, as the Milanese were likely to do, and leaving the Venetians isolated, it was not a prospect to delight the heart of a Venetian sympathizer like Tommaso. Consequently, while Lorenzo opened negotiations with both Milan and Naples, Tommaso pursued his own course of trying to persuade his fellow citizens to maintain the Venetian connection. While Tommaso was Standardbearer of Justice in November and December 1479, there were reports that certain leading figures of the regime were attempting to convince their fellow citizens that Venice would provide the support which hitherto had not been forthcoming.[55] However, the news from Tommaso's replacement in Venice, Luigi Guicciardini, indicated that the Venetians were unlikely to prove any more cooperative than before, and on the basis of this report Lorenzo intensified his negotiations with Naples and Milan.

---

ambassador in mid-October that he had decided to be home for All Saints' Day: Leonardo Botta to the Duke and Duchess, 1, 16 Oct. 1479, ASMi, SPE, Venezia, 369; Medici, *Lettere*, iv. 233; the *Dieci* to Tommaso, 13 Oct. 1479, Dieci, Miss., 10, fo. 125ᵛ.

[53] Filippo to the Duke and Duchess, 27 Oct. 1479, ASMi, SPE, Firenze, 298.

[54] Giovanni Lanfredini to Lorenzo, 5 Nov. 1479, MAP, xxvi, 37. However, the threat of a Hungarian incursion into Friuli and the Venetians' suspicions that both their allies would desert them soon altered their attitude.

[55] Cf. Medici, *Lettere*, iv. 398.

As Tommaso saw the rift between the two republics inexorably approaching, he was torn between frustration at the Venetians' blindness and annoyance with his fellow citizens. As he exclaimed to the Ferrarese ambassador at the end of November 1479, God must have deprived the Venetians of their senses, for if they wished, they could be the masters of Italy.[56] Increasingly desperate to get the Venetians to act, Tommaso decided at the end of November 1479 to make a last effort to obtain a definite promise of support. He decided to write directly to a friend in Venice, revealing that Florence was on the point of making peace, and therefore requesting a definitive response regarding what assistance the Venetians would offer in the coming year. However, Tommaso's overture was ineffectual, for his friend felt unable to make any commitment on behalf of the Venetian government.[57] In any event, it was by then too late, for, dissatisfied with the terms of his negotiation, Lorenzo de' Medici had already decided to go personally to Naples to negotiate peace. On 5 December 1479, he dramatically announced his departure in a move which, since the King had ostensibly conducted the campaign to remove him from Florence, possessed an element of self-sacrifice as well as desperation.[58]

Tommaso's eagerness to maintain Florence's connection with Venice was undoubtedly inspired in part by self-interest. According to Francesco Guicciardini, both Tommaso and Luigi Guicciardini feared that, since they had a decade earlier chosen to support Milan instead of Naples and had subsequently furthered connections with Venice to Ferrante's exclusion, the King might insist on their expulsion from Florence as one of the conditions of the peace.[59] Nevertheless, his position in government required Tommaso to further Lorenzo's approach to King Ferrante. As a member of the *Dieci* Tommaso helped to ensure that Lorenzo was provided with the appropriate powers to negotiate in Florence's

[56] Antonio da Montecatini to Ercole d'Este, 19 Nov. 1479, ASMo, Carteggio degli ambasc., Firenze, 2.
[57] Alberto Cortese to Ercole d'Este, 4 Dec. 1479, ibid., Venezia, 2.
[58] On Lorenzo's decision to go to Naples, cf. Medici, *Lettere*, iv. 249–51, 391–400; Cecchini, 'La guerra', 291–301; Guicciardini, *Memorie di famiglia*, 25–6.
[59] Ibid., 26.

name.[60] Moreover, as head of government, Tommaso was responsible for announcing and explaining Lorenzo's decision to the foreign representatives in the city. Although he could not have relished justifying Lorenzo's action to the Venetian ambassador, he performed his task, according to his colleagues, very suitably.[61]

Lorenzo's absence from Florence during his mission to Naples from December 1479 to March 1480 gave Tommaso a responsibility and freedom of action which he would otherwise not have possessed. On the one hand, the authority of the regime was called into question, for the removal of direct Medici influence, and the possibility that the head of the Medici house might fail in his effort to bring peace, emboldened the enemies of Medici supremacy to voice their discontent. Tommaso, along with other Medici friends, must have done his best to repress these complaints. During his term as Standardbearer of Justice, he may have been partially responsible for the arrest of two citizens of standing who were accused of having slandered the leading citizens of the regime.[62] Meanwhile, Tommaso could use his political position in his own interest. According to Alamanno Rinuccini, Tommaso was principally responsible for the annulment of a tax levied in December 1479, which would have fallen particularly heavily on the leading citizens. Consequently, Rinuccini wrote, Tommaso and some other *principali* arranged to have it cancelled, and this example of Tommaso's placing private above the public interest led Rinuccini to a wholehearted denunciation of the Standardbearer as a terrible citizen, an avaricious old man, iniquitous and tyrannical.[63] Although Rinuccini was particularly hostile towards

---

[60] Bartolomeo Scala to Lorenzo, 15 Dec. 1479, in Roscoe, *Lorenzo de Medici*, 111; Medici, *Lettere*, iv. 269–70, 297–8, 367–8.

[61] The *Dieci* to Lorenzo, 6 Dec. 1479, Dieci, Miss., 11, fo. 47ʳ. Cf. Medici, *Lettere*, iv. 257.

[62] On the disturbances which occurred during Lorenzo's absence, see Guicciardini, *Memorie di famiglia*, 37; Brown, *Scala*, 90–6; Medici, *Lettere*, iv. 288, 322–3.

[63] Rinuccini, *Ricordi storici*, pp. cxxx–cxxxi. However, Marks suggests that this tax was revoked because of widespread protest against continued heavy taxation ('The Development of the Institutions of Public Finance at Florence During the Last Sixty Years of the Republic, *c.* 1470–1530', D.Phil. thesis, Oxford, 1954, p. 73).

the Medici group, his assessment of Tommaso was undoubt-edly shared by other citizens of a similar political persuasion. Meanwhile, by March 1480 Lorenzo had succeeded in reaching agreement with King Ferrante on the terms of a peace. Although these were by no means as favourable as the Florentines had been hoping, Lorenzo could still return to a hero's welcome, for he had averted the military catastrophe which might have subjugated the city to foreign control. However, some members of the regime, including Tommaso, were probably unhappy about the alliance with Naples and Milan to which Lorenzo had agreed, while the fact that the restoration of occupied Florentine lands had been left to the King's discretion raised the possibility of future problems in the implementation of the peace. This in turn created the prospect of future discontent with Medici leadership, which had already made itself felt during Lorenzo's absence. It was probably, then, a desire to strengthen the position of the Medici circle which induced the leading citizens to introduce further constitutional changes soon after Lorenzo's return.

As was by now usual, these institutional innovations of April 1480 were effected through a short-term *Balìa*, which performed a long-overdue scrutiny.[64] Although the immedi-ate purpose of the *Balìa* was ostensibly to deal with financial problems created by the war, its major objective was undoubtedly to create yet another permanent council, which was intended to serve as a more effective instrument of the inner circle than the *Cento* had proved. In the implementa-tion of these changes, particular authority was granted to thirty individuals, described as the 'wisest and most reputed' citizens of Florence. They constituted the nucleus of the *Balìa*, of which they also chose the remaining members. Moreover, they were authorized to select forty other citizens qualified for the office of Standardbearer of Justice to join them in acting as the new council, which, although initially established for five years, became a permanent fixture of the Medici regime. To a degree, this Seventy, as it was called,

---

[64] On the political changes of Apr. 1480, see Rubinstein, *Government*, 197–203; Ricchioni, *La constituzione politica*, 55 ff, 86 ff, and the relevant legislation in Balìe, 31, fos. 91ʳ–95ᵛ, 97ʳ–100ᵛ.

superseded the *Cento*, as it voted on all major legislative proposals before they could be presented to the other councils. In addition, it assumed the duties of the *accoppiatori*, as each year half the Seventy determined the candidates for the Signoria. Even more importantly, every six months the Seventy chose from among its own members two new magistracies, the *Otto di Pratica* and the *Dodici Procuratori*, who took charge of foreign policy and matters affecting the city's form of government and of internal affairs respectively. Thus, although the Signoria officially remained the city's principal executive magistracy, major policy decisions were now made by these two committees of the Seventy. The Signoria, which had for centuries represented the majesty of Florentine republican government, now became of secondary importance, as had the older legislative assemblies a decade earlier, while power had been concentrated in bodies more representative of the upper echelons of the Medici regime.

While these institutions strengthened the position of a small group at the vertex of the regime, they enhanced Medici authority in particular. As the Ferrarese ambassador pointed out, there were very few men in the Seventy who would dare to disagree with Lorenzo if he said it was raining when the sun was shining.[65] This implied that Lorenzo's influence could prove paramount in the formation and execution of government policy, as it could in important political appointments. Apart from electing the *Dodici Procuratori* and the *Otto di Pratica*, the Seventy now determined who would be chosen for the Signoria. They even decided who gained entry to the Seventy, for although these councillors eventually held their positions for life, they could co-opt citizens to replace dead members, and could decide whether each Standard-bearer of Justice who took office should or should not be included in their august company. Thus, they exerted extensive control over entry to the highest political ranks, and their fellow citizens must therefore have felt a pressure to win their goodwill and to support their policies. As Jacopo Pitti later argued, citizens were prepared to go along with what the *principali* wanted in the hope of eventually gaining the same position themselves.[66] Since the Seventy were in turn generally willing to follow Lorenzo's lead, the new system must ultimately have strengthened Medici patronage and influence throughout the whole Florentine political class. Given the implications of the 1480 changes, it is understandable that opinion regarding them was varied. Citizens close to the major figures of the regime, especially those reliant on Lorenzo, could hope for advancement through this system, and must on the whole have favoured it. Moreover, the developments of the preceding decades had accustomed Florentines to accept a greater concentration of political authority and to see in it progress towards a more efficient and stable government. Thus, one citizen could, even if with reserve, describe the measures as 'well suited to our life today', as well as 'to the stabilization of those who govern'.[67] However, to others, who remained committed to the city's traditional constitution and political principles, the legislation of April 1480 represented the final destruction of the popular elements in Florence's constitution. As that confirmed enemy of Medici ascendancy Alamanno Rinuccini phrased it, the new system meant that the liberty of the people was 'overwhelmed and totally lost'.[68]

Tommaso's position between these two poles of opinion is not totally clear. Always hungry for power, he undoubtedly appreciated the fact that he, like Lorenzo de' Medici, was among the thirty citizens who wielded such authority in creating the *Balìa* and the Seventy. Moreover, the new system guaranteed him a permanent position of power. Besides being a member of the Seventy for the remaining years of his life, he could, as one of the most authoritative figures in that council, expect to be appointed to the Seventy's sub-committees. He was, for example, included in the first *Otto di Pratica* appointed on 20 April 1480, and was selected for the same magistracy two years later.[69] Nevertheless, fleeting

[66] Pitti, *Istoria*, 25.
[67] Piero del Tovaglia to Federigo Gonzaga, 13 Apr. 1480, ASMa, Carteggio degli inviati, Firenze, 1101.
[68] Rinuccini, *Ricordi storici*, p. cxxxiii.
[69] Tratte, 82, fo. 108ʳ.

references suggest that Tommaso was not completely happy with the system introduced in 1480. For example, he had apparently become accustomed to warn his fellow citizens 'You will place yourselves in danger,' but stopped doing this in about July 1480. When asked why by a fellow citizen, he responded 'You have already endangered yourselves,' as though he felt that the recent political changes would arouse sufficient discontent in the city to place the leading citizens' position in danger. In fact, as the Ferrarese ambassador pointed out, the Florentines were showing extreme discontent at this time, and some of it at least was directed against the creation of the new Seventy.[70]

Although such references are inconclusive, it is possible that Tommaso felt that the changes of 1480 had gone too far. In the light of his earlier comment that Lorenzo had no one to tell him the truth, it seems probable that he was annoyed at the manner in which the new system of government increased Lorenzo's power. As in 1476, he might argue that concentrating so much authority in one person would destroy the broader consensus which he, in line with Florentine tradition, felt to be essential for good government. In addition, from a personal perspective, an increase in Lorenzo's power meant a decrease in his own, and this could not have been welcome to him. As the Ferrarese ambassador wrote in November 1480, Tommaso was one of the few citizens who possessed 'intelligence and authority', and would give his own opinion rather than doing as he was told.[71] The fact that he was in such a lonely position, however, meant that his freedom of action was much reduced.

After 1480 there are fewer references to Tommaso's role in the Florentine government. In part this is a result of his advancing years, which left him with less energy for public

---

[70] Antonio da Montecatini to Ercole d'Este, 3 July 1480, ASMo, Carteggio degli ambasc., Firenze, 2. Cf. Rubinstein, *Government*, 201. In that same dispatch Antonio da Montecatini also mentioned that, when describing the Sienese government's efforts to satisfy its people, Tommaso touched the citizen next to him, as though indicating that Florence should be doing the same.

[71] Antonio da Montecatini to Ercole d'Este, 30 Nov. 1480, ASMo, Carteggio degli ambasc., Firenze, 2.

affairs.[72] However, it was also a product of Lorenzo's confirmed ascendancy, and of the creation of the Seventy and its two committees, which meant that deliberation of public policy was concentrated in the hands of small bodies who worked more collegially, and apparently more secretly, than the older magistracies had done.[73] Nevertheless, the growing silence surrounding Tommaso does not mean that he abandoned politics or abdicated political responsibility to Lorenzo. Throughout his life Tommaso constantly abided by the patrician principle of service to the state, and he continued to pursue Florence's interests as he saw them. In turn, his contribution was highly appreciated by his fellow citizens right up until his death. When he died in October 1485, for example, he was a member of that most powerful of magistracies, the *Dieci di Balìa*. Already a member of the *Otto di Pratica* in 1482, he and his colleagues had been converted into the *Dieci* in order to guide the city during a conflict between Venice and Ferrara, in which the Milan–Naples–Florence alliance fought on Ferrara's side. It is an indication of Tommaso's readiness to bow to government policy that he thus helped conduct a war against his beloved Venice. Indeed, he did so for nearly three years, for, with the regime's tendency to concentrate authority for longer periods in fewer hands, the term of this *Dieci* was repeatedly renewed.[74]

Whether a member of the *Otto di Pratica* or the *Dieci di Balìa*, Tommaso distinguished himself by his stubborn commitment to his city's interests. When the King of Naples proved reluctant to restore the Florentine towns captured during the Pazzi War, Tommaso emerged as one of the principal spokesmen of a hard-line policy which made Florence's support for Ferrante contingent on the restoration of

[72] Cf. Antonio da Montecatini to Ercole d'Este, 9 Apr. 1484, ibid., 3: For some months Tommaso had been reluctant to attend the *Dieci*'s meetings because of his age.

[73] In this as well the Florentines had envied the Venetians and may well have tried to imitate them.

[74] Cento, 2, fos. 76ᵛ–77ʳ, 84ʳ⁻ᵛ, 88ʳ⁻ᵛ, 92ᵛ–93ʳ, 94ᵛ–95ʳ, 97ᵛ–98ᵛ, 101ʳ–103ʳ; Rubinstein, *Government*, 200. The *Dieci*'s powers did not finally lapse until 31 Oct. 1485, by which time Tommaso was dead.

the occupied lands.[75] Moreover, when Tommaso felt that the city's new allies were proving too neglectful of Florence's wishes, he was the first to advocate abandoning them for a closer union with Venice. On one occasion in January 1481 he was even prepared to forget his age and the inclement weather, as he offered to go in person to Venice to revive the earlier alliance.[76] However, although many other Florentines also tended to look longingly towards Venice whenever they felt frustrated by the city's existing alliance system, Tommaso's influence was never strong enough to turn the balance of opinion within the ruling group. The alliance with Naples and Milan which Lorenzo had negotiated in 1480 remained Florence's permanent foreign alignment throughout the last years of Tommaso's life.

As was appropriate for a Florentine so devoted to political affairs, Tommaso finally died while in office, not just as a member of the *Dieci*, but also as Captain of Pisa. It is a tribute to his interest in the Pisano and to the high salary attached to this particular post that, at the advanced age of 82, Tommaso should have abandoned Florence to serve in it. However, the malarial fevers of this coastal town apparently proved too much for him, and soon after he took up the post he was forced to return to Florence to die, as he had always wanted, in his own bed.[77]

Although Tommaso's death went virtually unrecorded by his contemporaries, he had had a remarkable career. In large part through his own abilities, he had succeeded in making himself the second citizen of Florence, and despite the repeated internal conflicts in which he had been involved, he had always managed ultimately to be on the winning side. Although he had been forced to subordinate his views and objectives to those of the Medici family, he had succeeded in generally collaborating with them in Florence's interests.

---

[75] Cf. Filippo to the Duke and Duchess, 22 June 1480, ASMi, SPE, Firenze, 299; Antonio da Montecatini to Ercole d'Este, 9 Dec. 1480, ASMo, Carteggio degli ambasc., Firenze, 2.

[76] Antonio da Montecatini to Ercole d'Este, 24, 28 Jan. 1481, ibid. On this issue of a Venetian alliance, cf. also Antonio to Ercole, 30 Nov., 3 Dec. 1480, ibid.

[77] For Tommaso's appointment as Captain of Pisa, Tratte, 69, fo. 1^r. Tommaso died on 26 Oct. 1485: ibid., 61, fo. 123^r.

Moreover, he had been able to use Medici authority to advance his own interests, as a result leaving his family in a position of prominence which few Florentine clans could match. Although many citizens blamed Tommaso for having subverted the city's liberty in the interests of a narrow élite, Tommaso might console himself that he had pursued what he felt to be Florence's interests, and that he had remained personally committed to the principles of public service and freedom of consultation throughout his life.

The measure of Tommaso's commitment to Florence's political tradition was provided by the careers of his and Dianora Tornabuoni's sons. Despite their early association with the Medici, they continued to take an independent line in politics, and even, in the end, to revolt against Lorenzo's son Piero. That Piero Soderini, when serving as head of the republic from 1502 to 1512, should have consciously sought to preserve Florence's tradition of broader government rather than opting for a more oligarchic system, suggests that devotion to the city's constitution may have remained deeply rooted within the family. However, in the end it was Tommaso who proved to be in the mainstream of Florence's constitutional development, for ultimately the broad government which had been established on the Medici's expulsion in 1494 was forced to yield, not just to a more oligarchic system, but eventually to a Medici prince. While this was an eventuality which Tommaso himself sought to avoid, he had nevertheless contributed to it through his pursuit of power and his willingness to promote Medici authority for this goal. Thus, although Florentine constitutional development eventually took a direction which Tommaso would have deplored, he and others like him had made a major contribution towards it by their pursuit of their own political interests throughout the fifteenth century.

Conclusion

Although the foregoing work has dealt principally with the careers of only two citizens, it suggests more general conclusions regarding the nature of politics in fifteenth-century Florence. Most obvious are its implications concerning that collection of citizens who co-operated most closely with the Medici family in political affairs and who made such an important contribution to the family's continued ascendancy. Tommaso's history is a confirmation of the arguments already so convincingly made by Dale Kent that the Medici consciously sought to build up a group of friends who would act as supporters and defenders of the family's political position. If Cosimo Favilla is to be believed, the principal concern of Cosimo de' Medici, and presumably of his descendants, was the danger in the degree of pre-eminence which their family had achieved, and thus the friends whom they cultivated were intended first and foremost as a means of defence. Tommaso's case further suggests that the Medici sought out as friends intelligent and competent citizens who were likely to be active in the political sphere, and who were prepared, for whatever reason, to attach themselves to the Medici star. By furthering these citizens' political careers and their personal interests, the Medici were able to expect from them the gratitude and support which they desired, and Tommaso's many years of loyalty to the family is ample testimony of the success of their policy. Indeed, it is clear from Tommaso's letters that he consciously regarded himself as a member of a group of 'Medici friends', with a responsibility not only to further the interests of the city's leading family but also to advance the careers of others willing to do the same.[1] In this way Medici influence and patronage did help to create a party in the sense that, although without formal organization or stable membership, its members acted together for the political security and advancement of all.

Yet, if Tommaso's career exemplifies the operation of such a group of Medici friends, it also indicates that this was not the only group through which he sought to achieve his political goals. As the oath of 1449 suggests, Tommaso saw himself also as a 'friend of the regime', or of the dominant political group after 1434. He was apparently one of those most anxious, for personal reasons, to advance the political interests of this group, and he formed *intelligenze* with other like-minded individuals to achieve mutual, specific goals. For obvious reasons, acting as a friend of the Medici was much the same as acting as a friend of the regime, and the goals, as well as the membership, of both groups were very much the same. Nevertheless, a different organization and a different method were involved, in that while Medici friends sought their goals by promoting Medici authority, these friends of the regime must often have been acting independently, relying on mutual co-operation. In fact, the oath of 1449 demonstrates how members of the regime could define their goals and organize their action apparently without any reference to the leading family of the regime.

Thus, this oath suggests that Florentines anxious for political advancement used diverse methods or strategies for achieving their political goals, of which friendship with the Medici was only one. From Tommaso's career, in fact, it would appear that he pursued some of the same strategies to reinforce his political authority as did the Medici. He also sought connections abroad, which would fortify a citizen's authority at home, as well as bring influence and importance throughout the country. He also relied on institutional controls to promote his career, for while he remained unpopular with the citizen body in general, his intelligence and commitment were highly valued by the leading citizens, and in particular by the Medici. In addition, Tommaso

---

[1] Cf. Tommaso Soderini's comment to Piero de' Medici when recommending Maso degli Albizzi, 21 Dec. 1459, MAP, xvi, 276, as quoted above, Chap. 5.

furthered the careers of his relatives and friends, and used institutional and personal patronage to strengthen his political position. The fact that his desire to be present for the scrutiny and to be appointed *accoppiatore* for it was expressed particularly strongly in 1471 may suggest that as the support of the Medici became less dependable, promoting his relatives and friends became correspondingly more essential to him. Thus, one strategy or another could become more important as circumstances changed, and the various means of gaining political authority represented diverse alternatives among those available.

Looking at Tommaso's relationship to the Medici as merely one strategy for advancement helps to explain how he could abandon his friendship with them so cold-bloodedly in 1470. For Tommaso, as presumably for other Medici supporters, his friendship with the city's leading family was more instrumental than sentimental, and therefore his loyalty to them remained constantly dependent on the relationship's continuing to serve his interests. For many years, particularly when he was less influential and therefore more in need of Medici aid, Tommaso evidently felt that siding with the Medici was the best means to secure himself the political and personal success which he sought. However, once he became more powerful, other methods offered better opportunities for advancing his political career, while Medici ascendancy became more an obstacle than an aid to his ambition. At that point, it is remarkable with what little compunction Tommaso forgot friendship, family ties, and benefits received in a calculation of how much more he might gain by opposing the Medici and undermining their authority. While Tommaso may have been more ruthless or ambitious than many of his fellow citizens, he was by no means exceptional in this change of heart. In fact, most of the Medici's principal collaborators eventually turned against them to a greater or lesser degree, suscitating major rebellions as in 1465–6 and 1470–1, or minor moments of tension, as in 1454. In all these cases, while factors such as a change in the head of the Medici house or the political situation of the time undoubtedly affected citizens' behaviour, it also seems true that, after years of collaboration with the Medici for mutual goals, citizens were eventually concluding that the balance between what they were gaining from and what they were losing to a growing Medici ascendancy was tipping too far in the latter direction. It was apparently for this reason that they decided they could better serve their own interests by changing direction and undermining the authority which for many years they had helped to defend.

Thus, if Tommaso's career demonstrates how the Medici used personal ties and patronage to build support, it also reveals the limitations and weaknesses of these bonds in the long run. Indeed, the Medici could never totally satisfy the ambition of their supporters, which would have meant renouncing their own ascendancy, while they were placed in the paradoxical position that the further they advanced their friends' interests the greater scope and the more reason they gave these very friends to turn against them. Similarly, Niccolò Soderini's career exemplifies the potentially temporary nature of the friendship bonds. After creating an obviously instrumental connection with the Medici in the early 1430s, his friendship with them declined once the political motivation behind it was removed, and, as the authority of the Medici and their friends became a betrayal of his principles and a block to his career, he went on, in the following decades, to become one of the Medici's most implacable enemies.

Thus by illustrating the potentially unstable nature of friendship ties, the careers of both Niccolò and Tommaso suggest that the Medici's continued success in maintaining and reinforcing their unofficial leadership could not have depended solely on such impermanent bonds. Indeed, the Medici themselves seem to have recognized the need to cultivate other bases of strength, whether support abroad, particularly at the Sforza court, or the wide popularity whose importance was mentioned by the Milanese ambassador at the end of 1469. Indeed, the vast—almost indiscriminate—patronage which the Medici dispensed seems unlikely to have been directed solely towards creating a compact group of friends, but was probably also intended to win the broadest goodwill possible. Apart from these strategies, the Medici, also relied on institutional changes which not only gave them the power to advance friends but also served to convince citizens to go along with the desires of the leading citizens of the regime if they wanted successful political careers. Yet the Medici were aware that institutional controls depended also on the will of other citizens, and could be turned against them by the *principali* with whom they shared power. Thus, even while they furthered oligarchic measures, the Medici also moved towards a more personal government, especially during Lorenzo's time. Just as institutional controls provided a means whereby the leading citizens could bypass the wishes of the less prominent, so a nascent personal government, based on the private use of less prominent individuals, enabled the Medici to reinforce their position by bypassing, to a degree, the opinions and desires of their fellow *ottimati*.

Perhaps the greatest strength of the Medici, however, lay in the fact that their wealth, their personal ability, and their willingness to dedicate themselves to government made them indispensable both to the city in general and to the leading citizens of the regime in particular. Apart from their financial contribution to the city, they possessed the contacts abroad through which to press the city's interests, and were prepared to sponsor difficult political decisions when others were unwilling to take the responsibility. The positive consensus which they received from their fellow citizens was based in part on the conviction that the Medici made an important contribution to the city, from which all benefited—that is, that they were benefactors of the republic, as the title of *Pater Patriae* given to Cosimo suggests.

The upper ranks of the regime had particularly strong reasons for appreciating the Medici's political contribution because their success in concentrating political power in their own hands depended on Medici support. Although the Medici were at times reluctant to further measures which might lose them popularity or give too much power to citizens who could combine against them, they nevertheless in the end always supported oligarchic measures. This was not only because they shared the same interests as other wealthy, prominent citizens, and needed political control even more than the others as a form of self-defence; it was undoubtedly also to satisfy their supporters and other prominent citizens who desired more power for themselves. Indeed, Tommaso's behaviour in late April 1471 is a rare, but presumably not isolated, instance of the pressure applied on the Medici by their supporters to intervene in the political system in their collective favour. Such appeals to the Medici arose from the fact that their authority was extremely important—at times essential—for achieving a consensus in favour of constitutional changes or for carrying them through. For example, in 1458, the leading citizens insisted on gaining Cosimo's approval for the changes which they planned, presumably knowing that he could ruin their plans if he chose, or assist them, as he ultimately did by placing foreign military support at their service. Moreover, as the events of 1454 suggest, Medici patronage could be useful to maintain citizens' dedication to narrower government, despite pressure from others who favoured a broader system, internal doubts about institutional controls, and jealousy of the increased authority which the narrower system brought to the Medici. When the then Gonfalonier of Justice, Dietisalvi Neroni, began to dismantle these controls, Tommaso exerted his influence to persuade him to change his mind, and to maintain the unity of the principal citizens in favour of restrictive measures. While his arguments that the '*Balìe*, *borse* and *catasto*' were interrelated, and served the interests of Dietisalvi as they did those of the rest of the regime, undoubtedly had some effect, Tommaso obviously felt that Medici influence would be more effective than his own. It was the Medici, he implied to Piero, who should have made it clear to Dietisalvi that no changes were to be made, while his suggestion that the Medici reinforce Dietisalvi's decision not to innovate further by giving him an inducement, is an example of how Medici patronage was used to maintain a consensus in favour of the institutional controls.

This implies that it was not only—possibly not principally—for the sake of Medici patronage that prominent citizens supported the city's leading family. They needed the Medici in order to achieve their collective interests. Indeed, while patronage may have been an important motive for less prominent citizens to support the Medici, and remained permanently important for unpopular ones like Tommaso, for eminent Florentines who had more means to achieve their personal goals, Medici patronage must have been less essential. Instead, it may have been the Medici's contribution, variously towards the government of the republic, the security of the regime, or the achievement of a political system more in their own interests, which formed the principal motive behind the support of such prominent citizens.

This leads us to the further consideration that the political groups formed in Florence during the fifteenth century were only partially patronage groups held together by personal ties. While personal bonds undoubtedly created connections which functioned in the political sphere by associating citizens' interests, it was this possession of common interests and goals which was the principal cement of political groups. The case of the Medici friends was somewhat unusual in that the group defined itself in terms of one exceptionally powerful family, and its members achieved their goals indirectly through them. Yet even here it was the satisfaction of common interests which maintained the group's unity, and while this goal was achieved in part through Medici patronage, it also depended on mutual collaboration. In the case of other political groupings, personal ties undoubtedly had an effect in determining who was drawn into them, but the groups themselves had specific political goals. The drive towards more oligarchic government, for example, which so united the leading citizens around the Medici, created a political group—often referred to in the preceding pages as 'the Medici group'—dedicated to the common goal of satisfying its political interests, which ultimately meant shifting the city's constitutional system in its own favour and it seems at times to have drawn the Medici after it rather than always following the Medici's lead. Other times groups were put together in which personal ties played a very minor role. The anti-Medici group which Tommaso helped to construct in 1470–1, for example, consisted of very disparate elements, held together only by their desire to reduce Medici authority. Even outright enemies, such as Tommaso and Antonio Ridolfi, could collaborate in this, much as Tommaso collaborated with Luigi Guicciardini at the end of 1469, putting his own rivalry with him aside in the interests of the unity and security of the regime.

The objectives of the political groups to which Tommaso and Niccolò belonged further suggest that the political conflicts of the fifteenth century concerned not just rival groups within a political élite, struggling among themselves for place and power. Rather, particularly until 1466, they also represented struggles between socio-economic groups— the traditional ones of the *maggiori* and *minori* or the *principali* and the *popolo*, as contemporaries might have phrased it. What the group of prominent citizens around the Medici were doing was seeking greater power for themselves in order to satisfy their interests, often at the expense of the less prominent or less wealthy Florentines. They were not seeking merely to gain more political posts—with the connected salaries, prestige, opportunities for profit and influence which might, for instance, assist them in the courts— but also to use their increased authority to pursue the interests of an economic group, the wealthy and in particular those involved in commerce. This is particularly evident in tax legislation, where the Medici group fought taxation which would have weighed more heavily on the rich and on liquid wealth. However, it is also evident in the manner in which the Medici regime insisted on the need to favour commerce and navigation, using the stabilization of their authority in 1458 to turn to such questions as port facilities and the state galley voyages. Such issues were of permanent importance to the city's commercial upper classes, to which most of the leading figures of the post-1434 regime (as of preceding regimes) belonged. However, pursuing those interests brought them into conflict with the broader strata of less wealthy citizens, who objected not only to the leading citizens' tax policy, but also to the purposes to which communal income was being put. This difference regarding economic policy is most evident in the movement of 1465–6, when 'popular' political ideas were also connected with a 'popular' financial policy, but it underlay also the struggle of 1458, and other conflicts over finances which Florence, like other Italian cities, so often experienced. It is a measure of the success of the leading citizens that such conflict was much less in evidence during the 1470s and 1480s, for by then they had established their ascendancy to such a degree that they were less constrained to take the wishes of the wider citizen body into account.

This, of course, does not mean that only economic factors influenced citizens' political behaviour. Florentines' actions were not determined by their economic position; other considerations could and did frequently intervene to motivate quite different behaviour. Wealthy patricians might, for example, espouse popular movements for their political purposes, as the leading figures of the Pitti group did in 1465. Vice versa, middle-status or lesser citizens could support the interests of the greater if they were so closely connected that what served the *maggiore*'s interests also served their own. Moreover, principle itself must have moved certain citizens to act as the common good required instead of pursuing their personal economic interests. Nevertheless, a conflict of economic interests did exist between the greater and lesser citizens of Florence, and this sort of socio-economic conflict remained a permanent element in Florentine politics. In fact, Niccolò Soderini's career suggests that even when a person might have seemed to be abandoning his natural socio-economic group for political purposes, economic motivation may also have lain behind his decision.

Thus, political conflicts in fifteenth-century Florence did involve major issues, even though they were sometimes hidden under personal rivalries and wrestlings for control. Even what might seem a pure power struggle was normally affected by wider questions, principles, and ideas. The conflict between Tommaso Soderini and Lorenzo de' Medici in 1470–1, for example, was profoundly affected by the issue of what power would prove Florence's best foreign ally, and Tommaso's admiration for Venice and the political ideas associated with it, as well as his sense of his own best interests, undoubtedly influenced his decision to opt for Venice and oppose Lorenzo. As regards the struggle over Florence's constitutional issues, self-interest was again an essential factor in dividing citizens into opposing groups. Yet connected ideas and even ideologies also played an important role. Those of the anti-Medici circles are undoubtedly most

obvious, for they could claim the traditional ideals of liberty
which were so deeply rooted in Florentines' consciousness,
and had been so clearly reaffirmed by the 'civic humanists'
of the late fourteenth and early fifteenth centuries. Not only
was Niccolò Soderini strongly influenced by these ideas, but
a great part of his success sprang from his ability to restate
them in terms which would move his contemporaries. Less
obvious are the ideas of the Medici circle who, although they
also initially claimed merely to be defending liberty (defined,
however, as the liberty of the regime), gradually moved
towards the elaboration of an oligarchic ideology which
better justified the political changes which they were institut-
ing. Although references to such ideas are rare, the debates
preceding the *parlamento* of 1458 indicate that the leading
citizens were by then arguing that the more restricted government which they were introducing meant better government
in that it gave political power to the 'better' citizens—that is,
those who were competent and well-intentioned, as well,
perhaps, as representing the upper ranks of Florentine society. Such citizens, Tommaso would argue, had Florence's
best interests at heart, and would pursue policies which
benefited the city as a whole. These arguments were clearly
self-serving, but they do indicate that the leading figures of
the Medici group were appealing to traditional patrician or
aristocratic assumptions, which, as Tommaso again suggests,
were gradually reinforced by the example of Venice, to cover
self-interest in a more acceptable cloak. Undoubtedly, at
some level, the *principali* sincerely believed in their arguments, particularly as they could find some foundation for
them in the manner in which election and special councils
did promote more efficient, more consistent, and possibly
more stable government by a group with political experience
and training. Moreover, their attitude was gradually accepted
by others, as is indicated by the praise given to the oligarchic
measures of 1480, and by the widespread respect for Venice
evident by the early 1480s.[2] This admiration for Venice could

---

[2] Cf. Piero del Tovaglia's comments regarding the changes of 1480, above,
Chap. 9, and Gilbert, 'The Venetian Constitution', 475.

hardly have been based on the two cities' political co-operation, which proved relatively unsuccessful during the second half of the fifteenth century, and therefore it must have depended on a growing community of political ideas.

Finally, a few words should be said regarding the motives which Tommaso displayed in his political activities and the sources of his political success. While it may not always have been obvious in the foregoing pages, a citizen like Tommaso, who dedicated his life to politics and served his city even when it meant something of a personal sacrifice, must have been truly devoted to his city's welfare. Like other Florentines, he would presumably have cited his city even before his family as an object of loyalty, and his response to his own son's conspiracy in 1468 confirms that he subscribed to this ideal. However, devotion to his city stands in sharp contrast to Tommaso's normal behaviour in political life, where his own advancement and that of his family seems so often to have taken precedence over the welfare of the community as a whole. Indeed, in his later years, Tommaso was even prepared to accept bribes and divert public money to his own use in a manner which fully justifies Rinuccini's denunciation of him as a '*pessimo cittadino, vecchio rapace, iniquo e tirannico*'.[3]

Some explanation of this contradiction can, perhaps, be offered by the attitudes of fifteenth-century Italians towards government and government service. As was apparently true for Venice as well as for Florence,[4] government was more identified with those who participated in it than is the case after the rise of the modern state. Members of the ruling group felt that they were the state, or had a share in it, and their proprietary attitude towards it is evident in their approach to offices, in their conviction that public authority should be used in the interests of family, neighbours, and friends, and in the sense expressed even by Florentine law,

---

[3] Cf. Chap. 9 above.
[4] Cf. Queller, *The Venetian Patriciate*, 17–18. Cf. also, for Florence, the comment of Manno Temperani in the *Pratica* of 14 Nov. 1465: '*ad primores et sapientores paucos referendum . . . ad quos plus pertinet res publica*': Pampaloni, 'Fermenti', 261.

that citizens should be getting something out of government—that is, the benefits (*onori* and *utili*) of public service—as well as supporting their share of the burdens.
Tommaso displays all these attitudes, as he also suggests that
there was some contemporary consensus regarding an acceptable limit up to which a citizen was justified in benefiting
from public service. Early in the 1460s he wrote proudly to
Piero de Medici that he had never taken advantage of his
political position for personal gain, 'beyond the ordinary'.
Although he did not define what 'the ordinary' meant, it
presumably included salaries of office, profit from state loans,
gifts to ambassadors, and the other emoluments which
accompanied public life. Beyond this, Tommaso had used his
position as *accoppiatore* to benefit himself and his family,
may have used his political influence to gain the property of
enemies of the Medici regime at a relatively low price, and
had used his relationship with the Medici to advance family
and friends, all of which may in his view have come within
the scope of 'ordinary'.

However, with time, Tommaso's use of his political position for private objectives went far beyond these limits. By
the beginning of the 1470s he was accepting money from
both the King of Naples and the Duke of Milan, retaining
government funds for his own use, and, if Rinuccini is
correct, cancelling taxes in order to protect his private purse.
It is not clear how Tommaso justified this behaviour to
himself. In the case of the bribes, he may have felt that the
money was appropriate payment for services rendered, while
he could salve his conscience by arguing that they had not
altered his political position or involved betraying Florence's
interests. Nevertheless, the fact remains that as he became
more powerful, and his financial need greater, Tommaso did
abandon his original self-declared abstemiousness and
behave in a way which even contemporaries regarded as
corrupt. He would therefore seem to provide a confirmation
both of the many accusations of corruption levied against
the Medici regime in the fifteenth century, and of the
argument that narrower government encouraged the placing
of private before public interest by reducing the controls over
the behaviour of officials which wider government was

supposed to impose. However, from the single example of Tommaso it is impossible to generalize concerning the whole regime, particularly as he was as exceptional in his greed and ambition as he was in his ability and the measure of power which he eventually obtained. Certainly other figures within the regime were less eager to use public power for private gain; Lorenzo de' Medici himself, according to the Milanese ambassador, was little interested in the financial advantages of power, preferring to concentrate on possessing its substance.⁵ Moreover, using political posts for private gain was nothing new in Florentine history; citizens in the past had turned public funds to their own use, as they had also taken advantage of military duties for profiteering. Even those most critical of the Medici regime and its corruption, such as Niccolò Soderini, were no less anxious than those whom they condemned to turn public authority to their own use, and seem equally to have seen public authority as a means to advance their private affairs, even though this so strongly contrasted with the idealism of their proclaimed views.

Finally, regarding the sources of the Soderini's political authority, it is obvious that for Niccolò briefly and for Tommaso permanently, connection with the Medici and their friends provided an important means of increasing their political importance by providing influential individuals or a group through whom they could affect Florentine politics. However, for both, the fundamental factors in their political success were their birth and their personal ability. The first gave them access to the Florentine political world, along with the possibility of winning an influential position within it, as within their local sphere in S. Spirito. The other allowed them to build on these advantages through intelligence and a talent for that fundamental quality in Renaissance politics— the power to persuade. Both Niccolò and Tommaso were repeatedly described as eloquent, and there are many testimonies to the power of Niccolò's rhetoric, which proved so effective during his embassies, as it did during his fateful period as Gonfalonier of Justice in 1465. To these qualities

⁵ Cf. Sacramoro to the Duke of Milan, 8 Aug. 1471, ASMi, SPE, Firenze, 283: Lorenzo is not anxious for '*il pasto*' but rather for '*la conditione*'.

must be added, in Niccolò's case, courage (carried at times to the point of recklessness), independence, and energy, which won the admiration of his fellow citizens, but nevertheless contributed to the débâcle of 1465. Tommaso's character, like his fate, was very different from his brother's, for in politics he displayed above all patience and a prudent caution, which warned him against revealing his true position, taught him to compromise for the sake of later success, and enabled him to pick a careful path through the pitfalls of Florentine politics with the successful results that we have seen. Tommaso was also much more willing than Niccolò to apply his intelligence to pragmatic questions, including how to achieve his objectives through the operation of the sometimes complex Florentine bureaucracy and the unpredictable shifts of republican politics. Repeatedly, the Milanese ambassadors bore witness to his ability in this area, as they did to his capacity to see the implications of events, and to take appropriate measures to deal with them. Such qualities made him extremely valuable not only to the Medici and to the other leading citizens, but also to powers abroad, whether the Duke of Milan, the King of Naples, or the Venetians, and therefore contributed to his influence both at home and throughout Italy. Indeed, it was this capacity to make such an effective political contribution which made him so essential to both the Sforza and the Medici that, despite his disloyalty in 1470-1 and the danger which he presented thereafter, they were prepared not only to tolerate his presence, but to work to recover his support, and to pay large sums of money to retain it.

Thus, while this history of Tommaso and Niccolò offers no single explanation of Florentine politics in the fifteenth century, it does illustrate not only the nature and basis of their connection with the Medici, but also the factors contributing to a Florentine's political success, and the complexity and variety inherent in Florentine politics as reflected in citizens' responses to the situation and developments of their times.

Bibliography

MANUSCRIPT SOURCES

FERRARA
Archivio di Stato
Archivio Bentivoglio

FLORENCE
Archivio di Stato
Archivio Mediceo avanti il Principato
Arti: Calimala
     Cambio
Atti del Capitano del Popolo
Atti del Podestà
Balìe
Capitani di Parte Guelfa
Carte Ancisa
Carte Strozziane (F. Giovanni, Ricordanze, ser. 2, 16 *bis*)
Catasto
Cento
Consulte e Pratiche
Corporazioni Religiose Soppressi
Dieci, Condotte e Stanziamenti
     Missive
     Missive, Legazioni, e Commissarie
Diplomatico, Acquisto Soderini
Libri fabarum
Manoscritti (B. Dei, Cronica, 119)
Mercanzia
Monte Comune
Notarile Antecosimiano
Otto di Guardia, periodo repubblicano
Provvisioni, Registri

Pupilli avanti il Principato
Signori, Legazioni e Commissarie,
    Legazioni e Commissarie, Risposte verbali di oratori
    Minutari
    Missive, 1*a* Cancelleria
    Missive, 2*a* Cancelleria
    Responsive, Copiari
Signori, Dieci, Otto, Legazioni e Commissarie, Missive e
    Responsive
Tratte
Archivio privato Niccolini
Biblioteca Moreniana
MSS Moreni (G. Baldovinetti, Sepoltuario, 339)
Biblioteca Nazionale di Firenze
Conventi Soppressi (Cosimo Favilla, 'De origine ordinis servorum
    et vita Beati Philippi de Benetiis' C. I. 145 and P. Petribuoni,
    'Priorista', C. 4. 895)
Ginori Conti
Fondo Magliabecchiano (M. Parenti, 'Ricordi politici di Firenze
    alla morte di Cosimo de' Medici', xxv, 272)
Fondo principale
Poligrafo Gargani

LONDON
British Library
MSS Egerton

MANTUA
Archivio di Stato
Carteggio degli inviati, Firenze
                    Milano
                    Venezia
Lettere della Signoria di Firenze e dei Medici ai Gonzaga

MILAN
Archivio di Stato
Archivio Visconteo–Sforzesco
Carteggio interno, Milano Città
Potenze estere, Firenze
               Genova
               Roma
               Venezia
Potenze Sovrane
Biblioteca Ambrosiana
MSS Ambrosiani

MODENA
Archivio di Stato
Carteggio degli ambasciadori, Firenze
                          Milano
                          Venezia

PARIS
Bibliothèque Nationale
MSS italiens

PISA
Archivio di Stato
Comune
Fiumi e Fossi

VATICAN CITY
Biblioteca Apostolica Vaticana
Codici Latini (Giovanni di Carlo, 'De temporibus suis', 5878)

VENICE
Archivio di Stato
Consiglio de' Dieci, Misti
Senato, Mar
Senato, Deliberazioni segrete (Senatus Secreta)

PRINTED PRIMARY SOURCES

Acta in consiglio secreto in castello Portae Jovis Mediolani, ed. A. R. Natale (Milan, 1963), 3 vols. (vols. 4, 7, and 16 of *Acta Italica*, published by the Fondazione italiana per la storia amministrativa).

AMMANATI, J., *Epistolae Jacobi Picolomini . . . una cum . . . Commentariis* (Milan, 1521).

BONINSEGNI, D., *Storie della città di Firenze dall'anno 1410 al 1460* (Florence, 1637).

CAMBI, G., *Istorie*, in *Delizie degli eruditi toscani*, ed. Ildefonso di S. Luigi, xx–xxiii (Florence, 1785–6).

CAVALCANTI, G., *Istorie fiorentine*, ed. F. Polidori, 2 vols. (Florence, 1838–9).

Cronaca di anonimo veronese, 1446–1488, ed. G. Soranzo, in *Monumenti storici pubblicati dalla R. Deputazione veneta di storia patria*, ser. 3, *Cronache e Diarii*, iv (Venice, 1915).

FILELFO, F., *Epistolae Francisci Philelfi* (The Hague, 1526).

GILLIODTS VAN SEVEREN, L. (ed.), *Cartulaire de l'ancienne étaple de Bruges*, 4 vols. (Bruges, 1904–6).

GUICCIARDINI, F., *Le cose fiorentine*, ed. R. Ridolfi (Florence, 1945).

—— *Memorie di famiglia*, in *Scritti autobiografici e rari*, ed. R. Palmarocchi (Bari, 1936).

LANDUCCI, L., *Diario fiorentino*, ed. I. del Badia (Florence, 1883).

MACHIAVELLI, N., *Istorie fiorentine*, in *Tutte le opere storiche e letterarie*, ed. G. Marzoni and M. Casella (Florence, 1929).

MALIPIERO, D., *Annali veneti dall'anno 1457 al 1500*, in *Archivio storico italiano*, 7, Parts I and II (1843–4).

MEDICI, L. DE', *Lettere*, ed. R. Fubini and N Rubinstein, vols. i–iv (Florence, 1977–81).

MORELLI, G., *Ricordi*, ed. V. Branca (Florence, 1956).

MORELLI, L., *Cronaca*, in *Delizie degli eruditi toscani*, ed. Ildefonso di S. Luigi, xix (Florence, 1785).

NERI DI BICCI, *Le ricordanze*, ed. B. Santi (Pisa, 1976).

NERLI, J., *Commentari dei fatti civili dal 1215 al 1537* (Trieste, 1859).

PALMIERI, M., *Annales*, ed. G. Scaramella, in *Rerum italicarum scriptores*, xxvi (Città di Castello, 1906).

PICCOLOMINI, A. S., *Commentaries*, ed. L. C. Gabel, trans. F. A. Gragg, in *Smith College Studies in History*, 22 (1936–7), 25 (1939–40), 30 (1947), 35 (1951), 43 (1957).

PITTI, J., *Istoria fiorentina*, in *Archivio storico italiano*, i (1842).

PULCI, L., *La giostra di Lorenzo de' Medici, messa in rima da Luigi Pulci* (Florence, 1518).

RINUCCINI, F., *Ricordi storici dal 1282 al 1460, con la continuazione di Alamanno e Neri, suoi figli, fino al 1506*, ed. G. Aiazzi (Florence, 1840).

RUCELLAI, G., *Giovanni Rucellai ed il suo Zibaldone*, i, ed. A. Perosa (London, 1960).

SIMONETTA, C., *I diari di Cecco Simonetta*, ed. A. R. Natale (Milan, 1962) (vol. i of *Acta Italica*).

Statuta Populi et Comunis Florentiae, 1415 ('Friburgi', 1778–83).

STEFANI, M., *Storia fiorentina*, ed. N. Rodolico, in *Rerum italicarum scriptores*, xxx, Part I (Città di Castello, 1903).

STROZZI, A. MACINGHI NEGLI, *Lettere di una gentildonna fiorentina del secolo XV ai figliuoli esuli*, ed. C. Guasti (Florence, 1877).

TRINCHERA, F. (ed.), *Codice aragonese* (Naples, 1866).

VAESEN, J., and CHARAVAY, E., *Louis XI, roi de France: Lettres . . .*, II vols. (Paris, 1883–1909).

VESPASIANO DA BISTICCI, *Vite di uomini illustri del secolo XV*, ed. L. Frati, 3 vols. (Bologna 1892–3).

SECONDARY PUBLISHED SOURCES

AMMIRATO, S., *Della famiglia de' Baroncelli e Bandini*, in *Delizie degli eruditi toscani*, ed. Ildefonso di S. Luigi, xvii (Florence, 1783).
—— *Delle famiglie nobili fiorentine* (Bologna, 1969).
—— *Istorie fiorentine* . . ., ed. L. Scarabelli, 7 vols. (Turin, 1853).
ARICI, Z., *Bona di Savoia, Duchessa di Milano, 1449–1503* (Turin, Milan, Padua, Florence, 1935).
ASHTOR, E., 'L'exportation de textiles occidentaux dans le Proche Orient musulman au bas Moyen Age (1370–1517)', in *Studi in memoria di Federigo Melis*, ii (Naples, 1978).
BARUCHELLO, M., *Livorno e suo porto, origini, caratteristiche, e vicende dei traffici livornesi* (Livorno, 1932).
BELOTTI, B., *La vita di Bartolomeo Colleoni* (Bergamo, 1951).
BONELLO URICCHIO, C., 'I rapporti fra Lorenzo il Magnifico e Galeazzo Maria Sforza negli anni 1471–3', *Archivio storico lombardo*, 91–2 (1964–5).
BRANCHI, E., *Storia della Lunigiana feudale*, 3 vols. (Pistoia, 1897).
BROWN, A., *Bartolomeo Scala, 1430–1497, Chancellor of Florence* (Princeton, NJ, 1979).
—— 'The Guelf Party in Fifteenth-Century Florence', *Rinascimento*, 2 (1980).
BRUCKER, G., 'The Medici in the Fourteenth Century', *Speculum*, 32 (1957).
—— *The Society of Renaissance Florence* (New York, 1971).
BUSER, B., *Die beziehungen der Mediceer zu Frankreich während der Jahre 1434–94* (Leipzig, 1879).
CALISSE, C., *Storia del diritto italiano*, 3 vols. (Florence, 1891).
CANESTRINI, G., *La scienza e l'arte di stato* . . . (Florence, 1862).
CASANOVA, E., 'L'uccisione di Galeazzo Maria Sforza e alcuni documenti fiorentini', *Archivio storico lombardo*, ser. 3, 26 (1899).
CATALANO, F., *Francesco Sforza* (Milan, 1983).
CECCHINI, G., 'La guerra della congiura de' Pazzi e l'andata di Lorenzo a Napoli', *Bollettino senese*, ser. 3, 14 (1965).
COHN, S., *The Labouring Classes in Renaissance Florence* (New York, 1980).
COLOMBO, E., 'Re Renato, alleato del duca Francesco Sforza contro i Veneziani', *Archivio storico lombardo*, ser. 3, 21 (1894).
COOPER, R. PESMAN, 'L'elezione di Piero Soderini a gonfaloniere a vita', *Archivio storico italiano*, 125 (1967).

DAINELLI, A., 'Niccolo da Uzzano nella vita politica dei suoi tempi', *Archivio storico italiano*, ser. 7, 17 (1932).

DELLA TORRE, A., *La storia dell' Accademia Platonica di Firenze* (Florence, 1902).

DE ROOVER, R., *The Rise and Decline of the Medici Bank, 1397–1494* (New York, 1966).

EDLER DE ROOVER, F., 'Andrea Banchi, Florentine Silk Manufacturer and Merchant of the Fifteenth Century', *Studies in Renaissance and Medieval History*, 3 (1966).

FABRONI, A., *Laurentii Medicis Magnifici vita* (Pisa, 1784).

FILIPPI, G., *L'arte dei mercanti di Calimala* (Turin, 1889).

FIUMI, E., *L'impresa di Lorenzo de' Medici contro Volterra (1472)* (Florence, 1948).

FOSSATI, F., 'Documenti sulle relazioni tra Galeazzo Maria Sforza e Federigo d'Urbino per l'assedio di Rimini', *Atti e memorie della R. Deputazione di storia patria per le province delle Marche*, NS 2 (1905).

—— 'Francesco Sforza e la "sorpresa" del 16 maggio 1452', *Archivio storico lombardo*, 61 (1934–5).

FUBINI, R., 'Osservazioni e documenti sulla crisi del ducato di Milano nel 1477 . . .', in *Essays Presented to Myron P. Gilmore*, i, ed. S. Bertelli and G. Ramakus (Florence, 1978).

GAMURRINI, E., *Istoria genealogica delle famiglie nobili toscane et umbre*, 5 vols. (Florence, 1668–85).

GELLI, A., 'L'esilio di Cosimo de' Medici', *Archivio storico italiano*, ser. 4, 10 (1882).

GILBERT, F., 'The Venetian Constitution in Florentine Political Thought', in *Florentine Studies*, ed. N. Rubinstein (London 1968).

GOLDTHWAITE, R., *The Building of Renaissance Florence* (Baltimore, 1980).

—— *Private Wealth in Renaissance Florence* (Princeton, NJ, 1968).

GUIDI, G., *Il governo della città-repubblica di Firenze del primo Quattrocento*, 3 vols. (Florence, 1981).

HEERS, J., *Family Clans in the Middle Ages*, trans. B. Herbert (Amsterdam, New York and Oxford, 1977).

HERLIHY, D., 'Family and Property in Renaissance Florence', in H. A. Miskimin, D. Herlihy, and A. L. Udovitch, *The Medieval City* (New Haven and London, 1977).

ILARDI, V., 'The Assassination of Galeazzo Maria Sforza and the Reaction of Italian Diplomacy', in L. Martines ed., *Violence and Civil Disorder in Italian Cities, 1200–1500* (Berkeley, Los Angeles and London, 1972).

JONES, P., 'Florentine Families and Florentine Diaries in the Fourteenth Century', *Papers of the British School at Rome*, 24 (1956).

—— *The Malatesta of Rimini* (Cambridge, 1974).

JORDAN, E., 'Florence et la succession lombarde, 1447–1450', *Mélanges d'archéologie et d'histoire de l'école française de Rome*, 9 (1889).

KENT, D. V., 'The Florentine Reggimento in the Fifteenth Century', *The Renaissance Quarterly*, 28 (1975).

—— *The Rise of the Medici: Faction in Florence, 1426–1434* (Oxford, 1978).

—— and KENT, F. W., *Neighbours and Neighbourhoods in Renaissance Florence:The District of the Red Lion in the Fifteenth Century* (Locust Valley, NY, 1982).

KENT, F. W., *Household and Lineage in Renaissance Florence: The Family Life of the Capponi, Ginori, and Rucellai* (Princeton, 1977).

—— *Letters to an Obscure Florentine: Bartolomeo Cederni and his Friends*, texts by Gino Corti and F. W. Kent (Florence, 1990).

KIRSCHNER, J., 'Pursuing Honor while Avoiding Sin: The Monte delle Doti of Florence', *Quaderni di studi senesi*, 41 (1978).

KLAPISCH-ZUBER, C., 'Parenti, Amici e Vicini: il territorio urbano d'una famiglia mercantile nel xv secolo', *Quaderni storici*, 33 (1976).

—— 'Zacharie ou le père évincé . . .', *Annales, Economies, Sociétés, Civilizations*, 34 (1979).

KLAPISCH-ZUBER, C., and HERLIHY, D., *Les Toscans et leurs familles: une étude du catasto florentin de 1427* (Paris, 1978).

KUEHN, T., *Emancipation in late Medieval Florence* (New Brunswick, NJ, 1982).

LIGHTBOWN, R. W., *Sandro Botticelli* (London, 1978).

LITTA, P., *Celebri famiglie italiane*, 15 vols. (Milan, 1819–1902).

LUZZATI, M., 'Contratti agrari e rapporti di produzione nelle campagne pisane dal xiii al xvi secolo', in *Studi in memoria di Federigo Melis*, i (Naples, 1978).

MALLETT, M. E., *The Florentine Galleys in the Fifteenth Century* (Oxford, 1967).

—— 'Pisa and Florence in the Fifteenth Century: Aspects of the First Florentine Domination', in *Florentine Studies*, ed. N. Rubinstein (London, 1968).

—— 'The Sea Consuls of Florence in the Fifteenth Century', *Papers of the British School at Rome*, 27 (1959).

MARKS, L., 'The Financial Oligarchy in Florence under Lorenzo', in *Italian Renaissance Studies*, ed. E. F. Jacob (London, 1960).

MARTINES, L., *The Social World of the Florentine Humanists, 1390–1460* (Princeton, NJ, 1963).
MAULDE-LA-CLAVIÈRE, R. de, *La Diplomatie au temps de Machiavel*, 3 vols. (Paris, 1892–3).
MOISE, F., S. *Croce di Firenze* (Florence, 1845).
MOLHO, A., 'Cosimo de' Medici: Pater Patriae or Padrino?', *Stanford Italian Review*, 1 (1979).
—— *Florentine Public Finances in the Early Renaissance, 1400–1433* (Cambridge, Mass., 1971).
—— 'The Florentine Oligarchy and the *Balie* of the Late Trecento', *Speculum*, 43 (1968).
—— 'The Florentine "Tassa dei Traffichi" of 1451', *Studies in the Renaissance*, 17 (1970).
—— and KIRSCHNER, J., 'The Dowry Fund and the Marriage Market in Early Quattrocento Florence', *Journal of Modern History*, 50 (1978).
MORANDINI, F., 'Il conflitto tra Lorenzo il Magnifico e Sisto IV dopo la congiura de' Pazzi', *Archivio storico italiano*, 107 (1949).
MORÇAY, R., *Saint Antonin* (Tours and Paris, 1914).
MUNICCHI, A., *La fazione antimedicea detta 'del Poggio'* (Florence, 1911).
NAJEMY, J., *Corporatism and Consensus in Florentine Electoral Politics, 1280–1400* (Chapel Hill, NC, 1982).
NICCOLINI, G., 'Lettere di Piero di Cosimo de' Medici a Otto Niccolini (1467–69)', *Archivio storico italiano*, ser. 5, 20 (1897).
—— *The Chronicles of a Florentine Family* (London, 1932).
PAMPALONI, G., 'Fermenti di riforme democratiche nella Firenze medicea del Quattrocento', *Archivio storico italiano*, 119 (1961).
—— 'Gli organi della repubblica fiorentina per le relazioni con l'estero', *Rivista di storia politica internazionale*, 20 (1953).
—— 'Il giuramento pubblico in Palazzo vecchio a Firenze e un patto giurato degli antimedicei (maggio, 1466)', *Bollettino senese di storia patria*, ser. 3, 23 (1964).
—— 'Nuovi tentativi di riforme alla Costituzione Fiorentina visti attraverso le consulte', *Archivio storico italiano*, 120 (1962).
PASSERINI, L., 'Sigillo del cardinale Francesco de' Soderini', *Periodico di numismatica e sfragistica*, 6 (1874).
PASTOR, L., *History of the Popes*, ed. F. I. Antrobus (London, 1949).
—— *Ungedruckte Akten zur Geschichte der Papste* (Freiburg, 1904).
PERRET, P.-M., *Histoire des relations de la France avec Venise du*

XIIIe siècle à l'événement de Charles VIII ..., 2 vols. (Paris, 1896).

PHILLIPS, M., 'A Newly Discovered Chronicle by Marco Parenti', *The Renaissance Quarterly*, 31 (1978).

PICOTTI, G. B., *La giovinezza di Leone X* (Milan, 1927).

—— *Scritti vari di storia pisana e toscana* (Pisa, 1968).

PINTOR, E., 'Le due ambascerie di Bernardo Bembo a Firenze e le sue relazioni coi Medici', in *Studi letterari e linguistici dedicati a Pio Rajna* (Florence, 1911).

PIVA, E., 'Origine e conclusione della pace e dell'alleanza fra i Veneziani e Sisto IV (1479–80)', *Nuovo archivio veneto*, NS ii, part 2 (1901).

PONTIERI, E., *Per la storia del regno di Ferrante I d'Aragona, Re di Napoli* (Naples, 1947).

RAZZI, S., *Vita di Piero Soderini* (Padua, 1737).

RENOUARD, Y., *Les Relations des papes d'Avignon et les compagnies commerciales et bancaires de 1316 a 1378* (Paris, 1941).

RICCHIONI, V., *La constituzione politica di Firenze ai tempi di Lorenzo il Magnifico* (Siena, 1913).

RICHA, G., *Notizie storiche delle chiese fiorentine*, 10 vols. (Florence, 1754–62).

RICHARDS, G. R. B., *Florentine Merchants in the Age of the Medici* (Cambridge, Mass., 1932).

ROCHON, A., *La Jeunesse de Laurent de Medicis, 1449–78* (Paris, 1963).

ROMANIN, S., *Storia documentata di Venezia* ..., 10 vols. (Venice, 1912–21).

ROSCOE, W., *The Life of Lorenzo de' Medici* (London, 1796).

ROSSI, L., 'Niccolò V e le potenze d'Italia, dal maggio 1447 al dicembre 1451', *Rivista di scienze storiche*, 3 (1906).

RUBINSTEIN, N., 'La confessione di Franceso Neroni e la congiura anti-Medicea del 1466', *Archivio storico italiano*, 126 (1968).

—— 'Michelozzo e Niccolò Michelozzi in Chios, 1466–7', in *Essays in Honour of P. O. Kristeller*, ed. C. H. Clough (Manchester, 1976).

—— *The Government of Florence under the Medici* (Oxford, 1966).

SACCHI, M. A., 'Cosimo de' Medici nell'acquisto di Milano allo Sforza', *Rivista di scienze storiche*, 2 (1905).

SALVEMINI, G., *La dignità cavaleresca* (Florence, 1896).

SANTORO, C., *Gli uffizi del dominio sforzesco, 1450–1500* (Milan, 1948).

SAPORI, A., 'Cosimo de' Medici e un "patto giurato" a Firenze nel 1449', *Eventail de l'histoire vivante: Hommage à Lucien Febvre* (Paris, 1953).

—— 'La compagnia dei Peruzzi', in *Storia dell'economia italiana*, i, ed. C. M. Cipolla (Turin, 1959).

—— *Studi di storia economica*, 3 vols. (Florence, 1955–67).

SETTON, K., *The Papacy and the Levant (1204–1571)*, 4 vols. (Philadelphia, 1976–84).

SORANZO, G., 'Lorenzo il Magnifico alla morte del padre e il suo primo balzo verso la Signoria', *Archivio storico italiano*, 111 (1953).

Storia di Milano, published by the Fondazione Treccani degli Alfieri, 16 vols. (Milan, 1953–66).

Stradario storico e amministrativo della città e Comune di Firenze (Florence, 1913).

TIRIBILLI-GIULIANI, D., *Sommario delle famiglie celebri tos- cane* i. (Florence, 1855).

TOMMASOLI, W., *Momenti e figure della politica dell'equilibrio (Federigo da Montefeltro e l'impresa di Rimini)* (Urbino, 1968).

UZIELLI, G., *La vita e i tempi Paolo dal Pozzo Toscanelli* (Rome, 1894).

VERDE, A. F., *Lo studio fiorentino, 1473–1503*, 3 vols. (Pistoia, 1977).

VOLPE, G., 'Luigi Pulci, studio biografico', *Giornale storico della letteratura italiana*, 22 (1893).

WACKERNAGEL, M., *The World of the Florentine Renaissance Artist*, trans. A. Luchs (Princeton, 1981).

WITT, R., *Hercules at the Crossroads: The Life, Work and Thought of Coluccio Salutati* (Durham, NC, 1983).

ZIMOLO, G., 'Le relazioni tra Milano e Napoli e la politica italiana in due lettere del 1478', *Archivio storico italiano*, NS 2 (1937).

ZIPPEL, G., *Il Filelfo a Firenze, 1429–1434* (Rome, 1899).

Glossary

accoppiator/e, -i: an official (officials) appointed originally at the time of a scrutiny to determine which citizens' names should be placed in the various election bags for later sortition for positions within the Signoria. After 1434 this group of officials was also repeatedly authorized to prepare election bags for every two-monthly drawing of the Signoria. Since they were required to place a limited number of name-tags in these bags, they gained considerable authority over the appointment of the principal magistracy of the city, and hence an unusual degree of political power.

a discrezione: literally 'at the discretion' of the company in question. The term was applied to interest given on deposits in banking or trading firms, which generally amounted to 8 per cent. However, to avoid the accusation of usury, the fiction was maintained that interest was not guaranteed, but at risk, i.e. given only when the owners of the firm considered profits large enough to distribute part as interest to the depositors.

a mano: the method whereby the Signoria was appointed when the *accoppiatori* were filling the election bags every two months. Instead of the election bags being filled with the names of all candidates successful in the scrutiny and then 'closed', they were kept open so as to be filled for each election. Hence the term *a mano*, or 'by hand', which meant that the bags were prepared by hand for every appointment.

benefici/o -ati: literally 'benefit' and 'benefited', these terms were applied to citizens whose near male relatives (fathers, grandfathers, and uncles) had been qualified for the highest offices of the republic—the Signoria and its two Colleges. The 'benefit' of this achievement was passed to their descendants in that the *beneficiati* were at times, for example, voted on in the scrutiny before other citizens and tended to have a higher rate of success.

borse/llino: the election bags in which the name-tags of citizens successful in the scrutiny were placed in preparation for the sortition of candidates for the various offices whenever the time for filling them arrived. There were different bags, or *borse*, for different series of offices, including separate ones for the Signoria. In addition, a special bag was created with a small number of names—hençe *borsellino*. When this bag was in use, three members of the Signoria were drawn from it, and so those whose names were placed in it possessed a greater chance of obtaining a post within the Signoria.

Calimala: the guild of the wool-finishers or of merchants in general. The oldest of the Florentine guilds, it had apparently been originally the sole commercial guild of the city, from which other, more specialized guilds later sprang. However, the earliest of Florentine industrial activity— that of finishing woollen cloth imported originally from Flanders— remained associated with this guild until the occupation declined or was suppressed, leaving its members with the occupation of general import and export trade.

catasto: a system of tax assessment first introduced in 1427 in order to respond to the need for a fairer type of taxation, and applied sporadic- ally during the 15th century. It required the declaration of all income- bearing possessions, from the total value of which debits were deducted, either of debts, permanent financial obligations, or, in the case of Florentine citizens, living expenses of family members. Of the resultant amount 0.5 per cent represented the tax-payer's assessment, although if several *catasti* were imposed during a year, he would pay multiple amounts of this sum.

Cento: a council created after the *parlamento* of 1458, with authority to vote before the older councils on such matters as scrutinies, appointment of officials, the form of the government, the hiring of soldiers, and taxes. It consisted of the Signoria and Colleges in office plus 100 members drawn from the *veduti ai Tre Maggiori*. In 1471 the *Cento* gained sole authority over those matters on which it had previously voted before the other councils, thereby effectively replacing the older legislative assemblies of the city.

condott/a, -iere: a military contract and a military captain hired by such a contract. Normally, the contract stipulated the period of service, the number of horse and foot with which the commander was to fight, the amount of pay, and other terms such as the captain's obligation to pass in review all the soldiers whom he was supposed to keep in service.

Consiglio Maggiore: literally 'Greater Council', the name applied in particular to the special council of 1444–9, in a possible reference to the Great Council or 'Maggior Consiglio' of Venice.

Dieci di Balìa: a magistracy of 10 citizens appointed with special powers, or *balìa*, in periods of war. During their six-month term, the *Dieci* possessed wide powers over military matters and diplomacy, including peace negotiations. Because of their connection purely with war, the creation of the *Dieci* was justly regarded as an official beginning of war.

Dodici Procuratori: a body of twelve citizens appointed by the Council of Seventy from the Seventy to deal with questions regarding the internal administration of Florence and her dominion. The office was created, along with the Seventy itself, by the constitutional changes of 1480.

gonfalone: one of the 16 administrative districts of Florence, of which there were 4 per quarter, each with its own symbol. The *gonfalone* acted originally as the basic unit of the military organization of the commoners, or *popolo*, under its district leaders, the *gonfalonieri delle companie* or standardbearers of the companies. Although the military function fell into desuetude, the *gonfalone* continued to serve as an administrative unit for such duties as the distribution of certain taxes and the compilation of lists of candidates for the periodic scrutinies. The *gonfalonieri* were communal officials of importance since they formed one of the Signoria's Colleges, whose consent was essential for all legislative proposals.

grandi: originally, the term applied to the Florentine magnates, or those citizens generally of noble origins who at the end of the 13th century were deprived of their political rights through the Ordinances of Justice. These laws designated as magnates certain families who had had knights among their members and who had exhibited violent behaviour, especially towards commoners. Thus, the Ordinances represented a political affirmation of the commoners against some of the older, aristocratic families. By the 15th century, however, many magnates had become commoners and as a group the *grandi* were no longer of political importance. In fact, by then the term *grandi* was at times applied to powerful citizens in general rather than the group of families designated as such in the late 13th century.

magnate: see *grandi* above.

marcheschi: a term used to signify the supporters or sympathizers of Venice, the city of St Mark.

Monte: the public funded debt, created in the 1340s after wars and a system of public finance based in large part on citizen loans had created a debt far beyond what could be repaid in the foreseeable future. As a result, a system was instituted in which citizens received credits equal to the sum which they had contributed to the debt. These credits bore interest, generally of 5 per cent, and became negotiable. Thus, a system of debt financing became permanent, despite sporadic efforts by the government to repay the loans and eliminate the debt. Later, various other *monti* were established, among which was the *Monte delle Doti*, set up in 1425 with the intention of guaranteeing girls' dowries in exchange for sums placed with the government for periods up to 15 years.

ottimati, *optimates*: the leading or 'better' citizens in the sense of the upper class of wealthier citizens, who were generally also those with the highest social status and the greatest political influence.

Otto di Guardia: a magistracy responsible for the maintenance of public order in Florence and her dominion. After 1434 it was repeatedly given extraordinary powers, or *balìa*, to proceed in cases in its competence, which included in particular crimes against the state. Hence the controversial nature of the *Otto* and its powers in e.g. 1465.

parent/e, -i, -adò: in-laws or relatives by marriage, and the marriage relationship itself, which was felt to involve the families on both sides and not just the couple themselves.

parlamento: a gathering of the whole body of citizens, which possessed full legislative powers in that it represented the will of the whole community. Although obsolete by the 15th century, the *parlamento* was used by the Medici regime to bypass normal legislative channels and thereby came to be associated with oligarchic intentions and heartily resented by a large section of the citizen body.

Podestà: a foreign official appointed to maintain order in a city, for which he was originally granted wide administrative, judicial, and military authority. By the 15th century the power of the *Podestà* in Florence had been reduced to the point at which he was merely a judicial official, but the *Podestà* whom Florence sent to represent her interests in her subject towns also retained some administrative and military powers.

popolo: literally, 'the people', the term was applied to the commoners as opposed to the aristocratic families. In the 13th century, the term differentiated the common citizens from the magnates, whereas by the 15th century *popolo* referred to the ordinary citizens as opposed to the *principali* or *ottimati*.*

Pratica: a discussion or debate called by and held under the auspices of the Signoria. Although the Signoria and its Colleges could theoretically invite whomever it wished to these meetings, there was a generally recognized group of leading citizens who were regularly invited. Thereby, although they might possess no official government position, these leading citizens could exercise a continuing influence on public policy.

principali: principal citizens, in the sense of those with the greatest political authority and influence.

Priorate: literally, the Priors (eight by the 15th century), who, along with the Standardbearer of Justice, composed the Signoria. However, by extension, Priorate came to mean the Signoria as a whole.

scrutiny: a periodic review of citizens' qualifications to office carried out by a council in whose composition the Signoria possessed the major say. In this review, lists of candidates, often prepared by the Standardbearers of the Companies, were presented to the scrutiny council for various groups of offices. If a candidate received a two-thirds majority of votes in the scrutiny council, his name was placed in the appropriate bags for eventual sortition.

* According to Guidi, *Il governo*, i. 13–14, in the 14th and 15th centuries the *popolo* meant only those citizens who possessed political rights, i.e. the right to hold public office. However, this interpretation seems contradicted by the fact that all those who formed part of the companies of the people also seem to have been included in the *popolo*, and not all of them possessed political rights.

Tre Maggiori: the Signoria (Priors and Standardbearer of Justice) and its two Colleges (the 12 *Buonomini* or Good Men and the 16 Standard-bearers of the Companies). Since these were the highest executive offices in the republic, they were given the title of the *Tre Maggiori* or the 'three greater' offices.

veduti ai Tre Maggiori: Since the results of the scrutinies were theoretically kept secret, the only way in which it was known that a citizen had been approved for the *Tre Maggiori* was if his name were actually drawn for a post in one of them. In that case, he became 'seen' or *veduto*, for the office, although he might not, for a variety of reasons, be able to fill it. Consequently, it was the *veduti* who best represented all the citizens eligible for these highest offices, and, since this was a considerable honour, the *veduti* gradually became a sort of élite political group which, from the late 14th century, was increasingly singled out for further political honours.

Index

Niccolò di Lorenzo: as ambassador 46–7, 48–9; as critic of the Medici regime 50–1, 58–9, 63–4, 88–91, 93–4; death 124, 171; exiled 93–4, 107, 124; knighted 107, 171; as one of *Otto di Guardia* 48; as Podestà of Castiglione della Pescaia 24; and plots against Medici régime 124, 126–7, 130, 154–6, 171; as secretary for the scrutiny of the Guelf party 29; as Standardbearer of Justice 45–6, 47, 80–7, 106, 272–3
Paolantonio di Tommaso di Lorenzo 119, 141, 142
Piero di Tommaso di Lorenzo 111, 119, 139, 177, 259
Tommaso di Guccio 15–17, 18–19, 96, 116
Tommaso di Lorenzo di Tommaso di Guccio: as *accoppiatore* 33–5, 42–3, 51, 56–7, 68, 79–80, 124, 131, 133, 148–9, 150, 218, 262, 271; as ambassador 69–76, 124, 133, 155–8, 165–71, 173–7, 200–1, 207–13, 216, 217, 218–29, 234–45, 246–50; among *Dieci di Balìa* 161–71, 245–52, 257; in financial offices 32–3, 35–6, 121; knighted 73–4; in offices at Pisa 66, 67, 68, 76, 108, 118, 228, 258; among *Otto di Guardia* 160–2, 198; among *Otto di Pratica* 255, 257; as secretary for the scrutiny of 1440 29; as Standardbearer of Justice 40–2, 54–5, 66–8, 148, 161, 250–3; among the Twenty directing the War of Volterra 217
Tommaso di Lorenzo di Tommaso di Lorenzo 127
Spinelli, Tommaso 142
Spoleto 219
Stefani, Marchionne 15
Strozzi, family 37, 119, 141

Agnolo di Palla Novello 27, 120, 146, 147–8, 151, 202
Alessandra, *see* Macinghi
Margherita di Strozza di Marcello 141
Marcello 141
Matteo 37
Palla di Nofri 15, 114, 147
Strozza di Marcello 141

Tazzi, Piero 145
Temperani, Manno 59 n, 79, 84 n
Tinucci, Ser Niccolò 20–1
Todi 219
Torelli, Jacopo 146
Tornabuoni, family 31, 138
Dianora 30–1, 115, 125, 128, 136, 138, 259
Giovanni 31
Lucrezia 31
Torrigiani, family 136
Giuliano 20
Maria 30–1, 114, 124, 125–6
Tranchedini, Nicodemo 81, 86, 90, 158
Turks 69–71, 73, 74, 164, 199, 224, 227, 246, 248
Tuscany 39, 76, 101, 102, 103, 140, 181, 243

Uliveto 102

Vada 102
Val di Serchio 118
Venice 3, 9–10, 12, 45, 51–2, 55, 69–72, 75, 90, 107, 110–11, 115, 154–6, 160, 164–78, 182, 184, 187–90, 192–5, 199–200, 203, 216, 218–19, 223–30, 241–2, 244, 246–52, 257–8, 268–70, 273 as model for political changes in Florence 27–8, 84, 269
Visconti, family 9, 45
Bianca 45, 163
Vitelli, Niccolò 219–20, 223
Volterra 112, 214–18

This is a study of politics in fifteenth-century
Florence. Paula C. Clarke's detailed account of
the careers of two brothers, Tommaso and
Niccolo Soderini, and their relationship with
the Medici family offers a new synthesis of the
political world of Renaissance Florence. The
Soderini were at different times supporters and
adversaries of the Medici, whose rise to power
remains the subject of historical debate.

Based on hitherto unpublished sources,
particularly from the archives of Florence and
Milan, *The Soderini and the Medici* examines the
nature of the ascendancy of the Medici and
opposition to them, the sources of their power,
the operation of their system of patronage, the
bonds connecting one of the most successful
political élites in Renaissance Italy, and the
development of the political institutions of the
Florentine state. It is an important contribution
to our understanding of the political and
constitutional history of Florence.

Paula C. Clarke is Assistant Professor of
History at McGill University, Montreal.